LIFE OF
JOSEPH SMITH
THE PROPHET

LIFE OF
JOSEPH SMITH
THE PROPHET

BY

GEORGE Q. CANNON

STRATFORD
BOOKS

Arlington, Virginia | Provo, Utah
2005

Life of Joseph Smith the Prophet
by George Q. Cannon

ISBN: 0-929753-09-7

Stratford Books, Inc.
Eastern States Office
4308 37th Road North
Arlington, VA 22207

Stratford Books, Inc.
Western States Office
P.O. Box 1371
Provo, UT 84603-1371

www.stratfordbooks.com

First printing: February 2005
Second Printing: August 2005

Printed on acid-free paper
in accordance with the guidelines of the
American Library Association

Foreword

This is the classic biography, long out of print, of the Prophet Joseph Smith by a contemporary, George Q. Cannon—the apostle who served as counselor to four of Joseph Smith's successors as President of the Church of Jesus Christ of Latter-day Saints. Clean, modern type speeds the reader along in perusing this highly readable biography that also serves as a compact, yet comprehensive summary of LDS Church history in Joseph's lifetime.

The tone of this biography is uplifting and faith promoting. The author stresses the heroic aspects of Joseph's character—his boldness, bravery, selflessness, and magnanimity—while delineating Joseph's countless prophecies that were fulfilled, many of which have been forgotten today.

Unlike biographers of our day, Cannon makes no attempt to get into his subject's mind or motivations; rather, he simply lays out the man's deeds and sayings, leaving the reader to form his own opinions.

He takes pains to be orthodox, although ironically some of the facts he presents might be edited out of official Church publications today. He rounds out the picture by presenting fascinating, candid assessments by contemporaries who observed Joseph firsthand—the small cadre of unbelieving but unbigoted writers who didn't know quite what to make of this charismatic founder of a new religious movement on the American frontier.

Cannon plays up the adage, "To know him was to love him"— or hate him. In his mind, people were polarized about Joseph. The "good" were attracted to him, the "evil" wanted to kill him.

(It is actually amazing how many wanted to kill him.) The virtually unrelenting threats that Joseph faced throughout his career from conspirators and religious bigots form a persitent undercurrent to the narrative.

Written for the most part while the author was in hiding from federal authorities during the persecution of polygamist Church leaders, this biography consistently emphasizes the persecutions, indignities, and sufferings that Joseph had to endure.

This book may not fit the mold of modern "balanced" biographical writing, but in the end, George Q. Cannon obviously cares only if it's true and if it reveals a prophet the way the Lord would want him portrayed, with all criticisms of Joseph cast aside as unimportant.

With the facts he has to work with—limited compared with today's available research but still voluminous considering he had full access to Church archives—Cannon manages to distill the most pertinent information from the mountains of original documents into a narrative that never loses focus or direction as it weaves through the tale of Church history that is inextricably linked with Joseph's life.

All the pieces really do make sense. Cannon makes it clear, for example, what was going on behind the scenes that led to Joseph's assassination, and the connections of those in Missouri who worked feverishly to take Joseph to his grave.

Then there are the political machinations of ambitious politicians, for whom truth, justice, and civil rights took a back seat (or no seat at all) to pandering for votes. The writer details the underpinnings of conspiracy. He unravels the efforts of governors in Missouri and Illinois who greased the skids for Joseph's death. Along the way we encounter blunt exposés of "the apostates"— those unique characters like John C. Bennett, William Law, and the Higbees—who thirsted for Joseph's blood.

Most readers are aware that Joseph Smith was running for President of the United States when he was martyred, but how many have heard what his platform was? Cannon reveals the prophet's bold, uninhibited vision for societal reform, his practical and—in hindsight—enlightened solutions to the thorniest issues of antebellum America, some of which have currency even today.

The opening chapters may seem like a piously bland rehashing of familiar territory in Church history, but this is perhaps attributable to a paucity of original source material available to the author regarding the early years of Joseph's life. Once we get to Kirtland, the narrative picks up, and as we progress through the travails of Missouri to the culminating scenes in Nauvoo, the account steadily increases in detail and intrigue.

Surprising and often humorous anecdotes pop up at almost every turn. Like the quick-witted boy flying a kite in Nauvoo, who, when confronted by a malevolent stranger inquiring as to Smith's whereabouts, cheekily covered for the prophet by replying that Joseph and Hyrum had flown to heaven on Joseph's old horse and that he was flying his kite to send them their dinner! Or how about the prophet's fearless rejoinder to Joseph Reynolds, the sheriff of Jackson County, Missouri, who stole across the border into Illinois and kidnapped Joseph: Tiring of hearing the fellow's repeated threats to shoot him on the spot, Joseph retorted: "Why do you make this threat so often? If you want to shoot me, do so." (To Joseph, death threats had become old hat by this time.) Then there is the incident on his trip to Washington, D.C., to seek redress from the federal government for the atrocities suffered by his people in Missouri, where he takes control of a runaway stagecoach, à la *Indiana Jones*, and wins the undying gratitude of his fellow passengers—that is, until they learn the identity of their rescuer. This volume is also rife with startling, intriguing utterances of the irrepressible prophet on matters religious, moral, and political.

You hold in your hand the first of only two biographies about the prophet ever to be written by an LDS General Authority, and the only one written in the same century in which Joseph lived by one who actually saw Joseph. In addition, it is the only biography by *any writer* who ever actually interviewed Joseph's closest friends at length. Cannon enjoyed a significant advantage over modern biographers: he was intimate with those who knew Joseph and whose memories were still vivid from having lived through these scenes themselves.

If your interest is in reading an authoritative biography of Joseph Smith that is factual, thorough, and faith promoting, you can hardly do better than read this volume. Nineteenth-century writers had larger vocabularies than today's, but George Q. Cannon's account of the life of Joseph Smith is straightforward, approachable, and eminently readable. Whether or not you agree with Joseph and his mission, you will be enlightened by this volume. And that's a promise.

RICHARD LLOYD DEWEY
26 November 2004

JOSEPH SMITH, JR.

HYRUM SMITH

Author's Preface

Joseph and Hyrum are now dead; but like the first martyr, they yet speak. Their united voice is one of testimony, admonition and warning to the world.

They lived men of God. They died pure and holy, sealing their testimony with their blood.

No men ever suffered greater persecution than they; no men were ever less understood by their generation.

It is in the hope that the Saints may find joy in reading of their beloved Prophet and Patriarch, and that the world may judge more fairly of these benefactors of mankind, that this book is written.

To the author its preparation has been a loving duty. In the midst of a somewhat busy and laborious life, he has found comfort in the contemplation of this great subject. The closing chapters, detailing the final sufferings upon earth of the Prophet of God and his ever-constant brother, were finished in prison for adherence to the principles which they taught, and for this, the life is invested with a dearer regard. To send the work away now is like being torn from a beloved companion, when most the solace of his friendly presence is needed.

In some respects this volume may be imperfect; the circumstances which surrounded its preparation were not favorable to the collection and arrangement of materials, but it is believed to be truthful and just.

To many friends the author is indebted for information here embodied; and he takes this occasion to thank them, hoping to live yet to meet them and express his gratitude in the flesh.

That the sublime example and inspired teachings of Joseph, the Prophet of the last dispensation, may be of eternal benefit to all who read this life, is the heartfelt wish of

THE AUTHOR.

October 1, 1888.

Contents

The
Ripened
Time

THE PROPHECY OF JOHN THE REVELATOR

Babylon the great is fallen, is fallen, and is become the habitation of devils, and the hold of every foul spirit, and a cage of every unclean and hateful bird.

For all nations have drunk of the wine of the wrath of her fornication, and the kings of the earth have committed fornication with her, and the merchants of the earth are waxed rich through the abundance of her delicacies.

... Come out of her, my people, that ye be not partakers of her sins, and that ye receive not of her plagues.

For her sins have reached unto heaven, and God hath remembered her iniquities.   (Revelation 18:2b–5.)

The Apostasy
and the Restoration

In the reign of Tiberius of Rome, the Lord Jesus was crucified. At the hour of the atonement, His gospel was to the dominant earthly power only "a deadly superstition,"[1] "a strange and pestilent superstition,"[2] sought to be crushed at any cost by the ruthless power of the pagan empire. Thus came the persecutions of the early Christians, lasting until after Christianity, with irresistible power, had "sprung up, even in Rome, the common reservoir for all the streams of wickedness and infamy."[1]

In the midst of these early tribulations, the plain and simple gospel was becoming involved and mystified by the many opposing sects which professed to believe in Jesus; and yet it retained so much of divinity as enabled it to resist persecution and idolatry, and made it, in the fourth century, the established religion of Rome.

This elevation was not achieved without some sacrifice of identity. And in the commingling with error, truth yielded much.[3]

The Roman emperor, Constantine I, was led to show favor to the unpopular people; but his friendliness to Christianity demanded and received its price. He sought as much the welfare of the state as the progress of the religion to which he had been only in part converted; and when he exacted concessions of creed and principle, the Fathers felt forced to comply. It was Constantine who called the first Council of Nicea. He presided over its opening

---

[1] Tacitus.

[2] Suetonius.

[3] Paganism, unable to oppose Christianity successfully, has done much to corrupt it, and in numberless ways had made inroads upon its purity. Prof. T. M. Lindsay, Glasgow.

session, and dictated its policy in accordance with his own imperial ambitions.[4]

From that time on, for twelve hundred years, the church of Rome grew in lustful power. The first great check was when the German monk Martin Luther, with bared feet, fled in disappointment from the debauched court of Pope Leo X. Luther's courage partly stripped the idol of its awe-invoking cloak of mystery and dread threats; and never more did the whole civilized world crouch in terror at the feet of Rome.

The freedom of thought heralded by the Reformation at last found its abuse in the Age of Reason and the blasphemy of the French Revolution. At first rejecting Christianity for a dream of paganism restored, the infidels, in turn, exchanged pagan mythology, with its gods many, for their own new mythology, with its gods none.

This tempest of profane unbelief was too violent to be enduring. A reawakening to religious fervor was manifest in Christendom. Men gladly blotted from their memories the dread of the *auto-da-fe*, the inquisition dungeons and racks of Spain and Italy, the funeral fires of England, the witch-hanging and Quaker-driving of the New World, and all the atrocities sacrilegiously practiced as ceremonies of worship. Mankind turned back by thousands to find satisfaction for their inherent necessity—belief in a Higher Power.

But that Higher Power was itself an unfathomable mystery. God had been misunderstood for centuries. Much of the world had known nothing of Him—His nature or His purposes—from the death of Christ's apostles. The men who had known Him walked no more in the midst of mankind. Prophets and apostles, while they lived, taught their fellow men that he was a distinct personality—a glorious Being in whose likeness man was created. Jesus Christ, the Son of God, was declared "to be made like unto his brethren"—"made in the likeness of men"—and "in the likeness of sinful flesh"; yet inspired men claimed Him as being "in the form of God"—"the express image of His person"—"the

---

[4] The interest of the emperor [Constantine] was still [at the Council of Nicea] primarily political and official rather than personal. W. Browning Smith.

image of the invisible God." But as generations and centuries passed, true knowledge concerning the Creator faded away. A spiritual meaning concerning His personage and attributes was given to the testimony of those who had known Him. Modern sectarianism taught the world that God the Father, of whose person Jesus was the "express image," was an all-pervading God of spirit—a Being who, without any tangible existence, is everywhere in the material world—a Being "without body, parts or passions," "whose center was nowhere and whose circumference was everywhere." Professing to have an understanding of the Deity, they differed but little from the Pantheists, who, rejecting a personal God, made bold avowal of an all-existing God of nature—the combined forces and laws which are manifested in the existing universe.

Thus blinded, how could mankind offer true worship to the Lord of heaven and earth?

The Eastern World had lost this knowledge of the Lord earlier than the Western Hemisphere. Upon the land of North America, four hundred years after the birth of our Savior and Master, there stood at least one man who knew the Lord God Almighty as a distinct personality, a Being capable of communicating Himself to man. That man was Moroni, the son of Mormon, whose testimony abides now and must abide through all the ages to come.[5]

---

[5] Behold, will ye believe in the day of your visitation—behold, when the Lord shall come, yea, even that great day when the earth shall be rolled together as a scroll, and the elements shall melt with fervent heat—yea, in that great day when ye shall be brought to stand before the Lamb of God then will ye say there is no God?

Then will ye longer deny the Christ, or can ye behold the Lamb of God? . . .

For behold, when ye shall be brought to see your nakedness before God, and also the glory of God, and the holiness of Jesus Christ, it will kindle a flame of unquenchable fire upon you.

O then ye unbelieving, turn ye unto the Lord; cry mightily unto the Father in the name of Jesus, that perhaps ye may be found spotless, pure, fair, and white, having been cleansed by the blood of the Lamb, at that great and last day.

And again I speak unto you who deny the revelations of God, and say that they are done away, that there are no revelations, nor prophecies, nor gifts, nor healing, nor speaking with tongues, and the interpretation of tongues;

Behold I say unto you, he that denieth these things, knoweth not the gospel of Christ; . . .

For do we not read that God is the same yesterday, today, and forever; and in him there is no variableness neither shadow of changing? (Mormon 9:2-3, 5-9.)

It was upon this land that Jesus last appeared to His brethren who dwelt in mortality; and it was predestined that upon this land man was to first receive a renewal of divine revelation. After the discovery of the hemisphere which had been so long concealed from the knowledge of those who had dwelt upon the other parts of the earth, nearly three centuries elapsed before a nation with a charter of liberty divinely ordained was established. In God's providence it was necessary that those who had been led here by His hand should receive political emancipation to prepare the way for the restoration of the gospel in its purity and the Church of Christ in the plenitude of its power. Political salvation had first been declared, that men's bodies might be free and their souls be filled with high aspirations to prepare for the greater enfranchisement and redemption which were to appear.

The period succeeding the Revolution was filled with a veritable Babel of religious creeds. Every obsolete tradition was revived; every possible human fancy of doctrine was promulgated; and each found its upholding sect. Confusion and doubt waxed fat, feeding upon human fears. No earthly wisdom could bring peace to the sects or make harmony among the creeds.

It became the ripe hour for the heavens to open and with their celestial light show to man the way out of the abyss into which he had fallen. It became the hour for the reestablishment of heavenly truth—the gospel of Christ and its direct communications between God and humanity: a religion which should cast off alike the skepticism of "reason" and the shackles of superstition; a religion which should be bold in righteous faith and convincing in its revealed philosophy. By divine aid the way had been paved for this renewal.

For the greater part of eighteen hundred years humanity had been perverting the gospel of Jesus the Anointed.

Then the Eternal Father and His Son Jesus Christ revealed themselves from heaven. This glorious manifestation was followed by the angel flying in the midst of heaven, who proclaimed that the restoration of the gospel had come.

Joseph Smith's Life and Work

JOSEPH SMITH AT NAUVOO
May 15, 1844

It is by no means improbable that some future textbook, for the use of generations yet unborn, will contain a question something like this: What historical American of the nineteenth century has exerted the most powerful influence upon the destinies of his countrymen? And it is by no means impossible that the answer to that interrogatory may be thus written: JOSEPH SMITH, THE MORMON PROPHET. And the reply, absurd as it doubtless seems to most men now living, may be an obvious commonplace to their descendants. History deals in surprises and paradoxes quite as startling as this. The man who established a religion in this age of free debate, who was and is today accepted by hundreds of thousands as a direct emissary from the Most High—such a rare human being is not to be disposed of by pelting his memory with unsavory epithets. . . . The most vital questions Americans are asking each other today have to do with this man and what he has left us. . . . Burning questions they are, which must give a prominent place in the history of the country to that sturdy self-asserter whom I visited at Nauvoo. Joseph Smith, claiming to be an inspired teacher, faced adversity such as few men have been called to meet, enjoyed a brief season of prosperity such as few men have ever attained, and finally, forty-three days after I saw him, went cheerfully to a martyr's death. When he surrendered his person to Governor Ford, in order to prevent the shedding of blood, the Prophet had a presentiment of what was before him. "I am going like a lamb to the slaughter," he is reported to have said; "but I am as calm as a summer's morning. I have a conscience void of offense and shall die innocent."

—JOSIAH QUINCY'S *FIGURES OF THE PAST*

The
"Choice Seer"

In the day of Jesus, every act and every circumstance of His life was ridiculed and belittled by His jealous enemies. But the record of His career, from which the present world of Christians makes up its judgment of Him, was not written until all insignificant or paltry things had been forgotten; and now His character, illuminated by the eternal sunshine of heaven, stands outlined against the blue vastness of the past in sublime simplicity. Let us view Joseph Smith in the same light—see him as he towered in the full radiance of his labors; see him the reconciler of divergent sects and doctrines, the oracle of the Almighty to all nations, kindreds, tongues and peoples.

Joseph Smith had been a retiring youth—the Spirit made him bold to declare to rulers and potentates and all mankind, the gospel again revealed. He had been a humble farmer lad—divine authority sat so becomingly upon him that men looked at him with reverent awe. He had been unlearned in the great things of art and science—he walked with God until human knowledge was to his eye an open book; the celestial light beamed through his mind.

His lofty soul comprehended the grandeur of his mission upon earth; and with divine fortitude he fulfilled the destiny which God had ordained for him before the world was.

When he had achieved the prime of his manhood, he seemed to combine all attractions and excellencies. His physical person was the fit habitation of his exalted spirit. He was more than six feet in height, with expansive chest and clean-cut limbs—a staunch and graceful figure. His head, crowned with a mass of soft, wavy hair, was grandly poised. His face possessed a complexion of such clearness and transparency that the soul appeared to shine through. He wore no beard, and the full strength and beauty of his countenance impressed all beholders at a glance. He had eyes which seemed to read the hearts of men. His mouth was one of mingled power and sweetness. His majesty of air was natural, not studied. Though full of personal and prophetic dignity whenever occasion demanded, he could at other times unbend and be as happy and unconventional as a boy. This was one of his most striking characteristics; and it was sometimes held up to scorn by his traducers, that the chosen "man of God" should at times mingle as a man of earth with his earthly brethren. And yet it is a false ridicule; for Savior and prophets must, like other men, eat, drink and wear apparel. They have the physical necessities and the affections and enjoyments which are common to other men. And it is this petty human fact—that a divine apostle with an earthly body has hunger and thirst to appease, that he cannot always be prophesying, but has hours to smile with the gay and to weep with the saddened—which leaves him "without honor in his own country."

But whether engaging in manly sport during hours of relaxation, or proclaiming words of wisdom in pulpit or grove, he was ever the leader. His magnetism was masterful, and his heroic qualities won universal admiration. Where he moved, all classes were forced to recognize in him the man of power. Strangers journeying to see him from a distance, knew him the moment their eyes beheld his person. Men have crossed ocean and continent to meet him and have selected him instantly from among a multitude.[6]

It was a part of Joseph Smith's great mission "to combat the errors of ages; to meet the violence of mobs; to cope with illegal

---

[6] It was the author's privilege thus to meet the Prophet for the first time. The occasion was the arrival of a large company of Latter-day Saints at the upper landing at Nauvoo. The general conference of the Church was in session and large numbers crowded to the landing place to welcome the emigrants. Nearly every prominent man in the community was there. Familiar with the names of all and the persons of many of the prominent elders, the author sought with a boy's curiosity and

proceedings from executive authority; to cut the Gordian knot of powers; to solve mathematical problems of universities with truth—diamond truth." He performed a work, "not pagan ire, nor tooth of time, nor sword, nor fire, shall bring to naught."

The Prophet's life was exalted and unselfish. His death was a sealing martyrdom, following after that which was completed upon Calvary for the redemption of a world.

---

eagerness, to discover those whom he knew, and especially to get sight of the Prophet and his brother Hyrum, neither of whom he had ever met. When his eyes fell upon the Prophet, without a word from anyone to point him out, or any reason to separate him from others who stood around, he knew him instantly. He would have known him among ten thousand. There was that about him which to the author's eyes distinguished him from all the men he had ever seen.

CHAPTER 1

The Prophet's Ancestry

Joseph Smith was of humble birth. His parents and their progenitors were toilers; but their characters were godly and their names unstained.

In the year 1638 Robert Smith, a sturdy yeoman of England, emigrated to the New World, the land of promise. He settled in Essex County, Massachusetts, and afterwards married Mary French. The numerous descendants of these worthy people intermarried with many of the staunchest and most industrious families of New England. Samuel, the son of Robert and Mary, born January 26, 1666, wedded Rebecca Curtis, January 25, 1707. Their son, the second Samuel, was born January 26, 1714; he married Priscilla Gould and was the father of Asael, born March 7, 1744. Asael Smith took to wife Mary Duty, and their son Joseph was born July 12, 1771. On the 24th of January, 1796, Joseph married Lucy Mack, at Tunbridge, in the State of Vermont. She was born July 8, 1776, and was the daughter of Solomon and Lydia Mack, and was the granddaughter of Ebenezer Mack.

The men of these two families, Smith and Mack, through several generations had been tillers of the soil. They were devout and generous, measurably prosperous in a worldly sense, and several of them were brave and steadfast soldiers through the early colonial campaigns and the Revolutionary struggle.

After the marriage of Joseph Smith with Lucy Mack, they settled, respected and happy, upon their own farm at Tunbridge. Here they were successful, financially, for a few years, until the dishonesty of a trusted friend and agent robbed them of their surplus means and left them plunged in debt. They freely sacrificed all of monetary value which they possessed, even homestead and Lucy's treasured marriage portion, and paid every just claim which was held against them. Left thus in absolute poverty, they sought to retrieve their loss of home; and Tunbridge, where they were known and respected, offered for a time a prospect of success. Soon afterwards, however, they removed to Sharon, where Joseph rented a farm from his father-in-law. This field he diligently tilled through the summer, and during the winter taught the village school. Comfort was restored to them; but they were destined to be still tried and sanctified by the tribulations of life. Honest and industrious, pious and benevolent, yet Joseph and Lucy saw themselves and their children pursued by poverty, illness and the cold neglect of their fellow mortals. They repined not at their chastenings, but they marveled.

God was teaching the parents the great lesson of personal humility; and they and their children were learning how fleeting is earthly wealth and how fallible is mere human friendship. For the choice seed which is to bring forth rich and perfect fruit, the Lord Almighty prepares the soil of His garden.

The paternal grandfather of the Prophet was Asael Smith, a man of the strongest religious convictions, and yet a man whose broad humanitarian views were repugnant to many of the sectarians of the day. Upon one occasion, before the Prophet's birth, Asael Smith had a premonition that one of his descendants should be a great teacher and leader of men. To quote his words, as they are remembered and recorded by one who knew and heard him speak: "It has been borne in upon my soul that one of my descendants will promulgate a work to revolutionize the world of religious faith."

It is not known if the young Joseph ever learned of this prophetic declaration until after his own career had been made manifest. But Asael lived to see the dawn of the fulfillment of his words. Just before his death, the Book of Mormon, then recently printed, was presented to him.

He accepted it, and with the light of inspiration which sometimes illumines the mind of man as the veil of eternity opens to his gaze, Asael solemnly warned his attendants to give heed to the book, for it was true, and its coming forth heralded a renewal of the gospel light.

CHAPTER 2

Religious Activity

The circumstances and surroundings of the elder Joseph were of the humblest, when unto his house was born, on the 23rd of December, 1805, Joseph, the Prophet of the last dispensation. The family was still living in the little town of Sharon, in Windsor County, Vermont; and was, at the time, greatly impoverished. Very early, therefore, was the future Prophet compelled to learn the lessons of labor, patience and self-denial. The father was striving with every faculty to repair his shattered fortunes, that he might educate his children and provide for their comfort and well-being; but successive disasters consumed his little savings. After a time he removed from Sharon, and later, in 1815, left the state of Vermont, locating at Palmyra, Ontario County, New York; in which place and the adjoining town of Manchester, whither the family moved four years afterward, they dwelt for several years. Here they engaged in clearing land and farming, the boys, including the young Joseph, giving their constant aid to the family work. With the severest toil they could only compass a frugal mode of life. But they wasted no time in useless repining. They were able to pay their obligations, to maintain their honest name, to live in happiness, and to devote some hours of each week to the rudimentary education of the younger children.

The offspring of Joseph and Lucy Smith, with the dates and places of their birth, are named as follow:[1]

Alvin, born February 11, 1798, at Tunbridge, Vermont.

Hyrum, born February 9, 1800, at Tunbridge, Vermont.

---

[1] See Note 1, Appendix.

Sophronia, born May 18, 1803, at Tunbridge, Vermont.

Joseph, born December 23, 1805, at Sharon, Vermont.

Samuel, born March 13, 1808, at Tunbridge, Vermont.

Ephraim, born March 13, 1810, at Royalton, Vermont.

William, born March 13, 1811, at Royalton, Vermont.

Catherine, born July 8, 1812, at Lebanon, New Hampshire.

Don Carlos, born March 25, 1816, at Norwich, Vermont.

Lucy, born July 18, 1821, at Palmyra, New York.

The first quarter of the nineteenth century was a time of intense religious excitement, and New York and surrounding states were the scenes of many revivals and much strife. Not only among preachers and exhorters was the enthusiasm manifested, but the people themselves became much exercised over their sinful condition and ran here and there in a wild search for the salvation for which their souls seemed to yearn. The movement originated with the Methodists; but it soon spread to other sects in the neighborhood until the whole region was infected by it and the greatest excitement was created, in which all the good effects of a revival were swallowed up in bitter contests of opinions and the strife of words between the adherents of the various creeds.

The Smith family inclined towards the Presbyterian faith, and the mother, two sons and a daughter united themselves with that church. Joseph was at the time in his fifteenth year—just at an age, with his limited experience, he might be deemed most susceptible to the example of others. He listened and considered, yet could not profess the faith of his family. The clergymen of other sects assailed him; but although he became somewhat partial to the Methodist creed, their soft words and direful threats were alike unavailing. The tempest could not reach the depths of the boy's nature. Unknown to himself he was awaiting the hour when the divine message should stir the waters of his soul.

CHAPTER 3

Answer
to Prayer

Joseph was earnest beyond his years; but he was not of a nature to become a prey to morbid feelings. He was neither terrified by the awful threats of the revivalists into a ready acceptance of their dogmas, nor driven by their divisions and strife into unbelief in revealed religion. The all-absorbing question with him was: Which of these churches is the church of Christ? Under the influence of his great desire to know the truth and the correct path which led to salvation, he made a thoughtful analysis of the proffered creeds. Can it be wondered at that he was bewildered in the labyrinth of paths, each of which claimed to be the heavenly way? When at divers times he thought of uniting himself with some one of the churches, his further investigation each time revealed some false mysteries. Dissatisfied with their claims and pretensions, and conscious of his own want of knowledge and how easily he might err in a matter of such vital and eternal importance, he was led to seek for guidance from a righteous source. He had recourse to the word of God.

Searching the scriptures for comfort and light, one happy and most fortunate moment he read these sacred words:

> If any of you lack wisdom, let him ask of God, that giveth to all men liberally, and upbraideth not; and it shall be given him. (James 1:5.)

Like a flash of sunlight through lowering clouds, the import of a mighty truth burst upon Joseph's mind. He had been vainly asking help from men who had answered him out of their own darkness. He determined now to seek assistance from God.

A modest fear might suggest: Who was he that he should dare to approach the great Creator's throne? But there was the plain promise. He could not doubt it without doubting his Maker. He felt that he lacked wisdom; and to such as he, asking of God, there was the divine pledge to hear and give without upbraiding.

It was one morning in early springtime of the year 1820, that Joseph felt the earnest prompting and adopted the holy resolve. He walked into the depths of a wood, which stood near his home, and sought a little glade. There in trembling humility, but with a faith which thrilled his soul—alone, unseen of man, he fell upon his knees and lifted his voice in prayer to God. While he was calling upon the Almighty, a subtle and malignant power seized him and stilled his utterance. Deep darkness enveloped him; he felt that he was in the grasp of Satan and that the destroyer was exerting all the power of hell to drag him to sudden destruction. In his agony he called anew upon the Lord for deliverance; and at the moment when he seemed to be sinking under the power of the evil one, the deep gloom was rolled away and he saw a brilliant light. A pillar of celestial fire, far more glorious than the brightness of the noonday sun, appeared directly above him. The defeated power fled with the darkness; and Joseph's spirit was free to worship and marvel at his deliverance. Gradually the light descended until it rested upon him; and he saw, standing above him in the air, enveloped in the pure radiance of the fiery pillar, two Personages of incomparable beauty, alike in form and feature, and clad alike in snowy raiment. Sublime, dazzling, they filled his soul with awe. At length, one, calling Joseph by name, stretched His shining arm toward the other, and said:

This is my beloved Son: Hear Him!

As soon as Joseph could regain possession of himself, to which he was encouraged by the benign and comforting look of the Son and by the heavenly bliss which pervaded his own soul, he found words to ask which of all the multitude of churches upon the face of the globe had the gospel of Christ; for up to this time it had never entered his mind to doubt that the true church of the Lamb, pure and undefiled, had an existence somewhere among men. But the answer came that no one of the creeds of earth was pure and that Joseph must unite himself with none of them. Said the glorious Being:

> They draw near me with their lips, but their hearts are far from me; they teach for doctrine the commandments of men, having a form of godliness, but they deny the power thereof. ("Joseph Smith's Own Story.")

Even in the transport of his vision, Joseph felt amazed at the instruction. But the Heavenly Personages continued to commune with him and repeated their command that he should not ally himself with any of the man-made sects. Then they and their enclosing pillar of light passed from his gaze, and he was left to look into the immensity of space.

The boy's faith in the promises of God had now deepened into knowledge. He had been assailed by the power of evil, until it seemed he must succumb—that the limit of human endurance was passed. And in that instant of deepest despair, he had been suddenly transported into the blaze of celestial light. He had seen with his own eyes the Father and the Son, with his own ears he had heard their eternal voices. Over this untaught youth at least, the heavens were no longer as brass. He had emerged from the maze of doubt and uncertainty in which he had so long groped and had received positive assurances on the matter nearest his heart from Him, whom to know was anciently declared to be life eternal.

Emboldened, satisfied, and happy beyond expression, Joseph's first thought was of his loved ones. He must impart the glorious truth to them. His parents and his brethren listened and were lost in awe at his straightforward recital. He next sought his old friends the ministers, those who had affected such an interest in his welfare and who would have so willingly acted as his guides toward heaven. His first experience with these gentlemen was somewhat discouraging. A Methodist preacher who had formerly cultivated the utmost friendship, and who probably had acquired considerable influence with him, was soon informed by Joseph of the heavenly manifestation. The pious man treated the communication with contempt, and curtly replied that there were no such things as visions or revelations in these days, they having ceased with the apostles, and that the whole thing was of the devil. Other ministers, and in fact the religious portion of the entire neighborhood, as the event became more widely known, united in the determination to overwhelm with ridicule and abuse that which they found themselves unable to silence by argument.

Joseph had been a great favorite among his neighbors; his gentle ways had made him beloved by all; he now was hated and reviled. He had been especially sought after by the clergy because of his diligence, earnestness and humility in striving to secure the grace of God; he now was stigmatized as a dissolute dreamer, a worthless knave and an arrant hypocrite. A boy of fourteen is seldom the object of universal conversation and comment in his locality; yet this youth's enemies did not rest short of lifting him to an eminence where he could the better be seen and scorned of all men.

His family were made to share the vindictiveness and contumely exhibited toward him, which at last reached such a pitch that an attempt was actually made to assassinate him. The family, on hearing the report of the gun, rushed from the house only to find the marks made by the crouching murderer at the side of the path, and the leaden missiles embedded a short distance from the spot.

But persecution, slander and cruel outrage were all unable to change the steadfast testimony of Joseph.

Three years passed away, during which time he was true to his trust—through toil and poverty, through scorn and tribulation. The heavens no more opened to his view in this trying period; but the youth, who was fast maturing—growing in strength and understanding—was able to show the staunchness of his nature while he waited in patience and humility for the additional light which he had been led to expect.

Yet Joseph was human, with human loves and human wants. He sorrowed to find himself and his kindred cast off by all their old associates, and he at times was forced into the society of persons who made few or no pretensions to religion. Doubtless the avowed infidels and unbelievers, whom he thus occasionally met, were no more lacking in genuine purity than were the self-righteous enthusiasts who shunned him except when they could devise some means for persecution and torture. But he had not yet learned to justly weigh the virtues and failings of others; and often he reproached himself with sinfulness because of his enforced associations. His quick conscience was apt to exaggerate every youthful foible, and he regarded many of his acts of thoughtlessness as offenses at which the heavens must frown.

At last he felt the imperative need of light and help from the source whence flows all truth. He acknowledged that he had fallen into many foolish errors and youthful weaknesses; and he prayed without ceasing for the pardon of every wrong which he had done. He pleaded earnestly that he might gain greater knowledge for his guidance, and asked for a manifestation, from which he might know concerning his state and standing before the Lord. Despite his own self-accusation, the answer to his prayer proves that his probationary period had been passed satisfactorily to the heavens and that he was still unstained by any dark offense.

CHAPTER 4

Cumorah's Treasure

It was on the night of the 21st of September, in the year 1823, that Joseph, having retired to his humble room, invoked an answer to his petition unto the Lord. While lying upon his bed thus seeking with all the power of his spirit, the usual darkness of the room began to fade away and a spreading glory appeared, which increased until the room was lighter than at noonday. In the midst of this light, which was most brilliant around his person, stood a radiant being, whose countenance was more bright than vivid lightning and was marvelously lovely. He seemed of greater stature than an ordinary man and moved and stood without touching the floor. He was clothed in a robe of intense and dazzling whiteness, far exceeding anything of an earthly character; and his hands and wrists and feet and ankles, as well as his head and neck, were bare. The glorious personage stood at Joseph's bedside; and to the awed youth, in a voice of tenderness and comfort, calling Joseph by name, the angel announced himself to be a messenger from the presence of the Almighty, and that his name was Moroni. The holy visitor then proceeded to unfold some of the grand purposes of the Lord. He said that through Joseph, God's power and kingdom were to be restored to earth; that Joseph's name should go out to all nations, kindred and tongues, to be blessed by the pure, reviled by the unholy—that it should be both good and evil spoken of among all people; that in the fulfillment of this mission, Joseph would be led to a hill, where was buried an ancient record engraved upon plates of gold, which record was a history of the nations that had inhabited the American continent, and furthermore contained the fullness of the gospel as given during the administration of Jesus on this land. He said that with the plates were hidden two sacred stones, set in a bow of silver fastened to a breastplate, and called Urim and Thummim, by the possession and use of which, men in ancient times had become seers, and by means of which, aided by the inspiration of heaven, Joseph also would become a seer and be able to read and translate the engraven record.

While the angel was thus speaking, Joseph was enabled in vision to see clearly and distinctly the holy hill and its environs, and the particular spot upon the hillside where the plates were held in silent trust. Moroni resumed his teachings, saying that the hour had not yet come for the translation of the record, but Joseph must prepare his mind by prayer and thought for the exalted duties and blessings which awaited him; and he most solemnly warned the youth, on penalty of sure destruction, against showing the hidden treasures to anyone except by commandment of God. Before taking his leave, the angelic messenger rehearsed much of ancient prophecy relating to the restoration of all holiness, the second coming of our Savior and His dominion upon earth; he explained many scriptural utterances; and of the wicked and unbelieving blasphemies, he spoke in such a sorrowful, yet terrible voice, that these words seemed to still the beating of the listener's heart:

> For behold, the day cometh that shall burn as an oven; and all the proud, yea and all that do wickedly shall burn as stubble!

Among many commands and promises, Moroni gave this assurance from the Lord to Joseph:

> Behold, I will reveal unto you the priesthood by the hand of Elijah the prophet, before the coming of the great and dreadful day of the Lord. ("Joseph Smith's Own Story.")

As the angel ceased to speak, all the light of the room gathered to his person. Above him all earthly things seemed moved away, and a shining pillar was stretching heavenward. With a look of hope and blessing upon the youth, Moroni ascended; and when he disappeared, darkness again fell about the bedside.

Powerful emotions crowded upon Joseph's mind as he recalled the things which had been revealed to him. And while he yet pondered, once more Moroni came and stood in a blazing glory and repeated solemnly the heavenly lessons to the listening youth, adding that great judgments were coming upon the earth and that grievous desolations should be poured out during this present generation.

Again Moroni ascended as before; and yet for the third time he returned to repeat the message of which he was the bearer. The solemn instructions were once more given, and with them a special warning concerning the plates of gold and the sacred stones. He told Joseph that by reason of the poverty of himself and family, Satan would try to tempt him to use them for the purpose of getting rich and that if he had any other motive than the glory of God, they would be withheld. Many hours had passed in this communion, and when the heavenly ambassador disappeared for the third time, Joseph heard the birds of the air heralding the coming of the dawn.

CHAPTER 5

Educating
a Prophet

At his usual hour of arising, Joseph left his bed, and according to his custom went to labor in the field. The experiences of the night had swept all color from his face. His mind was filled with thoughts unutterable, and his attention was fixed beyond his earthly toil. His father observed that the boy seemed weak and acted strangely, and told him to go home. Joseph started from the field towards the house, but on his way, in attempting to cross a fence, he sank helpless to the earth. He was recalled from a partial swoon by a voice which gently spoke his name. He looked up and saw the same glorious messenger standing above his head, clothed about with an effulgence which eclipsed the splendor of the noonday sun.

Once more the angel told the truths of the night before, with their commands and warnings, and he instructed Joseph to return to his father and impart to him that which he had learned of the purposes of God. He obeyed at once, and standing there in the harvest field, related to his father all that had passed. The inspiration of heaven rested upon the elder Joseph as he heard the lad's words; and when the account was finished, he said "My son, these things are of God; take heed that you proceed in all holiness to do His will."

Having the consent and blessing of his earthly father, Joseph departed to visit the hill. And now, within a few hours of its utterance, was one of the angel's predictions fulfilled. During the journey of two or three miles beyond Manchester toward the hill which had been pointed out to him in vision, Joseph was made to feel within him the striving of two invisible powers. On the one

hand the evil one presented alluring prospects of worldly gain
from the possession of the plates of gold—on the other, the better
influence whispered that the record was sacred and must only be
used for the glory of God and the fulfillment of His purposes. In
this frame of mind he approached the spot which he had seen
in vision. It was on the west side and near the top of a hill which
stood higher than any other in that neighborhood.[1] He easily
recognized the exact place which held the holy treasure; and upon
reaching it, he saw the rounded top of a stone peeping from the
ground, while all the edges were encased in the earth. He speedily
moved the surface soil, and with the aid of a lever raised the stone,
which proved to be the covering of a rock cavity or box. Into this
box he looked and found that it did indeed contain the promised
plates of gold and the Urim and Thummim.

Joseph could see that the box had been fashioned by
cementing stones together to form the bottom and sides; while the
rock which he had lifted away, beveled thin at the edges but thick
and rounded at the center, had formed a close-fitting cover to the
sacred receptacle. Within and across each end of the bottom of
the box lay a stone; and upon these the plates and other treasures
rested.

Carried away for a moment by admiration and his eager desire
to learn further, Joseph stretched forth his hands to remove the
records, but instantly the messenger was by his side and stayed his
touch. Moroni informed him that four years must elapse before he
could be permitted to hold and examine the contents of the box;
in the meantime he must prove faithful as he had proved in the
past, and on each succeeding anniversary of that day, during the
intervening years, he must appear at the spot to view the sacred
records, renew his covenants and be instructed from the Lord.

Many precious truths the angel now imparted to him: telling
him that he, Moroni, while yet living, had hidden up the plates in
the hill, four centuries after Christ, to await their coming forth in
the destined hour of God's mercy to man; that he, Moroni, was the

---

[1]   See Note 2, Appendix.

son of Mormon, a prophet of the ancient Nephites, who had once dwelt on this land; that to the Nephites this sacred hill was known as Cumorah, and to the Jaredites (who had still more anciently inhabited this continent) as Ramah; and much more did he impart to Joseph concerning the mysteries of the past, and the future purposes of Almighty God in the redemption of fallen mankind.

Then the kingdom of heaven, in all its majesty, and the dominion of the prince of darkness, in all its terror, were brought to Joseph's vision, and Moroni said:

> All this is shown, the good and the evil, the holy and the impure, the glory of God and the power of darkness, that you may know hereafter the two powers, and never be influenced or overcome by that wicked one. ("Joseph Smith's Own Story.")

Joseph restored the cover to the box and replaced the earth; and when the heavenly messenger had ended the counsel and disappeared, the youth again sought his home, marveling greatly at the goodness and infinite power of his Creator.

Happily for the comfort of the chosen Prophet, at this hour he met help within the family circle. He imparted to his parents and the older children all that he had been empowered to reveal; and their understanding and faith were quickened to the acceptance of the truth. They learned to know of a surety that God had spoken and that Joseph must obey.

On each recurrence of the twenty-second day of September during the next three years, Joseph visited the Hill Cumorah. Each time he opened the box, viewed its precious contents, and then restored the hiding place to its former appearance. Each time, the messenger visited him on that consecrated spot; chastening him to patience, exacting anew a covenant of self-sacrificing fidelity to the trust, and extending the counsels and instructions pertaining to the reestablishment, at the proper hour, of the Church of Christ upon the earth.

This continued communion wrought God's purpose with Joseph. It gave him a comprehension of the destiny of man, both

earthly and eternal; unfolding to his view the progression of his
race, from heaven through the probation of this world and back
to the judgment seat of Omnipotence. It filled him with a burning
zeal, and a higher wisdom than that taught in the schools began
to expand his intellect; he was learning the sublime principle of
just government; he was being fitted to become the instrument
to reestablish the Church which should endure until the coming
of Christ to reign thereby in glory. Out of His all-compassing
power, the Lord gave to this unlearned youth, from year to year,
knowledge according to the hour of his need; and the bestowal
of this heavenly wisdom was continued to Joseph through all the
vicissitudes of the mortality which culminated in that awful day at
Carthage.

CHAPTER 6

Marriage
to Emma

When Joseph first stood upon the sacred Hill Cumorah, he was in his eighteenth year. The time in which the human character most strongly assumes its shaping was to be with him the ensuing four years.

Wondrous as had been the vision of the host of heaven and the ranks of Lucifer; exalting as were the communications from the Lord; mighty as was to be the mission of translation; yet Joseph had day by day the humble labors of life to perform. Without a murmur he accepted his lot of toil, working with his hands to aid in the family maintenance, while his mind was busy with eternal truths. There is always a heroism in the honest, uncomplaining home toil of youth: a necessary heroism, indeed, for without the early formed habit of industry for man, the Almighty's purposes concerning mankind would fail. And that heroism is doubly beautiful in the life of Joseph, who knew already his destiny, divinely ordained. Left much to itself in the selfishness of earth, a weaker or an unsustained soul would have wasted its powers in vain dreamings or found its destruction in pride and self-glory.

The sweat of the face, therefore, was at once a necessity and a salutation: a requisite for the family welfare and comfort; a protection from enervating dreams. No husbandman of all that neighborhood was more industrious than he; and, except for the hatred bred against him by false teachers and their followers, no one would have had a better reputation.

As the younger sons of the family grew into vigor, the small farm and the home duties less exacted the diligence of Joseph; and when an opportunity came, in his twentieth year, for remunerative employment at a distance, he willingly accepted the offer. The engagement carried him to Susquehanna County, State of Pennsylvania, where the employer, Josiah Stoal, though dwelling in New York State, had some property upon which Joseph worked, while he boarded at the neighboring house of Mr. Isaac Hale. Stoal conceived the idea that there were signs of a silver deposit in his land, and he put his farming men to the work of mining. It was soon evident that he had become infatuated with the hope of achieving sudden and extraordinary wealth and was squandering his means in a pursuit which gave no promise of an adequate return. Joseph, who had become a favorite with Mr. Stoal because of industry and good judgment, remonstrated with him, and finally influenced him to withdraw from his sordid and fruitless project.

Isaac Hale had a daughter, Emma, a good girl of high mind and devout feelings. This worthy young woman and Joseph formed a mutual attachment, and her father was requested to give his permission to their marriage. Mr. Hale opposed their desire for a time, as he was prosperous while Joseph's people had lost their property; and it was on the 18th day of January, 1827, the last year of waiting for the plates, before Joseph and Emma could accomplish their desired union. On that day they were married by one Squire Tarbill, at the residence of that gentleman, in South Bainbridge, in Chenango County, New York. Immediately after the marriage Joseph left the employ of Mr. Stoal and journeyed with his wife to his parental home at Manchester, where during the succeeding summer, he worked to obtain means for his family and his mission. The time was near at hand for the great promise to be fulfilled and for his patience and faithfulness to be rewarded.

As the hour approached for the delivery of the ancient record into his hands, Joseph prayed earnestly for humility and strength. He had not failed in any of his prescribed visits to Cumorah. Even when at work in Pennsylvania, he had obtained temporary release that he might journey to the hill and meet his heavenly teacher.

His wife, his parents and brethren were made participants in his hopes, and they added their faith to his, and gave their hearty support to his labor and preparation.

The 21st day of September, 1827, completed the fourth year since Moroni first appeared at Joseph's bedside, and the occasion was deemed a fitting hour for prayer and thanksgiving. In that humble home God's chosen servant and his kindred offered their adoration to the beneficent Father. It was also a time for the review of the trying years since the call first came to Joseph. The family had remained in honest lowliness, unmoved by the assaults and ridicule of the world. Alvin, the eldest son of Joseph and Lucy, had died on the 19th of November, 1823, with a firm belief in the coming of the new dispensation and with words of comfort and blessing for his brother Joseph upon his lips. The faithful Hyrum, like Joseph, was happily wed. And the younger children were nearly all at years of understanding.

Quiet came with the darkness, and peace dwelt upon the house and by the pillows of this devoted family. The tranquility of the night was long remembered, for it was almost the last time they had on earth in unfearing and undisturbed enjoyment of each other's society.

CHAPTER 7

Martin Harris
Aids

For the fifth time Joseph stood by the place of deposit of the stone box and its precious contents, which for fourteen centuries had remained concealed from human vision and undisturbed by mortal hand. It was the morning of the twenty-second day of September, in the year of our Lord one thousand eight hundred and twenty-seven. For the last time he removed the soil and lifted the stone cover, while he prayed that he might be as faithful to his trust as had been the inanimate hillside. The angel of the Lord was at his side and bade him stretch forth his hands and take from their long hiding place the Urim and Thummim and the record.

Joseph touched them and his being was thrilled with a divine joy. He lifted them to the surface and examined their beauty.

The Urim and Thummim was as the angel had described it—two precious stones set in an arch of silver which was fastened to an ancient breastplate, curiously wrought.

The plates, also of gold, were of uniform size; each was slightly less in thickness than a common sheet of tin and was about eight inches in width; and all were bound together by three rings, running through one edge of the plates. Thus secured, they formed a book about six inches in thickness. A part of the volume was sealed; the other leaves Joseph turned with his hand. They were covered on both sides with strange characters, small and beautifully engraved.

Moroni instructed Joseph that he must not attempt to open that part of the book which was sealed, for the hour had not come wherein it was destined to be made known; but in God's accepted time he would bring that portion of the record to the knowledge of His children. Then the angel repeated all that he had formerly said in advice and blessing. Joseph was told that the Lord expected him to shield the record from profane touch and sight, even with his life, until his work of translation should be completed and the plates restored to the hands of Moroni; that all the former guardians had relinquished their trust and he alone would be held accountable for their safety; that efforts would be made to rob him of the holy writings, but if he proved faithful the heavens would give their aid to his support and he would come off triumphant. And he was finally and solemnly warned that if he should betray his mission he must be cut off and destroyed.

With a crowning promise to Joseph that he should not be left to grope in darkness, and that upon the conclusion of the labor of translation, the angel would visit him and again receive the plates, Moroni disappeared, and the Prophet of the last dispensation stood alone upon Cumorah, clasping to his bosom the priceless trust.

Joseph folded the golden record of past generations beneath his mantle and sped homeward. The words of Moroni had been prophetic; three different times in the brief journey to his house the chosen minister of salvation was assailed by unknown men— emissaries of the evil one, who sought to strike him to the earth and rob him of his precious charge. Once they dealt him a terrific blow with a bludgeon, but he did not fall. He was a man of rare physical endowments, yet on this occasion his own strength and activity, without the help of the Lord, would not have delivered him or been sufficient to cast his assailants one by one prone in the dust with the irresistible force which he used against them.

With the plates unharmed, but himself bruised and panting from the contest, Joseph reached his home.

After this important hour the powers of darkness arrayed all their subtle and murderous influences against him. Abominable falsehoods were cunningly circulated against him and his father's family, the purpose being to excite the rage of the populace against them. Constantly the Prophet's life was beset by assassins;

the sacred record was sought by robbers. Each hour brought some new menace. Men, lurking by his pathway, discharged deadly weapons at his person; and mobs attacked him and invaded his home. Wherever the plates were supposed to be hidden, there were the despoilers breaking through bolts and walls. Open force failing, subtle stratagems were devised for the destruction of the Prophet's life and the abstraction of the plates.

These numerous efforts all failed to accomplish the ends at which they were aimed. But they prevented Joseph from obtaining the safe leisure necessary for his labor of translation. Anxious to pursue his heaven-appointed work without the interruption of these continued attacks, he was led to the idea of removing from Manchester. Personal fear was not an element of his nature, and no selfish motive prompted his resolve; but in no other visible manner could his sacred instructions be fulfilled. The home of Emma's parents, in Susquehanna County, Pennsylvania, was the place which he selected, and thither he determined to journey.

Poverty seemed, however, to present an insurmountable barrier; but it was suddenly removed. Martin Harris, a prosperous and respected farmer of Wayne County, New York, and who was destined in the providence of God to afterwards fill an important part in connection with the divine record, was inspired to come to Joseph with a free offer of help. By the aid thus extended, the Prophet was able to take his departure to Manchester, carrying with him his wife and the sacred plates. As Joseph and Mary were warned to flee with the infant Jesus into Egypt to escape the destruction which Herod had planned, so the Prophet was led to seek another place of residence for the performance of his labor.

But Satan was not idle. Twice while on the journey was the servant of God stopped by officers, who, under a pretended warrant of law, searched his wagon for the plates. But the angel of the Lord blinded the eyes of the wicked, and they found not what they sought.

It was in the month of December, 1827, when Joseph reached the house of Isaac Hale in Pennsylvania; and without delay he began his inspired work of translation by the aid of the seer stones.

It may seem strange and unaccountable that such extraordinary efforts should be made to destroy this young man and to get possession of the plates with which he had been entrusted. But his whole life from this time forward until he sealed his testimony with his blood was filled with incidents of the most remarkable character. The words of the angel were that God had a work for Joseph to do, and that his name should be had for good and evil among all nations, kindreds and tongues; or that it should be both good and evil spoken of among all people; and they were fulfilled to the letter. No man of this generation was so passionately loved; no man was so cruelly hated. Satan knew that if the work of which God had chosen Joseph to be the founder should prevail, his power and dominion should be overthrown. Against this Prophet, therefore, the profoundest depths of hell were stirred up. While he lived he was the target at which the most deadly shafts of Satan were directed. For the succeeding sixteen or seventeen years from the time of which we write, his steps were beset by peril. Violence and murder lurked in his pathway. He was never free from menace. Through his life he enjoyed peace, but it was the peace that came from above and not that which arises from auspicious surroundings and undisturbed quiet. He was a happy man; but his happiness was never due to worldly favor or popularity. God had endowed him with a buoyancy of spirit and a strength of faith that the most deadly opposition and the most threatening difficulties could not repress; with a courage which, in the midst of brutal mobs howling for his blood, never faltered or was quenched. His was a stormy career; but he was amply qualified for it. As he himself said on one occasion:

> And as for perils which I am called to pass through, they seem but a small thing to me, as the envy and wrath of man have been my common lot all the days of my life, and for what cause it seems mysterious, unless I was ordained from before the foundation of the world for some

good end, or bad, as you may choose to call it. Judge ye for yourselves. God knoweth all these things whether it be good or bad. But nevertheless, deep water is what I am wont to swim in. It has all become a second nature to me, and I feel like Paul, to glory in tribulation, for to this day has the God of my fathers delivered me out of them all, and will deliver me from henceforth; for behold, and lo, I shall triumph over all my enemies, for the Lord God hath spoken it. ("Joseph Smith's Own Story.")

CHAPTER 8

Charles Anthon

Joseph's first labor with the plates was in obedience to the general command given to him through Moroni. The particular means by which the translation was to be effected and given to the world had not been made known; and this young, untaught, impoverished man was at that hour unable, within his own resources of education and purse, to arrange for the consummation of the work. He devoted every available moment, however, to his sacred task, constantly praying to the Almighty for aid; and yet the progress was slow.

In every step which Joseph took as the chosen messenger of God, human struggle and sacrifice, to overcome perplexing difficulties and delays, seemed necessary. In this way more than any other was he taught a patient trust, and was sanctified for the exalted destiny which awaited him. Though he had been instructed by Moroni that Jehovah designed the record to be translated for the edification and blessing of the race, he did not experience the direct interposition of God in the accomplishment of the work—except only as the power of the heavens was manifested through the Urim and Thummim. And much he marveled that the Lord should permit His holy purposes to depend upon weak and slow-moving man. But the Prophet lived to learn and to demonstrate that God commits His decrees to His earthly children for fulfillment; and though He may often work miracles in their behalf, yet are they required to give their best endeavor— even though weak and human—to the appointed deed; and out of their trials, their stumblings, their failures and their ultimate successes, will he bring the triumph of their devotion and His word.

Joseph had leisure and safety, after establishing himself at the house of Isaac Hale, in Harmony, Susquehanna County, State of Pennsylvania, in the month of December, 1827, to examine the sacred history and treasure which had been committed to his ward. And he very soon began a somewhat desultory labor of copying the different styles of strange characters found upon the plates and translating some of them by the aid of the Urim and Thummim. He thus prepared a considerable number of characters on sheets; some of them being accompanied by translations and others being alone. It does not appear that he had any more definite object in this superficial work than to seek, half-blindly, to fulfill the command delivered by the lips of Moroni, the angel of the record. But the purpose, wisely ordained, was latter apparent.

Joseph continued his efforts until some time in the month of February, 1828. Then the man, Martin Harris, who had once before befriended him, appeared at the Hale homestead.

Martin Harris had been deeply affected by his former interview with Joseph; and he had come, in the depth of winter from his home near Lake Ontario, to seek out the young Prophet and to learn more of his wondrous mission. Harris tarried a brief time with Joseph at the house of Isaac Hale; and then in this same month of February, 1828, with the Prophet's permission, he carried away some of the various copies and translations which Joseph, laboriously and patiently, had made. It was the purpose of Martin Harris to submit the characters to scientists and linguists; and possibly by their verdict to decide to establish or withdraw his half-yielded faith. In pursuance of this plan, he went to New York City, and there visited Charles Anthon, a professor of languages at Columbia College.

Anthon examined first a sheet of characters accompanied by Joseph's translation; and declared that the characters were ancient Egyptian and that the interpretation was correct—more complete and perfect than any other translation of that language which he had ever seen. He then looked at the other sheets, not accompanied by translations, and pronounced the characters to be genuine specimens of various ancient written languages. He wrote a certificate which embodied the foregoing assertions and presented it to Martin Harris.

Afterward, Anthon made inquiry of Martin regarding the origin of the characters; and then for the first time the learned professor discovered what endorsement he had bestowed upon an unlearned youth who had received from the hands of an angel a golden record filled with these ancient writings. Anthon hastily demanded the certificate which he had given to Harris; implying in his request that he wished to give the paper a final examination or to add something to it. And as soon as the professor received it again into his hands, he destroyed it, saying: "There is no such thing in these days as ministering of angels."

He asked that "the book which the young man had dug up" might be brought to him; and stated that out of his worldly learning he would translate the whole work. Harris replied that a considerable portion of the record was sealed and might not be opened to human gaze. Then Anthon contemptuously responded.

I cannot read a sealed book!

And thus was fulfilled the word of Isaiah who wrote twenty-six centuries ago:

And the vision of all is become unto you as the words of a book that is sealed, which men deliver to one that is learned, saying, read this, I pray thee: and he saith, I cannot; for it is sealed. (Isaiah 29:11.)

When the conference with Professor Anthon was ended, Martin Harris carried his manuscripts to one Dr. Mitchell, who claimed a knowledge of some of the characters; and learning what Anthon had said concerning their genuineness, the learned doctor endorsed the statements of the other scholar.

Harris returned to the Prophet's home, fully convinced. This man—generous, skeptical naturally, but honest—was seized upon by the spirit of the work. When he met Joseph he related the convincing occurrences of his visits to the learned men, and he proffered his services as a writer for the Prophet, in the great work of translation.

The proposal was gladly accepted; and Martin proceeded to Palmyra to arrange for a long absence from home. It was the 12th day of April, 1828, when he returned to Harmony, prepared to serve as a scribe.

From this time forward until the 14th day of June, 1828, Joseph dictated to Martin Harris from the plates of gold; as the characters thereon assumed, through the Urim and Thummim, the forms of equivalent modern words which were familiar to the understanding of the youthful Seer.

Martin Harris was a critical man without superstition. Listening to the words dictated day by day, and becoming familiar with Joseph, he sought to make another test.

The work progressed through the two months from April until June—not steadily, for Martin was much called away. But at the expiration of that time, on the 14th day of June, 1828, Martin had written one hundred and sixteen pages foolscap of the translation.

And at this hour came a test, bitter in its experiences and consequences to the Prophet of God.

A woman wrought a betrayal of the confidence reposed in Martin Harris and a temporary destruction of Joseph's power.

The wife of the scribe was desirous to see the writings dictated to her husband by Joseph: she importuned Martin until he, too, became anxious to have in his own possession the manuscript. Long before the 14th day of June, he began to solicit from the Prophet the privilege of taking the papers away that he might show them to curious and skeptical friends; and thereby be able to give convincing proof to doubting persons, of Joseph's divine mission.

A simple denial was not sufficient, and he insisted that Jehovah should be asked to thus favor him. Once, twice, in answer to his demands, the Prophet inquired; and each time the reply was that Martin Harris ought not to be entrusted with the sacred manuscript. Even a third time Martin required that Joseph should solicit permission in his behalf; and on this occasion, which was near the 14th day of June, 1828, the word of the Lord came that Joseph, at his own peril, might allow Harris to take possession of the manuscript and exhibit it to a few other persons who were designated by the Prophet in his supplication. But because of Joseph's wearying application to God, the Urim and Thummim and seer stone were taken from him. Accordingly the precious manuscript was entrusted to the keeping of Martin Harris; and he bound himself by a solemn oath to show it only to his wife; his brother, Preserved Harris; his father and mother; and Mrs. Cobb, his wife's sister. After entering into this sacred covenant, Martin Harris departed from Harmony, carrying with him the inspired writings.

Then came about the punishment of Martin for his importunity and of Joseph for his blindness. Wicked people, through the vanity and treachery of Martin's wife and his own weakness, gained sight of the precious manuscript, and they contrived to steal it away from Harris, so that his eyes and the eyes of the Prophet never again beheld it.

For his disobedient pertinacity in voicing to the Lord the request of Martin Harris, Joseph had been deprived of the Urim and Thummim and seer stone; but this was not his only punishment. The pages of manuscript which contained the translation he had been inspired to make, and which thereby became the words of God, had been loaned to Martin Harris and been stolen; and now the plates themselves were taken from him by the angel of the record.

The sorrow and humiliation which Joseph felt were beyond description. The Lord's rebukes for his conduct pierced him to the center. He humbled himself in prayer and repentance; and so true was his humility that the Lord accepted it as expiation, and the treasures were restored to his keeping.

Martin Harris was also shamed and grieved; and he repented in anguish the violation of his trust. But, though a measure of confidence was restored to him, he was never again permitted to act as a scribe for the Prophet in the work of translation.

While Joseph was mourning the loss of the manuscript, the Lord revealed to him many truths regarding the situation to which he had brought himself, and also warned him of the designs of wicked men who plotted to overthrow him and to put the name of God and His newly revealed record to shame in the land.

A rebuke was given at this time in words which Joseph always remembered:

> . . . although a man may have many revelations, and have power to do many mighty works, yet, if he boasts in his own strength, and sets at naught the counsels of God, and follows after the dictates of his own will and carnal desires, he must fall and incur the vengeance of a just God upon him. (D&C 3:4.)

While these momentous events were in progress, Joseph and his wife were called to mourn. In July, 1828, a son was born to their house, but the babe died after a brief time, leaving its mother at the door of dissolution. The needs of the little household now required that the Prophet should give a time to toil; and he went forth to labor humbly and uncomplainingly.

While he was thus engaged, in the month of February, 1829, he received a comforting revelation from the Almighty:

> Now behold, a marvelous work is about to come forth among the children of men; . . .
> For behold the field is white already to harvest, and lo, he that thrusteth in his sickle with his might, the same layeth up in store that he perish not, but bringeth salvation to his soul. (D&C 4:1,4.)

Joseph's desire to atone for his loss of the first manuscript impelled him to constant exertion. After his manual toil was ended each day, he contritely devoted his hours to the work of translation; and his young wife aided him by writing at his dictation. In this way some progress was made. But Emma was bowed with bodily suffering and with sorrow for her babe; and often the holy task languished, causing Joseph to pray earnestly to God for a writer who could give his whole time to the work.

CHAPTER 9

Oliver Cowdery

Almost a year had passed from the day which Martin Harris began his service as a scribe for Joseph, when once more an earthly messenger of help appeared to the Prophet.

It was at the hour of sunset on the Sabbath day, April 5th, 1829, when Oliver Cowdery came to the Prophet's door—in Harmony, Susquehanna County, state of Pennsylvania. This young man, Oliver Cowdery, a schoolteacher, had been carried in the autumn of the year 1828, in fulfillment of an engagement, to the town of Manchester, New York. Hearing there of the angelic visitations to the unlearned farm lad, Joseph Smith, he was led to a deep and prayerful investigation of the subject. A powerful conviction that Joseph had been ministered to by heavenly beings, as he had testified, was wrought upon Oliver's mind, and he asked the Lord for direct guidance. His prayer was answered, and the Lord made plain to him that his would be the privilege and the duty to aid the young Prophet as a scribe or secretary. Situated as Oliver Cowdery was, he needed inspiration from the Almighty to enable him to decide to accept such a mission; for around and within the little village of Manchester at that dark hour surged the spirits of hatred, cruelty, falsehood and even murder, and no man from any selfish wish would have cared to ally himself in acts or sympathetic words with the cause and the man condemned by all the power of the pulpit. As soon as he could gain honorable release from his school duties, Oliver journeyed to Pennsylvania and presented himself to Joseph as one who had a wish to serve God and aid His chosen servant.

This was the first conversion by the testimony of the Spirit of one who had not seen the Prophet. The Church speaks for itself of the hundreds of thousands of honest souls who have had the testimony of the Holy Ghost since that hour.

Joseph accepted Oliver as the embodied answer to his prayer for help; and on Tuesday, the 7th day of April, 1829—two days after they had first beheld each other in the flesh—the Prophet began dictating to Oliver in continuance of the work of translation. While they labored, the revelations of God came to them in guidance of their daily work, in support of their hopes and in the enlargement of their understandings concerning the principles of salvation.

As they progressed, they encountered a passage of the revealed record which spoke of baptism for the remission of sins. Deeply imbued with the sense of their great responsibility, Joseph and Oliver felt as if a personal message had come to them, requiring their compliance with some sacred observance. They talked together long and earnestly upon the subject; and one day in the month of May, 1829, they went into the woods together and knelt before the Lord. They asked Him for light concerning the matter of baptism for the remission of sins. While kneeling with uncovered heads and lifting up their voices in supplication, a messenger of heaven, clothed in dazzling glory, descended before their eyes. As in the other visitations which had come to the Prophet alone, this personage was also surrounded by a supernal light. He stated to them that he was John, known as John the Baptist at the time of Christ; and that he had come to minister to them, being under the direction of Peter, James and John, the apostles who still held the keys of the priesthood after the order of Melchizedek. He laid his hands upon their heads and said:

> Upon you my fellow servants, in the name of Messiah, I confer the Priesthood of Aaron, which holds the keys of the ministering of angels, and of the gospel of repentance, and of baptism by immersion for the remission of sins; and this shall never be taken again from the earth, until

the sons of Levi do offer again an offering unto the Lord in righteousness. (D&C 13.)

Then this heavenly personage, concerning whom the Savior Himself had said: "Among those that are born of women, there is not a greater prophet than John the Baptist," and whose unique and glorious privilege it had been while in mortality to administer the ordinance of baptism to the Son of God, instructed them in the duties of the Aaronic Priesthood to which they had just been ordained. He said to Joseph and Oliver that the Aaronic Priesthood did not possess the authority to bestow the gift of the Holy Ghost by the laying on of hands, but that such power belonged to the priesthood of Melchizedek, which in due time would be conferred upon them. John then commanded them that they should go forth unto the water; and by the authority which he had transmitted to them they should each baptize the other—Joseph to immerse Oliver first, and then Oliver to perform the same office for Joseph; and that each should, following baptism, reordain the other to the priesthood after the order of Aaron. Later, they would receive the Melchizedek Priesthood and be ordained as elders; Joseph to be first and Oliver second.

When John left them and ascended in his encircling pillar of light, they went straightway to perform the command which they had received. Joseph led Oliver down into the water, and, by authority which he had received, the Prophet immersed his companion for the remission of sin. As soon as this was done, Oliver immersed Joseph in the same manner and by the same authority. They came up together out of the water and ordained each other to the Aaronic Priesthood.

No sooner had they fulfilled the requirements left with them by John than they felt the power of holiness resting upon them. Each one of them had instantly the gift of mighty prophecy. Joseph saw and foretold the establishment of a Church founded upon the rock of righteousness; having the everlasting gospel; proclaiming the truth to all the nations of the earth; fulfilling the destiny designed by God in the redemption of humanity from darkness and misery. Oliver, too, prophesied of many glorious things, both for his own comfort and that of Joseph.

Thus filled with sublime delight, entertaining more hope and courage than ever before, they returned to their labor of translation. If anything had been wanting to banish every worldly thought from their minds and to fill them with a zealous desire to hasten the work, the promise of John supplied that requirement. Having so far been permitted to partake of the blessings and ordinances enjoyed by the chosen servants of Christ in another age, and having a promise that through faithfulness they should enjoy other gifts of this holy nature, nothing could restrain their ardor.

The bitter experience which Joseph had endured, through communicating so freely the glorious manifestations which he had received, taught him caution. When he received his first communications from heaven, he had supposed that he could relate what had occurred, and the tidings would be gladly received; but he soon learned, as so many of those who have since espoused the truth have also learned, that the words of caution given by the Lord Jesus to His disciples, concerning giving that which is holy unto the dogs and casting their pearls before swine, were as applicable to these times as they were when He gave them. There was a class of persons who would trample such precious things under their feet and would turn again and rend those who presented the truth to them. Except, therefore, in things of this sacred character which he was commanded of the Lord to make known, he kept them to himself. So he and Oliver hid within their breasts the fact of John's visitation and their baptism, and the joy arising therefrom. Yet, notwithstanding their caution, every step taken by the Prophet in fulfillment of God's purposes in this dispensation, however quietly he had acted, had been followed quickly by a new outburst of persecution. The dawn of a new era was visible, and the evil one must exert every power he possessed to becloud the minds of men. The hatred of the people dwelling in the vicinity of Harmony was kindled, unaccountably even to themselves, against the two young men. A mob spirit reigned in the neighborhood; and a murderous attack upon Joseph and Oliver was only prevented by the influence of Isaac Hale and his family, who gave sympathy and help at this hour to the Prophet.

Joseph and Oliver, in the midst of their labors, did not fail to pray for that help and guidance which they needed. From the record itself they gathered a large store of religious truths; and their minds being opened to comprehend the principles of salvation, they also searched the other scriptures, the Old and New Testaments, with great profit to themselves. As a result much blessing came to them through their devotion and industry. Joseph's concentration upon the work entrusted to him had such effect upon members of the Hale family, that they united in giving to him the assurance that he should be protected from the mob; and that he should be saved from all unlawful persecution, so far as their influence and strength could avail to defend him. They also extended to Oliver a promise similarly to protect him so long as he remained to assist Joseph.

After a little time the Spirit led the Prophet to impart to his friends and acquaintances some of the information which he had gained. Though at this time he was far from possessing the comprehension of the truth which he afterwards had, he was still rich in knowledge and blessings, compared with the people who surrounded him and who were enthralled by the ignorance and intolerance which had been growing through all the ages since the ruin of the early church.

CHAPTER 10

Hyrum Smith Baptized

While thus busily engaged, Samuel H. Smith, a brother of Joseph, came down from Manchester to Harmony. Joseph proclaimed to him the truth, so far as it had been revealed; presented to his view the translation of the Book of Mormon, so far as it had been completed; and then besought him to gain by prayer to Almighty God a knowledge for himself concerning the divine origin of that which he had heard and seen. Samuel, a man of integrity and singleness and fixity of purpose, was not easily convinced. Finally, however, he consented to ask for light from heaven. For this purpose he retired to the woods and humbled himself in supplication before the Lord. A convincing answer came to his prayer, and he hastened to Joseph with his tidings of joy. At the request of the Prophet, Oliver Cowdery administered to Samuel the ordinance of baptism for the remission of his sins, and later he was confirmed. The same signs followed in this case; and Samuel was filled with the spirit of prophecy and praise. He uttered many sublime truths of which his mind, up to that moment, had never conceived. Desiring that his kindred might be made partakers of his joy, he journeyed quickly back to Manchester to give to the family the news of Joseph's extended calling. Hyrum Smith came to Harmony immediately afterward to inquire of Joseph concerning these wondrous things. The young Prophet declared to his elder brother that an angel from heaven had restored to earth the power to baptize for the remission of human sin; and that he himself and Oliver had been made the recipients of this authority.

Hyrum Smith was a noble man, filled with earnest desire for truth and holiness. He asked Joseph to obtain further light, and at his request the Prophet solicited a direct revelation from the Lord on Hyrum's behalf. The desire was answered in a revelation given to Hyrum through the Prophet. In that revelation these words occur:

> ... Hyrum, my son; seek the kingdom of God, and all things shall be added according to that which is just.
>
> Build upon my rock, which is my gospel;
>
> Deny not the spirit of revelation nor the spirit of prophecy; for wo unto him that denieth these things. (D&C 11:23–25.)

Hyrum believed and awaited the proper hour for baptism.

While the light of truth was thus breaking upon the world, all the powers of hell allied themselves against it, with the determination that it should be extinguished. Mobs increased in strength and hatred. Added to this constant menace, Joseph once more found himself almost destitute of means. He would soon have been compelled to relinquish the glorious work of translation to engage again in manual toil for the sustenance of his family and to provide maintenance for himself and Oliver, had not Providence again raised up a friend to come to his aid.

In this eventful month of May, 1829, a man named Joseph Knight appeared at Harmony and sought out the Prophet. Mr. Knight had heard of Joseph's work and desired to contribute out of his means to the progress of the cause. He brought food and such other comforts as would enable the Prophet to continue his work of translation without being interrupted. Not only upon this occasion, but more than once subsequently, Joseph Knight journeyed from his home in Broome County, New York, a distance of thirty miles, to bring supplies to the Prophet's house.

Also in this month of May, Joseph received a revelation from God instructing him that the manuscript lost by Martin Harris had fallen into the hands of wicked men, who had made alterations with intent to bring shame and confusion upon Joseph, and distrust upon the word of the Lord; that the portion which was thus lost and changed was only a translation of an abridgment of certain records; and that, instead of translating once more this part of the work, Joseph should translate "... the engravings which are on the plates of Nephi, down even till you come to the reign of king Benjamin,—and behold you shall publish it as the record of Nephi" (D&C 10:41–42)—thus giving a more complete presentation of that portion of the history and thus preventing the wicked from bringing forth their forgery and casting discredit upon the Prophet by its means.

But the persecution did not cease, and the mobs seemed to be gathering their forces with some definite determination. At the opening of the month of June, 1829, immediate danger threatened the Prophet and his charge. But at this time a young man, calling himself David Whitmer, presented himself at the residence of Joseph and announced that he came with a message from his father, Peter Whitmer, of Fayette, Seneca County, New York. The message was an invitation from the elder Whitmer to Joseph, requesting him to remove with his work and his assistant to Fayette and there enjoy the hospitality of the Whitmers and the protection which they would be able to afford him, until his labor could be completed.

The young man, David, also related to Joseph a marvelous interposition which had enabled him to deliver his message so early. When David first felt an impression that he ought to journey to Harmony in search of Joseph, he questioned the wisdom of such a course; because his farm work was in such a condition that much loss must ensue, he feared, if he departed at a time apparently so inopportune. He was pondering his doubts upon the subject when he was instructed by the whispering of the Spirit that his duty required him to go down to Harmony as soon as his field labor should reach a certain state. He toiled during the ensuing day to harrow in the wheat of a large field; and at night he found that he had done more in a few hours than he could usually accomplish in two or three days. The next morning he went out to spread plaster, according to the custom of that region, upon another field. When he reached the spot where he had formerly deposited large heaps of the plaster, he found that it had been carried upon the field and spread just as he would have laid it by his own hand. He marveled much. His sister dwelt near the place, and he asked her who had done the work. She answered him that three strangers had appeared at the field the day previous and had scattered the plaster with wonderful skill and speed. She and her children had viewed with amazement the progress made by the men; but she had said nothing to them as they were strangers, and she presumed that David had employed them to help him through his rush of work.

Both Peter Whitmer and his son regarded these events as miraculous interpositions to aid David to hasten down into Pennsylvania. The young man therefore departed with his horses and wagon the next morning and journeyed to Harmony, a distance, as traveled, of one hundred and fifty miles, in two days.

This aid came providentially; and Joseph, after receiving instruction in answer to prayer, accepted the invitation. When the Prophet was prepared to depart from Harmony, he asked the Lord to direct the manner in which the plates should be carried to Fayette. He was told in response that the angel would receive the treasures and, after the arrival of Joseph at the home of Peter Whitmer in Fayette, would again deliver them into his hands. Thus relieved, Joseph went serenely forth; and in a few days he was safe in Fayette. In the garden adjoining the Whitmer residence, the Prophet was visited by the angel and once more was given possession of the record.

The family of Peter Whitmer, and some other persons in the neighborhood, were very earnest inquirers after truth. The supernatural instruction and aid which David had received to go down into Pennsylvania and offer his father's house as a refuge to Joseph amazed all who heard of the occurrence. Therefore Joseph found many people at Fayette anxious to receive him. Peter Whitmer and all the members of his household accorded to Joseph and also to Oliver every help and comfort within their bestowal; and thus, without further anxiety as to their maintenance or safety, they were enabled to progress with the translation of the sacred history.

While they were not laboring upon this work, they were praying and teaching among the people. Thus the Prophet and his assistant Oliver wrought much good. Several honest, God-fearing souls became convinced that Joseph Smith was entrusted with a divine mission. And in this month of June, 1829, three persons were baptized in Seneca Lake, after the pattern and under the authority received from John, the forerunner of our Savior. Hyrum Smith and David Whitmer received this ordinance under the hand of the Prophet himself, and John Whitmer, a brother of David, was baptized by Oliver Cowdery.

The work of translation went on rapidly. When Oliver's hand would grow weary after some hours of writing, either John or David Whitmer would take his place and continue at the Prophet's dictation.

CHAPTER 11

Witnesses
to Truth

After establishing himself at the home of David Whitmer, and early in the month of June while engaged in translating, Joseph was instructed that three special witnesses should be blessed of God with a revelation of the truth of the book and should be permitted to examine the plates. This was also in fulfillment of predictions published in the Book of Mormon. When this promise became known to Oliver Cowdery and David Whitmer, they begged that they might be numbered among the three witnesses. While they were still making their petitions for this favor, Martin Harris came to Fayette. Impelled by repentance and a desire to gain forgiveness, he had followed Joseph. Martin humbled himself in prayer to God and solicited the entreaties of Joseph in his behalf. Joseph joined with Martin in praying to heaven that his humility and contribution might be accepted and that he might be received again into favor. The Lord answered Joseph that if Martin continued faithful and humble, and refused to be led away again by evil counsels or the vanity of the world, his sins would be forgiven. Then Martin, learning that witnesses were to be chosen to behold the plates of gold bearing the engraved record, and to give testimony to all the world concerning this work of God, most penitently and anxiously solicited that he might be one of the witnesses with Oliver Cowdery and David Whitmer. Much supplication was offered by these three men; and Joseph prayed to the Lord on their behalf. Soon the Prophet received a reply that through prayer and humility, Oliver and David and Martin should witness this manifestation of the power of God; that they should view the plates of gold upon which were written the sacred records; that they should see the Urim and Thummim and the breastplate; and that they should be permitted to behold the sword of Laban, which Nephi carried away from Jerusalem. After this promise was given in a revelation through the Prophet, he and his three fellow servants, Oliver Cowdery, David Whitmer and Martin Harris, withdrew into a retired spot in the woods, and there bowed themselves in humble prayer. Joseph first offered a supplication to the Lord, and he was followed by the others in succession; all asking that the witnesses might be purified and forgiven before heaven and be permitted to view the plates and the other treasures. At first they received no manifestation of divine favor; and they contritely and fervently repeated their solicitations. Still there came no answer. Martin Harris then arose and confessed that his presence was the cause of their failure. He said that he realized, through the whispering of the Spirit, that his presence was objectionable because of the sins he had formerly committed, and that the Lord designed this as a rebuke to him and an admonition that he must continue to humble himself before heaven. He proposed that he should withdraw to a little distance, beyond the sight of his companions, and engage in silent prayer while they should continue their joint supplications for the favor of God.

After Martin had left, the others knelt down again and engaged once more in prayer. While they were beseeching the heavens, a light of exceeding brightness changed the shadowed air above their heads into wondrous brilliancy and soon descended around about them. Within a pillar of radiance stood the angel holding the treasures in his hands. He turned over the leaves of the unsealed portion of the record one by one and displayed to the gaze of Oliver and David the golden plates. So bright was the light that they could plainly discern the engraved characters. The angel also showed to them the other promised treasures. While the light was still about them, the voice of heaven declared to them the divinity of the work of which they were the witnesses. And after they had been admonished to be forever faithful to the testimony bestowed upon them, the vision withdrew.

Joseph left Oliver and David engaged in thanksgiving to God for His infinite mercy, while he hastened away to find Martin Harris. At a little distance, still within the wood, Joseph discovered Martin praying hopelessly. He had not been able to obtain an answer to his supplication, and he earnestly entreated Joseph to join with him in his appeal to the Lord. Meekly they prayed to God; and at length came an answer in the renewal of the vision. Once more the holy personage descended in dazzling brightness and exhibited to Martin the plates and the other treasures as they had been shown to Oliver and David. And again the voice of heaven gave testimony and admonition. So great was the glory of the vision that Martin Harris had not strength to sustain his ecstasy long; and he fell upon his face, crying,

"It is enough! Mine eyes have beheld of the glories of God!"

All the witnesses then returned with the Prophet to the house of Peter Whitmer. Later they gave to the world the testimony which has since gone forth with the Book of Mormon: declaring to all nations, kindreds, tongues and people that through the grace of God the Eternal Father and His Son Jesus Christ, they had seen the plates containing the holy record; that an angel of God came down from heaven and laid before their eyes the plates; that they beheld the engraving thereon; and that the voice of God had declared unto them for a surety that the holy record was true and had been faithfully translated; and to this testimony they added the solemn words:

> And we know that if we are faithful in Christ, we shall rid our garments of the blood of all men, and be found spotless before the judgment seat of Christ, and shall dwell eternally with him in the heavens. (Testimony of the Three Witnesses.)

The great happiness which the three witnesses experienced in thus being permitted to view the sacred treasure, and the great desire they evinced from this hour to aid the work of the Lord, made Joseph anxious that others who were worthy might, in part at least, participate in that blessing. He therefore obtained permission from the Lord to show the plates of gold to eight other faithful persons: Christian Whitmer; Jacob Whitmer; Peter Whitmer, Jr.; John Whitmer; Hiram Page; Joseph Smith, Sr.; Hyrum Smith; and Samuel H. Smith. And these men also gave to the world a testimony which has linked their names forever with the Book of Mormon and the cause of Christ. They saw, and testified to seeing, the plates of gold and the engravings of curious workmanship upon them. And they closed their simple declaration with these words:

> And we give our names unto the world, to witness unto the world that which we have seen. And we lie not, God bearing witness of it. (Testimony of the Eight Witnesses.)

At length the translation was completed, and Joseph and his friends arranged to have the book printed. A contract was made with Egbert B. Grandin of Palmyra, Wayne County, New York. And soon this sublime work, which details the history of the peoples who anciently inhabited the continents of North and South America; which describes the dealings of God with the nations of the past upon these lands; and which recounts the ministrations of Christ in this part of His vineyard after His crucifixion at Jerusalem, was opened to the gaze of the world. It is a marvelous book and a wonder. Its pages portray the history of powerful nations which flourished for hundreds and even thousands of years; and yet, despite the brevity of the work, this history is more complete and graphic than any that was ever penned by the unaided hand of man. The book also contains a record of a sublime system of religion and religious government, as perfect as any enjoyed by man upon this earth.

After the work of translation was ended, Joseph recommitted his charge to the care of the angel of the record; and Moroni received it back into his keeping, to bring forth the yet unsealed portions of it only when God shall so decree.

Joseph and Oliver, under the Prophet's direction, labored assiduously to spread the truth among the people. And, though the powers of evil were often manifested against them, they still were blessed with much success. They had not waited for the completion of the work of translation in order to engage in preaching. They felt that the command was already definite and that the need of the world was urgent. As they became more acquainted with the glorious truths which had been opened to their minds through the bestowal of the Aaronic Priesthood upon them, they became eager to obtain a better understanding of the work of God and to enjoy further blessings and gifts in accordance with the promise made to them.

Some time in the month of June, 1829, Peter, James and John, the ancient disciples of our Lord and Savior, and who, under Him, held the keys of that dispensation, appeared in glory to Joseph and conferred upon him the apostleship to which they themselves had been ordained by the Lord Jesus while in mortality. Then these holy personages ordained Oliver to the same priesthood. After they had departed, Joseph reordained Oliver, and also accepted a reordination himself at Oliver's hands. Thus was the Melchizedek Priesthood in purity and power again received on earth. The gift of the Holy Ghost was sealed upon the heads of the Prophet and his fellow servant, and they enjoyed its fullness of blessing. A momentous revelation soon followed from the Lord; directed not only to Joseph, but to Oliver Cowdery and David Whitmer, making known the calling of the apostles of the last dispensation and bestowing instructions concerning the building up of the Church of Christ, according to the fullness of the gospel.

So passed some months of blessing and industry. Truth was constantly developed by study and reflection upon God's goodness and the mysteries of His kingdom through the aid of revelation from Him. Much time was also given to inquiring acquaintances and strangers who came to seek for light. Whenever any person, being convinced of the truth of the mission to which Joseph Smith had been called, solicited baptism at the hands of the apostles, if Joseph became convinced of the sincerity and worthiness of the applicant, the ordinance was administered in faith and power. It never failed to produce its promised result.

Emma, the wife of the Prophet, had remained in Pennsylvania. After the manuscript translation had been placed in the printer's hands, Joseph found time to visit his wife. As fast as the truth was made known to him through revelation, he communicated it unto her; he desired that she might partake with him of the gifts which heaven was bestowing. He paid two or three visits to Harmony during the autumn of 1829, and the succeeding winter; while Oliver, under Joseph's direction, gave close attention to the printing and publishing of the Book of Mormon. Early in the spring of 1830, the work was completed and the first edition of the book was given to the world.

And at this time the hour was come for the establishment, after the order revealed by God, of the Church of Christ once more upon the earth.

CHAPTER 12

Believers
and Mobsters

The Church of Jesus Christ of Latter-day Saints was organized on the 6th day of April in the year of our Lord one thousand eight hundred and thirty, in Fayette, Seneca County, in the state of New York. Six persons were the original members: Joseph Smith the Prophet; Oliver Cowdery; Hyrum Smith; Peter Whitmer, Jr.; Samuel H. Smith; and David Whitmer. Each of the men had already been baptized by direct authority from heaven. The organization was made on the day and after the pattern dictated by God in a revelation given to Joseph Smith. The Church was called after the name of Jesus Christ because He so ordered. Jesus accepted the Church, declared it to be His own, and empowered it to minister on earth in His name.

The Sacrament, under inspiration from Jesus Christ, was administered to all who had thus taken upon them His name.

This was a day of great joy to Joseph—a joy which was shared by those who became thus united with him in a holy work. It is also a day now reverenced by hundreds of thousands of the human family; a day to be held in sacred veneration throughout all the time to elapse until the Messiah Himself shall come in glory to accept the kingdom from the hands of His authorized servants, and to give reward for all the woes and the persecutions which men have heaped upon His chosen ones.

Joseph was at this time twenty-four years of age. A period of ten years had passed since the hour in which the Father and Son had first appeared in answer to his prayer. During the most of this time he had been in close communication with the heavens, and the organization of the Church was but the accomplishment of a definite purpose of the Almighty. Joseph had been led along, himself not knowing in complete fullness to what great result his life and labors were tending. He had only known to do the will of heaven as expressed to him and patiently to await the future. Doubtless at this hour of the organization, he looked back with thanks and marvel at all which God had given for the benefit of His children. From out of the false religions of the earth the Lord had lifted this His servant, and had trained him from boyhood in the way most pleasing to Him.

In the very manner of the restoration of the gospel, Joseph learned that God requires even His elect to defer to the order and authority instituted by Christ. The power by which Joseph Smith was baptized was the same power by which every man must be baptized who has a membership in the Church of Christ. That power had been taken from the earth, leaving the human family without the authority to administer the ordinances of the gospel during many centuries. No earthly being could restore it, and none could use it until John the Baptist conferred it in its fullness upon Joseph and also upon his fellow servant Oliver. There is something significant in the fact that the authority to baptize was bestowed upon Joseph and Oliver by the same personage who had stood in the waters of the Jordan about 1800 years before, to immerse in that stream the earthly tabernacle of God's Only Begotten. As Joseph had not been permitted to officiate in baptism or to confer the Aaronic Priesthood until John had visited him and transmitted that authority from heaven, so after even this blessing had become his own, he was unable to seal the gift of the Holy Ghost or to ordain an elder until after Peter, James and John had endowed him with the priesthood after the holy order of Melchizedek. And even after both these holy orders of priesthood were given to him, and he had ordained Oliver unto them; even after he had beheld in vision the establishment of the work of righteousness, he knew not how nor when the organization of the Church should be accomplished. It was necessary that God should define the mode and the principle of organization and should direct each step to be taken in this establishment of His kingdom;

and it was not until He did this that Joseph knew in what manner to obtain the restoration of the power which belongs to the body of the Saints in Christ.

Joseph proceeded carefully and exactly according to the instruction of the Almighty, and he laid the foundation of a work which will endure as long as earth shall last.

The people who thus became associated with Joseph were generally his seniors, but there was no hesitation on their part in yielding him the respect due to the representative of Christ on earth, and they united in giving him a devotion which supported and blessed him from hour to hour. Joseph was no longer an uncouth village lad, for the exalted course of his life during the years in which he had walked under God's guidance had elevated him intellectually until he was already the peer of any man. No doubt at this hour he was lacking, as he had been in his earlier youth, in the technical teachings of the schools; but he had a deeper knowledge and a finer judgment than any possessed by the most favored of all the students of the colleges. As a boy he may have been no more potent in swaying the feelings and judgment of those with whom he came in contact than were his fellow youths; but as a man of God, clothed upon with the priesthood, filled with zeal, noble in carriage, majestic in deportment, no person could view him without bestowing veneration. Such is the testimony of all who knew him at this time. It is true that he had not yet received that broad culture; he had not penetrated to the depths of theology, astronomy, and all the higher sciences which govern the kingdom of Christ, and unto which the Spirit of God eventually led him; but from his almost transparent face there shone a light of such beauty and power, and from his lips there came such words of divine promise to mankind, that his associates accorded to him a greater respect than could have been elicited by the most learned minister of earthly churches, or the most powerful ruler of earthly kingdoms.

The men who were thus associated with him, and who thus freely tendered him, as the vicegerent of God on earth, the highest devotion of their souls, were not naturally enthusiasts in the matter of religion; nor were they men who could be deceived. They were of Puritan ancestry and demanded the conviction of their reason before yielding their faith.

That reason once convinced, they were men of such exalted courage that they dared the ridicule of the pulpit and the anger of mobs to voice their convictions and to yield their adherence to the gospel. The witnesses to the Book of Mormon and the men who supported Joseph in his fulfillment of the divine command to organize the Church of Christ in these last days have left no room for a doubt of their sincerity. Conservative in character, thrifty in habits, they were not of a class who would venture from any slight motive to excite the hatred of a world which they knew would deem itself outraged by their avowal. Each one of them knew enough of the early experiences of Joseph to feel certain that he, too, would become the object of clerical ridicule and the vindictive persecution of the masses, incited by jealous religious leaders. At every step since Joseph's encounter with the intolerant spirit of the community in which he lived, he had been obliged to call upon the Lord to aid him with more than mortal courage, to meet and withstand the cruel assaults of his enemies. In thus joining him, the witnesses and early members of the Church provoked the hostility already raging against him, and they were obliged to seek the same source for the same reinforcement of their natural strength, moral and physical.

In this inception of the work, its character was defined to a marvelous degree. Joseph himself, and much less his companions, may not have fully understood the divine simplicity and sublime comprehensiveness of the organization of the Church of the Lamb of God, which he was commanded to effect upon that memorable day; but their minds were enlightened by the Spirit of God, and by the gift of prophecy they were inspired to foretell the grandeur of the results that would be accomplished through this organization. Standing at this distance of time from that day, the observer can clearly see how beautifully adapted it is for the purposes for which it is designed. Suitable in the beginning for the government of a Church of six members, and for branches of the Church composed of any number of members, experience has demonstrated that it is capable of furnishing heavenly government for the entire race of man. Coming from Deity, it possesses divine perfection and admits of magnificent and infinite expansion. No officers necessary for the correct government of the Church and for the growth and full development of its members were omitted, and their spheres of operation and labor were so well defined that, while they retain the Spirit of the Lord, there can be no conflict or even friction between them. Fully recognizing the free agency of man, the Lord designed that the officers should derive their power to control, and the system its wonderful elasticity and strength, from the cheerfully yielded obedience of its members. In this way the requisite authority to govern, the power to enforce and maintain order, and complete personal freedom are harmoniously blended in the organization of the Church as revealed to the Prophet Joseph.

The gospel, as revealed in part and promised in full to him at that early day, was a pure and simple gift to all men upon the face of the earth who would make themselves worthy. It neither contemplated unrighteous espionage of thought and personal action, nor unholy servitude or worship of man by man. The barbarity of power, which characterized the apostate churches which swayed the world of Christendom for so many long centuries, did not exist in this divine plan for the salvation of the human race. Such gloomy tenets as infantile damnation or accountability, and the consigning of the soul to a place of eternal misery and torment from which there could be no deliverance and to which there could be no alleviation, embodied in the systems of religion which were taught and vouched for by their teachers as divine, were absent from this simple gospel. At the time of the organization of His Church, God made known His gospel in all the simplicity and fullness of truth, sublime and symmetrical as taught by the Redeemer, not as it had been perverted for ages. All the dark and cruel mysteries which had enshrouded so-called religion were swept away. Joseph had learned by most glorious and satisfactory experience that it was possible for man to approach and know God for himself. He taught his fellows that this is the true foundation of the gospel of salvation; that it is every human being's privilege to lift his eyes to God, to obtain revelation and every good gift from Him through obedience to His laws. Who can measure the great blossoming of human character which has already appeared and the rich fruitage which the coming generations will yet yield through the enforcement of this grand truth? One of the accusations brought against the Savior, and for which His enemies sought to stone Him, was that He, being a man, made Himself equal with God. To a generation such as they, from whom God was so far removed that all communication between them had ceased, such a relationship between man and the great Creator, as the Lord Jesus taught as existing, was offensive and blasphemous. It was this elevating and ennobling truth that the Prophet Joseph taught to the world. He taught a gospel of man's worship to God, and not man's servitude to his fellow. One of its grand principles is that each soul must be accountable to its Creator for its deeds; and no person who has not reached the years of individual accountability is condemned for the nonperformance of ceremonies or ordinances which he can neither understand nor attend to. Infants are all saved in Christ and need no penance, no baptism, no church membership. But a man who has heard the word of God is personally responsible for his own life and must bear the consequences of its rejection in his own person.

The full recognition of God's authority as bestowed by Him and man's equality with his fellow man constitute the vitality of the kingdom of God. But Satan prompts man to establish creeds of man worship, in which priestcraft, as opposed to priesthood, prevails. He appeals to the avarice and ambition of men and divides society into classes, making worldly learning, the possession of wealth, and the "accident of birth" the distinctions which command respect and honor. The theology of the churches, which flourished in the region where Joseph dwelt from boyhood to maturity, flowed from the muddy stream. But he was not influenced by it. Through the revelations of Jesus, the theology which he was inspired to teach was utterly unlike any system taught by man.

Instead of being lifted up by the favor which had been shown to him, Joseph was made to feel his own weaknesses. Chosen to be a prophet and the leader of God's people, he was conscious that he was only human, subject to human temptations and human frailties. Having the honesty and courage inspired by the Spirit of the Lord, he dared to confess this openly; and, under the same inspiration, acknowledge his transgression and make his contrition known. He was not above any law which applied to his fellow man. Of his responsibility to God and his brethren of the Church, he was required by the law revealed through himself to the Church, to give as strict an account as any other member. They who participated with him in authority owed it not to him as an individual, but to the eternal power to which they were alike responsible.

The grandeur of Joseph's character is most shown in his lack of pretension. Christ declared Himself the head of the Church; and though Joseph was to be our Savior's representative here on earth, he exacted no homage from his fellow believers, but only such respect as the gospel required them to pay. The thought of gaining glory for himself appears never to have entered his mind. His conduct in the beginning, in execution of the requirements of the Lord, was but a type of his whole life. The commands of God came through him to earth, and he gave them voice firmly and fearlessly. Speaking as a prophet of God under the influence of the Spirit, he brooked no opposition; but in his personal relations with his fellow apostles and elders he gave them, according to their station and their desserts, as much deference as he asked, or was willing to receive for himself. This characteristic gave him power in the beginning. Only he who knows how to obey is worthy to command; only he who yields to others their due can expect compliance with his own order, however lawful it may be.

From this time of the organization of the Church, the revelations of God have come constantly through Christ's chosen representative, to guide, to instruct, to admonish and to warn the people; and from this source the body of the Saints has received its daily life.

CHAPTER 13

The Church Organized

Joseph saw his mission now in its full significance. The instruction which came to him when he first prayed in the woods at Manchester did not mean that he alone should find salvation outside of the creeds of man; but that the error of the ages was to be overthrown by the hand of God and the way opened for the redemption of a race.

The organization of the Church, therefore, meant that the chief apostle of Christ in this last dispensation should take upon himself the cross and bear it through life. The people must be edified and perfected, and the gospel must be extended freely to the acceptance or rejection of all nations, kindreds, tongues and people.

Joseph knew now that through prayer to heaven he must seek stores of wisdom for his own guidance and for the secure establishment and the perfect government of the Church of our Lord and Savior. He was not obliged to search the worldly records of the past for knowledge and inspiration. If at this hour all the histories of earthly governments and religious organizations, with the books of philosophy and moral truths—accepted by the world, had been blotted out, Joseph Smith and his mission of enlightenment would have abated not one tittle of their power and significance. The light of God's all-comprehending wisdom was shining upon the Prophet's soul.

The first public meeting of the Church after the day of its organization was held at the house of Peter Whitmer in Fayette, on the 11th day of April, 1830. On that occasion Oliver Cowdery, under Joseph's direction, proclaimed the word of God for the comfort and instruction of Saints and strangers. The appointment for this meeting had gone forth through all the neighborhood; and many persons came to hear what wonderful things were to be spoken by the men who professed to be called directly of God to the ministry. This was the first public discourse delivered by an authorized servant of God in these last days. At the conclusion of the services, a number of persons demanded baptism and membership among the people of God. They professed to have faith in Christ, avowed their penitence for all evil done by them, and asked to be baptized that they might obtain the remission of their sins. The ordinance was administered to such as were worthy.

Following this meeting, which gave him joy and called forth praise from his heart to heaven, Joseph journeyed to Colesville, the home of the kindly Mr. Knight whose bounty had been extended to the Prophet and to Oliver in an hour of need. Joseph desired to make known to the family of Mr. Knight all that God had spoken in way of command and promise. Mr. Knight and several members of his family were Universalists. They were firm in their conviction, but were glad to listen to the message delivered by Joseph. It was a plain statement; for Joseph made no attempt to lend earthly adornments to the pure word of Christ. Joseph Knight listened and then argued with the Prophet. But he was deeply impressed and solicited Joseph to hold meetings in which the public might hear the young apostle and have opportunity to judge of the doctrines which he avowed. Newel, a son of Joseph Knight, became much interested in the Prophet's words. Many serious conversations ensued, and Newel became so far convinced of the divinity of the work that he gave a partial promise that he would arise in meeting and offer supplication to God before his friends and neighbors. But at the appointed moment he failed to respond to Joseph's invitation. Later he told the Prophet he would pray in secret, and thus seek to resolve his doubts and gain strength. On the day following, Newel went into the woods to offer his devotions to heaven; but was unable to give utterance to his feelings, being held in bondage by some power which he could not define. He returned to his home ill in body and depressed in mind. His appearance alarmed his wife, and in a broken voice he requested her to find the Prophet quickly and bring him to his bedside. When Joseph arrived at the house, Newel was suffering most frightful distortions of his visage and limbs, as if he were in convulsions. Even as the Prophet gazed at him Newel was seized upon by some mysterious influence and tossed helpless about the room. Through the gift of discernment, Joseph saw that his friend was in the grasp of the evil one, and that only the power of God could save him from the tortures under which he was suffering. He took Newel's hand and gently addressed him. Newel replied, "I am possessed of a devil. Exert your authority, I beseech you, to cast him out." Joseph replied, "If you know that I have power to drive him from your soul, it shall be done." And when these words were uttered, Joseph rebuked the destroyer and commanded him in the name of Jesus Christ to depart. The Lord condescended to honor His servant in thus exercising the power which belonged to his priesthood and calling, for instantly Newel cried out with joy that he felt the accursed influence leave him and saw the evil spirit passing from the room.

Thus was performed the first miracle of the Church. Many people were present and witnessed it, and when they would have ascribed to Joseph honor and praise, he checked them, saying:

"It was not done by man, nor by the power of man, but was done by God and the power of His godliness; therefore let the honor and the praise and the dominion and the glory be ascribed to the Father, the Son, and the Holy Spirit for ever and ever."

Since that hour thousands of miracles have been performed by the elders of the Church, through the power of the priesthood restored from heaven and in fulfillment of the promises made by the Lord Jesus. But those who have been honored in performing them have not administered unto their fellow men to gratify any wish to behold a miracle—a sign sought for by "a wicked and adulterous generation"; but to comply with the command of the Lord in administering an ordinance designed for the healing of the faithful sick and to comfort them and strengthen them in their faith.

Newel Knight believed and was made whole. He became enrapt in contemplation of the goodness of God, and the visions of eternity were opened to his view. He saw such a world of glory that he lost his sense of earthly things. His physical being participated in the exaltation, and while his spirit soared beyond the narrow confines of his earthly house, his body was caught up and suspended in the air. When the vision passed he sank, weak but happy, to the floor. So much was he overcome that it was necessary to carry him to his bed and leave him to some hours of repose.

Of the many persons who witnessed these events, nearly all subsequently became members of the Church.

When Joseph had completed a brief ministry among the people in that region, he returned to Fayette and found that much excitement prevailed there because of the coming forth of the word of God. "The Book of Mormon was accounted as a strange thing"; and persecution was heaped upon the adherents of the Church and all who would entertain friendly relations with them.

The first appointed conference of the Church of Jesus Christ in this dispensation was held at Fayette on the 1st day of June, 1830. Thirty members were present on the opening day; and scores of people were there who already believed, or came with the desire to hear the principles taught by Joseph Smith. The Sacrament of the Lord's supper was administered to all the members of the Church in conference assembled; and the faith of the congregation was so mighty that the heavens were opened to their view, and many beheld the glory of the celestial kingdom. Newel Knight was one of the believers present, and he saw, through the parted veil of eternity, the Lord Jesus Christ seated at the right hand of the Majesty on high. Prophetic vision flooded his soul with light, and he saw the mighty work of the dispensation carried to its fulfillment; he saw Joseph Smith laboring, as the instrument of God's choice, to redeem man and lead him back to the presence of his Creator. The effect of these visions upon Newel Knight and the others who beheld them was to deprive them of their natural strength, and they were carried to couches, upon which they rested for a brief time. When their strength was restored, they arose and shouted, "Hosannah, to God and the Lamb," and then, to the wonder and joy of all who heard them, they rehearsed the glories which they had beheld.

Many baptisms followed. Those of the brethren who were most suitable were ordained to the ministry and received instantly the spirit of their holy calling. Joseph returned to his own home at Harmony. Later, accompanied by his wife and three of the elders, he went again to Colesville. Here they found many people awaiting baptism. Joseph prepared to accede to their demand. A suitable portion of a little stream in that locality was prepared for the purpose of the administration of the ordinance; but in the night sectarian priests, fearful of losing their congregations and their hire, instigated evil men to desecrate the spot and to destroy all the preparations of the elders. But the candidates for baptism remained faithful and were confirmed in their belief by this sign flowing from the hatred of the ungodly; and a few days later the ordinance was administered by Oliver Cowdery to thirteen persons at Colesville. Among them was Emma, the Prophet's wife, who believed and humbly went forth to perform the requirement of heaven. The joy of Joseph when he welcomed his wife into the Church was unspeakable.

While the baptisms were in progress, an angry mob collected and threatened destruction to the elders and believers. The mob surrounded the houses of Joseph Knight and his son Newel and railed with devilish hatred at the inmates. The Prophet spoke to them and made an effort to calm their passion, but without avail. Wearied with their own impotent wrath, the mobs departed; but only to concoct new plots.

That night a meeting was to be held, and when the believers and sympathizers had assembled, and Joseph was about to offer them instruction and consolation, a constable approached and arrested him on a warrant charging him with being a disorderly person, for setting the country in an uproar by circulating the Book of Mormon and by preaching a gospel of revelation. The officer was a kind man, and some time after the formal arrest he stated to Joseph that the object of the warrant was to place the prisoner in the hands of the mob who were determined to destroy him. These words were verified immediately after; because when the constable was taking Joseph away from Mr. Knight's house in a wagon, they found the mob in ambush awaiting the appearance of the Prophet, and ready to act murderously upon a signal from the constable, whom they vainly believed was in sympathy with them. The baffled mob, more enraged than ever, pursued the wagon a considerable distance, but were unable to overtake it; and the constable soon reached South Bainbridge, in Chenango County, with his prisoner. The hour was late and they went to an inn, where they were lodged in an upper room. Joseph occupied a bed and slept peacefully, after communing silently with his Maker. The officer threw his body across the entrance to the room and slumbered lightly. He held a loaded musket in his hands, ready to defend his prisoner from unlawful assault.

The next day was a time of intense excitement. A court was convened to consider the strange charges brought against the young man, Joseph Smith; and hateful lies, of every form which the father of falsehood could devise, were circulated to create popular dislike. But Joseph Knight appeared at the court with two of his neighbors, James Davidson and John Reid, outspoken men, learned in the law and standing high in public esteem, who were to appear on behalf of the Prophet. The bitter feeling of endangered priestcraft was visible throughout the trial; but all the accusations which were made were but lies, and none were sustained. The court declared an acquittal. The evidence in the trial was a high tribute to the character of Joseph Smith. Evidently preparations had been made to deal his influence a fatal blow; and people were brought from great distances who knew him intimately as a boy and as a young man. It was hoped by the inciters of the outrage that these former neighbors of Joseph would heed the public clamor against him and testify that his nature was evil. But on the contrary, all these witnesses declared that in all their association with the Prophet, his life had been above reproach.

Unheeding this emphatic demonstration in Joseph's behalf, his enemies determined that they would not withhold their hands. They declared that he had committed other offenses in Broome County, and they must have a warrant for him in the interest of the public weal. This paper was secured on the oath of a sectarian bigot; and no sooner was Joseph acquitted by the court in Chenango County, than he was seized under the new warrant and dragged back to Colesville. The officer in charge this time was a sympathizer with the mob. He refused food to his prisoner and refused to allow him to call at the houses of his friends or to see his wife. This constable carried him to a tavern and then invited a number of persons to unite in abuse and ridicule of the Prophet. The rabble jeered and spat upon their victim. They pointed their fingers at him, crying, "Prophesy! Prophesy!" Joseph offered security for his appearance on the following day and asked to be released; but the officer would not consent.

The only favor which he would grant to Joseph was to bring to him a cup of water and a crust of bread.

When the morning came, Joseph was arraigned before the magistrate's court of Colesville. Arrayed against him were some of the people who had been discomfited at the trial in Chenango County. This time they were determined to secure a conviction. By the side of the Prophet were his friends and advocates who had aided him in the former trial. Despite the vindictive effort of the mob, the court discharged the Prophet, declaring that nothing was shown to his dishonor. Even the cruel constable who had abused his little authority to make Joseph's lot more miserable became convinced of the entire innocence of his charge, and he besought the forgiveness of his former prisoner. He gave information to Joseph that a plot was in progress to secure his person.

The inciters of these outrages were two prominent Presbyterians of that region—Cyrus McMaster and one Dr. Boyington. The creature whom they secured to make oath against Joseph was also a Presbyterian; his name was Benton.

The honest and courageous man John Reid, who successfully defended the Prophet before the courts, himself had testified to the remarkable manner in which he was engaged in the case. A messenger came to his house and requested him to appear before the magistrate on behalf of Joseph Smith. Mr. Reid was busy at the time; he had never seen the young man Joseph Smith; and he determined not to enter the case. But before he could decline aloud, a low, strange voice uttered these words: *"You MUST go to deliver the Lord's anointed!"* He was thrilled with awe at the mysterious sound. He knew that the messenger had not spoken; and upon inquiry Mr. Reid learned that the voice had been to himself alone. The impression caused by this experience was such that Mr. Reid hastened to the place of trial. While he was engaged in the case, his mysterious emotion increased; and when he arose to defend the Prophet in argument, he was inspired to an eloquence beyond himself, and which was irresistible.[1]

When Joseph was freed from custody after the second trial, the constable extended his aid; and thus the Prophet was enabled to escape while his enemies were organizing unlawfully to get him into their clutches. Joseph had been two days without food; and when released, his friends told him that he must flee at once, for the mob had organized and was determined. Night had already come; and he traveled until daylight the next morning, when he reached a place of safety at the house of an acquaintance many miles distant from Colesville. Here he found Emma, and they journeyed to Harmony without further molestation. But a few days later, when he returned to Colesville to confirm the persons who had been baptized, the mob assailed him with greater violence than ever before; and it was with difficulty that his friends aided him to preserve his life from the attacks of the sectarian priests through their bigoted followers.

Upon returning once more to Harmony after this last visit to Colesville, the Prophet engaged in the labor of making a record, in proper order, of the revelations which had come to him from the

---

[1] It is worthy of notice here that Hon. Amos Reid, who, in early days, was secretary and, part of the time, acting Governor of Utah Territory, was the son of this honest man, John Reid, and always referred with pleasure and pride to the part his father took in behalf of the Prophet on these occasions.

Lord. In this work he was aided for a time by Oliver Cowdery; but later Oliver went to Fayette, and Emma, under commandment of the Lord, once more served her husband as a scribe.

While Joseph was thus laboring in Pennsylvania, Parley P. Pratt visited Fayette to learn something of the young Prophet. Not finding Joseph, the seeker after truth made his investigations alone. He became convinced that he had found the gospel; and he asked and received baptism at the hands of Oliver Cowdery in Seneca Lake.

This was a momentous event.

CHAPTER 14

Disharmony

The peaceful and blessed hours which the Prophet had hoped to enjoy in the performance of his holy work at his home in Harmony were quickly intruded upon. Satan had been able already to excite Joseph's enemies to a frenzy and to make the conversion of even honest inquirers difficult, and in many cases impossible. Not satisfied with this, the evil one stirred up the hearts of some of Joseph's friends and associates to feelings of jealous vanity and fear.

Oliver Cowdery, at Fayette, was the first victim within the fold of the assaults of the adversary. While the Prophet, aided by his wife, was transcribing the revelations, he received a startling letter, couched in stern and disrespectful terms, addressed to him by Oliver from Fayette. The letter demanded that Joseph should erase certain words from one of the commandments given by God to the Church, alleging that they had been incorrectly written. The Prophet was shocked and grieved because he saw therein the snare which Satan had set for the feet of some of the flock of Christ. He knew, too, how prone Oliver was to be lifted up in the pride of his heart; and he saw in this a concession to evil by Oliver which must soon be checked and withdrawn, or Oliver, and those who had sympathy for him, would soon be cast out. Joseph wrote a letter, full of loving admonition, and yet rebuking firmly the error to which Oliver was yielding. Joseph informed him that the revelation had been correctly written—it was the command of God, and no man had authority to take from it a single word.

Joseph soon followed his letter and visited his associates at Fayette. He found there a most deplorable state of affairs. Oliver

Cowdery had yielded to the power of darkness. In the vanity of his heart he had set himself up against the Prophet of the Lord, and by skillful persuasion and flattery, had succeeded in winning the Whitmers to a belief in his views. Joseph felt that they were hardened toward him and that the spirit which possessed them must at once be subdued and cast out, else they would be lost to the cause of Christ. He prayed for help and labored earnestly and lovingly to show to Oliver and the others the error of their way. None of them at first would listen to his words. The influence which possessed them was perfectly aware that if they gave attention to Joseph's words they would soon discover their mistake; and it encouraged in them an obstinate and hateful feeling. After some time Christian Whitmer became convinced of their error. He saw the abyss into which the archenemy had endeavored to drag him; and he joined with Joseph in supplication to the Lord that his father and brothers and Oliver Cowdery might be turned aside from their evil course and brought back into the right way. One by one they yielded to the voice of truth, and finally all—including Oliver Cowdery—confessed that they had been misled by Satan, and that they knew the Lord's words were not within the power of man to enlarge or diminish.

Thus, promptly met, was an error rooted out. If unchecked it would have led away some of those to whom angels had administered. This showed to Joseph and to all who were with him that constant vigilance was necessary to protect even the best from the devices of the evil one. They saw that it was against the elect that Satan directed his strongest efforts; and that, when blinded by his temptations, they were unable to see the way of righteousness from which they were departing or the mire of wickedness into which he was leading their feet. For some of them the lesson was long effective; but with others it was of but temporary avail. These latter seemed unable to long restrain their own eager ambition and vanity or to close their ears to the tempting whispers of the adversary, who constantly plotted their downfall.

While Joseph was laboring in Fayette to restore peace to his brethren and prosperity to the cause, the sectarian preachers were stirring up the minds of the people at Harmony to think and act evilly toward the Prophet and his work. As soon as Joseph went back to his home, he found that some persons who had been his friends now spoke and bore themselves coldly toward him. A Methodist minister in the neighborhood, taking advantage of Joseph's absence, had spoken all manner of evil things concerning him and had succeeded in making the people distrust the Prophet and the work of God. Isaac Hale and his family were thus led away. When Joseph had left them to go to Fayette, they were filled with kindness toward him and his wife. They promised and accorded him protection and help; and they were examining the principles of the gospel so earnestly that Joseph hoped soon to welcome his wife's family into the fold. But the Methodist minister, who was influential with Isaac Hale, had whispered such untruths concerning the absent Prophet, and Satan had worked so effectively to blind the eyes and becloud the understanding of the people of Harmony, that nearly all were ready in persecution against Joseph. Isaac Hale and his family were turned from the work and became from that hour its bitter opponents.

But Joseph must not falter in his labor. The branch of the Church at Colesville was also suffering persecution; and the Prophet had to forget for the time all his personal afflictions. In the latter part of August, 1830, he called to his company John Whitmer, David Whitmer and Hyrum Smith, and went to comfort and instruct Joseph Knight and those who were associated with him. Such fierce threats had been uttered by the mobocrats who sympathized with the Presbyterian ministers that Joseph and his brethren felt that they were risking their lives in thus journeying to Colesville. They joined together in mighty prayer, beseeching God that He would blind the eyes of their enemies and permit them to go and come without recognition by the wicked. The Prophet informed his companions that their prayer would be answered, and the angel of the Lord would protect them and cover with a veil the vision of the murderous mob. They made no effort to disguise themselves but traveled through Colesville to the house of Joseph Knight in broad day, meeting a score of their persecutors. A reward had been offered to anyone who would give information of Joseph's return; and among those whom they met were many who would gladly have earned the money, even at the expense of the Prophet's life. But no one said a harsh word to Joseph and his companions, and they were treated merely as ordinary strangers passing through the village. A meeting of the branch was held that night, and the Spirit of God was poured out upon the believers in rich abundance. They were all made firm by the blessing given and filled with a determination to yield nothing of their faith, though the anger of the wicked should be visited upon them through robbery or even death.

The next morning Joseph and his party started back to Harmony. A few hours after they were gone, a howling mob descended upon the house of Joseph Knight and demanded the persons of the Prophet and his companions—swearing to visit vengeance in case of a refusal. This mob was composed of some of the persons who had been incited by sectarian ministers on other occasions to offer violence to the Prophet. This time they were more fierce than ever before. All day long they surged around the houses of Joseph Knight and his son Newel, cursing and threatening. Nothing apparently would appease them until, exhausted by their own evil passions, they were forced to disperse.

The situation in Pennsylvania was not improved; and soon it became apparent that the Prophet could not work in the vicinity of Harmony with any degree of vigor and freedom. Persecution flourished on every side. But while the Prophet was suffering all this in body and in spirit, a messenger brought an invitation from Peter Whitmer, asking Joseph once more to come to Fayette and establish his home. The peace of the Holy Spirit had filled the hearts of the brethren at Fayette, and they desired to have the Prophet among them, to bless him with their faith, and aid him by their works in the accomplishment of his ministry. After a brief time Joseph Knight came to Harmony. Seeing the situation of the Prophet, he offered his wagon and horses for the conveyance of

Joseph's family to Fayette; and in the last week of August, 1830, the Prophet found himself established once more in the house of Peter Whitmer.

Wearied with the buffetings of the world, Joseph would have been glad to enjoy a little season of peace; but on his arrival at Fayette he found that the old spirit of vanity had gained an entrance, even while he was journeying from Harmony. One of the brethren named Hiram Page, had been inspired by the evil one to make known revelations which he declared he had received for the Church, through a stone he had, which were utterly at variance with the spirit of the gospel and opposed to the commands of God, previously given through Joseph, the ordained Prophet. These tempting declarations made by Hiram Page had met with the favor of Oliver Cowdery and some of the Whitmers. They were deceived by him; they had not yet fully learned that Satan could give revelations. Joseph rebuked again, and this time more sternly, the childish folly of these people. They were anxious to do right; and yet, without his presence, they were certain to do evil. He demanded that they should forsake the false doctrines which Hiram Page was promulgating, and that all should unite with him in asking God to reveal to them His will concerning the manner in which His commands should be given to the world. The answer to this petition was that revelation, given to Oliver Cowdery early in September, 1830, establishing once and forever the order of heaven concerning God's revelations to men.

It was made known to Oliver therein that God had but one head for His Church, and that head was His chosen servant Joseph Smith. No one else should be appointed by the Church, until God should so direct, to receive commandments; for Joseph held the keys of the mysteries and the revelations which were sealed, and through him alone should they be given, until some other should be chosen by the Lord in his stead. Oliver's place was defined to him: He should receive revelations, but not to be written by way of command to the Church. It was his duty to labor in secret with his brother Hiram Page and declare to him that the things which Hiram had written as revelations from that stone, were not of God and that Satan was deceiving him. When these things should be finished, Oliver was told, it would be his duty to go to the land of the Lamanites, or Indians, among whom the gospel must be proclaimed, and by whose borders a city should be built.

The word of God had its effect, and the evil which had been done was repented of by all. Hiram Page and the Whitmers forsook that which had been condemned and asked forgiveness.

Besides settling the grand principle that individuals can receive revelations for their own comfort, but not as commandments for the Church, and that the chosen Prophet who stands at the head shall alone have that authority, the Lord in this revelation informed His children of a purpose which to them must have been a source of amazement. It was within this divine purpose that a city of the Saints should be built; and yet here was but a handful of people, with a Prophet persecuted, threatened, driven, until he had no place to lay his head, except through the charity of his brethren.

Doubtless these people, who were now reconciled to heaven and united with each other, felt wonder that they should be called upon to engage in any labor likely to attract anew the vengeful feeling of mobs. But whatever worldly fear may have assailed them, they were soon blessed and encouraged by another revelation, which followed in a few days. It came through Joseph in the presence of six elders at Fayette; and it declared that they were chosen out of the world to proclaim the gospel of Jesus Christ with the sound of rejoicing as with the voice of a trump. They were informed that their duty would be to bring to pass the gathering of God's people upon the earth. This was the spiritual inception of that great missionary movement designed by God to bring out from every nation, kindred, tongue and people to the land which He should designate as a place of gathering, every honest soul who would have faith and accept the requirements of the gospel.

CHAPTER 15

Lamanite
Mission

The second general conference of the Church opened at Fayette, on the 1st day of September, 1830. Joseph Smith presided, and he was supported by the presence, the faith and prayers of nearly all the members of the Church. The conference lasted three days and was remarkable for the power of the Spirit which was exhibited.

At the conference Joseph Smith showed one of his greatest characteristics, which was an especial willingness to meet any issue which might be involved within his labor as a prophet, or his life as an individual. He had already won Oliver Cowdery and the Whitmers to a rejection of the destroying revelations enunciated by Hiram Page; and Hiram, himself, had abandoned these false manifestations. But the Prophet knew that the people must learn within their own individual experience to be guided by holy influence, and to know the voice of Christ and, for their individual rejection, the tempting whisper of the evil one. His confidence in the inspiration which flowed from heaven, and then from heart to heart within the congregation, was not mistaken. Every soul present at this conference realized for himself that Satan had been lying in wait to ensnare the feet of God's children,and to bring upon their heads a greater condemnation than the unbelieving world could know. Therefore the conference officially and unanimously renounced the false and pernicious doctrines sought to be foisted upon the Church and heard with joyful acceptance the revelation from God declaring that His commands should come only through His Prophet.

The men who held the Holy Priesthood in the new and everlasting covenant were learning to love one another with a love greater than that of brothers. Separated from the world no less by its hatred and murderous persecution than by their own determination to keep the commandments of God, they realized that they must seek within one another's society on earth the comfort and peace necessary to sustain them through the waters of tribulation. And at this conference was felt an unspeakable influence of union and mutual regard. People attracted by the wondrous tidings had come from afar to Fayette, and many of them listened and believed. Baptisms for the remission of sins, confirmations for the gift of the Holy Ghost, and ordinations to power and priesthood were numerous, and the Sacrament was administered to every person who was present claiming membership in the body of Christ. Faith and hope and charity abounded in the midst of the congregation of Israel.

Revelations to David Whitmer; Peter Whitmer, Jr.; and John Whitmer; and to Thomas B. Marsh, were received through the Prophet, announcing the will of the Lord concerning these brethren. Of Peter Whitmer it was decreed of God that he should soon journey with Oliver Cowdery towards the land of the Lamanites. David was rebuked for being worldly-minded; and he was ordered to attend to the ministry in the Church and before the people dwelling in the regions around about Fayette, until the Lord should give unto him further commandments.

The revelation formerly given through the Prophet to Oliver Cowdery, enunciating the divine decree concerning the Lamanites and the work to be accomplished among them, created great interest in the minds of the elders of the Church. The desire to learn more of this important matter was intensified by the harmony which prevailed during the conference, and the flow of the Spirit resulting therefrom. Joseph and his brethren realized that the purposes of God toward the Indians of this land were great and far-reaching; and that the time would come when they must receive the gospel and enjoy its blessings.

Many of the elders expressed a desire to take up the work of the ministry among their brethren bound in darkness and ignorance through the curse laid upon their fathers; but before appointing anyone to aid Oliver and Peter Whitmer in this mission, Joseph inquired of the Lord. His answer was a revelation appointing unto Parley P. Pratt and Ziba Peterson that they should go with Oliver and Peter into the wilderness, among the Lamanites. Our Lord and Savior promised them that He would go with them and be in their midst, and that nothing should prevail against them; but they were commanded to pretend to no power or revelation except that which was given to them by God and unfolded by the Holy Spirit to their understanding.

In the month of October, 1830, the elders appointed to this work departed from Fayette, carrying with them a copy of the revelations concerning their mission. Their mission was more than to journey westward to the land of the Lamanites; for each one of them was also under the special command and ordination to proclaim the gospel of Jesus Christ to every listening ear. And from the hour that they departed from Fayette, they lifted up their voices by the wayside and left their testimony in every village through which they passed.

In this same month of October, a revelation was given through the Prophet to Ezra Thayre and Northrup Sweet, calling them to labor in the vineyard, for the eleventh hour had come. They were promised that speech sacred and powerful should be given unto them if they would have faith to open their mouths before congregations. And in November, 1830, Orson Pratt—a youth of 19 years, a brother of Parley P. Pratt—came from his home in Canaan, New York, to Fayette, to ask of the Lord for light and help concerning his individual duty. The Prophet complied with the youth's desire and inquired of the Lord for him; and in response a revelation was given in Orson's behalf, which has since had a wondrous fulfillment in his life:

And blessed are you, because you are called of me to preach my gospel— ...

For behold, verily, verily, I say unto you, the time is soon at hand that I shall come in a cloud with power and great glory.

And it shall be a great day at the time of my coming, for all nations shall tremble.

But before that great day shall come, the sun shall be darkened and the moon be turned into blood; and the stars shall refuse their shining, and some shall fall, and great destructions await the wicked.

Wherefore, lift up your voice and spare not, for the Lord God hath spoken; therefore prophesy, and it shall be given by the power of the Holy Ghost. (D&C 34:5, 7–10.)

These revelations to individuals concerning their duty were necessary in that hour. Men, however faithful and devoted to the Church, had not yet learned the order of the gospel and its requirements upon them. And, that they might not be suffered to rest in their own ignorance and led astray by the wiles of Satan, the Lord, through His Prophet, marked out the plain path which they were to follow. The rich heritage of knowledge, which belongs now to every faithful member of the Church, had to be gained little by little through long and continuous prayer to God, by the early acceptors of the gospel.

The Lord suffered none to go astray for lack of commandment. And, in the subsequent history of the men whose names appear as early recipients of divine revelation, can be traced their faithfulness to heavenly requirement, or their yielding to the whispers of the evil one. The Lord in His revelation through Joseph Smith gave a mission to Orson Pratt which was nobly fulfilled. No less particular and comprehensive was His commandment to other elders, but in many instances far different was the result.

The work which the Prophet directed under these revelations shows that the plan decreed by God for the building up of His Church was understood by Joseph. Viewed from a human standpoint, the intention of the Prophet to send missionaries throughout all the land, bearing proclamation concerning the new Church, would have been a surprising ambition. What was he that he should declare a gathering place in the West; that he should command men to lay down their daily toil and go forth as ministers proclaiming religious truth to a skeptical world; that he should decree the building up of a city upon the Lamanite borders? Had Joseph Smith, at the hour when he sent forth Oliver Cowdery and Parley P. Pratt, with their companions into the western wilderness, made avowal of such intentions, prompted by vanity and a self-conceived desire to give himself and his cause prominence, complete and humiliating would have been his failure. But if the declaration which he made had originated from such a source, he could not have been subjected to greater ridicule than fell upon him when he avowed that he and his coadjutors were but fulfilling the will of God—who would not suffer His purposes to fail one jot or tittle. To call men, untrained by education and special preparation, to go forth without purse or scrip to preach the gospel, was a departure from accustomed methods that in many minds excited derision and contempt. True, this was the practice in apostolic days, and was the course taken by the Savior in the calling and sending out of His disciples, but the fashion had become obsolete. Education had become more essential for ministers than the Holy Ghost; a salary than a faith that would trust the Lord to supply food and clothing.

Teaching of the doctrine of the gathering also was a new announcement to the world. The belief common in Christendom was that man was as near to God in one place as another, and He could be worshiped everywhere alike. The idea, therefore of converts abandoning home, with all its delightful associations and ancestral memories, and going to a new land, remote from kindred and friends, as a religious duty, was a startling one and came in contact with all preconceived views. Under the inspiration, however, of the Lord, Joseph made it known as a movement required of true believers by the Almighty to prepare them for coming events. It was a bold proclamation and, viewed from a human standpoint, was likely to interfere with successful conversions. But it was from the Lord, and honest seekers after truth were led to look to Him for the evidence of its heavenly origin. The result came in due time, and should have been convincing to every human soul. Of all the commandments enunciated through Joseph Smith, nothing failed.

The Prophet, during the months of October and November, himself labored in the ministry, encouraging all by his upright and zealous life, making many converts, and spreading heavenly wisdom among all the honest-in-heart who would give ear to his words.

In the meantime, the missionaries to the West were progressing with their labor. They reached Kirtland, Ohio, and there made a brief stand, because the field seemed promising. Many persons were converted to the truth and accepted the gospel. The elders wrote at once to the Prophet, informing him of these facts, and he directed John Whitmer to proceed at once to Kirtland and preside over the branch of the Church there.

When the elders left Kirtland to proceed farther into the wilderness, one of the new converts, Frederick G. Williams, accompanied them. They went as far as Independence, Jackson County, Missouri; and were the first of God's chosen servants in this dispensation to set foot upon that consecrated soil.

CHAPTER 16

A Gathering Place

In December, 1830, two men came from Kirtland, Ohio, to visit the Prophet at Fayette. They were Sidney Rigdon and Edward Partridge. Both had accepted the gospel, as declared to them by the western missionaries, and Sidney Rigdon had been baptized. After reaching Fayette, Edward Partridge demanded and received baptism under the Prophet's hands. These two men offered to Joseph, for the work of the Lord, their time, their talents, and all they possessed. Like all the early members of the Church, having not yet gained full understanding of the purposes of God, having not yet gained confidence in their own ability rightly to determine their conduct, they desired that the Lord should give them His special commands. Joseph prayed for revelation on their behalf,and was speedily answered.

The Lord revealed many comforting and exalting truths to Sidney Rigdon and Edward Partridge. To Sidney He gave a special command that he should write for Joseph. The Lord made known to Sidney what Joseph already understood—that the scriptures should be given, even as they were in God's own bosom, to the salvation of His elect. And soon after this time Joseph began a new translation of the scriptures. While he labored, many truths, buried through scores of ages, were brought forth to his understanding, and he saw in their purity and holiness all the doings of God among His children, from the days of Adam unto the birth of our Lord and Savior. But before the close of December, after Sidney had been aiding Joseph some little time, the Lord required the Prophet to cease temporarily his work of translation. The enemy of all truth was drawing his forces around about

Fayette to achieve the destruction of the Prophet and the downfall
of the newly founded Church. But they were to be foiled. Fayette
was not the region where the Lord designed His people to settle.
Joseph's mind had been led to look to the western country for
that purpose. Contact with Sidney Rigdon and Edward Partridge
confirmed his inclination in that direction. The time had now
arrived when it appeared necessary for the accomplishment of
God's purposes, that His people (now increased to several score)
should have an abiding place. It was made known to Joseph by
revelation from the Lord where this new resting place should
be. He himself did not expect to escape personal suffering or
persecution by this new move; nor was this in the providence of
God concerning him. But he knew that every migration made by
him under the direction of the Almighty had been followed by
prosperity and increase to the work, and he, therefore, obeyed the
command to move to the place designated by the Lord, without
hesitation or doubt.

In the revelation now referred to, it was commanded that the
people of God should assemble in the State of Ohio and there
await the return of Oliver Cowdery and his fellow missionaries
from their eventful journey into the wilderness. Thus early in
the history of the Church was the destiny of the people outlined.
Kirtland was to be a stake of Zion; blessed by the presence of
God's anointed Prophet and the apostles of our Lord Jesus Christ;
glorified by a temple built to the name of the Most High; and
worthy to receive the ministrations in person of the Only Begotten
Son of the Eternal Father. And yet it was to be but a temporary
resting place; for even while the Saints were to gather to Kirtland,
the western missionaries were viewing the region in Missouri, yet
to be known as the center stake of Zion, which was to be built up
and beautified for the visible presence of our Lord and Savior.

Before organizing his company for the migration from Seneca
County, New York, into Ohio, the Prophet called a conference
of the Church to be held in Fayette on the 2nd day of January,
1831. With the opening of the year, the Prophet saw a glorious
prospect for the welfare of the kingdom. And at this conference

all present seemed to partake of his faith and of the power of the Holy Spirit. In a revelation given for the comfort and sustenance of the Saints on this occasion, the Lord made known that in secret chambers there was much plotting for the destruction of the Saints of God. The command was renewed that they should go into Ohio, and some of the reasons for this movement were made known. Encouragement was also given to the people that the Lord intended to give unto them a land of promise—a land upon which there should be no curse when the Lord should come. If they would seek it with all their hearts, the Lord made a covenant with them that it should be the land of inheritance for themselves and their children, not only while the earth shall stand, but in eternity, no more to pass away. It is upon this and kindred promises that is founded the hope so tenaciously clung to by the Latter-day Saints amid all the vicissitudes of their checkered career, that they will yet inherit that land where the center stake of Zion is to be built.

In the latter part of January, 1831, Joseph departed for Kirtland. In his company were his wife, and Elders Sidney Rigdon, Edward Partridge, Ezra Thayre, and Newel Knight. Before leaving Seneca County, and later at several points on their journey, they preached in public meetings to many searchers after the truth. On every occasion new converts came forward and accepted baptism at their hands. They reached their destination in the opening of February; Joseph and his wife at once found entertainment and comfort in the house of Elder Newel K. Whitney, one of the converts made in Kirtland by the western missionaries. For some weeks the Prophet dwelt here, solaced and sustained by the faith and prayers of some dear friends. But outside this little circle he found much to cause him concern of mind.

The branch of the Church at Kirtland had become numerically strong, for it numbered nearly one hundred members. But they had been led into strange errors and darkness. False spirits had crept in and had manifested themselves in the subjugation of the physical and mental powers of their victims—as Newel Knight had formerly been controlled and possessed by the evil power at Colesville. The Saints at Kirtland, not having had experience to enable them to distinguish between the powers of light and the powers of darkness, and believing these things to be divine manifestations, were yielding to them and imperiling their earthly and eternal salvation, when the Prophet came and by his presence and the prayers and faith of those elders who accompanied him, banished all these dark influences from the congregation of the Saints. When the faith of the Saints was aroused and exercised, the miracle which had been wrought at Colesville was here repeated. Joseph, by the power of God, rebuked the vile one and his crew; and his brother Hyrum, under the Prophet's direction, laid his hands on the sufferers' heads and cast out the devils.

Immediately following the reconciliation wrought among the Saints of God by their faith and these miracles, a revelation was given from the Lord directing what the elders should do to receive His law, that they might know how to govern His Church, and informing them that he who received his law and doeth it is His disciple; but he that saith he receiveth it and doeth it not, is not His disciple, and should be cast out from among them: and also appointing unto Edward Partridge that he should be ordained a bishop, to leave his own affairs and devote his time to the service of the Lord. This was on the 4th of February, 1831. Five days later the word of the Lord again came to the elders of the Church, saying:

> And ye shall go forth in the power of my Spirit, preaching my gospel, two by two, in my name, lifting up your voices as with the voice of a trump, declaring my word like unto the angels of God.
>
> And ye shall go forth baptizing with water, saying: Repent ye, repent ye, for the kingdom of heaven is at hand.
>
> And from this place ye shall go forth unto the regions westward; and inasmuch as ye shall find them that will receive you, ye shall build up my church in every region—
>
> Until the time shall come when it shall be revealed unto you from on high, when the city of the New Jerusalem shall be prepared, that you may be gathered in

one, that you may be my people and I will be your God. (D&C 42: 6-9.)

In this revelation instruction was given that no one was to preach or to build up the Church of Christ without being properly ordained by one having authority; the elders were taught the principles which they should declare, and they were particularly enjoined to teach by the Spirit of the Lord; and if they received it not, they were told not to teach; the moral law was plainly declared and the dreadful consequence of unchastity was strongly emphasized; he that sinned and repented not was to be cast out; consecration of property to sustain the poor was enforced; home manufacture was encouraged by the requirements that dress should be plain and its beauty the beauty which the Saints' own labor gave it; cleanliness was commanded and idleness was condemned; the proper treatment of the sick and the mourning for the dead were made known: that glorious promise—the complete fulfillment of which has been a solace and a source of unbounded joy to the Latter-day Saints through all the years which have intervened since it was given—was made, "that those that die in me [Jesus Christ] shall not taste of death, for it shall be sweet unto them"; to those who had various infirmities and had faith, miraculous healing was promised; honesty of dealing was enjoined; instructions concerning the new translation of the scriptures were given; when asked for, revelation upon revelation and knowledge upon knowledge were promised; the converts in the East were to be taught by the elders to flee to the West to escape future trouble: the Saints were to receive Church covenants sufficient to establish them in Ohio and in the New Jerusalem; he that lacked wisdom was encouraged to ask and he should be given liberally and without upbraiding; commandments were given respecting fornicators, adulterers, and other transgressors, and the manner they should be dealt with.

Altogether this was a most important revelation. It threw a flood of light upon a great variety of subjects and settled many important questions. Faithful men and women were greatly delighted at being members of a Church which the Lord acknowledged as His own and to which He communicated His word through his inspired Prophet, as he did at this time.

While Joseph was thus administering among the people, in the same month of February, 1831, the Lord commanded him to call the elders of the Church together from the east and the west, and from the north and south, to receive in solemn assemblage the pouring out of His Spirit upon them. Pursuant to this requirement a general conference of the Church was appointed to be held in Kirtland on the 6th day of June, 1831.

At no time during the Prophet's career did the care of the poor escape his attention or become a matter of indifference to him. He was a man of large benevolence, and his sympathies were quickly aroused by any tale of sorrow or appeal for relief. In the most busy and trying periods of his life, those who went to him for counsel in their troubles always found him willing to listen, and they were sure to receive encouragement and assistance. To extend comfort to the bruised spirit, and to help the needy and distressed appeared a constant pleasure to him. His hospitality, also, was a marked feature in his character. His house was always open to entertain the stranger. One of the most cherished recollections of many of the old members of the Church is the kindness with which they were treated by "Brother Joseph," and the warm welcome he gave them to his house upon their arrival at Kirtland and other places where he lived.

In the revelation above referred to, the Lord said:

> ... ye must visit the poor and the needy and administer to their relief, that they may be kept until all things may be done according to my law which ye have received. (D&C 44:6.)

In other revelations which the Lord gave to Joseph, frequent mention was made of the poor and the provisions which should be made for their sustenance. Before leaving Fayette, New York, the Church was commanded to appoint certain men to look to the poor and the needy and administer to their relief that they should not suffer. Directly after reaching Kirtland, Joseph received a revelation in which the Church was told by the Lord to remember the poor and consecrate properties for their support, that every man who had need might be amply supplied and receive according to his wants. Again the command was given to "remember in all things the poor and the needy, the sick and the afflicted, for," the Lord said, "he that doeth not these things the same is not my disciple."

A clear exposition of the duty laid upon every believer in the gospel as revealed in this last dispensation, if he had been blessed with abundance, to share of his wealth with the poor, was given in a subsequent revelation in the following striking language:

> Wo unto you rich men, that will not give your substance to the poor, for your riches will canker your souls; and this shall be your lamentation in the day of visitation, and of judgment, and of indignation: The harvest is past, the summer is ended, and my soul is not saved! (D&C 56:16.)

In this way the duty of the Saints towards the poor—this practical and essential part of true religion—was deeply impressed upon them and kept constantly before them. In numerous paragraphs of the revelations given to the Church during those early days, were the members taught that the Lord intended His people to be equal in temporal things—that class distinctions should not exist among them because of the riches of some and the poverty of others. The effect of those early revelations and teachings upon this subject has been visible upon the people from the time they were given to the present. There has been a continued yearning for such a higher life—such a blessed and heavenly condition of society—as the practical adaptation and realization of the truths of the revelations will bring about. Amid the dangers with which many of the faithful members have thought the Church has been menaced through the increase of wealth of some of their number, they have always been cheered by the assurance that the day was not far distant when the injunction

would be carried out, which the Lord gave in the days of which
we write: "Let every man deal honestly, and be alike among this
people, and receive alike, that ye may be one, even as I have
commanded you."

This has been the ideal condition to which all have lifted
their eyes. The effect has been that the wide difference which
exists in the world between the rich and the poor—with the one
class wealthy beyond all safety and reason, and the other class
wretchedly poor even to starvation—has always been felt to be
terribly wrong and contrary to the will of God. It was this bond
of union and mutual help in a temporal sense, established by
the command of Jehovah, and constantly taught by the Prophet
Joseph and his co-laborers, which enabled the Saints through all
the succeeding persecutions to move and endure as one family,
all suffering measurably alike. Since the days of the Savior there
has never been, until Joseph Smith's time, a system of social life
in which honorable poverty received such consideration and such
help. Concerning the poor at this early day the Lord said:

> . . . they shall see the kingdom of God coming in power
> and great glory unto their deliverance; for the fatness of
> the earth shall be theirs.
>
> For behold, the Lord shall come, and his recompense
> shall be with him, and he shall reward every man, and the
> poor shall rejoice;
>
> And their generations shall inherit the earth from
> generation to generation forever and ever. (D&C 56:18-20.)

The Church at Kirtland soon began to assume an importance
which alarmed its opponents. Previous to this time falsehood and
persecution had been directed almost entirely against the Prophet
himself. But as the work extended and the Church increased in
its membership, the father of lies did not confine his attacks to
Joseph; he sent forth his countless emissaries to provoke hatred
and wrath against the Church itself. Yet nothing tangible, up
to this time, could be alleged against the Prophet Joseph or the
Church which God organized through his instrumentality. Here

at Kirtland, and at this time, however, the foes of truth united in formulating and publishing to the world all the calumnies which their wicked imaginations could devise. None were more active in this infamous business than certain fearful and lying priests and their bigoted adherents; and it is from this fruitful source of accusation and slander that subsequent defamers of the Prophet's early life have drawn many of their falsehoods.

To the Saints, however, there was compensation for these attacks in the word of the Lord which they received in plainness and power at this time through the Prophet. He was inspired to write many revelations which were of priceless value to the Church. Principles and doctrines, instructions and warnings, promises and prophecies, were given with a simplicity and clearness suited to the capacity of the humblest understanding, and yet the truths they contained are so sublime as to furnish instruction and food for profound thought to men of the highest attainments and the most extensive cultivation.

Among several revelations given during this month of March, 1831, there was one of more than ordinary interest to the Saints then, and the lapse of time has only added to its importance in the minds of all believers. It was upon that never-failing subject of interest—the second coming of the Savior. The signs which should precede His coming and the wonderful manifestations which should accompany it—making the event the most awful and yet the most glorious witnessed since the dawn of creation—were described with divine clearness. In this revelation the Lord said:

> Wherefore, hearken and I will reason with you, and I will speak unto you and prophesy, as unto men in days of old.
>
> And I will show it plainly as I showed it unto my disciples as I stood before them in the flesh, and spake unto them, saying: As ye have asked of me concerning the signs of my coming, in the day when I shall come in my glory in the clouds of heaven, to fulfill the promises that I made unto your fathers. (D&C 45:15–16.)

A rehearsal is then given of instructions and predictions which He gave to His disciples, similar, but in greater fullness to those recorded in the 24th chapter of Matthew in the New Testament. For the comfort of His ancient disciples He made promises, from which Saints in every age can derive satisfaction and hope. He said:

> And it shall come to pass that he that feareth me shall be looking forth for the great day of the Lord to come, even for the signs of the coming of the Son of Man. . . .
>
> But before the arm of the Lord shall fall, an angel shall sound his trump, and the saints that have slept shall come forth to meet me in the cloud.
>
> Wherefore, if ye have slept in peace blessed are you; for as you now behold me and know that I am, even so shall ye come unto me and your souls shall live, and your redemption shall be perfected; and the saints shall come forth from the four quarters of the earth.
>
> Then shall the arm of the Lord fall upon the nations.
>
> And then shall the Lord set his foot upon this mount, and it shall cleave in twain, and the earth shall tremble, and reel to and fro, and the heavens shall also shake. . .
>
> For they that are wise and have received the truth, and have taken the Holy Spirit for their guide, and have not been deceived—verily I say unto you, they shall not be hewn down and cast into the fire, but shall abide the day.
>
> And the earth shall be given unto them for an inheritance; and they shall multiply and wax strong, and their children shall grow up without sin unto salvation.
>
> For the Lord shall be in their midst, and his glory shall be upon them, and he will be their king and their lawgiver. (D&C 45:39, 45–48, 57–59.)

In the months of April and May, 1831, the Prophet continued to labor among the people and numerous commandments came from the Lord to him and other elders, especially directing their ministrations and constantly resolving their doubts and removing their difficulties. The harvest was being gathered; the Saints from New York and other places had come up to Kirtland to join with their fellow worshipers; constant accessions were being made, until on the 1st of June, 1831, a few days preceding the appointed general conference of the Church, the congregation of the Saints numbered nearly two thousand souls.

CHAPTER 17

New Jerusalem

From all the dwelling places of the Saints throughout the land came representatives to attend the fourth general conference of the Church. It opened on the morning of the 6th of June, 1831, in Kirtland, Ohio, under the Presidency of Joseph Smith, the Prophet of God. Fourteen months had elapsed since the organization of the Church with six members. Now the congregation numbered two thousand souls. For the marvelous manifestation of His power which had brought these people to a knowledge of the truth and had enabled them to become the recipients of saving ordinances, the conference offered praise to Almighty God. There was a great outpouring of the Spirit upon the assemblage, and the Lord displayed His power in the firm establishment of His word in the hearts of His children. Joseph himself says, "The Lord gave us power in proportion to the work to be done." Several were selected by revelation and ordained to the High Priesthood after the order of the Son of God, which is after the order of Melchizedek. This was the first occasion this priesthood had been conferred upon the elders in this dispensation. The cause was no longer the work of a single family. Its glory, its promise and its tribulation, as it must endure, were shared by a considerable community; but if the Saints had been all one family in the flesh, they could not have been more united and harmonious than they were on the occasion of this conference. Peace was in the household of faith, and through humility and prayer the blessings of heaven were generally enjoyed.

In the midst of the congregation the Lord made known, through Joseph, that their next conference should be held far

away, in the State of Missouri, upon the spot consecrated by God
unto the children of Jacob, the heirs of His covenant. In the same
revelation the Lord directed the Prophet and Sidney Rigdon to
prepare for their journey into the land of Zion; promising to them
that through their faith they should know the land which was to
be forever the inheritance of the Saints of the Most High. Special
instructions were also given to others of the elders, commanding
them to go forth two by two in the proclamation of the word
of God by the way, to every congregation where they could get
a hearing. Though the western frontier of Missouri was their
destination, they were commanded to take different routes and
not build on each other's foundation or travel in each other's track.

At this time the branch of the Church in Thompson, Ohio,
fell into darkness, and messengers came to the Prophet asking
him to inquire of the Lord for them. This branch was composed
of Saints who had moved from Colesville, New York, and who
had received instructions from the Lord, through the Prophet at
the request of Bishop Partridge, as to the manner in which they
should organize themselves to conduct their temporal affairs.
In response to the supplication which Joseph addressed to the
Lord upon this subject, humility and contrition were required
from the Saints at Thompson for their transgression, and they
were directed to take their journey into the regions westward, to
near the line of the state of Missouri and the then Indian country.
Word had been received from Oliver Cowdery and from Parley
P. Pratt, announcing their ministrations in the West, and giving
information concerning the Indians or Lamanites, who dwelt in
the wilderness across the line from Missouri.

While Joseph was preparing to depart on the western journey
which he had been commanded to take, William W. Phelps, a man
of considerable prominence in the Church afterwards, came with
his family from afar and offered himself to do the will of the Lord.
He had not yet been baptized, but he was promised the remission
of his sins and the gift of the Holy Ghost by the laying on of hands,
if he would submit to the ordinances with the proper feeling, and
he was to be ordained to do the work of printing for the Church;

and for this cause was required to take his journey with Joseph and Sidney Rigdon to the West.

It was on the 19th day of June, 1831, that Joseph Smith departed from Kirtland, Ohio, to go up into Missouri, the place promised as an inheritance for the Saints and at which the New Jerusalem should sometime be established. The Prophet was accompanied by Sidney Rigdon, Martin Harris, Edward Partridge, W. W. Phelps, Joseph Coe and A. S. Gilbert and wife. As rapidly as possible they journeyed by wagon and stage and occasionally by canal boat to Cincinnati, Ohio. From the latter point they went to Louisville, Kentucky, by steamer, and were compelled to remain there three days waiting for an opportunity to get to St. Louis; they reached St. Louis by steamer and there made a brief pause. From this city on the Mississippi, the Prophet of God walked across the entire state of Missouri to Independence, Jackson County, a distance of nearly three hundred miles as traveled. This journey, through the blazing heat of June and July, was sweet to Joseph. There was a charm about it which lightened toil. The pains and burdens were unworthy of notice in the delightful anticipation of seeing the land for which the Lord, as had been shown to him by vision and prophecy, had reserved so glorious a future.

He was accompanied by Martin Harris, William W. Phelps, Edward Partridge and Joseph Coe; while Sidney Rigdon and A. S. Gilbert and wife went up the Missouri River a few days later by steamboat. It was about the middle of July when the Prophet and his party reached Independence. During the month of their journey Joseph had taught the gospel, in the cities, the villages and the country places, in vigor and simplicity.

Joseph himself says that the meeting with his brethren, who had long awaited his arrival upon the confines of civilization, was a glorious one, moistened by many tears. It seemed good and pleasant for brethren to meet in unity and love after the privations which, for the sake of obeying the commands of God, they had endured since their separation.

CHAPTER 18

Missouri Temple Site

When will the wilderness blossom as the rose? When will Zion be built up in her glory? And where will Thy temple stand unto which all nations shall come in the last days?

The cry of the ancient prophets was repeated by the Prophet of the last dispensation as he looked out upon the wilderness; and the Lord answered the supplication with words of comfort and instruction. In a revelation given immediately after Joseph's arrival with his party in July, 1831, the Lord designated Independence and the lands surrounding as the promised spot, appointed and consecrated for the gathering of the Saints. It was the revealed purpose of the Almighty to give to His devoted Saints an everlasting inheritance in that region. Independence was to be the center place of Zion, and the voice of the Lord indicated the exact spot upon which He would have a temple erected to His glory.

In this revelation the Prophet and his brethren were informed, also, concerning the division of lands among the Saints, that all might be planted in their inheritances; and special instruction was given to such of the elders as were required to perform special duties.

On the first Sunday after the Prophet reached Independence, William W. Phelps preached a sermon over the western boundary line of the United States, Joseph and the other elders being present. The strangers in the congregation were Indians, Negroes and many white citizens who dwelt in the borders of the wilderness.

Before the meeting adjourned, two believers were baptized into the Church.

Within a week after this time, the members of the Colesville branch of the Church, who had been instructed to establish themselves in the land of Zion, arrived at Independence. About the first of August the word of the Lord was received, in which was made known many of His purposes concerning this land; that it should be the place upon which the Zion of God should stand, and where a feast of fat things should be prepared for the poor.

God promised that unto this land all nations should be invited:

> First, the rich and the learned, the wise and the noble;
> And after that cometh the day of my power; then shall the poor, the lame, and the blind, and the deaf, come in unto the marriage of the Lamb, and partake of the supper of the Lord, prepared for the great day to come.

It was in this revelation that the Lord made known His will concerning all rightful submission of His Saints to earthly powers. He said:

> Let no man think he is ruler; but let God rule him that judgeth, according to the counsel of his own will, . . .
> Let no man break the laws of the land, for he that keepeth the laws of God hath no need to break the laws of the land.
> Wherefore, be subject to the powers that be, until he reigns whose right it is to reign, and subdues all enemies under his feet.
> Behold, the laws which ye have received from my hand are the laws of the church, and in this light ye shall hold them forth. (D&C 58:10–11, 20–23.)

There was a disposition on the part of many, now that God had raised up a Prophet through whom the word of the Lord could be given, not to act upon their own agency, nor even exert their own powers in many directions, unless they received a command from the Lord, or counsel from His servant to do so. The great anxiety of the people to comply with the will of the Lord engendered this disposition. But there was danger of this being carried too far. The Prophet could, under the inspiration of the Almighty, give general laws and counsel for the government and guidance of the Church, and as occasion might require, receive special revelations making known to individuals the will of the Lord concerning them and their labors. But as the Church increased in numbers, there was necessarily a limit to this. It was not the design of the Lord to keep His people in leading strings; but to develop in them the attributes of Deity inherited from Himself. It was for them, therefore, to seek for His inspiration for themselves, and to exercise their own faculties ever subject to the general laws which He would give through him whom He had chosen as the leader of His people.

Upon this subject His word came to the Prophet at this time on this wise:

> For behold, it is not meet that I should command in all things; for he that is compelled in all things, the same is a slothful and not a wise servant; wherefore he receiveth no reward.
>
> Verily, I say men should be actively engaged in a good cause, and do many things of their own free will, and bring to pass much righteousness;
>
> For the power is in them, wherein they are agents unto themselves. And inasmuch as men do good they shall in no wise lose their reward.
>
> But he that doeth not anything until he is commanded, and receiveth a commandment with a doubtful heart, and keepeth it with slothfulness, the same is damned. (D&C 26–29.)

It was also declared that by the voice of Sidney Rigdon the land should be consecrated and dedicated unto the Lord and that the temple site should be blessed and set apart. Further, the Lord commanded that Joseph and Oliver and Sidney, after the conference meeting of the Church at Independence, should return to Kirtland and pursue their work there.

> ... verily, the sound [of the gospel] must go forth from this place into all the world, and unto the uttermost parts of the earth—the gospel must be preached unto every creature, with signs following them that believe.
> And behold the Son of Man cometh. (D&C 64–65.)

The first log for a house as a foundation for Zion was laid at Kaw Township, Jackson County, Missouri, twelve miles west of Independence, on August 2, 1831. In honor of the twelve tribes of Israel, it was carried and placed in position by twelve men, the Prophet being one of that number. This act was performed by the Saints of the Colesville branch, whose settlement in this region had been dictated through revelation by the Almighty, and they were directed and assisted in the same by Joseph himself. On the same day Sidney Rigdon offered the dedicatory prayer, in which this was consecrated to be the land of Zion and to be a gathering place of the Saints. The promise of that inspired prayer "will yet," according to the words of the Prophet, "be unfolded to the satisfaction of the faithful." It seemed to Joseph that when the curse should be taken from this land, it would become one of the most blessed places on the face of the earth.

On the following day, the 3rd of August, the spot for the temple was dedicated. Only eight men were present, but the Prophet says that the scene was most solemn and impressive. The elders who were named by Joseph as having been so favored as to participate with him in this most important work were Sidney Rigdon, Edward Partridge, W. W. Phelps, Oliver Cowdery, Martin Harris and Joseph Coe. The prayer of dedication was offered by the Prophet himself; and his promises and supplications to heaven upon that spot have sanctified it for all time, and while earth shall endure.

On the fourth day of August, 1831, the fifth conference of the Church and the first conference in the land of Zion was held at the house of Joshua Lewis, in Kaw Township; Joseph presided, and nearly if not quite all of the members of the Church in that region were present.

These events which we have described—the selection and dedication of the center place of Zion and the spot upon which the temple was to be erected, the formal laying of a foundation for the first building, the holding of a conference, and the establishment of some of the Saints in the land—attracted but slight attention at the time outside of the little circle of God's people. To merely human eyes, and viewed from the standpoint of men who had no faith in the promises of God, these must have seemed insignificant and, perhaps, contemptible proceedings to be the beginning of such great works as were predicted. But from the day that land was thus dedicated, unshaken confidence in the perfect fulfillment of every promise made concerning it, has filled the heart of every faithful member of the Church. Towards it the eyes of thousands upon thousands have been directed, around it their dearest hopes for themselves and their posterity have clustered, and their daily prayer has been that the Lord would hasten the redemption of Zion and build up the center stake thereof.

Having fulfilled the requirements of the Almighty, Joseph and ten companion elders departed from Independence Landing on the Missouri River, for Kirtland, Ohio. It was on August 9, 1831, that they started to row down the river with a flotilla of sixteen canoes, carrying themselves and their provisions.

The Prophet departed on this journey as cheerfully as he had left the land of civilization for the wilderness. If he knew the persecutions and tribulation into which he was advancing, he made no sign to his fellow voyagers. After three days of rowing down the Missouri, Joseph and Sidney and Oliver were directed to journey by land speedily to Kirtland, while the others were instructed to proceed with the canoes.

On the day following this division, the 13th of August, Joseph met several elders who were on their way to Independence. A meeting was held in which joy abounded. After this the elders parted, the Prophet and his two companions continuing their journey and the others advancing toward the land of Zion.

It was on the 27th day of August, 1831, that the Prophet and Sidney and Oliver reached Kirtland. During their eventful absence they had enjoyed the Spirit of inspiration to a great extent and had witnessed many manifestations of God's power. Their faith had been strengthened, and the purposes of the Almighty had been made more clear to their comprehension. They had also gained greater knowledge of the effort which Satan was making to hide the light from the eyes of mankind. The Lord had said to them:

> . . . ye are blessed, for the testimony which ye have borne is recorded in heaven for the angels to look upon, and they rejoice for you. . . . (D&C 62:3.)

After the return of the elders to Kirtland, the Saints sought most earnestly for further instruction concerning Zion and the gathering; and Joseph received a revelation in which many things were made plain upon these subjects, and they were shown the proper manner of securing the land of Zion to the best advantage.

There had been some seeking after signs, and the Lord said:

> Wherefore, verily I say, let the wicked take heed, and let the rebellious fear and tremble; and let the unbelieving hold their lips, for the day of wrath shall come upon them as a whirlwind, and all flesh shall know that I am God.
>
> And he that seeketh shall see signs, but not unto salvation. . . .
>
> But, behold, faith cometh not by signs, but signs follow them that believe. (D&C 63:6–7, 9.)

The ensuing few days were spent in earnest labor among the Saints in Kirtland, many of whom were preparing to go up to Zion, hoping to start in the ensuing October. Joseph and Sidney were making ready to remove to the town of Hiram in Portage County, Ohio, where the Prophet intended to reengage in the work of translating the Bible. On the 12th day of September, 1831, Joseph departed from Kirtland to take up his abode at Hiram, and here encountered anew and in violence the malicious spirit which, too often, accompanied those who seek after signs.

CHAPTER 19

First LDS Paper

Joseph had learned and taught to his brethren that the mission of the gospel was to bring peace and salvation to all mankind. He himself ministered in the utmost humility among the Saints as well as among strangers, for he was well aware that faith, meekness, patience and tribulation went before blessing, and that God required lowliness of heart before He exalted men; but the lesson which was so plain to him was never learned by some who became associated with the Church in that early day. One of the first of those who sought for signs was Ezra Booth, a man who had been a Methodist priest and had become suddenly converted to the gospel by seeing a miracle performed. Soon afterwards he asked that he might be granted power of God that he might smite men and make them believe the gospel of Christ. His conversion had been by a sign, and he sought to minister by means of signs. He wanted to go forth with the power to bless in one hand and the power to curse in the other, and save souls after a fashion he thought would be successful, and entirely different from the way ordained by the Lord. Early in the month of September, 1831, Ezra Booth became disappointed and yielded to the spirit of apostasy. Later he wrote a series of false and malignant letters which aroused hatred against Joseph and the cause and which culminated in a murderous attack.

It was on the 12th day of September, 1831, that the Prophet took up his abode with his family at Hiram, Portage County, Ohio, at the residence of John Johnson, a member of the Church, and father of Luke S. and Lyman E. Johnson, who afterwards were chosen to be two of the Twelve Apostles. His daughter Marinda was the wife of Orson Hyde, another of the Twelve. Hiram was about thirty miles in a southeasterly direction from Kirtland. His first work was the preparation to continue the translation of the Bible. In the meantime conferences were held and the word of the Lord received. At the first conference, held at the house where Joseph resided, October 11, 1831, it was decided that William W. Phelps should go to Missouri, and on his way, at Cincinnati, should purchase a press and type for the publication of a paper at Independence, to be called *The Evening and Morning Star.* This conference was adjourned until the 25th day of that month, to meet at the house of Serems Burnett, in Orange, Cuyahoga County, Ohio. During the interval, certain elders were designated and directed to go forth among the other branches of the Church and collect means to aid the Prophet and Sidney Rigdon while engaged in translation of the scriptures.

At Orange there were in attendance at the adjourned conference twelve high priests, seventeen elders, four priests, three teachers, and four deacons, in addition to a large congregation of other members.

While at Orange, William E. McLellin, one of the prominent elders, desired the Prophet to obtain the will of the Lord concerning him. Joseph complied, and through the word of the Lord which came as an answer to his prayer, William E. McLellin received much encouragement for what he had done; but he was commanded to repent of some things and was warned against adultery, a sin to which, it appears, he was inclined. He was promised great blessings if he should overcome. This instruction, direct from the Almighty, seemed to affect him for a time, but the words did not sink deep into his heart, because he soon rebelled and attempted to bring reproach upon the Church of Christ. He joined with others, in whom the spirit of discontent was brooding, to find fault with the revelations of the Lord which Joseph received.

When the Prophet returned to Hiram, the Lord condemned the folly and pride of McLellin and his sympathizers, and said to them that they might seek out of the Book of Commandments even the least of the revelations, and appoint the wisest among them to make one like unto it from his own knowledge. Filled with vanity and self-conceit, McLellin sacrilegiously essayed to write a commandment in rivalry of those bestowed direct from God upon the Church. But he failed miserably in his audacious effort, to the chagrin and humiliation of himself and his fellows. The attempt was not without its benefits, however, for the Saints were enabled to recognize the difference between the works of God and the presumptuous efforts of men. Upon this subject the Lord had said that the elders should be under condemnation if they failed to bear record to the truth of His commandments, should the one who attempted to imitate them not succeed in his effort; "for," He said, "ye know there is no unrighteousness in them, and that which is righteous cometh down from above, from the Father of lights." The elders obeyed this behest of the Lord and declared in strength and power their absolute knowledge that the revelations which had been bestowed upon the Church were from God.

The Prophet held many special conferences during October and November, 1831, with different branches of the Church. He also pursued his work of translating the Bible, Sidney Rigdon writing at his dictation. Important revelations continued to be received for the comfort of the Saints. On the 3rd day of November the commandment now known and published in the book of Doctrine and Covenants as Section 133 was given to the Prophet at Hiram. Some of its sublime passages are as follows:

> Hearken and hear, O ye inhabitants of the earth. Listen, ye elders of my church together, and hear the voice of the Lord; for he calleth upon all men, and he commandeth all men everywhere to repent.
>
> For behold, the Lord God hath sent forth the angel crying through the midst of heaven, saying: Prepare ye the way of the Lord, and make his paths straight, for the hour of his coming is nigh—

When the Lamb shall stand upon Mount Zion and with him a hundred and forty-four thousand, having his Father's name written on their foreheads.

Wherefore, prepare ye for the coming of the Bridegroom; go ye, go ye out to meet him,

For behold, he shall stand upon the mount of Olivet, and upon the mighty ocean, even the great deep, and upon the islands of the sea, and upon the land of Zion.

And he shall utter his voice out of Zion, and he shall speak from Jerusalem, and his voice shall be heard among all people;

And it shall be the voice as of the voice of many waters, and as the voice of a great thunder, which shall break down the mountains, and the valleys shall not be found.

He shall command the great deep, and it shall be driven back into the north countries, and the islands shall become one land;

And the land of Jerusalem and the land of Zion shall be turned back into their own place, and the earth shall be like as it was in the days before it was divided.

And the Lord, even the Savior, shall stand in the midst of his people, and shall reign over all flesh.

And they who are in the north countries shall come in remembrance before the Lord; and their prophets shall hear his voice, and shall no longer stay themselves; and they shall smite the rocks, and the ice shall flow down at their presence.

And an highway shall be cast up in the midst of the great deep.

Their enemies shall become a prey unto them,

And in the barren desert shall come forth pools of living water; and the parched ground shall no longer be a thirsty land.

And they shall bring forth their rich treasures unto the children of Ephraim, my servants.

And the boundaries of the everlasting hills shall tremble at their presence.

And there shall they fall down and be crowned with glory, even in Zion, by the hands of the servants of the Lord, even the children of Ephraim.

And they shall be filled with songs of everlasting joy.

Behold, this is the blessing of the everlasting God upon the tribes of Israel, and the richer blessing upon the head of Ephraim and his fellows.

And they also of the tribe of Judah, after their pain shall be sanctified in holiness before the Lord, to dwell in his presence day and night, forever and ever.

And now, verily saith the Lord, that these things might be known among you, O inhabitants of the earth, I have sent forth mine angel flying through the midst of heaven, having the everlasting gospel, who hath appeared unto some and hath committed it unto man, who shall appear unto many who dwell on the earth.

And this gospel shall be preached unto every nation, and kindred, and tongue, and people.

And the servants of God shall go forth, saying with a loud voice: Fear God and give glory to him, for the hour of his judgment is come; . . .

And unto him that repenteth and sanctifieth himself before the Lord shall be given eternal life.

And upon them that hearken not to the voice of the Lord shall be fulfilled that which was written by the prophet Moses, that they should be cut off from among the people.

And also that which was written by the prophet Malachi: For, behold, the day cometh that shall burn as an oven, and all the proud, yea, and all that do wickedly, shall be stubble; and the day that cometh shall burn them up, saith the Lord of hosts, that it shall leave them neither root nor branch.

Wherefore, this shall be the answer of the Lord unto them: In that day when I came unto mine own, no man among you received me, and you were driven out.

When I called again there was none of you to answer; yet my arm was not shortened at all that I could not redeem, neither my power to deliver.

Behold, at my rebuke I dry up the sea. I make the rivers a wilderness; their fish stink, and die for thirst.

I clothe the heavens with blackness, and make sackcloth their covering.

And this shall ye have of my hand—ye shall lay down in sorrow.

Behold, and lo, there are none to deliver you; for ye obeyed not my voice when I called to you out of the heavens; ye believed not my servants, and when they were sent unto you ye received them not.

Wherefore, they sealed up the testimony and bound up the law, and ye were delivered over unto darkness.

These shall go away into outer darkness, where there is weeping, and wailing, and gnashing of teeth. (D&C 133: 16–38, 62–73.)

In November Joseph arranged the commandments of the Lord to the Church which he had received, in their proper order, and sent them up into Missouri by the hands of Oliver Cowdery and John Whitmer, the purpose being to issue a printed edition of them for their dissemination among the Saints.

Though the translating of the scriptures occupied his attention at this time, yet the Prophet was not permitted to confine himself entirely to this labor; he was often required to go out and preach the gospel. Sidney Rigdon accompanied him, and wherever they went they overcame all opposition, confounding their enemies by a simple declaration of the truth and putting to shame such of the sectarian preachers as opposed them.

On the 4th day of December, 1831, while the Prophet was at Kirtland, Newel K. Whitney was called by revelation from the Lord to be a bishop in that part of the vineyard, and his duties in that important office were specified.

Ezra Booth had succeeded in securing space in the columns of the Ohio *Star*, in which to publish his slanderous denunciations and falsehoods concerning Joseph and the Church. In replying to these, and in vindicating the people against them, the Prophet and Sidney Rigdon were closely occupied for some weeks. Satan was busy arousing enmity, and he used the apostate Booth and others as his instruments to provoke persecution. They were successful in filling the minds of many with darkness and prejudice; but Joseph and Sidney, wherever they appeared, were enabled to allay much of the excited feeling of bigotry.

At Hiram, on the 16th day of February, 1832, the "vision," which is recorded in the Doctrine and Covenants, Section 76— one of the grandest revelations given by God to man, in which the different degrees of glory held in reserve by the Almighty for His children and the dreadful fate which awaits the sons of perdition, were described with felicitous clearness—was given to Joseph and Sidney Rigdon. In writing this vision they leave this momentous testimony:

> And now, after the many testimonies that have been given of him [Jesus Christ], this is the testimony, last of all, which we give of him: That he lives!
>
> For we saw him, even on the right hand of God; and we heard the voice bearing record that he is the Only Begotten of the Father—
>
> That by him, and through him, and of him, the worlds are and were created, and the inhabitants thereof are begotten sons and daughters unto God. (D&C 76:22–24.)

As the numerical strength of the Church increased, the Lord renewed his instructions concerning the welfare of the poor of His people. In a revelation given in the month of March, 1832, it was declared that a storehouse must be established for the needy among the Saints. This revelation also declared the Lord's will and purpose to yet establish a city in the land of Zion to secure equality of earthly blessings among the Saints.

The wondrous enlightenment wrought by the revelations and the instructions of the past year had been shared by Joseph with his brethren. Nor did the knowledge of the great work stop with the Prophet and the believers. It extended to the opponents of the Almighty's purposes, and they were stirred up to intensity of hate. The wider the influence of the Prophet and his mission, the greater the scope of salvation thus ordained, the fiercer flamed out the fire of persecution. The murderous spirit of evil which had followed close upon Joseph's footsteps for several years threw its shadow on his humble home at Hiram. He had received a letter from Missouri announcing the arrival of the brethren at Independence and containing a prospectus for *The Evening and Morning Star,* and he was making preparation to visit the land of Zion when the fury of mobocratic violence broke loose upon him.

During his residence at Father Johnson's, he had held many meetings in the evenings and on the Sabbath and had baptized a number of persons. Olmsted Johnson, a son of Father Johnson, who had come upon a visit, heard the gospel from Joseph's lips; but the young man would not accept it. Joseph was led to warn him that if he rejected the truth and should depart without obeying the requirements of the gospel, he should never return nor see his father's face more in this life. Olmsted was obdurate and left Hiram for the Southern States and Mexico. On his way homeward he was stricken with illness in Virginia and died there—a literal fulfillment of the warning he had received.

Ezra Booth exerted a baleful influence upon three others of the Johnson boys who had already accepted the gospel, and they grew weak in the faith, and finally, together with Simonds Rider, apostatized and opposed the Prophet.

CHAPTER 20

Persecution Renewed

When the Prophet went to Hiram, he carried with him twin children, the offspring of John Murdock, whom Emma adopted when they were nine days old, intending to rear them in place of twin children of her own who had died. These babes were now eleven months old. On the 25th of March they were very ill, and the Prophet and his wife were anxiously nursing them and getting only a little broken rest. At a late hour of the night, Joseph was lying down and slumbering heavily from weariness, when Emma heard a gentle tapping on the window. Her senses were dulled by sleepiness, and she paid little attention to the noise and made no inquiry nor investigation. A few moments later an infuriated mob burst the door open and surrounded the bed whereon Joseph lay in deep slumber. Ten or twelve of them had seized him and were dragging him from the house when Emma screamed. The cry awakened the Prophet, and in an instant he realized his position. As they were taking him through the door, he made a desperate struggle to release himself. Getting a limb clear for a moment, he kicked one of the mob with such force as to fell the wretch to the ground. But before Joseph could bring his superior physical powers to bear, he was confined again within the grasp of numerous hands; and with a torrent of oaths in which the mobbers profaned the name of Deity, they declared that they would kill him if he did not cease his struggles. As they started around the house with him, the mobocrat whom he had kicked came thrusting his bloody hands into the Prophet's face and shrieked at him with frightful execrations. Then they seized his throat and choked him until he ceased to breathe. When he recovered his senses from this inhuman attack, he was nearly a furlong from the house, and there he saw Sidney Rigdon stretched upon the ground where the mob had dragged him by the heels. The Prophet thought that his companion was dead.

These fiendish men continued to curse him and to blaspheme the name of Deity. They told him to ask his God for help, for they would give him none. They then dragged him nearly another furlong into a meadow and began calling to each other, continuing, however, to utter threats and oaths at him. By this time many additions had been made to their number. One cried out asking if Joseph was not to be killed. A group gathered at a little distance to hold a council and fix upon the Prophet's fate, while several of their number held him suspended in the air lest his person should touch the ground and thereby give him an opportunity to get a spring and wrench himself loose. After the council was concluded, the leading mobocrats declared that they would not kill him but would strip him naked and whip and tear his flesh. One cried out for a tar bucket, and when it was brought another exclaimed with a wicked oath, "Let us tar up his mouth!" They thrust a reeking tar paddle into his face and attempted to force it down his throat, but he kept his teeth tightly clenched. Then they tried to force a phial containing aqua fortis into his mouth, but it broke between his lips. Not content with inflicting all this violence upon the Prophet's helpless form, one of the inhuman wretches, as though he was a devil incarnate, fell upon him and began to tear like a wildcat, at the same time screaming with a curse, "That's the way the Holy Ghost falls on folks!"

While the mob were bruising him they mentioned two names that were familiar to him, "Simonds" and "Eli."

After they left Joseph, he attempted to rise, but fell back again from pain and exhaustion. He succeeded, however, in tearing the tar away from his face so that he could breathe freely, and shortly afterward he began to recover. Arising, he made his way toward a light and found that it was from the house of Father Johnson where he lived. Emma saw his bruised form covered with tar, and thinking him to be fatally mangled she screamed and fainted.

Securing some covering for his person, the Prophet entered the house and spent the night in cleansing his body and dressing his wounds.

Before making the assault upon Joseph, the mob had locked Father Johnson in his room. He had called for his wife to bring his gun, saying that he would blow a hole through the door, and at this the mob fled. As soon as he could force an egress, Father Johnson rushed from the house, seizing a club as he ran. He overtook the party which had captured Sidney Rigdon, and knocked one man down, and was about to smite another to the earth, when the mob deserted their first victim to attack the heroic old man. This diversion saved Sidney only for a brief time. The mob soon returned to him and inflicted serious pain and indignity upon him. They dragged him by his heels and left his head to strike upon the rough and frozen ground. By such barbarous treatment his scalp was lacerated and his body bruised, and he was driven into a delirium.

The next morning, being the Sabbath, the people assembled at the usual hour of worship. With them came some of the mobbers, Simonds Rider, an apostate and Campbellite preacher, leader of the mob; one McClentic, son of a Campbellite minister; and Pelatiah Allen, Esq., who had given the mob a barrel of whisky to fill them with the devilish daring necessary for their crime. Many others of the mob were also in attendance.

With his flesh all bruised and scarred, Joseph went to the meeting and stood before the congregation, facing his assailants of the previous night calmly and manfully. He preached a powerful sermon and on the same day baptized three believers into the Church.

This mob was chiefly composed of religious men, principally sanctimonious Campbellites, Methodists and Baptists, besides several apostates from the Church. They continued to watch the house of Father Johnson, and even the death of one of the helpless little children, which occurred on the Friday following from the exposures of the night of the attack, could not dissuade the demoniac men from their purpose. Indeed, the death of this poor little infant seemed to act upon them like a taste of blood upon a tiger. It drove them to a murderous frenzy. The spirit of mobocracy spread through all that region of country and was particularly fierce at Kirtland. Sidney Rigdon fled to the latter city from Hiram, taking his sick family; but after a brief rest was compelled again to flee and went to Chardon. The Prophet himself remained in Hiram during another week.

CHAPTER 21

Book of Commandments

On the 2nd day of April, 1832, Joseph started from Hiram for Missouri. He was carried by Elder George Pitkin in the latter's wagon to Stubenville, whence the Prophet and Sidney, who had joined him in the meantime, took passage on Wednesday, April 5, 1832, on board a steamboat for Wheeling, then in the state of Virginia.

After departing from Hiram, Joseph directed his wife to go to Kirtland and await his return; and this she did, finding help and consolation with his friends.

From Wheeling he soon resumed his journey towards Zion, and reached there on the 24th day of April, 1832.

Two days later, in a solemn assemblage of the Church, Joseph was sustained as President of the High Priesthood. Bishop Edward Partridge extended the right hand of fellowship and recognition to Joseph in the office to which he had been elected, and the Saints ratified the deed in an impressive and unanimous manner.

The Prophet found the Saints in Zion surrounded by people filled with the spirit of murder and rapine, and he sought with all the vigor and faith of his soul to unite the people in the bonds of love and mutual trust and help, that thus they might be enabled to withstand the assaults of their enemies. It was characteristic of him and of the revealed work, that he should teach his brethren at this hour, as always before and always after until the hour of his death, the potency of union. His purpose was then, as ever, to show the Saints the strength of a passive defense, coupled with kindness toward all humanity. Joseph had the personal strength and courage which, when not controlled by some mighty influence, make a man ambitious to overcome and punish any cruel foe by the arm of flesh, and yet in all his sufferings and ministrations he never advised or permitted any aggression upon the law or any insult to rightful authority.

The Prophet visited the Saints in Kaw Township and was received with delight. The people there loved him and rejoiced in his presence and in his teachings.

On the 1st day of May, 1832, the council of the elders was continued at Independence, and the order was made that three thousand copies of the Book of Commandments should be printed.

Five days later Joseph departed from Independence for Kirtland in company with Sidney Rigdon and Newel K. Whitney. On their return, Bishop Whitney, while attempting to jump from the coach as the horses were running away, had his leg and foot broken in several places. Joseph had succeeded in getting out unhurt, and he took the bishop to a public house at Greenville, Indiana, remaining with him there while Sidney went forward to Kirtland. Four weeks elapsed and still Newel was unable to proceed. Several times during that period, when the Prophet walked out into the adjoining woods, he saw newly made graves; and one day at dinner he was seized with a spasm caused by poison which had been administered to him in his food with murderous intent. He rushed to the door and quantities of blood and poisonous matter gushed from his mouth. The muscular contortion induced by the agony was so great that his jaw was dislocated. When the convulsion had partially passed, he wrenched his jaw back to its place with his own hands and made his way to the couch of Bishop Whitney as speedily as possible. The bishop administered to him, and he was healed instantly, although the poison had been so quick and strong in its effect as to loosen the hair upon his head.

The Prophet felt that they must flee from this spot at once, and asked his helpless brother to promise that he would be ready to start for Kirtland the next morning. Joseph declared to Bishop Whitney that if he would agree to this plan a wagon should be in waiting the next morning to transport them to the river bank, where they should find a ferryboat to take them quickly across. On the other side they should meet a carriage ready to convey them directly to the boat landing. Here a steamer should be ready to start, and at ten o'clock in the morning they should be steaming up the river. When the Prophet was led to make this prediction no arrangements had been made, neither were there any afterwards made by him to carry out this program of travel. But animated by faith, Bishop Whitney gave his promise, and Joseph remained with him all night. Early the next morning they departed, and at ten o'clock, after having found the way opened, exactly as the Prophet was led to promise, they were sailing up the river, with the bishop's limb sound enough to bear the journey without pain.

It was June, 1832, when they arrived at Kirtland, where Joseph found his wife awaiting him.

CHAPTER 22

Brigham Young Joins Church

While the Prophet was on his way to Missouri in the month of April, 1832, an event occurred afar off in Mendon, Monroe County, New York, which was the forerunner of mighty help to Joseph and strength to the Church. It was the baptism of Brigham Young on the 14th day of April, 1832, by Elder Eleazer Miller. This destined successor of the Prophet had heard and accepted the truth. His sincerity and force of character were visible at his conversion, and after his confirmation at the water's edge as a member of the Church of Jesus Christ, he was ordained on the same day to the Melchizedek Priesthood.

In the month of June, when Joseph returned to Kirtland from Missouri, he met and gave the hand of fellowship to Brigham Young, who had journeyed to Kirtland to hear the voice of the Prophet of God. A most memorable meeting was this of these two men whose names and fame were to become so indissolubly united! Of all the men of their generation, they were to be the most loved and hated, their words and deeds were to be heralded to every corner of the earth and, beyond those of all their contemporaries, were to make the deepest impress upon the world. If the fact be not fully recognized and acknowledged today, the hour is not far distant when it will be, that Joseph Smith and Brigham Young were the two greatest men of their time. Providence had assigned each his labor, and each faithfully performed the allotted task. Joseph, under the direction of the Almighty, marked out the design and laid the foundation deep and strong; and Brigham, inspired from the same source, built upon it carefully and judiciously. The labor of one was designed to be the fitting complement to the other.

At this first visit the Prophet Joseph heard, for the first time, the gift of speaking in tongues. Brigham had received this gift, and at a meeting in the evening the Spirit rested upon him and he spoke in tongues. The Prophet received the gift of interpretation, and he said it was the language spoken by our Father Adam. The Spirit also rested upon him and he spoke in tongues. After this the gifts of speaking in tongues and interpreting tongues were received and enjoyed by many of the Saints at Kirtland and elsewhere.

From that day Joseph and Brigham were friends, attached to each other by a tie stronger and closer than that of earthly kinship. From that time on for twelve years Brigham gave earnest help to Joseph and demonstrated by his consideration and devotion that he knew the authority under which the younger man was acting. There was a time to come when Oliver Cowdery—the fellow apostle of Joseph, who, with him, had received the Aaronic Priesthood under the hands of John the Baptist, and the Melchizedek Priesthood under the hands of the apostles Peter, James and John, heavenly messengers sent expressly to confer these two priesthoods upon them—would waver in his fidelity to the truth and would oppose Joseph and leave the Church.

Not many years from the time of which we write Sidney Rigdon, the trusted counselor, the eloquent spokesman of the Prophet, who with him had beheld in vision the glories of the eternal world and borne solemn testimony that he had seen the Savior and knew that He lived, would turn his back upon and be ready to desert Joseph and to conspire against the Church. But not so with Brigham Young; but not so with the Prophet's brother Hyrum, and many others less eminent than these two. Hyrum Smith was the embodiment of unswerving fidelity and fraternal love. Ever by his brother's side to aid and comfort him, life had no charms for him when danger threatened the Lord's anointed. He had a mother to whom he always rendered dutiful and loving obedience; he had a wife and children upon whom he lavished a wealth of affection; he had brothers and sisters to whom he was kind, considerate and helpful; but for his brother Joseph he had a love which overmastered all these affections; it surpassed the love of woman. When death stood in the pathway and menaced with its fearful terrors Joseph and those who stood by him, the Prophet besought Hyrum to stand aside and not accompany him. But, however obedient he might be to the slightest wish of his brother in other directions, upon this point he was immovable. If Joseph died, they would die together. As in his life, so in his death, Hyrum Smith exhibited the perfection of human love.

With similar fidelity and unshaken integrity Brigham Young, from the time of this meeting in Kirtland, cordially sustained the Prophet Joseph in all his ministrations up to the day of his martyrdom. Many times during the ensuing twelve years, and especially during the great defection and apostasy at Kirtland, he had occasion, because of his devotion to Joseph, to exhibit the decision of character and moral courage for which he was so distinguished in after life. When hesitation and doubt were far too common, and many leading men faltered and fell away, Brigham stood in the midst of the storm of opposition like a tower of strength. The remark which he made concerning some of his brother apostles at Nauvoo, after the death of the Prophet Joseph, when he said "their hands had never trembled and their knees had never shaken in maintaining and defending the principles of righteousness" applied with peculiar significance to himself and his own past connection with the work of God. But it was not in Joseph's lifetime alone that Brigham manifested his admiration for and devotion to his great friend. During the long period—thirty-three years—which he outlived the Prophet (when a common man under his circumstances might have been tempted to criticize the acts or peculiarities of his predecessor, or to contrast his own management of affairs with that of Joseph's) no one ever heard a word drop from his lips that was not worthy of the two men. His own success and great and worldwide prominence never diminished nor obscured the deep-rooted love and loyalty he felt towards the man whom God had chosen to hold the keys of this last dispensation and to be his file-leader in the priesthood.

It appears that the Prophet must have had something shown to him on this occasion concerning the future of Brigham Young; for Heber C. Kimball and Joseph Young, who both accompanied Brigham to Kirtland, each testified in his lifetime that the Prophet Joseph said to those who stood around him, "that man," pointing to Brigham Young who was a little distance off, "will yet preside over this Church." Levi W. Hancock, also, frequently testified that he heard the Prophet make this same statement concerning Brigham.

In July Joseph was gratified to receive the first number of *The Evening and Morning Star* from Independence. Light was already beginning to radiate from the land of Zion.

A few weeks later elders began to come in from their missionary labors in the Eastern States. Their reports were interesting, as from them could be gathered the nature of the difficulties to be contended with in bringing the people to a knowledge of the truth. The importance of this missionary work was apparent. The message which the Lord had given to His servants had to be declared to all people. The Prophet sought for definite instructions concerning this labor. On the 22nd and 23rd of September, 1832, he received the word of the Lord defining some of the powers of the priesthood and giving consolation and strength to such as should be called to go forth in the ministry.

> ... let no man among you, ... from this hour take purse or scrip, that goeth forth to proclaim this gospel of the kingdom. . . .
>
> And whoso receiveth you, there I will be also, for I will go before your face. I will be on your right hand and on your left, and my Spirit shall be in your hearts, and mine angels round about you to bear you up. . . .
>
> ... search diligently and spare not; and wo unto that house, or that village or city that rejecteth you, or your words, or your testimony concerning me;

For I, the Almighty, have laid my hands upon the nations, to scourge them for their wickedness.

And plagues shall go forth, and they shall not be taken from the earth until I have completed my work, which shall be cut short in righteousness—

Until all shall know me, who remain, even from the least unto the greatest, and shall be filled with the knowledge of the Lord, and shall see eye to eye, and shall lift up their voice, and with the voice together sing this new song, saying:

The Lord hath brought again Zion;
The Lord hath redeemed his people, Israel,
According to the election of grace,
Which was brought to pass by the faith
And covenant of their fathers.

The Lord hath redeemed his people;
And Satan is bound and time is no longer.
The Lord hath gathered all things in one.
The Lord hath brought down Zion from above.
The Lord hath brought up Zion from beneath.

The earth hath travailed and brought forth her
    strength;
And truth is established in her bowels;
And the heavens have smiled upon her;
And she is clothed with the glory of her God;
For he stands in the midst of his people.

Glory, and honor, and power, and might,
Be ascribed to our God; for he is full of mercy,
Justice, grace and truth, and peace,
Forever and ever, Amen.

... go ye forth ... reproving the world in righteousness of all their unrighteous and ungodly deeds, setting forth clearly and understandingly the desolation of abomination in the last days.

For, with you, saith the Lord Almighty, I will rend their kingdoms; I will not only shake the earth, but the starry heavens shall tremble.

For I, the Lord, have put forth my hand to exert the powers of heaven; ye cannot see it now, yet a little while and ye shall see it, and know that I am, and that I will come and reign with my people. (D&C 84:86, 88, 94–102, 117–119.)

Early in the month of October the Prophet departed with Bishop Whitney for the Eastern States, and made hurried visits to the cities of Albany, New York and Boston, returning to Kirtland on the sixth day of November, 1832. Three days previous to the latter date, on November 3, a son was born to him, whom he named Joseph.

To one not divinely sustained, the burden of work now laid upon Joseph would have been oppressive. The little time he could snatch from the labors of the ministry was devoted to diligent labor upon the translation of the Bible; and in addition he was planning for the further progress of proselyting work and for the upbuilding of Zion in Missouri. Upon this latter subject he bestowed much anxious thought. He communicated with the elders there by letter, and gave them careful instruction concerning the distribution of inheritances to the Saints and the general management of affairs in that land.

On the 25th day of December, 1832, the following revelation and prophecy were given to Joseph at Kirtland, Ohio:

Verily, thus saith the Lord concerning the wars that will shortly come to pass, beginning at the rebellion of South Carolina, which will eventually terminate in the death and misery of many souls;

And the time will come that war will be poured out upon all nations, beginning at this place.

For behold, the Southern States shall be divided against the Northern States, and the Southern States will call on other nations, even the nation of Great Britain, as it is called, and they shall also call upon other nations, in order to defend themselves against other nations; and then war shall be poured out upon all nations.

And it shall come to pass, after many days, slaves shall rise up against their masters, who shall be marshaled and disciplined for war.

And it shall come to pass also that the remnants who are left of the land will marshal themselves, and shall become exceeding angry, and shall vex the Gentiles with a sore vexation.

And thus, with the sword, and by bloodshed the inhabitants of the earth shall mourn; and with famine, and plague, and earthquake, and the thunder of heaven, and the fierce and vivid lightning also, shall the inhabitants of the earth be made to feel the wrath, and indignation, and chastening hand of an Almighty God, until the consumption decreed hath made a full end of all the nations; . . .

Wherefore, stand ye in holy places, and be not moved, until the day of the Lord come; for behold it cometh quickly, saith the Lord. Amen. (D&C 87:1–6, 8.)

This revelation was made known at that time to the Saints and was a subject of constant remark in the Church; in 1851 it was published to the world and obtained a somewhat wide circulation. Nearly twenty-nine years after its date, its wondrous fulfillment began when the first gun was fired at Fort Sumter, South Carolina. Since that time wars and rumors of wars have prevailed throughout the world. Peace has fled, and in view of all the Lord has said, it is not too much to expect it has fled, no more to return till the reign of righteousness shall begin.

It is strange that the solemn warning uttered by Joseph in 1832 should have gone unheeded. His prophecy was not without its purpose. The Lord inspired his mind with visions of the future and with power to view the paths by which the nation might escape the impending disasters, but like other parts of His message of salvation to the human race this warning also was rejected.

CHAPTER 23

Word of Wisdom

The warnings, of which he had been the chosen proclaimer
to the world, imbued the Prophet with a sense of mankind's
physical danger, as he had formerly been made to understand
their spiritual jeopardy; and we find from all his writings and
utterances of this period that he repeated often and in various
ways the message of alarm.

It was a busy winter of 1832–3 for Joseph. He organized a
school of the prophets, wherein such of the members of the
Church as held the Melchizedek Priesthood and were worthy
were permitted to assemble and receive instruction day by day in
the things of God. He continued his translation of the scriptures;
he directed letters to the Saints in Zion, exhorting them to
repentance, to faithfulness and purification, admonishing them
of the punishment in store for workers of unrighteousness; and
he sat in many conferences in which the gifts of the gospel were
made manifest in recognition and blessing of the humility of the
people.

On the 22nd day of January, 1833, there were many
manifestations of the Holy Spirit at a conference at Kirtland.
The Prophet and many of his brethren of the higher priesthood,
together with several other members, both men and women,
spoke in tongues. The restoration of this gift to man gave great
joy to those who received it; but the gift of speaking in tongues
was esteemed by the Saints of that early day as a reward to patient
trust and meekness and not as a necessary sign or proof of truth.

On the second day of February, 1833, the Prophet completed,
for the time being, his inspired translation of the New Testament.

No endeavor was made at that time to print the work. It was sealed up with the expectation that it would be brought forth at a later day with other of the scriptures. Joseph did not live to give to the world an authoritative publication of these translations.[1] But the labor was its own reward, bringing in the performance a special blessing of broadened comprehension to the Prophet and a general blessing of enlightenment to the people through his subsequent teachings.

The Lord revealed His purpose in this matter when He said to Joseph at a later time:

And, verily I say unto you, that it is my will that you should hasten to translate my scriptures, and to obtain a knowledge of history, and of countries, and of kingdoms, of laws of God and man, and all this for the salvation of Zion. (D&C 93:53.)

On the 27th day of February, 1833, the Prophet received the revelation known as the Word of Wisdom, warning the people to abstain from impurities and grossness in their food and drink, and promising them rich blessings of physical strength and protection from the power of the adversary as a reward for their obedience. The requirement of bodily pureness, to be gained by clean and wholesome living, was not more directly made upon the children of Israel anciently than upon the Latter-day Saints through the Prophet Joseph. This revealed Word of Wisdom embodies the most advanced principles of science in the condemnation of unclean or gluttonous appetites; and if it were implicitly obeyed by the human family, it would be a power to aid in a physical redemption for the race. Its delivery to Joseph marks another step in the divine plan for man's eventual elevation to divine acceptability—a plan which had already proved itself of heavenly origin by its sublime character.

And now we are brought to the time when the Lord designed that the authority and power of the presidency of the Church

---

[1] We have heard President Brigham Young state that the Prophet, before his death, had spoken to him about going through the translation of the scriptures again and perfecting it upon points of doctrine which the Lord had restrained him from giving in plainness and fullness at the time of which we write.

should be shared by others and should be conferred upon them by Joseph. An intimation concerning the First Presidency of the Church was given in a revelation which the Prophet received in March, 1832, in which Frederick G. Williams was called of the Lord to be a counselor to Joseph. In previous revelations, also, mention was made by the Lord of the First Presidency of the Church, and some of the duties which belonged to that body. But it was not until the 8th day of March, 1833, that the Lord revealed His further will concerning this organization. At that time two men were designated to be associates of the Prophet—to be his counselors and members with him of the First Presidency of the Church. They were Sidney Rigdon and Frederick G. Williams, and on the 18th day of March, 1833, in the school of the prophets, at Kirtland, obedient to the revealed word, Joseph ordained these men to this office, to take part with him in bearing the burden of the kingdom of God, and to assist in the presidency of the High Priesthood. In this way was the first presiding quorum formed to administer in the Church; and it was not dissolved during the Prophet's life. But when the frightful deed at Carthage took place in after years, the Lord had provided an authority, equal in power to the complete first quorum, to hold the gifts and to carry the responsibility of the work.

Joseph's glad submission to the will of the Lord respecting the distribution of authority is sufficient proof of his unselfishness. And the conception of this plan for the guidance of the Church proves that the system had its origin beyond and above the petty ambitions of humanity.

Sidney Rigdon and Frederick G. Williams, with the successors of the latter as counselors, ever received proper consideration from Joseph; and though often they were a thorn in the flesh, because of their own ambitions or misdoings, he bore with them patiently, knowing that they were the chosen of the Lord, and forgave their failings as willingly and as humbly as he besought forgiveness of his own frailties. The Prophet was never more watchful of his own ordained prerogatives than of the power similarly conferred upon his brethren. He showed by his example to the Saints then and for all time how a man could defer to proper authority without cringing to his fellow man.

The full beauty of the organization and the means by which the authority of the priesthood would be perpetuated in the Church was not made fully known at that time. It came later, notably when the Quorum of Apostles was organized. But this creation of the First Presidency was of great moment in demonstrating the exalted nature of his calling, and the Lord blessed it in the eyes of the assembled priesthood. On the occasion when the ordination was solemnized, the Sacrament was administered by the Prophet under the promise that the pure in heart should see a heavenly vision; and after the bread and wine had been partaken of in prayer and humility, the Savior appeared before their eyes, accompanied by concourses of holy angels. It was thus that the faithful were comforted in their meekness and blessed in their devotion.

While looking forward to the building of Zion in Missouri, it was still deemed necessary for the Saints to have a resting place for some time to come in Kirtland. And very soon after the ordination of Sidney Rigdon and Frederick G. Williams, a council of the priesthood was called, by which it was decided to purchase lands in and around Kirtland for the use of the Saints upon which they were to be established. This plan was not vacillation, however it might have seemed at that time to an unbeliever. Nor was it without its accomplishments and great benefits. Hopeful as Joseph and the Saints were to perform the work of establishing the center stake in Jackson County, and earnest as they were in their endeavor, the administration of ordinances, the endowment of the worthy Saints, and the ministration of heavenly beings, which afterwards took place in the temple at Kirtland, would necessarily have been delayed if the sole effort had been to erect a temple in Missouri, because the hatred against the truth soon became so violent there that the fulfillment of this purpose was, for the time, impossible.

But while Kirtland was being strengthened and plans were being made to beautify the city and to enrich it for the benefit of the Saints, Zion in Missouri was also coming under the good influence. Joseph was gratified to learn that every dissension among the elders and members in Jackson County had ceased and that all was peace within that branch of the Church. There had been no serious difficulties, but so far removed from his direct guidance, some of the traveling elders had exalted their own authority to conflict with that exercised by the resident presidency in Zion and misunderstandings ensued. This had all been corrected after Joseph had sent an epistle to the Saints in that region, and with the opening of April, 1833, there was much joy and hope at Kirtland, and much union and love in Jackson County.

Later in the spring and in the early summer of 1833, revelations were received concerning the erection of a temple at Kirtland, and with this and attendant work the Prophet was constantly engaged.

CHAPTER 24

To Clay County

Eighteen hundred years after the crucifixion of our Savior, His Church in this last dispensation celebrated the third anniversary of its establishment. The ceremonies took place on the sixth day of April, 1833, on the banks of the Big Blue River in the western part of Jackson County, Missouri. Few as were the Saints then gathered in the land Zion, the event was impressive in its solemn recall of the past, and sublime in its exalted promise for the future of Christ's people. Joseph himself was not there; but eighty men who had received the priesthood and also many other members of the Church were present to enjoy this reawakening in modern times of the power of the Son of God.

This was not to be the only reawakening. The spirit of insensate murder which Jesus had encountered and which had culminated on Calvary was aroused in all its intensity against these His humble and chosen followers in the latter days. In the same month that witnessed the glorious reunion of the Saints, a mob consisting of three hundred men congregated at Independence and swore with much blasphemy to drive the people of God from their homes in that region and to destroy that branch of the Church. News of these dreadful threats was brought to the leading elders at Independence; and in solemn assemblage they prayed that God would stay the hand of the wicked. The supplication was granted for a time; and the drunken rabble became filled with mutual hatred and distrust, so that they scattered from the meeting and carousing place, mingling with their maledictions against the Saints much vile language and many execrations concerning each other.

When the Prophet learned of these manifestations in Jackson County, he was filled with much concern for his brethren; but his duty, as commanded by the Lord, required for a time his presence at Kirtland and in the East. And at Kirtland, despite the poverty of the people and the menace made by a wicked world against them, preparations were made to build the house unto the Lord as required in the revelations.

The spirit of persecution which raged was doubtless permitted, if for no other reason than that it had the effect to purify the Church, and the members were also admonished thereby to sweep all unworthiness from their midst and to exclude from Church membership all willful and persistent wrongdoers. Few and poor as were the Saints, it was the rule that no man, whatever his attainments or wealth, should retain his fellowship if his conduct proved that his soul was vile. It was not and is not now the practice of the Latter-day Saints to cover the sins of their members from the gaze of an unbelieving world and to harbor the wrongdoer rather than to subject the entire body to the reproach of scoffers. With charity such as Christ commanded for all the frailties of a humanity struggling toward goodness, the Church has ever been an uncompromising punisher of willful wickedness. In June, 1833, one Dr. P. Hurlburt was tried by the council of high priests upon a charge of impure conduct with women while acting as a missionary in the East; and although he contested the case, as he desired for his own selfish purposes to continue for a time in relation with the Church, his guilt was fully established; he was cut off; and the world was warned against him as an insidious enemy of female chastity. This man Hurlburt, being filled with hatred by the exposure of his true nature, showed himself a vindictive enemy of the Prophet and the Church, and in later times his name became associated with the notorious Spaulding story, and with threats and attempts upon Joseph's life.

It was by such men, dishonorable apostates, suborned and aided by a jealous clergy, that the early falsehoods were propagated and the early persecutions were incited against the Church which would not condone their impurities. And it is the

wicked untruth, started in that age and added to by the same
class of men in later times, which is circulated today and which
deceives the world concerning a people whose sole desire is to
live in purity and in peace with all mankind. It was then, as it is
now, noted that, in many instances, the charges against Latter-
day Saints have varied according to the varied character of their
originators. Men whose profession is divining for money, whose
trade is deceiving human souls to gratify their own avarice, joined
in the cry that Joseph Smith and his fellow apostles were selfish
seekers after the things of this world. Men whose souls felt no
repugnance to the butchery of defenseless men, pure women
and innocent little children originated the awful lie that murder
was practiced and condoned by this Church. Impure wretches,
looking with lustful eyes upon females, originated the untruth
that woman was degraded and her virtue held in light esteem by
the Latter-day Saints; and among the most prominent persecutors
and prosecutors of this people have been lechers. Dishonest
and disreputable men circulated the absurd falsehood that
Joseph Smith and his followers sought to despoil others of their
possessions instead of acquiring homes by the labors of their own
hands. It is one of the most peculiar experiences of the Saints that
in most instances the charge brought against them has been one
of which the originator would himself be glad to be guilty.

So it was at Independence in the summer of 1833.

The first effort of the mob failed. They lacked a leader
sufficiently base to unite them in their plans for robbery and
murder. But in July of that year a man named Pixley, a paid
agent of a sectarian missionary society, was dwelling in that
region under the pretense of helping the Indians to the light
of Christianity. He defamed the Saints to their fellow citizens
of Missouri and sent malicious lies to the eastern states to stir
up the older communities of the nation to a feeling of dislike.
He misrepresented the Saints to the Indians and to the wilder
white men of the border, with the hope to inflame these
ungoverned and lawless people to attack and destroy the little
handful of Church members. The number of the Saints in the

center stake of Zion at this time was twelve hundred. They were law-abiding and industrious. But they were intent upon the work commanded of the Lord, and they did not assimilate readily nor join in unworthy pursuits with the surrounding people, white and red and black. This self-isolation or exclusiveness constituted their sole offense. It is not surprising that the Saints should have striven to keep their skirts clean from close contact with the vicious element abounding there, nor that this same vicious element should have been easily aroused against a people so singular in their demeanor and so unworldly in their lives and aspirations.

Pixley, himself the teacher of a false religion, proclaimed against Joseph Smith as a false prophet. Pixley, himself the leader of deceived converts, proclaimed against the Saints as deluded followers. Pixley, himself a dishonest creature, proclaimed that the purpose of the Saints was to steal the possessions of other settlers, to steal their Negroes, or to incite them to run away. The Latter-day Saints were men from the eastern states— Yankees—and consequently open to the suspicion of being abolitionists. In upper Missouri in those days no charge could be made that would arouse more intense hatred and violence than that of being an abolitionist. The mere whisper of such a suspicion was sufficient to inflame anger and arouse a mob. By such cries Pixley and others of his kind induced every dissolute idler in that region to join in an onslaught for plunder. They all hoped safely to annihilate the Church and to seize the lands of the Saints under cover of a Pharisaical cry, "False prophets, deluded followers, idle vagabonds, land thieves!" With this man Pixley were united professed ministers of the gospel, officers of the law, politicians and many individuals of less personal importance, if not less vindictiveness. They succeeded in so exciting the public mind that a mass meeting to devise some unlawful plan against the Saints was held at Independence, on the 20th day of July, 1833, at which a great horde of five hundred persons were in attendance. Not only were the scum of that wild region gathered, but men holding high official positions were also present, for individuals with political aspirations are often ready to join the lowest and most depraved in any popular movement. Amazing as it may seem, Lieutenant-Governor Lilburn W. Boggs, the second officer of the state of Missouri, was personally cognizant of the proceedings and aided every movement against the Saints.

Colonel Richard Simpson was chairman of the meeting, and James H. Flournoy and Colonel Samuel D. Lucas were secretaries. A committee appointed for the purpose prepared and presented a manifesto, which was adopted by the meeting. It denounced the Saints for their poverty and for their peculiar religious belief, but it did not dare to charge a single specific violation of law against them. It closed with the declaration that no Latter-day Saint should in future be permitted to settle in Jackson County; that such as then resided there should remove; that *The Evening and Morning Star* should no longer be published, and the business of printing by the Saints should be discontinued in that county; and "that those who failed to comply with this requisition are to refer to those of their brethren who have the gift of divination and of unknown tongues to inform them of the lot that awaits them."

Not a single voice was recorded against the adoption of this infamous edict. It was unanimously accepted; and immediately a committee of thirteen persons was appointed to see that the decree was enforced. The space of two hours was allowed by the meeting for the delivery of the terms of this manifesto to the presiding officers of the Church, for their answer to this demand, and for the return of the committee to the meeting. Scant time, indeed, for the expatriation of twelve hundred law-abiding men, women and children! The Saints asked for delay for a pitiful ten days, in which to consider the awful decree. The answer was, "Fifteen minutes are enough."

The mob were terribly, murderously earnest. When the committee returned to the reconvened meeting after a lapse of that brief two hours, they reported that the leaders of the Saints and the editor of the paper had asked time for consultation, not only among themselves, but also with their fellow believers and the Presidency of the Church in Ohio. A yell of hate greeted this announcement, and the meeting instantly and unanimously resolved to wreak instant vengeance upon the Saints and the paper. Headed by a red flag to signify their bloody purpose and their defiance of law, they rushed upon their prey. The house of William W. Phelps, the editor, containing the printing establishment, was razed to the ground. His press and type and other materials were seized and carried away by the mob. The papers and books were destroyed, and the family and furniture of the editor were cast off the premises. An infant child of Elder Phelps was dangerously ill in his wife's arms, but mother and babe were thrust out as brutally as the rest. An attack was made upon the store for the purpose of plundering it, but the mob was induced to forego their purpose to engage in more sanguinary delights. Bishop Edward Partridge and Charles Allen were stripped and tarred and feathered because they would not deny the truth nor agree to leave the county at once. With the tar was mixed some powerful acid which burned their flesh frightfully. Several of the brethren were threatened with whipping and even worse. But it was growing dark and the mob concluded that enough had been done for one time; so the mass meeting, which this inhuman rabble was called, adjourned for three days until the 23rd of July, 1833. And Lilburn W. Boggs addressed some of the Saints saying, "You now know what our Jackson boys can do, and you must leave the country."

Even a greater number of people assembled on the 23rd of July, as agreed, to renew the persecution of the poor Saints. A new committee was appointed to consult again with the presiding officers of the Church; and, not being entirely dead to humanity, this committee agreed to give the Saints time—one half until the 1st day of January, 1834, and the remainder until the 1st day of April of the same year, in which to remove themselves from Jackson County. Further, it was settled that the *Star* was not to be published again nor a press set up by any Latter-day Saint in the county, and that any members of the Church then journeying toward Jackson County should be stopped on the road and only permitted to have a temporary shelter until such time as all the Saints could remove from Jackson County to some new gathering place. A solemn pledge was given by the committee that, meanwhile, the people should not be again assailed. The mass meeting, upon receiving this report, ratified it in a formal manner. Concluding that their great mission—to which they had devoted "their bodily powers, their lives, fortunes and sacred honors"—had been accomplished, the rabble adjourned *sine die*.[1]

Oliver Cowdery was at once dispatched to Kirtland with full information. When the Prophet Joseph heard of this wanton attack upon the Church and the sad situation of the people at Independence, he wrote, "Man may torment the body; but God in return will punish the soul."

---

[1] See Note 3, Appendix.

CHAPTER 25

Work at Kirtland

No work of murderous mobs or judicial persecution has ever been able to stay the cause inaugurated under divine direction through Joseph Smith. At the very hour when the mob, on the 23rd day of July, 1833, were issuing their mandate of exile to the Saints in Jackson County, the cornerstone of the Lord's house in Kirtland was being laid according to the order of the Holy Priesthood of Christ. It was not that the purpose had shifted, that the center stake was to be removed from Missouri to Ohio. The command had been given; it will not be annulled. But long before manifestation of mob violence in Jackson County, the Lord had directed the building of a temple at Kirtland and the establishment of a stake of Zion there.

And while the future, to human appearance, seemed to be growing darker and darker, Joseph received a revelation in which the Lord declared His immutable covenant that the Saints should be rewarded and blessed according to His promise, and that their afflictions should eventually be turned to their everlasting good. And, while the wickedness of the mobs in Missouri was still agitating the hearts of Joseph and the Saints and making the weak among the people to tremble and the strong to feel deep indignation, the Lord commanded His Saints to renounce war and proclaim peace and to bear afflictions patiently, until the third time of their being smitten by the wicked. He promised them that whoso should lay down their life in the cause of Christ should find it again, even life eternal.

On the 11th day of September, 1833, a council under the presidency of the Prophet was held in Kirtland, and it was decided that a printing establishment should be opened there for the publication of the persecuted *Evening and Morning Star* and for a new paper to be called the *Latter-day Saints' Messenger and Advocate*. About the same time Elders Orson Hyde and John Gould were sent to Jackson County as messengers from the First Presidency to the Missouri Saints in their tribulation.

The Prophet felt that the field of souls was white for the harvest and that it was incumbent upon him to thrust in his sickle and gather the honest in heart. On the 5th day of October, 1833, he departed from Kirtland upon a missionary journey to Canada, in company with Sidney Rigdon and Freeman A. Nickerson. At various places on the road, they stopped and proclaimed the word of the Lord unto the inhabitants. In some villages they found already members of the Church. In others they found God-fearing men and women who were praying for light and were willing to obey when the simple gospel was presented before the eyes of their understanding. On the 12th day of October they arrived at Perrysburg, New York, where they halted for a little time. Here the Prophet received a revelation in which the Lord instructed him that Zion must be chastened yet for a season, although she would finally be redeemed. When they reached Lodi, New York, they preached in the evening and made a further appointment for the day following at a Presbyterian meetinghouse, the use of which had been promised to them. But when many people had assembled outside the hall to hear Joseph, they were refused admission by the jealous sectarians in charge, and the indignant congregation went home in great confusion. On the 17th day of October the Prophet and his companions reached the home of Freeman A. Nickerson at Mount Pleasant in Upper Canada; and at this place and the adjoining town of Brantford and the villages of Colburn and Waterford they held several meetings which were blessed by a great outflow of the Spirit of God and by the presence of many honest-hearted people. Upon one occasion at Colburn they were beset very tumultuously at one of their meetings by a Wesleyan Methodist who was determined that the assembled people should not hear the gospel. But his own lack of logic and courtesy injured himself rather than the persons against whom his violent efforts were directed. On the 26th day of October, after preaching to a large congregation at Mount Pleasant, Joseph baptized twelve persons, and on each of the two following days he baptized two persons, all of whom were confirmed as members of the Church. The Prophet also ordained E. F. Nickerson to be an elder; and he gave much instruction to the newly converted Saints concerning the truth and the constant necessity for watchfulness and humility. This labor made a considerable opening in this region for the further preaching of the truth. It was not, however, the first proclamation of the gospel in Canada, because as early as July 20th of the same year, 1833, Elder Orson Pratt had preached to the people in Patten.

On the 29th day of October, the Prophet and his companions departed from Mount Pleasant for Kirtland; and on Monday, the 4th day of November, the Prophet reached his home and found his family in peace, as had been promised in the revelation given to him at Perrysburg.

The inhabitants of Geauga County, Ohio, in which Kirtland was situated, began now to partake of a persecuting and mobocratic spirit, and threatened the Saints resident there with similar afflictions to those which had been visited upon their brethren in Missouri. The Prophet knew of the hate that was hanging around him, but he calmly viewed the situation, and in writing to Bishop Partridge at Clay County, Missouri, under date of December 5, 1833, he said:

The inhabitants of this county threaten our destruction, and we know not how soon they may be permitted to follow the examples of the Missourians; but our trust is in God, and we are determined, by His grace assisting us, to maintain the cause and hold out faithful unto the end, that we may be crowned with crowns of celestial glory, and enter into the rest that is prepared for the children of God.

On the 16th day of December, 1833, the Lord revealed to Joseph the divine purpose concerning the Saints in Missouri, saying:

I, the Lord, have suffered the affliction to come upon them, wherewith they have been afflicted, in consequence of their transgressions;

Yet I will own them, and they shall be mine in that day when I shall come to make up my jewels.

Therefore, they must needs be chastened and tried, even as Abraham, who was commanded to offer up his only son.

For all those who will not endure chastening, but deny me, cannot be sanctified.

And they that have been scattered shall be gathered. And all they who have mourned shall be comforted.

And all they who have given their lives for my name shall be crowned.

Therefore, let your hearts be comforted concerning Zion; for all flesh is in mine hands; be still and know that I am God.

Zion shall not be moved out of her place, notwithstanding her children are scattered. . . .

They that remain, and are pure in heart, shall return, and come to their inheritances, they and their children, with songs of everlasting joy, to build up the waste places of Zion—(D&C 101: 2–5, 13–18.)

And immediately after the revelation was received, the Prophet sent William Pratt and David W. Patten as messengers to the scattered Saints of Missouri to give them words of comfort and instruction.

Early in the month of December, 1833, Bishop Newel K. Whitney and Oliver Cowdery had brought to Kirtland a new printing press, and on the 18th day of the month a printing office in Kirtland was dedicated to the Lord and His purposes, and Oliver Cowdery began the publication of *The Evening and Morning*

Star, which had been cast out of Missouri. On the day that Joseph dedicated the printing establishment to the services of the Lord, his father, Joseph Smith, Sr., was ordained to be the Patriarch to the whole Church. On that day Joseph wrote:

And blessed is my father, for the hand of the Lord will be over him, for he shall see the afflictions of his children pass away; and when his head is fully ripe, he shall behold himself as an olive, whose branches are bowed down with much fruit; he shall also possess a mansion on high.

In view of all that has since occurred, it is a remarkable fact that the Prophet recorded in his journal of the 31st of December, 1833, the fact that "Wilford Woodruff was baptized at Richland, Oswego County, New York, by Zera Pulsipher." And this was before the Prophet and the future apostle and President had ever met in the flesh. This is not the only mention of Wilford Woodruff in Joseph's diary prior to their meeting. In one place the Prophet notices that Wilford had been ordained a teacher. It was the 25th day of April, 1834, when Wilford Woodruff visited the Prophet at Kirtland, and from that time on until Joseph's death they were intimately associated. It was clear that Joseph felt the staunch worthiness of his young brother, and in relying on him the Prophet was leaning upon no weak or broken reed, for Wilford Woodruff had been and had ever shown the fidelity of a Saint and the integrity and power of an apostle of Jesus Christ. He was one of the most faithful of all the men who were gathered near to the Prophet's person to share his trials and his confidences. Wilford Woodruff never made any attempt to cultivate showy qualities, and yet he was always marked among his fellows; his characteristic humility and unswerving honesty being sufficient to attract the attention of all who had known him. His is another of the names to be recorded with that of Joseph, and it is worthy to stand side by side with the names of Brigham Young and John Taylor, for he was as loyal to them as he and they were to Joseph, the first Prophet of this dispensation.

CHAPTER 26

Violence
in Missouri

"Be still, and know that I am God. . . ." (Psalm 46:10.)

These are the words with which the Almighty answered Joseph when he importuned heaven concerning the woes of the Saints in Missouri. And so he was wont to solace himself and his brethren with the remembrance of the revealed word that "After much tribulation cometh the blessing." How many years of the people or days of the Lord must elapse before the Saints would be planted in power in Zion, the Prophet could not learn; but this he did know, that after her term of affliction and purification had passed, she would be redeemed and beautified, and this is the promise that he uttered to his brethren in Kirtland and wrote to the Saints in Missouri.

While Joseph had been traveling in the missionary field, momentous events took place in the far west. The truce which the mob had made, the mob had broken. Assaults upon the houses of the Saints were of constant occurrence. Satan was not satisfied that the people of the Lord should peacefully migrate with their few possessions into some other region, and the more turbulent spirits in the rabble began to threaten the lives of leading men at Independence and to declare that all of the people—men, women and children—should be whipped out of the county. An attempt was made to establish a colony in Van Buren County, in the south. Some of the Saints settled there and began to labor diligently in the fields, but the spirit of mobocracy had spread, and a mob rose in arms, threatening to drive the Saints farther into exile.

On the 28th day of September, 1833, a petition was addressed to His Excellency Daniel Dunklin, Governor of the state of Missouri, by the persecuted people in Jackson County; and it was carried to the executive office in Jefferson City by Elders Orson Hyde and William W. Phelps. In this eloquent document a recital was made of the woes to which the people had been subjected, of the patience with which they had borne these outrages, of the utter subversion of the principles of law and humanity, and of the participation in these outrages by leading men in the state, civil and military officers, politicians and preachers. The final appeal in this petition was as follows:

> Knowing, as we do, that the threats of this mob, in most cases, have been put into execution, and knowing also that every officer, civil and military, with a very few exceptions, has pledged his life and honor to force us from the county, dead or alive; and believing that civil process cannot be served without the aid of the Executive; and not wishing to have the blood of our defenseless women and children to stain the land which has once been stained by the blood of our fathers to purchase our liberty; we appeal to the Governor for aid, asking him, by express proclamation or otherwise, to raise a sufficient number of troops, who, with us, may be empowered to defend our rights, that we may sue for damages in the loss of property—for abuse—for defamation, as to ourselves; and if advisable, try for treason against the government, that the law of the land may not be defied, nor nullified, but peace be restored to our country:—And we will ever pray.

Not one word in this petition had been set down in malice; it was temperate and respectful; and though its utterances were strong, they were borne out by incorruptible testimony, as well as, mainly, by the admissions of the mob themselves.

After such an appeal the Saints were entitled to prompt action and help. The Governor merely replied that the attorney general of the state was absent, and upon his return a response would be prepared and sent by mail to Independence. The messengers from Zion journeyed back with empty hands, and awaited, amidst the tide of persecution, which was rising higher and higher around them, the signal of succor, from the executive office.

About the 26th of October, 1833, a reply was received from Governor Dunklin, in which he says:

No citizen, nor number of citizens, have a right to take the redress of their grievances, whether real or imaginary, into their own hands. Such conduct strikes at the very existence of society and subverts the foundation on which it is based. *Not being willing to persuade myself that any portion of the citizens of the state of Missouri are so lost to a sense of these truths as to require the exercise of force, in order to ensure respect for them,* after advising with the attorney-general, and exercising my best judgment, I would advise you to make a trial of the efficacy of the laws; the judge of your circuit is a conservator of the peace. If an affidavit is made before him by any of you, that your lives are threatened and you believe them in danger, it would be his duty to have the offenders apprehended, and bind them to keep the peace.

Such was the redress offered by the man whose sworn duty it was to see that the laws were faithfully executed. The lamb was sent back by the lion to ask protection from the wolf! It has often happened since in the history of the Saints, as it was then, that the men who should have been their vigilant protectors against plunderers and murderers, have been among the thieves and assassins.

But Governor Dunklin's letter contained a promise that, in the event of a failure to get proper execution of the law in Jackson County, he would, upon official notification, take further steps to enforce its faithful observance. Upon this slight hope, the Saints began to restore their houses to comfort and to labor in the fields for their maintenance.

The Saints had engaged four lawyers to aid them in obtaining a redress of their grievances, and as soon as this fact became known, the event occurred which Governor Dunklin should have foreseen. With tenfold intensity the fire of hatred raged against the people. On the night of October 31 an armed mob attacked a settlement of the Saints west of Big Blue, tore the roofs from many of the dwelling houses, whipped the men and drove the women and children screaming into the wilderness. The profanity of the mob was appalling. None of the Saints were armed, and the resistance which they might have offered with sticks was forbidden by their captors under penalty of death. Satiated with brutality, the mob at length retired, leaving orders that the Saints—men, women and children—should leave the county. The next day was the first of bleak November; and when the cold morning dawned, the Saints crept out of their hiding places whither they had fled for safety, and came back to their despoiled homes to find their habitations and their gardens in ruins. The women wept for their scourged and bleeding husbands. Children sobbed with hunger, cold and fear. How were these plundered people to find means for journeying to a land of safety? And whither were they to go? Asylum had already been denied them in the adjoining county; adequate protection had been practically denied to them by the civil power of the state; and they had no hope that any section of Missouri would harbor them.

Such scenes of horror were repeated night after night at Independence and every dwelling place of the Saints in that county. At Independence, on the 1st of November, one of the mob was caught in the very act of robbing the store of Gilbert & Whitney, and was carried before Samuel Weston, a justice of the peace; but despite the boast of the Governor, Mr. Weston refused to issue a warrant or to entertain the case, and the robber was turned loose to join his fellows in a continuation of murderous work. Other efforts were made to secure the aid of judicial power to stop the horrible work of the rabble, but in vain. Such of the officers of the law as were not allied with the mob dared not assert their authority. And so the work of rapine went on until it ended in murder.

The 3rd day of November, 1833, was Sunday, and the Saints hoped for a cessation of hostilities, but none came. Word went out among the mob that Monday would be a bloody time. On November the 4th, the day of Joseph's return to Kirtland from his Canada mission, a large party of the mob fired upon some of the Saints west of Big Blue. Several of the Saints were wounded, two desperately. These were young men named Barber and Dibble, who were thought to have been fatally injured; but Philo Dibble finally recovered, and at the time of this writing is still living, a respected citizen of Utah Territory. After lingering in great agony, Barber died the next day. Three times and more the Saints had permitted their enemies to smite them, and three times and more they had submitted patiently. They had appealed to civil and military power in vain, and now the sight of blood thus wantonly shed aroused in them a strong spirit of resistance. When the mob continued the massacre, they were greeted by shots from such of the Saints as had guns, and two of the mob fell dead. One of them, Hugh L. Brazeale, had often boasted: "I will wade to my knees in blood but that I will drive the Mormons from Jackson County."

The men who had caught the mobber in the act of plundering Gilbert & Whitney's store were arrested upon a fictitious charge of assault upon that wretch. Apparently the mob had no difficulty in obtaining process of court and securing its services. An effort was made to kill these prisoners while they were in the charge of the officers of the law, and shots were fired at them, and they had to be placed in jail to protect their lives.

And now comes the most diabolical feature of all the persecution in Missouri up to that date. On the 5th day of November, 1833, Lieutenant-Governor Boggs permitted the mob to organize as a militia, and placed them under the command of Colonel Thomas Pitcher. While the Saints showed no intention of resisting, the rabble did not feel the need of such organization; but when it was found that, driven to the last extremity, the Saints would fight for their lives, Boggs clothed the mob with military power, that resistance to them might be charged against the Saints as insurrection against the legal authorities of the state of Missouri.

Colonel Pitcher demanded that the Saints should give up their arms; that certain men who had been engaged in the fight west of Big Blue should be delivered into his hands to be tried for murder; and that the people should leave the county forthwith. It was clear that the alternative was death to the men and outrage to the women and children. And so the Saints yielded under solemn promise of protection. As soon as the demand was complied with, the mob rushed like demons in various directions, bursting violently into houses and threatening the women and children with massacre. One party of the mob was headed by Rev. Isaac McCoy, and other preachers joined in the rabble. Men, women and children fled to the prairie and to the river banks, seeking in the wilderness, amidst all its terrors, a peace denied them by civilized men. Husbands and wives and children were separated, and one knew not whether his beloved kin were dead or alive.

Who can say that a restoration of the gospel of Peace was not necessary in such an age?

After a time most of the scattered Saints gathered in Clay County, where a court of inquiry was ordered by Governor Dunklin, but the murderers and robbers who slew the Saints and took their substance in Jackson County, Missouri, went unwhipped of justice. Clay County was the only section of the state which received the Saints with any degree of charity. From Van Buren and Lafayette and other counties they were forced to flee as they were from Jackson.

In Clay County, where many of them had found a haven of rest among noble-hearted citizens, the Saints prepared and sent up to Governor Dunklin such piteous appeals as might have melted a heart of adamant. They had been stripped of all their worldly substance; winter was upon them; they even lacked food and raiment; and from hour to hour they were in expectation of further assaults. It was their supplication to the Governor that he would use the power of the state to restore them to their lands and possessions, and to give a sufficient guard to a court of inquiry, which might examine into the whole history of the outrages made against them. The court of inquiry was held, and Colonel Pitcher was arraigned and ordered for further trial by court-martial. But it soon became clear that the Saints could not be restored to their lands in Jackson County under existing conditions because the mob swore that if they returned there would be a wholesale massacre of Mormons, and the Governor, it was said, had not the constitutional right to establish a permanent guard for the persons and property of the defenseless Saints.

Messengers had gone at various times from the scenes of the outrage in Missouri to the Prophet at Kirtland, and when he heard the dreadful news, he burst into tears and sobbed aloud:

"Oh, my brethren, my brethren; would that I had been with you to share your fate. Almighty God, what shall we do in such a trial as this?"

CHAPTER 27

Plight
of Saints

With the opening of the year 1834, Joseph recorded his prayer that the Lord would deliver Zion and gather in His scattered people to possess it in peace, and that, in their dispersion, He would provide for them that they might not perish of hunger and cold.

At the same time he was pursued by threats against his own life. The apostate, Dr. P. Hurlburt, was determined to wreak his rage upon Joseph's person. Hurlburt had circulated vile falsehoods and presented lying affidavits among the people in the towns surrounding Kirtland, in the hope of exciting mobocratic violence. If personal considerations alone had been involved in these attempts of Hurlburt's to destroy him, the Prophet might have taken no steps to restrain him or to bring him to justice. But his duty to the Church demanded his preservation, and by his consent, process of court was secured against Hurlburt, and later, on the 9th of April, 1834, that infamous creature was found guilty of threatening to kill, and was by a court at Chardon, Ohio, placed under bonds.

Many high councils exist in the Church at the present time, there being one in every stake of Zion. It was on the 17th day of February, 1834, at Kirtland, however, that the Prophet organized the first high council of the Church. This tribunal consisted of twelve high priests, and it was presided over by the Prophet and his two counselors, Sidney Rigdon and Frederick G. Williams. Its duty was to hear all matters of dispute between members of the Church who sought equity, and to decide such issues according to the principles of eternal justice. The plan of settling disputes and preventing litigation among brethren, which the Prophet was then inspired to introduce, has grown with the growth of the Church, and the high council has performed an important mission in the years which have followed. It has worked without fees; it has known no coercion; the honesty of its decisions have been beyond question; and often it had been appealed to by men not of the faith, that their disputes might be settled with fairness and economy. It has never usurped the function of the criminal courts; it has never sought to enforce its judgment by any civil process. It has only decreed according to clear and unmistakable justice and has left the parties to accept the judgment, and if not complied with or appealed from, to have Church fellowship withdrawn from them. The rules which the Prophet established to control its proceedings under divine guidance were delivered to it at the time of organization, and they, speaking of all the high councils which have since been organized, are still governed by them. To confirm the twelve chosen men in their places, the Prophet laid his hands upon each one's head and blessed him with the gifts and authority necessary for his calling.

The first act of the high council at Kirtland was to declare Joseph Smith the President of the Church with Sidney Rigdon and Frederick G. Williams as the other members of the First Presidency.

All this time the cry of the exiled Saints in Missouri was ascending to heaven for the redemption of their homes and for their own release from oppression. In a revelation given to the Prophet February 24, 1834, the Lord made known that the wicked had been permitted to fill up the measure of their iniquities that those who are called after His name might be chastened for a season; because in many things they had not hearkened unto His commandments. He declared that in His own due time the punishment of his wrath should be poured out upon the persecutors of His Saints, and He promised the elect that they should repossess the goodly land from which they had been driven. The Prophet was commanded to gather up the strength of the Lord's house to journey to the land Zion to assist the scattered

Saints. Two days later he departed for the East to obtain assistance for the work of the Lord. Other elders were also called to perform similar missions. The Prophet traveled as far as Geneseo, New York, reaching there on the 15th day of March, 1834. On the way he preached to many of the congregations of Saints and also to many assemblages of unbelievers. On the 19th of March he began his return journey to Kirtland, which place he reached on the 28th. On the 18th day of April, 1834, while Joseph was journeying in company with Sidney Rigdon, Oliver Cowdery and Zebedee Coltrin to New Portage for the purpose of gathering up help for Zion, an effort was made by a party of men to capture them as they traveled along the road after darkness had fallen. By driving rapidly, they escaped the hands of the bandits who sent a torrent of curses after the Prophet's party.

It was the 5th day of May, 1834, when Joseph, having gathered clothing and food for his brethren and sisters in Missouri who had been robbed and plundered of their effects, departed, with a company of brethren, from Kirtland to find and succor the distressed Saints. His party consisted of about one hundred men, nearly all young and nearly all endowed with the priesthood. At New Portage they were joined by fifty men, some of whom had gone in advance of the main body from Kirtland. A careful and harmonious organization of the company was made that the progress of this Camp of Zion might be in steadiness and order.

The wagons of the party numbered twenty and were filled with provisions and clothing and such arms as the company needed for the securing of game and for defense. Nearly all of the men were compelled to walk, and Joseph cheerfully led their journey. They traveled sometimes forty or fifty miles in a day, resting always on the Sabbath and holding religious services. Every night they retired to their tents at the sound of the trumpet, and every man bowed to the Lord in thanksgiving for the blessings of the day and in supplication for the welfare of the families they were leaving behind and the poor Saints they were going to meet. And every morning at the sound of the trumpet every man arose and fell upon his knees before heaven, invoking its watchful care during the day.

The march was necessarily one of great hardship. The men waded rivers, struggled through marshes and tramped across hard stretches of hill and sandy plain. Many of them suffered from bruised and bleeding feet. Often they were harassed by evil men who suspected their mission and sought to prevent its fulfillment.

A few persons in the camp had proved unruly, and while they were in the vicinity of the Illinois River, Joseph was led to utter a solemn warning against the dissensions of some of his brethren. He exhorted them to faithfulness and humility, and told them that the Lord had revealed to him that a scourge must come upon them in consequence of their disobedience. Still if they would repent and humble themselves before the Lord, a part of the severity of the scourge might be turned away.

Joseph and his brethren reached the banks of the Mississippi on the 4th day of June and encamped at a point where the river was a mile and half in width. Having but one ferryboat, two days were required in which to make the passage of the entire party from Illinois into Missouri. Besides, they were delayed, though not prevented, by the menace of numerous enemies who swore that they should not pass beyond the Mississippi.

One of the instructions given by the Prophet during this journey was that his brethren should not kill an animal of any kind, unless it became absolutely necessary to save themselves from starvation. On one occasion, while the Prophet's tent was being pitched at camp, the men saw three rattlesnakes and were about to kill them, but Joseph forbade the act. He asked the elders how would the serpent ever lose its venom while the servants of God made war upon it with desire to kill. He said: "Men themselves must first become harmless before they can expect the brute creation to be so. When man shall lose his own vicious disposition and cease to destroy the inferior animals, the lion and lamb may dwell together and the suckling child play with the serpent in safety." It was a deep philosophy and contrary to the preconceived notions and early lessons of his brethren; but they obeyed. And soon they experienced the truth of his words. One of the members of the camp, by the name of Solomon Humphrey, lay down on the prairie one day to rest. He fell asleep with his hat in hand. While he slumbered a large rattlesnake crawled up and coiled between him and his hat, and when Elder Humphrey awoke he found the serpent's head not a foot from his own. He did not harm it, and when some of his brethren would have killed it, he stayed their hands, saying: "No, I will protect him, for he and I have had a good nap together." Although the rattlesnake was roused, it made no effort to strike.

CHAPTER 28

Zion's Camp Marches

While the Prophet was encountering and overcoming many difficulties to bring succor to the Saints, the latter were engaged in a vain struggle to secure their rights. Correspondence passed between their leaders and the civil officers, from the judges up to the President of the United States. Many of the appeals brought polite replies, but they resulted in no effective aid. Governor Dunklin sent several communications recognizing and deploring the wrongs inflicted, but stating he could not, without transcending his power, order a military force to maintain the Saints in their Jackson County possessions. The latter sentiment was also the substance of the reply from the Secretary of War in behalf of the President of the United States. It is worthy of note that in all of the correspondence upon this question not a single charge is made against the Saints. It proves that in all things they were the sufferers from wrong, and not the doers of wrong; because the men to whom they appealed would have been quick to offer an excuse for their failure to extend redress.

Possibly the Governor thought he had done enough when he filled his correspondence with high-minded and sympathetic sentiments; but of what avail was it to the Saints for him to say to them as follows?

On the subject of civil injuries, I must refer you to the courts; such questions rest with them exclusively. The laws are sufficient to afford a remedy for every injury of this kind, and, whenever you make out a case, entitling you to damages, there can be no doubt entertained of their ample award. Justice is sometimes slow in its progress, but it is not less sure on that account.

This is but a repetition practically of what he had said before without avail. Was not this almost a mockery of the people's disasters? It was at least a satire upon the persistent denial of the judicial officers in Jackson County to do justice. Later a court of inquiry was convened at Independence, under military guard; but the mob defied all the authority of law, scoffed at the Governor's order, subdued the court into a state of terror, and laughed at the troops as they were withdrawn. A court-martial was convened, and it found Colonel Pitcher guilty of calling upon the militia to repress an insurrection where there was no insurrection, and decided that he had taken arms from the citizens who were lawfully seeking to defend themselves against unlawful aggression; but the Governor in vain commanded the officers to restore the arms to the people from whom they had been stolen. Although repeated orders were issued by his Excellency, those arms never were and to this day have not been returned.

The assaults of the mob on the scattered Saints and their property in Jackson County continued. In the latter part of April, 1834, one hundred and fifty houses were torn to the ground by the rabble.

Joseph and his party found a branch of the Church at Salt River, in the state of Missouri, where they encamped to spend Sunday, the 8th of June. Here they were joined by Hyrum Smith and Lyman Wight with another party which had been gathered in the state of Michigan and surrounding regions; and the Camp of Zion with this addition now numbered two hundred and five men and twenty-five wagons well laden. Several days were devoted to much needed recuperation, for the greater part of this devoted band of men had traveled nine hundred miles in a little more than a month's time, the journey being largely made on foot amidst all the natural hardships of a wild country where constant watchfulness had to be exercised.

On the 18th of June they pitched their tents within one mile of Richmond in Ray County. Two days previous to this time a mass meeting had been held at the courthouse in Liberty, Clay County, to consider propositions made by the people of Jackson County to the exiled Saints. Flaming war speeches were delivered by civil officers and by sectarian priests from Jackson County who had hoped to arouse the hospitable people of Clay against their inoffensive guests, the Saints. Because General Doniphan and the chairman of the meeting, a Mr. Turnham, counseled peace and decency, the old spirit of savage violence broke loose with all its virulence on the part of the representatives from Independence, and the meeting ended with a stabbing affray between two members of the former mob, in which one of them was dangerously wounded. The leading men among the Saints presented an answer in which they asked for time and in which they deprecated any hostilities upon either side during the pendency of the negotiation. It was at once manifest that the proposition of the mobocrats had been but a sham to cover further violence. The news of the approach of the Prophet and his brethren in an organized camp had reached the ears of these infuriated men, and they felt that he was putting himself in their power. They counted with entire certainty upon the inability of the officers of the law to prevent their carrying out any fell purpose which they might adopt against the Latter-day Saints. If there was an officer who did not justify them in their attacks upon the believers in this unpopular religion, they expected to overawe him; but from the Governor down they knew they had secret sympathy, if not their active aid. With all their innocence and excellence, therefore, the Latter-day Saints could place no reliance upon the laws and the safeguards of civilized society to protect them if these desperadoes chose to attack them.

The sole purpose of Joseph and his brethren was to bring succor to their suffering friends; but this their inhuman enemies were determined they should not do. Fifteen of the most violent mobocrats, with Samuel C. Owens and James Campbell at their head, started to raise an army to meet and overpower the Camp of Zion. James Campbell swore as he adjusted his pistols in the holsters, "The eagles and turkey buzzards shall eat my flesh if I do not fix Joe Smith and his army so that their skins will not hold shucks, before two days are past." That night as twelve of these mobocrats were attempting to cross the Missouri River their boat was sunk and seven of them were drowned. Among the lost was Campbell, whose corpse floated down the river several miles and lodged upon a pile of driftwood, where ravenous birds did indeed pick his flesh from his bones, leaving the hideous bare skeleton to be discovered three weeks later by one Mr. Purtle.

On the night of the 19th, unobserved by a large party of their enemies who intended to fall upon them and murder them, the members of Zion's Camp passed through Richmond in the darkness and pitched their tents between two branches of Fishing River.

While the members of the camp were making preparations for the night, five armed desperadoes appeared before them and, with many blasphemies, said: "You will see hell before morning. Sixty men are coming from Richmond, and seventy more from Clay County to utterly destroy you." More than three hundred bloodthirsty men had engaged to concentrate at this point and attack Joseph. But to the subsequent unbounded thankfulness of the members of the camp, the Lord interposed. When night came a mighty hurricane arose, throwing the plans of these savages into confusion, scattering them in the utmost disorder, and melting their courage into abject fright in the presence of the awful elemental strife. The severity of the storm was not felt to the same extent where Joseph and the camp had rested, but around them hail fell like grapeshot, spreading terror among the people and devastation amidst all the work of human hands.

While the surrounding region was in this state of consternation, Joseph and his party took refuge in a log meetinghouse near their camp, being compelled to enter the building through a window. When the commotion was over and they emerged from their retreat, the Prophet gave orders that the parties to whom the house belonged should be visited and tendered an explanation of the intrusion and remuneration for any fancied damage. So scrupulous was he not to trespass upon the rights of others.

When the tornado burst, only forty of the mob had been able to cross Fishing River. They afterwards swore that the little Fishing River rose thirty feet in thirty minutes, separating them from their companions, and making them glad to flee back among their lawless friends in Jackson County. The larger party of the mob, thus foiled in their purpose to cross the river, also fled. The Big Fishing River had risen nearly forty feet in one night. One of the mob had been killed by lightning.

On Saturday, the 21st of June, Colonel Scounce and two other leading men of Ray County visited Joseph, and begged to know his intentions, stating: "We see that there is an Almighty Power that protects this people." Colonel Scounce confessed that he had been leading a company of armed men to fall upon the Prophet but had been driven back by the storm. The Prophet, with all the mildness and dignity which ever sat so becomingly upon him, and which always impressed his hearers, answered that he had come to administer to the wants of his afflicted friends and did not wish to molest or injure anybody. He then made a full and fair statement of the difficulties as he understood them; and when he had closed, the three ambassadors, melted into compassion, offered their hands and declared that they would use every endeavor to allay the excitement.

On the 22nd day of June, 1834, while encamped on Fishing River, Joseph received a revelation in which the Lord declared that the elders should wait for a season for the redemption of Zion; that he did not require at their hands to fight the battles of Zion, for he would fight their battles; and this he addressed to the camp which had come up from Kirtland and other places into Missouri to do His will and with the hope that they might contribute to the redemption of His afflicted people. The Lord rebuked many among the Saints in the branches of the Church in the different states for their failure to join the Camp of Zion in response to the call which He had made upon them. The Lord had required the churches abroad to send up wise men with their moneys to purchase lands in Missouri, and thus assist in the redemption of Zion; but they had not hearkened unto His words. After renewing the promise that the day of redemption should surely come, and promising those who had hearkened to His words that He had prepared a blessing and an endowment for them if they would continue faithful, the revelation concluded:

> And inasmuch as they [the Saints] follow the counsel which they receive, they shall have power after many days to accomplish all things pertaining to Zion.
>
> And again I say unto you, sue for peace, not only to the people that have smitten you; but also to all people;
>
> And lift up an ensign of peace, and make a proclamation of peace unto the ends of the earth;
>
> And make proposals for peace unto those who have smitten you, according to the voice of the Spirit which is in you, and all things shall work together for your good.
>
> Therefore, be faithful; and behold, and lo, I am with you even unto the end. Even so. Amen. (D&C 105: 37–41.)

CHAPTER 29

The Law
of Tithing

The scourge came as had been foretold, and the Camp of Zion felt its terrible effects. Moanings and lamentations filled the air. In the divine economy it is not infrequently the case that the innocent suffer with the wrongdoers. "The Lord suffereth the righteous to be slain that His justice and judgment may come upon the wicked." In this attack some faithful men fell victims under the awful power of this scourge, and the entire camp suffered more or less. In organized bodies of Saints, experience has proved that it is not always the element which is guilty of transgression which alone has to endure the consequences, but the entire body which harbors or permits the impurity has to suffer. If it were not so, there would not be such imperative reason for a community to look well to the work of self-cleansing. It is when the judgment of heaven falls upon the obedient as well as the careless and disobedient of any organization that the people are taught to strive unceasingly, not alone each for his own, but all for the general purification. Some of the men who went down from Kirtland with Joseph and who had joined him on the road were among the noblest of humankind. They were of such exalted faith and courage that their righteous fame stands with that of the greatest disciples of old. They adhered to the Lord's commandments and to His prophet with all the fidelity of their souls. But other men—unjust, selfish, rebellious by nature—were also among the number of Zion's Camp; and as soon as they became wearied by hardships they betrayed their own lack of innate nobility. It was this latter class of men which brought affliction upon the camp.

It was about the 22nd day of June, 1834, when the cholera appeared in Zion's Camp at Fishing River. During the next week it raged in the midst of the party. Sixty-eight of the Saints were attacked and thirteen of them died. Among the fatal cases was that of Algernon Sidney Gilbert, a man of talent and many good works, though not always able to subdue self. Just before the destroyer seized him, the Prophet called him to journey to Kirtland to receive there his endowments and from there to proclaim the everlasting gospel of redemption. Elder Gilbert's answer was: "I would rather die than go forth to preach the gospel to the Gentiles." When he thus answered the Prophet of God he was full of strength and health; but in a few hours after the scourge had breathed upon him he was dead. Joseph and Hyrum administered assiduously to the sick, and soon they were in the grasp of the cholera. They were together when it seized them; and together they knelt down and prayed for deliverance. Three times they bowed in supplication, the third time with a vow that they would not rise until deliverance from the destroyer was vouchsafed. While they were thus upon their knees a vision of comfort came to Hyrum. He saw their mother afar off in Kirtland praying for her absent sons, and he felt that the Lord was answering her cry. Hyrum told Joseph of the comforting vision, and together they arose, made whole every whit. In ministering to their other brethren, they discovered that to dip an afflicted person in cold water afforded great relief, and this was practiced generally until the scourge had run its threatened course and had left the camp.

During the days of the scourge, the Prophet had moved his party from Fishing River. On the 23rd of June, they had reached within five or six miles of Liberty in Clay County, when General Atchison and several other persons went out from the town to meet the Prophet. They begged him not to go to Liberty as the people had become much enraged. Accepting the advice, Joseph turned from the road to Liberty and encamped on the banks of Rush Creek.

On the 25th of June the Prophet announced by letter to General Atchison and party that he had concluded to disperse his company, in order to allay the prejudice and fear on the part of citizens of Clay County. He requested the gentlemen to whom his note was addressed to inform the governor of the action thus taken; because the Prophet knew that Dunklin's ears were being filled with the most malicious rumors concerning the purpose entertained by Zion's Camp. In execution of his promise, Joseph disbanded his party, and the brethren scattered themselves among the Saints of that region.

The next day a report was received from one S. C. Owens, a leader of the Jackson County mob, in which he declared that his people would not accept the proposition of the Saints—to buy the lands of the men who objected to the Saints returning to their homes in Jackson County—nor anything akin to it. He coolly recommended that the Saints "cast their eye" on a distant and uninhabited spot which he named, "to see if that was not a country calculated for them."

One appeal after another was being made to the governor of the state; but so far as practical help was concerned, all were unanswered. Active hostilities in a general sense against the Saints had ceased for the time being, and there was some reason for hoping that they would be allowed to remain in Clay and surrounding regions. All the honest and fair-minded settlers in that land were forced to recognize the good qualities of the exiles from Jackson. The Saints were industrious, charitable and thrifty. Among them were no drunkenness, brawls nor crimes which too often gave a bad character to other border communities.

To this prospect of peace, the Prophet's personality had greatly contributed. In all the march through Missouri, his magnificent qualities had impressed themselves upon the people whom he met. His course had been that of a worthy leader among men. He had shown in all his association with the inhabitants of Missouri the utmost courage and generosity. It was his nature to extend consideration and kindness towards others, and he was as regardful of the rights of his fellow men at this time as always before and always after during his lifetime. The leading men of Clay County who were brought into contact with him felt that he possessed remarkable power. There was that in his dignified deportment and in the fearless glance of his blue eyes which warmed the souls of other men to his own, and they submitted to his charm of manner, even when they had come to oppose him. And when at last, to allay the fears of his avowed enemies, he dispersed his party, while surrounded by vindictive mobs who sought his life and the lives of his associates, he evinced a courage and a wisdom as grand as they were rare.

Jackson County was alive with men who had sworn to assassinate him if he ventured within their reach. What could have been more admirable than his noble disregard of all their threats! On the 1st of July, 1834, unattended except by two or three personal friends, he crossed the Missouri River from Clay into Jackson County, visited Independence and saw all that goodly land which the Lord had promised as a Zion, but which now was under the desecration of murder, rapine and a veritable reign of terror.

He stood among the ruins of once peaceful homes and gazed upon once fruitful fields which wicked men had laid waste, and his great heart swelled nigh to bursting. Did any premonition come to him of that awful hour when he should next look upon these scenes; when in chains he should be carried through the streets of Independence, as captive kings of old were dragged at their victor's chariot wheels to make the populace shout with cruel joy! Well might Joseph, Prophet of God, have indescribable emotions as he gazed upon this spot, hallowed in his mind by so many tender recollections and so many promised glories. Mobs had done their work, Zion was desolate. Joseph himself was free. But the day was not far distant, when he should, as a captive, be brought to Independence and his enemies should gloat over the tortured hero and his pale but undaunted face.

The Prophet had gone to Independence without ostentation, but without fear. While he prayed there, the eyes of the wicked were blinded, that they knew him not; and when he returned to his brethren he was unscathed.

On the 3rd day of July, the Prophet organized a high council near Liberty, in Clay County, and for several days he was engaged in imparting instruction to the members of that body, and such others as desired to listen to his words of wisdom.

An appeal was made and published to the world regarding the grievances of the Saints and asking for the restoration of their rights and for the privilege to live in peace.

On the 9th day of July, Joseph, in company with his brother Hyrum and Frederick G. Williams and others, departed for Kirtland. Returning, the journey was as toilsome as at first. The distance to be traversed was one thousand miles, and but few of the comforts of civilization existed for them along the path. Heat, thirst, hunger and pain of body alike oppressed them and were alike endured with patient fortitude. About the 1st day of August Joseph reached his home.

In leaving the Saints in Missouri, the Prophet had hoped that for a time, at least, they would be blessed with protection from their enemies, and that the brethren would be accorded the opportunity to gain a maintenance for their suffering wives and children. Although before he parted with them many appeals had been made for a restoration to their possessions in Jackson County, it is not probable that he entertained any hope that Governor Dunklin would accomplish such a courageous act. Joseph's subsequent zeal in building up Kirtland seems to indicate that he had prescience of the continued exile of the Church from the land of Zion.

Shortly after the Prophet's return to Kirtland, he submitted before the high council some charges which had been made against himself by one of the rebellious spirits in Zion's Camp. This man, Sylvester Smith, had become angered on the march by Joseph's rebukes, which were only uttered in kindness and to secure proper discipline and mutual concession and forbearance among the brethren; and in his rage Sylvester had declared that the Prophet was corrupt in his heart. The complaint made by Sylvester did not include any specific charge of impurity, and the Prophet might have passed it by without notice. But he wanted to teach the brethren that no man was above the law of God, and he cheerfully and patiently submitted to an investigation.

It was made fairly and fully, with no undue favor to him; and the result was a complete vindication of the Prophet's character and eventually a confession by Sylvester Smith of his own injustice, wrongdoing, and evil inspiration. Thus, by his own example, Joseph showed to his brethren the saintly course for the settlement of difficulties.

Joseph gave another evidence of his devotion to the work and his personal humility at this time. Labor upon the house of the Lord in Kirtland was in progress, but the poverty of the people and the surrounding difficulties made the advancement very slow. Only thirty families of Saints were then resident in Kirtland, and the toil and self-denial of the little handful cannot be described. Joseph gave his services as foreman in the temple stone quarry and labored day after day with his own hands in bringing out the materials for that important structure. At the same time Hyrum was showing similar evidence of his industry and meekness. It was he who lifted the first spadeful of earth for the foundation trench, and he continued from that time on to watch and work and pray for the success of this sacred undertaking.

Having placed all things in order in Kirtland for the progress of the Lord's house, Joseph departed on the 16th of October, 1834, with his brother Hyrum and others to visit the Saints in the state of Michigan. They went by water, and on board the steamer they met a man who called himself Elmer. Not knowing who they were, in the course of conversation he said: "I am personally acquainted with Joe Smith; I have heard him preach his lies, and now since he is dead I am glad. I heard Joe Smith preach in Bainbridge, Chenango County, New York, five years ago, and knew him because he had such a dark complexion." Then he continued his exultations at the supposed death of the Prophet. This is an illustration of the malice and ignorance which prevailed at that time. Joseph was not dead; his complexion was not dark; he had never been in Bainbridge. Elmer had probably heard the tirade of some sectarian minister against Joseph Smith and thought he was praising God when he lied about the Prophet, and that he was doing Christ's service by exulting in his supposed death.

After preaching to the Michigan Saints for a brief time and giving and receiving comfort in their society, Joseph and his companions returned to Kirtland, reaching there about the last of October. During the month of November, with so many labors upon his hands, Joseph found every moment of time occupied. He was able to accomplish prodigious labors because he obeyed the rule which he had established over his life and which he tersely states:

When the Lord commands, do it.

His scrupulous regard for the interests of others is shown by a circumstance which occurred during the last of November, 1834. Some brethren and sisters representing a branch of the Church in the East called at Kirtland. They had in their possession means with which to purchase lands in Zion; but in view of the action of mobs and the inaction of officials, they could not well proceed to Missouri. The money was offered to the Church in Kirtland, or to Joseph as its President; but as this was not the purpose for which the means had been donated, he would only take it in trust to be paid back with interest in the ensuing spring; and he gave proper security for the fulfillment of these conditions. The means thus obtained were not devoted to his personal use, but were entirely employed in the furtherance of Church works.

It was with the close of 1834 that a pledge of tithing was first given, and the custom now in force was begun, the doctrine having been foreshadowed in previous revelations from the Almighty. The principle of tithing as now practiced very properly began with the Prophet. On the 29th day of November, 1834, Joseph united in prayer with Oliver Cowdery for a continuation of divine blessings; and being filled with joy on this occasion, they entered into a covenant with the Lord as follows:

That if the Lord will prosper us in our business, and open the way before us, that we may obtain means to pay our debts, that we be not troubled nor brought into disrepute before the world, nor His people; after that, of all that He shall give us, we will give a tenth, to be bestowed upon the poor in His Church, or as He shall command; and that we will be faithful over that which He has entrusted to our care, that we may obtain much; and that our children after us, shall remember to observe this sacred and holy covenant; and that our children and our children's children may know of the same, we have subscribed our names with our own hands.

JOSEPH SMITH,
OLIVER COWDERY.

And now, O Father, as thou didst prosper our father Jacob, and bless him with protection and prosperity wherever he went, from the time he made a like covenant before and with thee; as thou didst, even the same night, open the heavens unto him, and manifest great mercy and power, and give him promises, so wilt thou do with us his sons; and as his blessings prevailed above his progenitors unto the utmost bounds of the everlasting hills, even so may our blessings prevail like his; and may thy servants be preserved from the power and influence of wicked and unrighteous men; may every weapon formed against us fall upon the head of him who shall form it; may we be blessed with a name and a place among the Saints here, and thy sanctified when they shall rest. Amen.

CHAPTER 30

Quorum of the Twelve

And this gospel of the kingdom shall be preached in all the world for a witness unto all nations; and then shall the end come. (Matthew 24:14.)

But before all these, they shall lay their hands on you, and persecute you, delivering you up to the synagogues, and into prisons, being brought before kings and rulers for my name's sake.

And it shall turn to you for a testimony. . . .

And ye shall be betrayed both by parents, and brethren, and kinsfolk and friends; and some of you shall they cause to be put to death,

And ye shall be hated of all men for my name's sake. . . .

And when these things begin to come to pass, then look up, and lift up your heads; for your redemption draweth nigh. (Luke 21:12–13, 16–17, 28.)

Our Lord and Master had His twelve special witnesses to the world when His gospel was offered to all mankind eighteen centuries ago. And so, in the reestablishment of the Church in this dispensation, twelve apostles were called and ordained to be witnesses of Christ, crucified and risen, and of Christ's gospel brought forth through the darkness of ages and now restored to stand forever.

The power, authority and scope of this apostleship are shown in the revelation given to the Prophet in Kirtland in the early part of the year 1835:

The twelve traveling councilors are called to be the Twelve Apostles, or special witnesses of the name of Christ in all the world— ...

And they form a quorum, equal in authority and power to the three presidents ... [the first presidency].

The Twelve are a Traveling Presiding High Council, to officiate in the name of the Lord, under the direction of the Presidency of the Church, agreeable to the institution of heaven; to build up the church, and regulate all the affairs of the same in all nations, ...

The Twelve being sent out, holding the keys, to open the door by the proclamation of the gospel of Jesus Christ, and first unto the Gentiles and then unto the Jews.

It is the duty of the Twelve, also, to ordain and set in order all the other officers of the church, agreeable to the revelation. ... (D&C 107:23, 24, 33, 35, 58.)

On the Sabbath day, February 8, 1835, Joseph invited Brigham and Joseph Young to his home and listened to some of their sweetest hymns. They were always noted for the excellence of their singing; but on this occasion with such wondrous power did their voices swell that the Prophet was lifted up in his soul and felt the Holy Spirit descending upon them. Joseph had seen in vision the brethren who had died of cholera in Missouri; and he related the vision to his visitors, saying: "If I get a mansion as bright as theirs, I shall ask no more." He wept at the recital, and could not speak again for some moments. When his composure returned, he told Brigham that he should be one of the twelve special witnesses, and said to Joseph Young: "The Lord has made you president of the seventies." Neither of the brothers Young fully understood the Prophet's meaning at that time, but later they learned.

On the 14th day of February, 1835, the Prophet called an assemblage at Kirtland of all the men who had formed the Camp of Zion. He said to call this meeting he had been directed by the Almighty. The elders who had passed through the trials and sufferings of the journey to Zion were to be ordained to the ministry to go forth and prune the vineyard for the last time before the coming of the Lord. Twelve men were to be chosen as apostles to bear testimony of the name of the Lord Jesus and to send it abroad among all nations, kindreds, tongues and people.

Under the hands of the Prophet, the three witnesses of the Book of Mormon, Oliver Cowdery, David Whitmer and Martin Harris, were blessed, by the direction of the Holy Spirit, to choose the twelve apostles of the Church. The men thus selected were all equal in authority, but in a later time the Prophet designated the order in which they should sit in council—that is, according to age the eldest first. And under this rule the first Quorum of the Twelve Apostles of the Church of Jesus Christ in these last days were: Thomas B. Marsh, David W. Patten, Brigham Young, Heber C. Kimball, Orson Hyde, William E. McLellin, Parley P. Pratt, Luke Johnson, William Smith, Orson Pratt, John F. Boynton, and Lyman E. Johnson.

The apostles had their mission of salvation divinely dictated unto them. How they have fulfilled its requirements, let answer the thousands from every continent and every isle of the sea who have heard the message in their native tongues!

It was the work which was great and which conferred greatness upon those who engaged in it. The world has never understood this. To man has been attributed the success which has attended the system of religion which Joseph Smith was the chosen earthly instrument to found. Joseph himself had a wonderful personality; and it was the custom to give him credit for the early growth of the Church numerically; and to ascribe its spread and the devotion of its adherents to his individual power of attraction. But he did not so esteem himself; and the work which the apostles have performed is proof that it is the Holy Spirit which animates and the Holy Spirit which convinces.

To the twelve it was not only a call to the ministry; for some of them it was also a call to martyrdom.

Of the disciples chosen then and of those since selected to keep the quorum complete, not one has escaped the afflictions of time.

With some the pains were too intense to be endured; the burdens too heavy to be borne; and they dropped aside from the on-marching ranks to find, as they hoped, repose and safety amidst the cooling shadows of that world from which they had been chosen to be special witnesses of the Son of God. Such are no longer His apostles.

But the others, with unshaken resoluteness, have gone forward in fulfillment of their high mission, under the scorching heat of fiery persecution. Joseph is their captain and their fellow soldier in the cause of Christ. With him and after him many of them have, with continuous and unyielding zeal, toiled steadily on until worn out in the performance of the duty assigned them by their Master Jesus; they have passed to the enjoyment of His promised rest. With Him they and the other faithful apostles will stand triumphant when human time shall be no more, and when the voice of the Eternal shall fill the universe with the thunder of His judgments. They shall not then be only twelve; for they who have been called of God to this holy calling and who endure faithful, though they may lay down their mortality, yet shall they not lose their apostleship; for it abideth with them in this world and in the worlds to come.

To proclaim the truth in all the earth for a witness, requires not only willingness but also numerical strength. And so the seventies were called by divine revelation. They are to preach the gospel and to be special witnesses unto the Gentiles, and in all the world; they are to act in the name of the Lord, under the direction of the twelve, in building up the Church and regulating all the affairs of the same in all nations—first unto the Gentiles and then unto the Jews.

> And they form a quorum, equal in authority to that of the Twelve . . . Apostles. . . . (D&C 107:26.)

On the 28th day of February, 1835, the Church in council assembled began the calling of the quorum of seventies from the members of Zion's Camp, and this devoted organization of the seventies speedily engaged in its appointed labors.

Thus was the Prophet blessed with efficient aids selected by the Spirit of God.

One day when Joseph had assembled the elders in Kirtland, soon after the establishment of the quorums of twelve and seventy, he said to them that the test had been made, the purpose of the journey to Missouri was now clear, and God had chosen his twelve and seventy from a body of men who had offered their lives, and who had made as great a sacrifice as did Abraham.

CHAPTER 31

Book
of Abraham

Joseph Smith was not only a prophet but a reformer—as able as Luther, as bold as Zwingli. And he was more than a reformer. He was a restorer—the greatest in his personality and in the character of his work since the day of the divine atonement.

Through him even the buried past reaches up to the listening present, and the distant future bends down to this gazing age. His work in revealing hidden truths spans the circle of all earthly time—stretching from the decree by which the world was rolled into space unto the moment when it shall become a purified and exalted sphere. This comprehension was the divine gift to the foreordained martyr.

Through him had been revealed the hidden truths concerning prehistoric America. From the hour when Joseph gave to the world the Book of Mormon, all ignorance concerning the ancient inhabitants of this land became willful. Then his labor of restoration reached another hemisphere and a remoter time.

Abraham, the friend of God, Abraham who died thirty-six centuries ago, Abraham who was buried in the cave of Machpelah, spoke through the modern prophet, his descendant; and the manner of that communication so manifestly shows the overruling hand of Providence that no one can doubt the divine direction.

While Joseph had been laboring in Kirtland, journeying to and from Missouri, teaching his brethren and being taught of God, there were moving to him from one of the catacombs of Egypt the writings of Father Abraham and of Joseph who was governor in Egypt.

On the 7th day of June, 1831, a French traveler and explorer penetrated the depths of a catacomb near the site of ancient Thebes. It had cost him time and treasure and influence to make the entrance. After securing the license to make his researches, he employed more than four hundred men for a period of some months to make the necessary excavation. When he was able at last to stand within this multipled tomb, he found several hundred mummies; but only eleven of them were in such a state that they could be removed. He carried them away but died on his voyage to Paris. By his will the mummies were bequeathed to Michael H. Chandler, his nephew, and in search of this gentleman they were sent through Ireland and finally across the sea. After two years of wanderings they found their owner. Hoping to discover some treasure of precious stones or metals, Mr. Chandler opened the coffins or embalming cases. Attached to two of the bodies were rolls of linen preserved with the same care and apparently by the same method as the bodies. Within the linen coverings were rolls of papyrus bearing a perfectly preserved record in black and red characters carefully formed. With other of the bodies were papyrus strips bearing epitaphs and astronomical calculations. The learned men of Philadelphia and other places flocked to see these representatives of an ancient time, and Mr. Chandler solicited their translation of some of the characters. Even the wisest among them were only able to interpret the meaning of a few of the signs. From the very moment when he discovered the rolls, Mr. Chandler had heard that a Prophet lived in the West who could decipher strange languages and reveal things hidden; and after failing with all the learned, and having parted with seven of the mummies and some few strips of papyrus bearing astronomical figures, he finally reached Kirtland and presented himself to Joseph with the four remaining bodies and with the rolls of manuscript. The Prophet, under inspiration of the Almighty, interpreted some of the ancient writings to Mr. Chandler's satisfaction. So far as the learned men of Philadelphia had been able to translate, Joseph's work coincided with theirs;

but he went much further, and in his delight Mr. Chandler wrote a letter to the Prophet certifying to this effect.

Later some of the friends of the Prophet purchased the four mummies, with the writings. Joseph engaged assiduously to interpret from the rolls and strips of papyrus. The result of his labor was to give the world a translation of the Book of Abraham. This book was written by the hand of Abraham while he was in Egypt and was preserved by the marvelous dispensation of Providence, through all the mutations of time and dangers of distance, to reach the hand of God's Prophet in this last dispensation. By this record the Father of the faithful makes known what the Lord Almighty had shown to him concerning the things that were before the world was; and he declares that he did penetrate the mysteries of the heavens even unto Kolob, the star which is nearest the throne of God, the Eternal One.

In the record of Joseph who was sold into Egypt is given a prophetic representation of the judgment, the Savior is shown seated upon His throne, crowned and holding the scepters of righteousness and power; before Him are assembled the Twelve Tribes of Israel and all the kingdoms of the world; while Michael the Archangel holds the key to the bottomless pit in which Satan has been chained.

At the time when Joseph, aided by the inspiration of the Almighty, was enabled to make these translations, he was studying ancient languages and the grandest sciences, while he was also imparting instruction in the school of the brethren in Kirtland, that others than himself might have their minds fitted to grasp the sublimities of truth in theology and history and the laws governing the universe. Joseph was now in his thirtieth year and was no longer an unlearned farmer lad. He was the leader of the people by the command of heaven, and he was the leader of the people by his growing intellectual greatness. The Prophet had already become a scholar. He loved learning. He loved knowledge for its righteous power. Through the tribulations which had surrounded him from the day when first he made known to a skeptical world his communion with the heavens, he had been ever advancing in the acquisition of intelligence. The Lord had commanded him to study, and he was obeying. Such branches of learning as he knew not, teachers were employed to communicate. His mind, quickened by the Holy Spirit, grasped with readiness all true principles, and one by one he mastered these branches and became in them a teacher.

Joseph Smith was the head of a committee which had been appointed in September, 1834, to compile the doctrines of the Church for publication. And in Kirtland, at a general assembly held on the 17th day of August, 1835, that committee reported by presenting the book of Doctrine and Covenants to the Church for the approval of the congregation. Solemn testimonies were given of the truth of the work and of the inspiration by which Joseph Smith had uttered the revelations from on high. The testimony of the twelve on this subject closed as follows:

> The Lord has borne record to our souls, through the Holy Ghost shed forth upon us, that these commandments were given by inspiration of God, and are profitable for all men, and are verily true. We give this testimony unto the world, the Lord being our helper: and it is through the grace of God, the Father, and His Son Jesus Christ, that we are permitted to have this privilege of bearing this testimony unto the world, in the which we rejoice exceedingly, praying the Lord always, that the children of men may be profited thereby.

At the same time there was presented and accepted the tenet of the Church concerning government and laws in which the following passages occur, showing that thus early in his career the Prophet's mind was trained in true statesmanship and social philosophy:

> We believe that governments were instituted of God for the benefit of man; and that he holds men accountable for their acts in relation to them, both in making laws or administering them, for the good and safety of society.

We believe that no government can exist in peace, except such laws are framed and held inviolate as will secure to each individual the free exercise of conscience, the right and control of property, and the protection of life....

We believe that religion is instituted of God; and that men are amenable to him, and to him only, for the exercise of it, unless their religious opinions prompt them to infringe upon the rights and liberties of others; but we do not believe that human law has a right to interfere in prescribing rules of worship to bind the consciences of men, nor dictate forms for public or private devotion; that the civil magistrate should restrain crime, but never control conscience; should punish guilt, but never suppress the freedom of the soul....

We believe that rulers, states, and governments have a right, and are bound to enact laws for the protection of all citizens in the free exercise of their religious belief; but we do not believe that they have a right in justice, to deprive citizens of this privilege, or proscribe them in their opinions, so long as a regard and reverence are shown to the laws and such religious opinions do not justify sedition nor conspiracy....

We do not believe it just to mingle religious influence with civil government, whereby one religious society is fostered, and another proscribed in its spiritual privileges, and the individual rights of its members as citizens denied. (D&C 134:1–2, 4, 7, 9.)

The Prophet was not present at the assembly, as he was visiting Saints in Michigan; but his hand was manifest in its proceedings, for he had all the time led in preparing the book for presentation to the Church.

With his staunch advocacy of truth, and his unyielding adherence to the commandments of God, Joseph was ever merciful to the weak and the erring. During the summer of 1835, he was laboring in councils and meetings in Kirtland and vicinity, and was chosen to take part in the proceedings against several members who were to be tried for utterances made against the presidency of the Church. Whether it fell to his lot to plead the cause of the accused or to prosecute, though he himself might have been the one who was wronged, he acted with so much tenderness and justice that he won the love of all.

At this time he labored under serious financial distress. The performance of the work laid upon him demanded many expenditures, and often it seemed that he would be involved in inextricable embarrassment. But the way was constantly opened to him. His brethren were kind and charitable, many of them presenting him or loaning him sums sufficient for the performance of his labors and to meet all his engagements; and all of these he blessed with the gratitude of his soul, and was especially scrupulous to pay at the time agreed upon.

Joseph was a dutiful son; his strong affection for his parents was ever a marked feature in his character. In the early part of October, 1835, his father was ill; and, though the Prophet was performing wearisome toil in traveling, preaching and other duties—exposed to chilling storms—he watched and waited on his parent with the utmost humility and tenderness. On the 10th day of October, the elder Joseph was failing very fast, so much that his life was despaired of. The Prophet prayed in secret most earnestly that his father's life might be spared, and on the morning of Sunday, the 11th of October, while he was still upon his knees, the Lord said to him:

My servant, thy father shall live.

That night Father Smith arose and dressed himself and shouted and praised the Lord for his recovery.

One of the most sorrowful passages in the Prophet's life opens with the 29th day of October, 1835. Joseph's brother William was a man of violent temper which he had not then nor ever afterwards subdued. Though not destitute of qualities, which, if properly used, would have made him a useful and noble man, he was willful and headstrong, and so impatient of contradiction and rebuke that he often forgot his own high station as an apostle of the Lord Jesus Christ, and forgot the kindness of his brother Joseph and the deference due him as a prophet of God. On the day mentioned, at a high council meeting, William abused Joseph in violent terms because of a just ruling made by the Prophet. The noble and faithful Hyrum, their elder brother, admonished William, but without avail. He left the building and soon after engaged in circulating evil reports against the Prophet. Every effort was made by his friends to correct the wrong and to bring him to a sense of his position. He made an outward show of humility but took an early occasion when the Prophet was a guest at his house to assault him with such violence that the effects were carried by Joseph to his grave.

Satan was indeed trying the Lord's chosen one. At home or abroad he was fated to have afflictions showered upon his devoted head. But of all the woes of his persecuted life, not one could have been more saddening to him than these attacks by his own brother in the flesh.

The Prophet harbored no malice; but with the humility and the godliness which permeated all his association with his fellow men, he freely forgave William. Such effect did the Prophet's kindness have upon William that he repented and expressed his contrition with great sincerity and earnestness. A reconciliation took place at which Father Smith and his brother John, with Hyrum, Joseph and William were present. The elder Joseph addressed them all in a pathetic manner, so much so that they wept. They all covenanted at that time to endeavor to build each other up in righteousness. Happy would it have been for William if he had then taken the advice of the Prophet and his father; but he violated his word, despised their counsel, and fell from his high estate.

Not only did Joseph show tenderness in his dealings with his brother, but also with others of the twelve. When Thomas B. Marsh, the president of the twelve apostles, complained that the Prophet, in chastening them for the wrongdoing of some of their number, had used harsh language, the Prophet readily begged their forgiveness if he had pained their feelings. And by his noble conduct he brought about a restoration of harmony and fellowship. If his brethren of the twelve had all been as mindful of the rule of righteousness as Joseph himself, the dissensions in that quorum which cost some of its brightest members their standing would not have occurred.

CHAPTER 32

Kirtland Temple

The building of the Kirtland Temple was accomplished by the utmost self-sacrifice. Nearly three years had been occupied in its construction; and during this time the Saints had given of their substance and had toiled without ceasing to make a habitation fit for the ministration of angelic visitants and of the Holy One, Himself. The consummation of this work had been very near to the Prophet's heart, especially since the tribulations in Missouri had shown that no house of the Lord could be erected speedily in the center stake of Zion.

Wondrous were the visions bestowed in that sacred edifice. Previous to its completion the glories of the heavens had been unfolded to the Prophet and his brethren while administering in the ordinances there. On the 21st of January, 1836, Joseph met with Sidney Rigdon and Frederick G. Williams, and his father, Patriarch Joseph Smith, Sr., at one of the finished schoolrooms in the building to anoint their heads with holy oil. They united in anointing and blessing the Prophet's father as the Patriarch and to anoint their heads; and each of the First Presidency was then anointed and blessed under the hands of Father Smith. While they were engaged in this labor, marvelous visions and revelations were bestowed.

The Prophet says:

The heavens were opened upon us, and I beheld the celestial kingdom of God, and the glory thereof, whether in the body or out I cannot tell. I saw the transcendent beauty of the gate through which the heirs of that kingdom

will enter, which was like unto circling flames of fire; also
the blazing throne of God, whereon was seated the Father
and the Son. I saw the beautiful streets of that kingdom,
which had the appearance of being paved with gold. I saw
fathers Adam and Abraham, and my father and mother,
my brother Alvin, who has long since slept, and wondered
how it was that he had obtained an inheritance in that
kingdom, seeing that he had departed this life before the
Lord had set his hand to gather Israel the second time, and
had not been baptized for the remission of sins.

Thus came the voice of the Lord unto me, saying—

All who have died without a knowledge of this gospel,
who would have received it if they had been permitted to
tarry, shall be heirs of the celestial kingdom of our God;
also all that shall die henceforth without a knowledge of
it, who would have received it with all their hearts, shall
be heirs of that kingdom, for I, the Lord, will judge all men
according to their works, according to the desires of their
hearts. (Joseph Smith, *History of the Church*, II, 380.)

Many other things did the Prophet see and hear. He beheld
that all children who died before reaching years of accountability
are saved in the celestial kingdom of our God. A holy comfort this,
which takes the place of all the black threats concerning infantile
damnation. He saw the twelve apostles of the Lamb in foreign
lands, standing in a circle, with their clothes tattered and their feet
swollen, with their eyes cast downward, and Jesus was standing in
their midst, but they did not behold Him, and the Savior looked
upon them and wept. Those of the brethren who received the
ordinances at this time saw most glorious visions. Some of them
beheld the face of their Redeemer; others were ministered unto
by holy angels; the spirit of prophecy and revelation was poured
out in mighty power; and loud hosannas saluted the heavens
from those who were communing with the sanctified hosts of the
celestial kingdom.

On other occasions, before the entire structure was completed and dedicated, similar visitations came to manifest the power of God and His gracious acceptance of this devoted labor.

On the morning of Sunday, March 27, 1836, the first temple ever built in this dispensation by the command of God was dedicated to His service. A large assemblage of the Saints had congregated in the building. Joseph presided, and he was supported by the priesthood. The Prophet himself made the dedicatory prayer, which he closed in the following words:

> ... hear us, O Lord! And answer these petitions, and accept the dedication of this house unto thee, the work of our hands, which we have built unto thy name.
>
> And also this church, to put upon it thy name. And help us by the power of thy Spirit, that we may mingle our voices with those bright, shining seraphs around thy throne, with acclamations of praise, singing Hosanna to God and the Lamb!
>
> And let these thine anointed ones, be clothed with salvation, and thy saints shout aloud for joy. Amen, and Amen. (D&C 109: 78–80.)

Joseph was acknowledged by the several quorums, standing upon their feet, as the Prophet and Seer of the Church, and they gave a solemn pledge to uphold him as such by their faith and prayers. This action was also ratified by the entire congregation of the Saints in the same manner. The Prophet then called upon the quorums and the congregation to acknowledge the other members of the First Presidency and the several quorums in their offices and callings, and the vote was unanimous in every instance.

After the administration of the Lord's Supper and the expression of many solemn testimonies, the dedication was sealed by shouting Hosanna, Hosanna, Hosanna to God and the Lamb, three times sealing it, each time with Amen, Amen, and Amen.

Brigham Young had the gift of tongues powerfully upon him and made an address, which David W. Patten interpreted.

Then the Prophet made a short exhortation, also in tongues, and afterward blessed the congregation in the name of the Lord, and the assembly dispersed.

The same evening the Prophet met the quorums in the temple. Brother George A. Smith stood up and began to prophesy, when a noise was heard like the sound of a mighty rushing wind which filled the building. All the congregation rose in an instant, being moved upon by an invisible power. Many began to speak in tongues and prophesy, others saw glorious visions. The temple was filled with angels. People from the neighborhood came running toward the temple, having heard an unusual sound and seen a brilliant light like a pillar of fire rising above the structure. These spectators were amazed at what they saw and heard.

On the 29th of March the Prophet met with many of the brethren in the most holy place in the Lord's house and fasted and prayed and performed sacred ordinances. In obedience to the commandment, they remained together throughout that whole day and the succeeding night. While they were there the Holy Spirit rested upon them; and they continued, until the morning light broke, to prophesy and give glory to God. The same services were repeated the day following.

Joseph said to the quorums that he had now completed the organization of the Church, having passed through all the necessary ceremonies, and that they were at liberty to go forth and build up the kingdom of God. At nine o'clock in the evening ,he retired from the temple and left the meeting in the charge of the twelve apostles, who remained to prophesy and speak in tongues until again the morning dawned. During the night the Savior appeared with a host of ministering angels. The Prophet said that it was a Pentecost long to be remembered, for the sound should go forth from that place unto all the world.

The next day, Thursday, March 31, the ceremonies in the temple were repeated for the benefit of those Saints who could not find room in the house on the preceding Sabbath.

On Sunday, the 3rd day of April, 1836, after the regular service of the day, the Prophet and Oliver Cowdery retired to the pulpit and dropped the veils by which it was separated from the body of the house, and bowed in solemn and silent prayer. After rising, a vision of supernal sublimity and beauty was opened to the eyes of their understanding. They saw the Lord standing upon the breastwork of the pulpit, and under his feet they saw a paved work of pure gold in color like amber. His eyes were as a flame of fire, the hair of His head was white like the pure snow, His countenance shone above the brightness of the sun, and His voice was as the sound of the rushing of great waters, even the voice of Jehovah, saying:

> I am the first and the last; I am he who liveth, I am he who was slain; I am your advocate with the Father.
>
> Behold, your sins are forgiven you; you are clean before me; therefore, lift up your heads and rejoice.
>
> Let the hearts of your brethren rejoice, and let the hearts of all my people rejoice, who have, with their might, built this house to my name.
>
> For behold, I have accepted this house, and my name shall be here; and I will manifest myself to my people in mercy in this house.
>
> Yea, I will appear unto my servants, and speak unto them with mine own voice, if my people will keep my commandments, and do not pollute this holy house.
>
> Yea the hearts of thousands and tens of thousands shall greatly rejoice in consequence of the blessings which shall be poured out, and the endowment with which my servants have been endowed in this house.
>
> And the fame of this house shall spread to foreign lands; and this is the beginning of the blessing which shall be poured out upon the heads of my people. Even so. Amen. (D&C 110:4–10.)

This vision closed, and then the heavens were again opened. Moses appeared and committed unto them the keys of the gathering of Israel. After this came Elias, who gave to them the dispensation of the gospel of Abraham. When this vision had closed, Elijah, the prophet who was taken to heaven without tasting death, appeared unto them, testifying that the time had fully come which was spoken of by the mouth of Malachi concerning the coming of Elijah—before the great and dreadful day of the Lord—to turn the hearts of the fathers to the children and the children to the fathers, lest the earth should be smitten with a curse.

During several weeks following the dedication of the temple, the Prophet and his associates were constantly engaged in measures for the spiritual advancement of the people and with the building up of Kirtland. A comforting thing came to Joseph at that time. It was in the month of May, 1836, when his uncles Asael and Silas Smith arrived in Kirtland with their families, bringing with them the Prophet's grandmother, Mary Smith. This noble woman was ninety-three years of age; she was the widow of Asael Smith, who had prophesied concerning the coming forth of Joseph and who had lived to accept the Book of Mormon. The aged Mary had traveled five hundred miles to see her grandson, the Prophet. For ten days all her relatives in Kirtland enjoyed the pleasure of her presence, and then she gently fell asleep in death.

On the 25th day of July, 1836, the Prophet departed with his brother Hyrum, Sidney Rigdon and Oliver Cowdery, on a mission to the eastern states. He labored diligently in the vicinity of Salem in Massachusetts, and while there received a revelation in which the Lord declared that many people from that part would in His due time be gathered out to journey to Zion.

Joseph returned to Kirtland in the month of September.

CHAPTER 33

Expulsion

They were eastern men, whose manners, habits, customs, and even dialect, are essentially different from our own. They are nonslaveholders, and opposed to slavery, which in this peculiar period, when Abolitionism has reared its deformed and haggard visage in our land, is well calculated to excite deep and abiding prejudices in any community where slavery is tolerated and protected.

This was the complaint raised against the Saints in Clay County on the 29th day of June, 1836, by a mass meeting of leading citizens who assembled at Liberty.

It will be remembered that when the mob had accomplished its awful work in Jackson County, the persecuted Saints had sought and found a temporary refuge in Clay. During all the intervening time of nearly three years, constant efforts had been made to secure a restoration of the Saints to their lawful possessions at Independence and vicinity; but all in vain, for the mob power triumphed over law, and murderous rapine still trampled upon law and justice.

Clay County had been the only one to show any available hospitality toward the plundered ones. But now the time had come when a feeling of self-preservation, as they called it, prompted the citizens of even this charitable region to send the Saints forth to renewed wandering.

The measures adopted were not intentionally cruel; it is pitiable even at this hour to read the resolutions of the mass meeting which decreed this exile; they show that the men who forced them were sinning against their own sense of justice, but for the sake of their own families and property.

At the meeting at Liberty, John Bird was chosen chairman and John F. Doherty secretary. The recorded minutes of that assemblage state that the reasons given in the opening of this chapter, with other similar causes, "have raised a feeling of hostility" against the Saints "that the first spark might ignite into all the horrors and desolations of a civil war, the worst evil that could befall any country."

Continuing, the document says:

> We therefore feel it our duty to come forward, as mediators, and use every means in our power to prevent the occurrence of so great an evil. As the most efficacious means to arrest the evil, we urge on the Mormons to use every means to put an immediate stop to the emigration of their people to this country. We earnestly urge them to seek some other abiding place, where the manners, the habits and customs of the people will be more consonant with their own.
>
> For this purpose we would advise them to explore the territory of Wisconsin. This country is peculiarly suited to their condition and to their wants. It is almost entirely unsettled; they can procure large bodies of land together, where there are no settlements, and none to interfere with them. It is a territory in which slavery is prohibited, and it is settled entirely with emigrants from the north and east.
>
> The religious tenets of this people are so different from the present churches of the age, that they always have, and always will excite deep prejudices against them in any populous country where they may locate. We, therefore, in a spirit of frank and friendly kindness, do advise them to seek a home where they may obtain large and separate bodies of land, and have a community of their own. We further say to them, if they regard their own safety and welfare, if they regard the welfare of their families, their

wives and children, they will ponder with deep and solemn reflection on this friendly admonition.

If they have one spark of gratitude, they will not willingly plunge a people into civil war, who held out to them the friendly hand of assistance in that hour of dark distress, when there were few to say, God save them. We can only say to them, if they still persist in the blind course they have heretofore followed in flooding the country with their people, that we fear and firmly believe that an immediate civil war is the inevitable consequence. We know that there is not one among us who thirsts for the blood of that people.

We do not contend that we have the least right, under the Constitution and laws of the country, to expel them by force. But we would indeed be blind, if we did not foresee that the first blow that is struck, at this moment of deep excitement, must and will speedily involve every individual in a war, bearing ruin, woe and desolation in its course. It matters but little how, where, or by whom, the war may begin, when the work of destruction commences, we must all be borne onward by the storm, or crushed beneath its fury. In a civil war, when our home is the theatre on which it is fought, there can be no neutrals; let our opinions be what they may, we must fight in self-defense.

We want nothing, we ask nothing, we would have nothing from this people, we only ask them, for their own safety, and for ours, to take the least of two evils. Most of them are destitute of land, have but little property, are late emigrants to this country, without relations, friends, or endearing ties, to bind them to this land. At the risk of such imminent peril to them and to us, we request them to leave us, when their crops are gathered, their business settled, and they have made every suitable preparation to remove. Those who have forty acres of land, we are willing should remain until they can dispose of it without loss, if it should require years. But we urge, most strongly urge, that emigration cease, and cease immediately, as nothing else can or will allay for a moment, the deep excitement that is now unhappily agitating this community.

. . .

That if the Mormons agree to these propositions, we will use every means in our power to allay the excitement among our own citizens, and to get them to await the result of these things.

That it is the opinion of this meeting that the recent emigration among the Mormons should take measures to leave this county immediately, as they have no crops on hand, and nothing to lose by continuing their journey to some more friendly land. (Joseph Smith, *History of the Church*, II, 450–452.)

This paper had the unanimous support of the meeting, and when this decree, mingling the sorrow of humane men with the cruel necessity of what seemed self-preservation, was entered, the meeting adjourned for three days. In the meantime a committee named in the resolution was to confer with the leaders of the Saints and obtain their reply.

When the Prophet heard of this new mandate of banishment he was on the eve of starting from Kirtland upon his journey to the East; but before going he forwarded a letter signed by himself, his counselors, his brother Hyrum, and Oliver Cowdery, to the committee of citizens at Liberty entrusted with the promulgation of the order of exile, in which letter the following passages occur:

Under existing circumstances, while rumor is afloat with her accustomed cunning, and while public opinion is fast setting, like a flood tide against the members of said Church, we cannot but admire the candor with which your preamble and resolutions were clothed, as presented to the meeting of the citizens of Clay County, on the 29th of June last. Though, as you expressed in your report to said meeting—"We do not contend that we have the least right, under the Constitution and laws of the country, to expel them by force,"—yet communities may be, at times, unexpectedly thrown into a situation, when wisdom, prudence, and that first item in nature's law, self-defense, would dictate that the responsible and influential part should step forward and guide the public mind in a course to save difficulty, preserve rights, and spare the innocent blood from staining that soil so dearly purchased with the fortunes and lives of our fathers. And as you have come forward as "mediators," to prevent the effusion of blood, and save disasters consequent upon civil war, we take this opportunity to present to you, though strangers, and through you, if you wish, to the people of Clay County, our heartfelt gratitude for every kindness rendered our friends in affliction, when driven from their peaceful homes, and to yourselves, also, for the prudent course in the present excited state of your community. But, in doing this, justice to ourselves, as communicants of that Church to which our friends belong, and duty towards them as acquaintances and former fellow citizens, require us to say something to exonerate them from the foul charges brought against them, to deprive them of their constitutional privileges, and drive them from the face of society.

They have been charged in consequence of the whims and vain notions of some few uninformed, with claiming that upper country, and that ere long they were to possess it, at all hazards, and in defiance of all consequences. This is unjust and far from a foundation in truth. A thing not expected, not looked for, not desired by this society, as a people, and where the idea could have originated is unknown to us. We do not, neither did we ever insinuate a thing of this kind, or hear it from the leading men of the society, now in your country. There is nothing in our religious faith to warrant it, but on the contrary, the most strict injunctions to live in obedience to the laws, and follow peace with all men. And we doubt not, but a recurrence to the Jackson County difficulties, with our friends, will fully satisfy you, that at least, heretofore, such has been the course followed by them. That instead of fighting for their own rights, they have sacrificed them for a season, to wait the redress guaranteed in the law, and so anxiously looked for at a time distant from this.

We have been, and are still, clearly under the conviction, that had our friends been disposed, they might have maintained their possessions in Jackson County. They might have resorted to the same barbarous means with their neighbors, throwing down dwellings, threatening lives, driving innocent women and children from their homes, and thereby have annoyed their enemies equally, at least—but this to their credit, and which must ever remain upon the pages of time, to their honor—they did not. They had possessions, they had homes, they had sacred rights, and more still, they had helpless, harmless innocence with an approving conscience that they had violated no law of their country or their God, to urge them forward—but, to show to all that they were willing to forego these for the peace of their country, they tamely submitted, and have since been wanderers among strangers (though hospitable) without homes. We think these sufficient reasons to show to your patriotic minds, that our friends, instead of having a wish to expel a community by force of arms, would suffer their rights to be taken from them before shedding blood. . . .

Another charge of great magnitude is brought against our friends in the west—of "keeping up a constant communication with the Indian tribes on our frontier, with declaring, even from the pulpit, that the Indians are a part of God's chosen people, and are destined, by heaven, to inherit this land, in common with themselves." We know of nothing, under the present aspect of our Indian relations, calculated to rouse the fears of the people of the upper Missouri, more than a combination or influence of this nature; and we cannot look upon it other than one of the most subtle purposes of those whose feelings are embittered against our friends, to turn the eye of suspicion upon them from every man who is acquainted with the barbarous cruelty of rude savages. Since a rumor was afloat that the western Indians were showing signs of war, we have received frequent private letters from our friends, who have not only expressed fears for their own safety, in case the Indians should break out, but a decided determination to be among the first to repel any invasion, and defend the frontier from all hostilities. We mention the last fact, because it was wholly uncalled for on our part, and came previous to any excitement on the part of the people of Clay County, against our friends, and must definitely show, that this charge is also untrue.

Another charge against our friends, and one that is urged as a reason why they must immediately leave the county of Clay, is, that they are making or are likely to make, the same "their permanent home, the center and general rendezvous of their people." We have never understood such to be the purpose, wish or design of this society; but on the contrary, have ever supposed, that those who ever resided in Clay County, only designed it as a temporary residence, until the law and authority of our country should put them in the quiet possession of their homes in Jackson County; and such as had not possessions there, could purchase to the entire satisfaction and interest of the people of Jackson County.

Having partially mentioned the leading objections urged against our friends, we would here add, that it has not been done with a view on our part, to dissuade you from acting in strict conformity with your preamble and resolutions, offered to the people of Clay County, on the 29th ult., but from a sense of duty to a people embarrassed, persecuted and afflicted. For you are aware, gentlemen, that in times of excitement, virtues are transformed into vices, acts, which in other cases and under other circumstances, would be considered upright and honorable, interpreted contrary from their real intent, are made objectionable and criminal; and from whom could we look for forbearance and compassion with confidence and assurance, more than from those whose bosoms are warmed with those pure principles of patriotism with which you have been guided in the present instance, to secure the peace of your county, and save a persecuted people from further violence and destruction?

It is said that our friends are poor; that they have but little or nothing to bind their feelings or wishes to Clay County, and that in consequence, have a less claim upon that county. We do not deny the fact, that our friends are poor; but their persecutions have helped to render them so. While other men were peacefully following their avocations, and extending their interest, they have been deprived of the right of citizenship, prevented from enjoying their own, charged with violating the sacred principles of our Constitution and laws; made to feel the keenest aspersions of the tongue of slander, waded through all but death, and are now suffering under calumnies calculated to excite the indignation and hatred of every people among whom they may dwell, thereby exposing them to destruction and inevitable ruin!

If a people, a community, or a society can accumulate wealth, increase in worldly fortune, improve in science and arts, rise to eminence in the eyes of the public, surmount these difficulties, so much as to bid defiance to poverty and wretchedness, it must be a new creation, a race of beings superhuman. But in all their poverty and want, we have yet to learn, for the first time, that our friends are not industrious and temperate, and wherein they have not always been the last to retaliate or resent an injury, and the first to overlook and forgive. We do not urge that there are not exceptions to be found: all communities, all societies and associations, are cumbered with disorderly and less virtuous members—members who violate in a greater or less degree the principles of the same. But this can be no just criterion by which to judge a whole society. And further still, where a people are laboring under constant fear of being dispossessed very little inducement is held out to excite them to be industrious.

We think, gentlemen, that we have pursued this subject far enough, and we here express to you, as we have in a letter accompanying this, to our friends, our decided disapprobation to the idea of shedding blood, if any other course can be followed to avoid it; in which case, and which alone, we have urged upon our friends to resist only in extreme cases of self-defense; and in this case not to give the offense or provoke their fellow men to acts of violence—which we have no doubt they will observe, as they ever have. For you may rest assured, gentlemen, that we would be the last to advise our friends to shed the blood of men, or commit one act to endanger the public peace.

We have no doubt but our friends will leave your county, sooner or later—they have not only signified the same to us, but we have advised them so to do, as fast as they can without incurring too much loss. It may be said that they have but little to lose if they lose the whole. But if they have but little, that little is their all, and the imperious demands of the helpless, urge them to make a prudent disposal of the same. And we are highly pleased with a proposition in your preamble, suffering them to remain peaceably till a disposition can be made of their land, etc., which if suffered, our fears are at once hushed, and we have every reason to believe, that during the remaining part of the residence of our friends in your county, the same feelings of friendship and kindness will continue to exist, that have heretofore, and that when they leave you, you will have no reflection of sorrow to cast, that they have been sojourners among you.

To what distance or place they will remove, we are unable to say: in this they must be dictated with judgment and prudence.

They may explore the territory of Wisconsin—they may remove there, or they may stop on the other side—of this we are unable to say; but be they where they will, we have this gratifying reflection, that they have never been the first, in an unjust manner, to violate the laws, injure their fellow men, or disturb the tranquility and peace under which any part of our country has heretofore reposed. And we cannot but believe, that ere long the public mind must undergo a change, when it will appear to the satisfaction of all that this people have been illy treated and abused without cause, and when, as justice would demand, those who have been the instigators of their sufferings will be regarded as their true characters demand.

Though our religious principles are before the world, ready for the investigation of all men, yet we are aware that the sole foundation of all the persecution against our friends, has arisen in consequence of the calumnies and misconstructions, without foundation in truth, or righteousness, in common with all other religious societies, at their first commencement; and should Providence order that we rise not as others before us, to respectability and esteem, but be trodden down by the ruthless hand of extermination, posterity will do us the justice, when our persecutors are equally low in the dust, with ourselves, to hand down to succeeding generations, the virtuous acts and forbearance of a people, who sacrificed their reputation for their religion, and their earthly fortunes and happiness to preserve peace, and save this land from being further drenched in blood.

We have no doubt but your very seasonable mediation, in the time of so great an excitement, will accomplish your most sanguine desire, in preventing further disorder; and we hope, gentlemen, that while you reflect upon the fact, that the citizens of Clay County are urgent for our friends to leave you, that you will also bear in mind, that by their complying with your request to leave, they surrender some of their dearest rights and among the first of those inherent principles guaranteed in the Constitution of our country; and that human nature can be driven to a certain extent, when it will yield no farther. Therefore while our friends suffer so much, and forego so many sacred rights, we sincerely hope, and we have every reason to expect, that a suitable forbearance may be shown by the people of Clay, which if done, the cloud that has been obscuring your horizon, will disperse, and you will be left to enjoy peace, harmony and prosperity. (Joseph Smith, *History of the Church*, II, 456–460.)

Nothing could be more admirable than the candor and gentleness of this letter. While Joseph's heart was bleeding for his injured brethren in the West, his sense of justice was so exalted that he could recognize every honest purpose among the men who felt forced to make the edict of expatriation. The Prophet also sent a letter of comfort to the elders in Clay, counseling peace and yet advising the protection at any cost of wives and little children.

No delay had been granted in which to receive such communication from Kirtland, and the leading brethren in Clay assembled on July 1, 1836, the second day following the mass meeting, and considered the proposition. William W. Phelps was chairman and John Corrill was secretary. A committee consisting of twelve—E. Partridge, I. Morley, L. Wight, T. B. Marsh, E. Higbee, C. Beebee, I. Hitchcock, I. Higbee, S. Bent, T. Billings, J. Emmett and R. Evans—was appointed to report a preamble with resolutions. These were presented and unanimously adopted as follows:

That we (the "Mormons" so called) are grateful for the kindness which has been shown to us by the citizens of Clay, since we have resided with them, and being desirous for peace and wishing the good rather than the ill will of mankind, will use all honorable means to allay the excitement, and, so far as we can, remove any foundations for jealousies against us as a people. We are aware that many rumors prejudicial to us as a society are afloat, and time only can prove their falsity to the world at large.

We deny having claim to this or any other county or country further than we purchase with money, or more than the Constitution and laws allow us as free American citizens. We have taken no part for or against slavery, but are opposed to the abolitionists, and consider that men have a right to hold slaves or not according to law.

We believe it just to preach the gospel to the nations of the earth, and warn the righteous to save themselves from the corruptions of the world; but we do not believe it right to interfere with bond servants, nor preach the gospel to, nor meddle with, or influence them in the least to cause them to be dissatisfied with their situation in life, thereby jeopardizing the lives of men. Such interference we believe to be unlawful and unjust, and dangerous to the peace of every government allowing human beings to be held in servitude.

We deny holding any communications with the Indians, and mean to hold ourselves as ready to defend our country against their barbarous ravages as any other people. We believe that all men are bound to sustain and uphold the respective governments in which they reside, while protected in their inherent and inalienable rights by the laws of such governments; and that sedition and rebellion are unbecoming every citizen thus protected, and should be punished accordingly. It is needless to enter into a further detail of our faith or mention our sufferings:

Therefore Resolved, For the sake of friendship, and to be in a covenant of peace with the citizens of Clay County, and the citizens of Clay County to be in a covenant of peace with us, notwithstanding the necessary loss of property and expense we incur in moving, we comply with the requisitions of their resolutions in leaving the county of Clay, as explained by the preamble accompanying the same; and that we will use our exertions to have the Church do the same; and that we will also exert ourselves to stop the tide of emigration of our people to this county.

Resolved, That we accept the friendly offer verbally tendered to us by the committee yesterday, to assist us in selecting a location and removing to it. (Joseph Smith, *History of the Church,* II, 452–453.)

The dread decree was met and accepted. The Saints were fully alive to the kindness of the people of Clay and were willing to sacrifice what little comforts they had been able to accumulate since their banishment from Jackson and to take up their sick and their helpless ones and journey—but whither? Nobly did they repay the charity which had been extended to them. If their presence was a menace to the well-being of men who had in the hour of affliction offered the hand of help, they would brave death in the wilderness rather than have it so any longer. It was an awful hour, but the alternative was exile or dishonor to their pledge. Let their choice speak for them throughout all the ages.

A home in civilization was denied to these afflicted Saints. The old mob organization in Jackson was still maintained. Only a few weeks previous to this time a committee of officials in Jackson had formulated recommendations to their fellow ruffians in case the Saints should attempt to come back to form a new settlement or to repossess their own property. The chief executive of the state, Daniel Dunklin, under date of July 18, made a miserable confession of his utter inability to help or protect them. And the settled counties adjoining Clay had already refused to permit them to live and labor within their borders.

But when the citizens of Clay witnessed the nobility of the long-suffering Saints, they adopted a resolution, urging the keeping of "the peace towards the Mormons as good faith, justice, morality and religion require." Committees were appointed by these citizens to aid the people in their removal. And before adjourning, the meeting adopted the following resolution:

That this meeting recommend the Mormons to the good treatment of the citizens of the adjoining counties. We also recommend the inhabitants of the neighboring counties to assist the Mormons in selecting some abiding place for their people, where they will be in a measure the only occupants and where none will be anxious to molest them.

In less than three months the Saints began their work of removal from Clay County into the wilderness. They had few of the facilities for extensive travel or for the establishment of comfortable settlements. To the north and east of Clay was Ray County, the upper part of which was almost entirely unoccupied. But seven men lived there, and these were bee-hunters who, having exhausted the honey of that region, were about to desert the place. The timber was poor and the land unattractive to ordinary settlers. Into this place, known as the Shoal Creek region, the Saints journeyed. They bought out the few possessions of the bee hunters and began to make homes. The natural poverty of the country rendered it for a time a place of safe refuge. But it was then, as it has been since, the case, that the Latter-day Saints are left in undisputed possession of a desert or a wilderness, until they have redeemed it from physical chaos and made it a delightful habitation for man—then their expulsion or oppression begins. Their industry and thrift are a temptation to the idle and dissolute.

With the simple hope of enjoying the life, liberty, and religious freedom guaranteed by the Constitution, the Saints immigrated into northern Ray County in considerable numbers. In December, 1836, they petitioned the legislature of the state of Missouri to incorporate the Shoal Creek region and surrounding lands, which were almost entirely unoccupied except by them, as a new county. The prayer was granted in that month, and the county was organized under the name of Caldwell. The city of Far West was laid out during the winter, and in the spring of 1837 preparations were made for the erection of a house of the Lord in that place.

CHAPTER 34

Missionary Movement

... I say unto all the Twelve: Arise and gird up your loins, take up your cross, follow me, and feed my sheep.

Exalt not yourselves; rebel not against my servant Joseph; for verily I say unto you, I am with him, and my hand shall be over him; and the keys which I have given unto him, and also to youward, shall not be taken from him till I come.

Wherefore, whithersoever they [the First Presidency] shall send you, go ye, and I will be with you; ... (D&C 112: 14–15, 19.)

This was a commandment given through Joseph Smith unto Thomas B. Marsh, at Kirtland, on the 23rd day of July, 1837, concerning the twelve apostles of the Lamb. It was necessary; for pride and disunion and the ambitions of the world were doing their work among some of their number, and they would heed neither the counsels of Joseph nor the direct behest of the Almighty.

Not for many generations had men been favored of the Lord as they had been. They had received heavenly manifestations sufficient, one would think, to keep them from ever turning away from the truth. But after receiving these glorious evidences of divine favor, like their master, Jesus, they were "tempted of the devil"; yet not like their Lord, some of these men yielded to temptation and fell from their high estate. They did not resist the allurements of Satan. The desire for the glory of the world, the wealth of the world, the vain things of the world, overcame them.

A mania to speculate, to make money, became almost universally prevalent. It was a general tendency in the United States, and especially in the west, at the time of which we write. Forgetting the visions of eternity they had beheld; forgetting the holy anointing they had received; forgetting their high callings and their dedication to the ministry of the Son of God, leading men became real estate dealers, merchants, organizers of "wildcat" schemes, and eventually deadly enemies of the work of God and of him whom He had chosen as His Prophet. Simultaneously with this spirit of speculation, came the spirit of apostasy and rebellion against the authority of heaven. So rife did this spirit become that those who rebelled were applauded, and men were glad to find excuse in the example of the twelve and other leading men for their own wrongdoing. The few of the apostles who were willing to fulfill the requirements of the gospel in all things were ridiculed, and every effort was made to dissuade them from the course they were pursuing. Jealousy and hatred of the Prophet cropped out on every hand. Those who disobeyed were called wise by all the disaffected spirits; and those who made every required sacrifice in humility were called foolish. But the generation had not passed away before the Lord repaid according to His promise. The men who had exalted themselves were abased into nothingness; while those who had bowed their heads in humility were exalted. Today the names of the proud and the vain of that time are almost forgotten, while the names of the apostles who endured all things faithfully are held in most solemn and sacred remembrance by the congregation of Israel.

It was a time of great trial. In the winter of 1836–7, preparations had been made to establish a bank to be known as the Kirtland Safety Society—an institution wisely designed to ameliorate the financial condition of the community. The society was established, but the Prophet's plan for its usefulness and the general prosperity failed through the envy and covetousness of some of the leading men. The sorrow which this brought to Joseph cannot be described. He had labored and advised with no other object than the general benefit, carrying upon his own shoulders a greater burden than was imposed upon anyone else. He had not sought self-aggrandizement, nor would he willingly permit the avarice of other men to gain advantage over the community's welfare.

He took part in every labor; and had assumed personally a large share of the work and care of the printing office, which was at that time a great responsibility and expense.

So many evil surmisings, so much disunion and apostasy followed in quick succession the spirit of speculation to which reference has been made, that the Prophet was led to exclaim:

> It seemed as though all the powers of earth and hell were combining their influence to overthrow the Church.

The integrity of all was tested. Instances of fidelity to the Prophet were not wanting, especially among the meek and humble, and when the Prophet met with these their presence and words brought solace and encouragement to his wounded spirit. Among the prominent men defection was too general. Several of them yielded to a spirit of mumuring and faultfinding who afterwards bitterly repented of their unstable and weak conduct and lack of integrity and courage. The feeling which Joseph had during these sorrowful days is illustrated by remarks which he made to Elder Wilford Woodruff, when the latter called upon him in the spring of 1837, on the eve of his departure on a mission to Fox Islands. At that time Elder Woodruff was one of the first seventy. The Prophet scrutinized him very closely, as though he would read his inmost thoughts, and remarked: "Brother Woodruff, I am glad to see you; I hardly know, when I meet those who have been my brethren in the Lord, who of them are my friends, they have become so scarce."

When Elder Woodruff reported to Sidney Rigdon, who was then the Prophet's first counselor, how strongly he was impressed to carry the gospel to Fox Islands, to a people who, he felt, were ready to receive it, Sidney said: "That is right; I wish you would go; for if you do, some of the devils who are now here in Kirtland will follow you, as they will every faithful man who goes out into the vineyard."

The enemies of the cause abroad were united with the spirits of dissension at Kirtland to produce disaffection against the Prophet himself and to attribute to him those evils which were solely caused by disobedience to his counsel and the command of God expressed through him. As we have seen, some of the twelve were so far blinded that they joined secretly with the enemy; but there was not a quorum in the Church that was entirely exempt from the evil influence.

Joseph was stricken with illness in June, 1837. And while he was wrestling with the adversary to overcome the physical affliction, the doubting members of the Church were taught by apostates that his woes had been sent upon him because of his transgressions. When the Prophet was once more restored through prayer and the blessing of the Almighty to his condition of health and power, he humbly said of his enemies:

The Lord judge betwixt me and them, while I pray my Father to forgive them the wrong.

While Satan was spreading this spirit of dissension through Kirtland, the Lord was directing to Joseph the magnificent missionary movement to the old world. About the first day of June, 1837, that devoted and ever-constant Apostle Heber C. Kimball was set apart by the spirit of prophecy and revelation to preside over a mission to England—the first in that dispensation. With him were associated Apostle Orson Hyde and Elders Willard Richards and Joseph Fielding; and when they reached New York, they were joined by three brethren from Canada, John Goodson, Isaac Russell and John Snyder. They sailed from the United States on the 1st day of July, 1837, on the ship *Garrick*, and landed in Liverpool on the 20th day of that same month.

This was the commencement of a glorious work, which has brought the honest in heart by tens of thousands from foreign lands, and which yet continues and must continue until the elect shall be gathered and the judgments of God are poured out upon the nations. Though this was the first missionary work of the Church performed in another hemisphere, self-denying brethren had up to this time been diligent in laboring in Canada, in the states and among the Indians on the border, that the people of this continent might have an opportunity to hear and obey.

It was a glorious overcoming of the evil which menaced the Church at that hour. Drawing strength and means from abroad to the cause, the missionary movement also opened a glorious opportunity for elders in Zion to forsake speculations, vanities, dissensions, and to prove their faith by their devoted efforts for the salvation of their fellow men.

Apostles Kimball and Hyde and Elder Richards and companions landed on this foreign shore absolutely moneyless. They did not have so much as a cent or a farthing, but they were not dismayed. The Prophet of God had pronounced upon their heads blessings which they knew could not fail. Immediately after landing at Liverpool they advanced to Preston, thirty miles distant. When they alighted from the coach they found unfurled above their heads a large flag bearing this inscription in letters of gold:

Truth Will Prevail.

The banner was floating in compliment to Queen Victoria who had but recently ascended the throne after the death of King William IV; but it was accepted as a promise and a good omen by the elders, and they were not disappointed.

Elder Joseph Fielding had a brother who resided at Preston, and with whom he and his sisters, one of whom afterwards became the wife of President Hyrum Smith, and the mother of his son, Joseph F. Smith, had corresponded. He was a minister of religion and was styled Rev. James Fielding. Three days after the elders landed in England they preached in Mr. Fielding's church, at Preston, and seven days later they baptized nine persons in the River Ribble near that place. The continuation of their work was marked by a noble zeal on their own part and a prosperity under the divine assistance almost without parallel.

The hatred against the Prophet took violent form at this time. Every possible effort was made by apostates and mobocrats to harass and injure him. On the 27th day of July, 1837, he departed from Kirtland with Elders Brigham Young, Albert P. Rockwood, Sidney Rigdon and Thomas B. Marsh for the purpose of performing a mission among the Saints in Canada. A considerable work was being done there, and the Prophet desired to give personal counsel and assistance to the Saints. But when they reached Painesville, a few miles from Kirtland, writs in civil action and warrants of arrest were served upon Joseph for the purpose of detaining him. These suits were vexatious and without any foundation in law or justice. Their purpose was stated by Sheriff Kimball, the man who served the papers upon the Prophet, to Elder Anson Call as follows:

> We don't want your Prophet to leave Kirtland, and he shan't leave.

Two or three times during the day the civil suits against him were dismissed, and he was discharged from the criminal warrants, their trumped-up character being evident. But this was only to make a show of justice; for the sheriff went after the Prophet as he was leaving Painesville, sprang into his carriage and served another writ upon him. Though this case was manifestly unjust as the others, he was held to bail in the sum of $700—quite a large amount in those days, considering the poverty of the people and the petty nature of the suit. It was decided by the court that no one who lived in Kirtland should be accepted as sureties upon the bonds. This order was made for no other purpose than to prevent the giving of bail, as it was hoped that Joseph could not secure it elsewhere and that his person would remain in the hands of his enemies. It was Anson Call, then living at Madison, who gave the necessary security for the Prophet's liberation, thereby permitting him to return to Kirtland. Some weeks subsequently, at the time appointed for the trial, the Prophet appeared in the court at Painesville; but as no one was there to maintain the charge against him, the falsifiers having in the meantime become frightened at their own perjury, he was acquitted.

On the night of July 28th, 1837, which was the day after the arrest at Painesville, Joseph started again for Canada with the brethren formerly named. On the afternoon of the 29th of July, having reached Ashtabula, they took a deck passage on board a steamer for Buffalo. They had very little money, and their accommodations and fare were of the humblest. They lay all night on the upper deck of the boat with their clothes on and with their valises for pillows. Despite the tribulations through which he had just passed and despite the rudeness of his couch, the Prophet slept serenely and restfully. When they reached Buffalo the party separated, Elders Brigham Young and Albert P. Rockwood going to the Eastern States, and Joseph—with Elders Rigdon and Marsh— departing for Upper Canada.

During the month of August, 1837, Joseph traveled among the branches of the Church in Canada, ministering counsel and comfort to the Saints. At Toronto he met John Taylor, who had been baptized by Parley P. Pratt, and who was then the president over the Church in Canada. The Prophet and the future president had a time of rejoicing together. Joseph was deeply impressed by the character of John Taylor. The latter had been a preacher in the Methodist church at Toronto, and had in that organization taken rank as a religious reformer. He declared apostolic doctrines before he ever saw one of the Latter-day Saints and had been brought to trial before a ministerial body for his heretical sermons. With the inspiration that was upon him, he had refused to recant, although his courageous act brought ostracism upon himself and family. It was this brave and scholarly man who welcomed Joseph and labored with him in Canada. It was this same hero who, after seven years of trial—during which he never flinched—was with his beloved Prophet at the martyrdom in Carthage Jail. Joseph's association with John Taylor, as with other leading men in the Church, shows how the Lord was directing the footsteps of His future apostles and seers of that generation, that they should come into communication and into living and loving companionship with the founder of the Church.

When the Prophet returned from Canada, he secured a horse and wagon at the city of Buffalo, with which to make the journey to Kirtland. Sidney was with him, and they traveled to Painesville without molestation; but while there, eating supper at the house of a Mr. Bissel, who had been the Prophet's advocate in the former lawsuits, a mob surrounded the house and yelled for Joseph's blood. Bissel knew that he himself might be a sufferer, but he was determined that murder should not be committed upon an unoffending man if he could prevent it. While the rabble was congregating in groups around the house, he led Joseph and Sidney quietly through the back door, and under cover of night they slipped between the assassin crowds and escaped. Scarcely were they gone when the mob discovered the fact and, mounting horses, pushed out upon the Mentor road. They posted sentinels and lighted bonfires all along this track, which they expected the Prophet and his companion would travel to get into Kirtland. But Joseph took to the fields. Sidney was weakened and almost helpless with illness and fear. Many swamps lay in their way; and Joseph waded through these and carried Sidney upon his back. He kept away from the road far enough to be secure in the darkness, while the fires which had been intended for his detection really aided him to avoid his bloodthirsty pursuers. After a toilsome and rapid journey, during which Joseph carried Sidney most of the way, they reached the end of the Mentor road which intersected with a highway leading two miles into Kirtland. The mob had not posted their sentinels or built their fires farther than this point; and, being well past their enemies, Joseph and Sidney were able to take the traveled road and to continue their journey with less pain and toil. It was very late on Saturday night when they reached their homes in Kirtland, greatly exhausted. None but their families heard of their arrival until the next morning, when Joseph appeared at meeting and preached a powerful sermon to the assembled Saints.

Immediately after this time, on September 3rd, at a conference held in Kirtland, Oliver Cowdery; Joseph Smith, Sr.; Hyrum Smith; and John Smith were sustained as assistant counselors to the First

Presidency, the congregation having declined to sustain Frederick G. Williams in the position which he held as second counselor to the Prophet. Objection being also made to three of the apostles, Luke Johnson, Lyman E. Johnson and John F. Boynton, they were by the voice of the Saints shorn of their apostolic rank and were disfellowshiped; however, as they subsequently made protestation of their repentance, they were received back into the Church and into their station. But their humility was either a mere pretense or was very volatile in its character; because not many weeks elapsed until they were once more engaged in an effort to ruin the Church and the Prophet.

Thus the first serious apostasy and the first great missionary movement of the Church started together. How unavailing the falsehoods and lack of fidelity have been and how glorious the efforts of the servants of God to spread the light of the gospel through every land, every chapter of the Church's history from that time to this speaks in eloquent tones.

In the August number of the *Messenger and Advocate* was published a prospectus for the *Elders' Journal* to be edited by the Prophet. In pursuance of this announcement, the publication of the *Messenger and Advocate* was suspended with the September number, and in October, 1837, the *Elders' Journal* was begun; but only two numbers were issued when, through the destruction of the printing office by fire, in December, 1837, work of this character was stopped.

CHAPTER 35

Divine Protection

After the apostasy became general at Kirtland, those who banded themselves against the Prophet and the faithful Saints set up a claim to the ownership of the temple. Scenes of a turbulent and even violent character were witnessed in the sacred building. Deadly weapons were drawn and flourished and lives were threatened by the members of the apostate party who sought by these means to overawe the peaceful members of the Church and to accomplish the ends they had in view.

After the visit which the Prophet, Sidney Rigdon and Thomas B. Marsh made to Canada, Elder John Taylor, with the view of making preparations to gather with the Saints and to provide a home for himself and family, repaired to Kirtland. While there he attended services in the temple. Faultfinding and accusation were indulged in by leading men in their remarks, and the Prophet was the target at which their shafts of censure were aimed. They looked upon him and spoke of him as a fallen prophet. These attacks aroused all the lion of John Taylor's nature—and all who ever saw him when strength and courage were demanded, can remember how grandly he could rise to the occasion and satisfy every expectation—and he arose and obtained the privilege of speaking from one of the stands. He was a stranger to the congregation; they knew not who he was nor whence he came, but the Saints saw in him a man of God. His fine presence, his courageous demeanor, the plainness and strength of his reasoning and the power of God which accompanied his words, made a great impression upon the entire audience. His address was a masterly exposition of the great truths which God had inspired Joseph to reveal—truths of which all the learned and religious world were in entire ignorance until they were brought forth by Joseph—and a defense of him as a prophet of God. The dissenters were rebuked, and the Saints were strengthened and encouraged, and all felt that a man had appeared upon the scene who would yet be a power among the Saints. This was President Taylor's first public introduction to the Saints at the gathering place.

Undaunted by the apostasy, and relying upon the promise of the Lord, Joseph knew that the work would surely grow and that places must be appointed for the gathering of the Saints in the last days. To every human appearance, in the spring and summer of 1837, the Church was in a state of dissolution; but all who were animated by the spirit of truth knew that the disunion at Kirtland was but the effort of the adversary, which, with patience and faithfulness, might be overcome.

In September, Joseph had not yet learned through any earthly medium of the marvelous work which was to be done abroad among the honest in heart; and yet, on the 27th day of that month, he and Sidney Rigdon began a journey to the west to visit the Saints in Missouri and to establish places into which might come converts from every land. They were accompanied on this journey by Vinson Knight and William Smith, while Hyrum was already at Far West, laboring with his accustomed energy and fidelity for the advancement of the gospel and the well-being of the Saints.

While the Prophet and his companions were on the way, Hyrum's wife Jerusha died at Kirtland, leaving five little children. Her dying message was full of faith in the gospel and was a comfort to her absent husband when he learned it, and it proved that she was worthy to be the consort of the destined patriarch and martyr.

A little over a month was consumed in the journey to Far West; and soon after the Prophet's arrival he began to hold meetings for the settlement of all difficulties which had arisen between the brethren there, the same evil spirit which had gained such sway in Kirtland having begun to assert its power in Missouri. On the 7th of November, 1837, a general assembly of the Church was held at Far West, at which Frederick G. Williams was rejected by the congregation as a counselor to the President of the Church; and, upon motion of Sidney Rigdon, Hyrum Smith was elected to fill the vacancy. The local organization was also perfected, and prayer was offered to God that this place might be a gathering spot for the Saints.

As it appeared to the Prophet that the regions surrounding Far West, occupied by other settlers, afforded yet much room, the plat of Far West was enlarged into the dimensions of a city, and every preparation was made to afford a refuge to such as might choose to gather to this new stake of Zion. It was also decided that the time had not yet come for the building of a temple at Far West but that the brethren should await the commandment of the Lord upon this subject.

About the 10th of November, Joseph left Far West to return to Kirtland, occupying a month in the journey and reaching his home on the 10th day of December.

While he had been absent, the spirit of apostasy had gained an ascendancy with men who had previously begged forgiveness from the Prophet. Warren Parrish, John F. Boynton, Joseph Coe and others—deeming that the absence of the Prophet afforded them an opportunity—banded themselves together to accomplish the overthrow of the Church. They renounced the Church of Jesus Christ, renounced the authority of the Prophet of God, and set up an organization for themselves. Denouncing Joseph and his faithful supporters as heretics, they became so violent at any opposition to their falsehoods that they even sought the lives of their former brethren.

Brigham Young always was one of the truest and most intrepid of men; and during all these Kirtland troubles he openly and fearlessly declared to all that Joseph Smith was a Prophet of God and had neither transgressed nor fallen from his divinely appointed place. His unswerving and undaunted attitude, the plainness of his declarations and the vigor of his defense of Joseph, and his exposure of the schemes of his enemies, aroused their fury. The apostates could not brook this boldness of the Apostle

Brigham; it interfered with their murderous designs against Joseph and their hateful purposes against the Church. Threats and cajolery having alike failed to intimidate or divert him, they determined to kill him. But he learned of their designs; and nearly two weeks after the Prophet had returned to Kirtland and was able to assert his own authority, Brigham Young departed for Missouri to escape the assassins who ravened for his life at Kirtland.

In the meantime the work abroad progressed gloriously. On Christmas day, 1837, a conference was held at Preston, at which the reports showed that already the branch of the Church in England numbered about one thousand souls.

The letters conveying these happy tidings had not yet reached the Prophet; and except as hope was inspired in his heart by the Holy Spirit, he had little comfort through the darkness of that night of 1837, for apostasy and transgression strove hard to rule the weak and ruin the staunch at Kirtland.

The experience of 1836–7 in the Church demonstrated as never before, that irrefragable testimonies concerning the divine origin of the gospel and the prophetic calling of Joseph were not alone sufficient to keep men faithful. Unflinching firmness and intrepidity were also indispensable; but preeminent above all other qualities, purity of life was absolutely essential. The half century which has since elapsed has abundantly confirmed this. The virtuous, humble men who possessed steadfastness and faith in the days of trial at Kirtland, have since grown to prominence among the Saints. The qualities which they then exhibited have had ample room for exercise in the subsequent vicissitudes through which the Church has passed.

The Lord has tried and proved them; they have acquired confidence themselves; and the people have ever looked to them as leaders who could be trusted and upon whose courage, judgment and integrity they could safely rely.

In this connection it is worthy of remark that the three men who have succeeded the Prophet Joseph as Presidents of the Church, were all distinguished during Joseph's lifetime for their love for the truth and their unswerving affection and loyalty to him as the Prophet of God. President Brigham Young, probably above all men in Kirtland, displayed these qualities during the stormy scenes of the last year of his residence at that place.

President Wilford Woodruff, though not so prominent in those days as he afterwards became, was expostulated with, coaxed and ridiculed by some of his old friends, notably Warren Parrish, who had been his fellow missionary in the Southern States, for the purpose of inducing him to join them and turn against the Prophet. But the integrity of the man was immovable, and all their efforts proved unavailing.

With the dawn of the new year, confusion and mobocratic power increased, and on the 12th of January, 1838, Joseph and Sidney were driven from Kirtland to escape mob violence. Their destination was Far West, and they were pursued more than two hundred miles by armed enemies seeking their lives. The weather was intensely severe, and Joseph and his companion, with their families who had joined them, suffered greatly in their endeavor to elude the murderous pursuit. Several times the pursuers crossed the Prophet's track. Twice they entered the houses where his party had gained a refuge, and once they occupied a room in the same building with only a partition between them, through which the Prophet heard their oaths and imprecations concerning him. Thus were they protected by divine power, else murder would have been done, for the long and unavailing pursuit had filled these would-be assassins with a fiendish desire for blood. Owing to the severity of the season, two months were occupied in the journey to Far West, which place the Prophet and his family reached on the 14th day of March, 1838, accompanied by Apostle Brigham Young, who had joined him on the way.

His arrival was very timely and necessary. Upon his previous visit objection had been raised to some of the local authorities, and they were only accepted by the congregation after having made humble confession of their sins and entered their solemn promise of repentance.

But as soon as the Prophet had turned his back upon Far West to go to Kirtland, the local presidency had again entered into transgression, acting selfishly and arbitrarily in the administration of financial affairs and completely losing the confidence of the body of the people.

While the Prophet had been journeying toward Missouri after escaping the Kirtland mob in January, 1838, a general assembly of the Saints in Far West was held on the 5th day of February, at which David Whitmer, John Whitmer and William W. Phelps were rejected as the local presidency; and a few days later Thomas B. Marsh and David W. Patten, of the Twelve, were selected to act as a presidency until the Prophet should arrive. Oliver Cowdery too had been suspended from his position. Persisting in unchristian-like conduct, W. W. Phelps and John Whitmer had been excommunicated by the high council in Far West, four days previous to the arrival of Joseph.

This was the sad situation as the Prophet approached the dwelling place of the Saints in Missouri. Many of the people went out to meet him, and at a distance of one hundred and twenty miles from Far West they found him and tendered him teams and money to help him forward. The joy they had in his presence arose from an absolute knowledge of his power and authority as a Prophet of God. They were certain that many of their difficulties would end with his presence, because he would give the light of truth by which to guide their footsteps.

On the eighth anniversary of the organization of the Church, a conference was held at Far West under the presidency of Joseph. On this occasion David W. Patten declared that he could not recommend William E. McLellin, Luke Johnson and John F. Boynton as members of the Twelve, and he was also doubtful of William Smith. His objection to these men was prophetic; all of them lost their standing, disgraced their calling, forfeited their knowledge of the truth and their promise of reward hereafter, and sank back into the mire of this world.

At the same conference Brigham Young, David W. Patten and Thomas B. Marsh were chosen to preside over the Church in Missouri.

On the 12th of April, 1838, Oliver Cowdery was found guilty of serious wrongdoing for which he had not made repentance, and he was excommunicated by the high council at Far West. Before the same tribunal, on the day following, David Whitmer was charged with persistent disobedience of the word of wisdom and with unchristian-like conduct, and he was also cut off. Luke Johnson, Lyman E. Johnson and John F. Boynton were excommunicated about the same time, and less than a month later a similar fate befell William E. McLellin.

It was a sorrowful day for Joseph when he lost the companionship of these men who had been with him during many trials and who had participated with him in the glorious understanding of heavenly things. But they were no longer anything but dead branches, harmful to the growing tree, and it was necessary for the pruner to lop them off. Oliver Cowdery and David Whitmer were two of the witnesses to the Book of Mormon, designated by the word of the Almighty to view the plates and to be ministered unto by the angel of the record. Oliver had stood with Joseph in the Kirtland Temple and seen the marvelous manifestations there. It was sad to see them thus shorn of power and blessing, but they had demonstrated their unworthiness to hold the positions which they had filled, and the penalty must fall upon them that the Church might escape the evil of their sins.

Had Joseph's faith in God and confidence in the mission which the Creator had entrusted to him been less than it was, he might have temporized with these men and not dealt with them in so strict and summary a manner. He was attached to them by many ties. They had been his aids and companions in days when he most needed help, sustenance and friendship. Through his ministrations of the gospel, God had enabled him abundantly to repay them. Still he never could forget their past associations. They were two of the heaven-selected witnesses who had testified that God's voice had declared to them that Joseph's translation of the Book of Mormon had been made by the gift and power of God. If they should be excommunicated from the Church, suppose that they, filled with anger thereat, should abandon themselves to the spirit of evil which so many men, so dealt with, yielded to in those days; what then? Like others, might they not renounce the truth, circulate all manner of falsehoods, deny the divinity of the work and even the solemn testimony which they had borne? These might be the reflections of an ordinary man under such circumstances; but such thoughts never troubled this Prophet of God. This Church was not the Church of man. Jesus Christ, its divine head, had promised He would take care of, sustain and defend it. However much, then, Joseph's affection and friendship might be for these men, he owed a paramount duty to his God to deal with transgressors in His Church according to the laws which He had given. This duty the Prophet performed without hesitation, leaving all consequences for the Lord to control.

Oliver Cowdery, David Whitmer and Martin Harris, the three witnesses of the divine origin of Joseph's translation of the Book of Mormon, were all severed from the Church. They became opponents of Joseph Smith and claimed he had fallen into transgression; but amid all their trials, temptations and vicissitudes they never hesitated or wavered in regard to the published testimony which they gave to the world concerning the Book of Mormon. Each of them to the day of his death, asseverated in the most solemn manner the truth of his testimony. All three are dead; but they still live as immutable witnesses of the truth and divinity of the record known as the Book of Mormon, and by their testimony will the world yet be judged.

In the sacred records which have come to us, there is no mention of any other man that was so highly favored as Oliver Cowdery was, falling from his exalted position and forfeiting his blessings and priesthood as he did. What a lesson and warning does his history convey! It is generally understood by those who knew him in the days of which we write, that he was guilty of unvirtuous conduct. This came to the Prophet's knowledge. He warned Oliver of the consequences which would follow if he did not repent. The warnings were unheeded. The Spirit of God withdrew itself from him and he fell into darkness; and from being the second elder in the Church, he lost his standing as a member and became an alien to the people of God. For years he remained in this condition. After the exodus of the Saints from Nauvoo and the city of Salt Lake had been founded, he arrived at Kanesville, made suitable acknowledgments in great humility to the Church there, and was admitted to it by baptism under the direction of Elder Orson Hyde. He was reordained to the Melchizedek Priesthood and shortly afterwards died at Richmond, in the state of Missouri.

Martin Harris also came back penitent to the Church, after being for years separated from it. He was restored to fellowship and the priesthood, and was strong in his testimony for the truth up to his death, which was at a very advanced age at Smithfield, Cache County, Utah Territory.

David Whitmer never rejoined the Church; but his testimony concerning the divine origin of the Book of Mormon was widely circulated through the newspapers of the country. He died at Richmond, Missouri.

Of the three apostles who were then excommunicated—Boynton and the two Johnsons—one only rejoined the Church. Luke Johnson came to Nauvoo at the time of the exodus and was again admitted to fellowship. He was one of the company of pioneers who, under the leadership of President Brigham Young, left Winter Quarters on the Missouri River in 1847, to find a home for the Latter-day Saints in the great West, and which resulted in the settling of Great Salt Lake Valley. Luke Johnson was a member of the Church when he died in Salt Lake City.

President Brigham Young related a conversation himself and some others of the twelve apostles had with Lyman E. Johnson on one occasion in Nauvoo. It was after the martyrdom of the Prophet Joseph. They were speaking of old times, when they were all engaged in the ministry and when Lyman E. Johnson was a zealous advocate of the truth. The bitterness he had exhibited in Kirtland had passed away, and he was softened by the association with his old companions. Speaking of the heavenly influence and spirit which had accompanied him in his labors in the ministry,

Lyman said, "I would give my right hand today if, by so doing, I could feel once more as I did then."

In the month of April, 1838, the Lord commanded His Saints, through Joseph, that the Church in these last days should be called the Church of Jesus Christ of Latter-day Saints. He also commanded His people to arise and shine that their light might be a standard for the nations, and that the gathering to Zion and her stakes might be a refuge from the storm and from the wrath which shall be poured out upon the whole earth.

During the spring and early summer of 1838, the Prophet was peacefully engaged in his labors at Far West and in the regions surrounding. He established a stake of Zion at Adam-ondi-Ahman in Daviess County, Missouri, at the spot where Adam had dwelt and where, according to Daniel the Prophet, the Ancient of Days shall sit. He assisted in the laying of the cornerstones of the house of the Lord at Far West on the 4th day of July. And during all this time he was busily engaged in collating data and recording facts relating to Church history, that the momentous events of the eight years preceding might not be lost to the coming generations.

On the 8th day of July, John Taylor, John E. Page, Wilford Woodruff and Willard Richards were appointed by revelation to fill the places of those who had fallen from the Quorum of the Twelve. On the same day the Lord declared the law of tithing to stand for the guidance of the faithful forever.

Joseph also labored in the preparation of the *Elders' Journal*, the publication of which was resumed in July, 1838, at Far West.

Apostles Heber C. Kimball and Orson Hyde had returned from England, reaching Kirtland in May, 1838, having left the English mission under the presidency of Joseph Fielding, with Willard Richards and William Clayton as his counselors.

On the 10th of March, 1838, the seventies at Kirtland had decided to remove their quorum in a camp to the West; and on the 6th day of July of this year, a large body of the Saints, numbering five hundred and fifteen souls—including and in the charge of the seventies—departed from Kirtland for Missouri. Many sufferings were endured by this devoted band. Their ranks were decimated by disease and persecutions. Some of them grew faint and faithless and fell by the wayside. But the majority persevered; and about two hundred of the original number reached Adam-ondi-Ahman in a body, while many of the others came as speedily as their circumstances would permit.

From that time on, until the mob once more triumphed and drove them forth, the gathering of the Saints continued.

CHAPTER 36

False Charges

In August, 1838, the appalling mob crusade began which resulted finally in the exile of the Saints from the state of Missouri.

Previous to this time lands had been purchased by some of the brethren in Daviess County, adjoining Caldwell on the north. The Saints who settled there were industrious and law-abiding citizens. But the murderous element in that region would not permit them to toil in peace and enjoy the rights of freemen. Some of the old mobbers were there, and they joined with the people who had sold farms to the Saints and who saw in this wicked conjunction of forces an opportunity to recover their possessions, without any other cost than the banishment or murder of the "Mormon" settlers. Colonel William P. Peniston, who had led the mob in Clay County against the Saints, was desirous of being returned to the state legislature as a representative from Daviess County. The election was to be held on the 6th day of August, 1838. Previous to that time Peniston and his friends had organized with a determination to prevent the Saints from voting, as it was believed that they would not aid their old enemy—persecutor and lawbreaker that he was—to a seat in the lawmaking body of the state. A friendly judge named Morin told some of the elders of the plot against them and advised them to go to the polls armed and ready to resist the unlawful aggression. But, though they were strong in their intention to exercise their rights as set forth in the Constitution and the laws, bitter experience had taught them that such an act on their part as carrying arms, merely for self-protection, would be called an unlawful demonstration and would be followed by a general assault upon them under cover of authority. So they went to the polling places with no other weapons than clean consciences, clean ballots and clean, strong hands. At Gallatin, the principal town of the county, twelve of them were preparing to cast their votes. But Peniston mounted a barrel and made an exciting, desperate speech. He was surrounded by an assemblage of ruffians numbering one hundred and fifty. To this inflammable material he applied the torch.

He said:

> The Mormon leaders profess to heal the sick, and you
> know that is a damned lie.

He declared his opposition to the settlement of the Saints in that region and told his hearers that if they suffered the "Mormons" to vote, they would deserve to lose their own suffrages.

Addressing the Saints he declared:

> I headed a mob to drive you out of Clay County and
> would not prevent your being mobbed now.

Incited to horrible rage by his incendiary tirade, some of the drunken men in the mob attacked the brethren, and when effective resistance was made by the courageous twelve, the entire rabble of one hundred and fifty set upon them. The brethren fought with desperate courage. They were defending the most sacred right of American citizenship. Before the well-directed blows from their stout arms and bare hands, scores of the mobocrats fell in the dust; but at last, overpowered by numbers, and warned by the authorities of the county that this attack had been premeditated and they would do better to withdraw, the brethren retreated.

Just outside of town they held a council to decide whether to return to the polling places or seek their homes. While they were debating this point, they saw crowds of mob recruits rush into the town armed with guns, pistols, knives and clubs; and knowing that these men intended to do murder upon them, the brethren hastened to their farms, collected their families and hid them in a thicket of hazel brush for the night. A heavy rain came on. The women and little children, drenched to the skin, were compelled to lie upon the chilling ground through all the stormy hours of darkness, while their husbands and fathers stood sentry at the edge of the copse, expecting every hour that the dread attack would come.

The next morning word was brought to Far West by friendly settlers that some of the brethren had been killed at Gallatin, while attempting to cast their votes, and that the mob power was again supreme and was determined to drive the Saints from the county of Daviess. It was reported that the murderers would not even allow the Saints to obtain the bodies of their dead nor direct their burial.

Without a thought for his personal safety and with that lion-like courage which ever distinguished him, Joseph and his no less heroic brother Hyrum, with fifteen or twenty others, started to aid the Saints in Daviess. On the way Joseph was joined by a few brethren from different places, some of whom were fleeing from the mob, and that night, having reached Colonel Wight's house in Daviess County, he was rejoiced to learn that although some of the brethren had been badly bruised, none had been killed.

Among the men who had sold lands to the Saints was one Adam Black, a justice of the peace and just then judge elect for the county. This man, a sworn officer of the law and an aspirant for further judicial honors, had joined himself with the mob, probably in the hope to recover his farm without cost. Joseph determined to see this treasonable man and remonstrate with him against the cruelty and dishonesty of his course. Upon visiting him the Prophet received a verbal confession of his alliance with the rabble. Being further pressed to declare what his future course would be concerning the Saints and solicited to sign an agreement of peace, he prepared and gave to the Prophet a document, of which the following is an exact copy:

> I Adam Black a Justice of the peace of Davies county
> do hereby Sertify to the people coled Mormin, that he is
> bound to suport the constitution of this State, and of the

United State, and he is not attached to any mob, nor will not attach himself to any such people, and so long as they will not molest me, I will not molest them. This the 8th day of August, 1838.

Adam Black J. P.

No force nor unkindness was used with Black. No threat was uttered against him. The Prophet merely visited him as he visited other men of prominence or notoriety in that region, in a manly endeavor to subdue the kindling flame. Whatever contempt Joseph felt for the wretch who, with a judge's dignity upon him, could connive with a lawless, murderous mob, he was able to suppress; his demeanor was that of dignity and repose. But, as subsequent events proved, Black could not forgive the Prophet for the humiliation which he had made him feel.

That night some of the leading citizens of the county called upon the Prophet, and together they agreed to hold a conference at Adam-ondi-Ahman the next day at 12 o'clock. Pursuant to this appointment, both parties met in friendly council, and entered into a covenant of peace to preserve each other's rights and to stand in their defense. For the Saints such men as Lyman Wight, John Smith, Vinson Knight, Reynolds Cahoon, and others resident there, gave this pledge. And for the other settlers, Joseph Morin, senator-elect; John Williams, representative-elect; James P. Turner, clerk of the circuit court; and other men of influence and character, made their solemn promise. Having accomplished so much, the assembly dispersed on terms of amity, and the Prophet and his companions returned to Far West.

The covenant of protection extended by the prominent men of Daviess County, who knew and by their acts admitted that the Saints had been unjustly dealt with and unlawfully threatened, was without avail. On the 10th day of August, 1838, William P. Peniston and several of his creatures made affidavit before Judge Austin A. King that a large body of armed men, whose movements and conduct he declared to be of a highly insurrectionary character, had been collecting in the county of Daviess under the leadership of Joseph Smith and Lyman Wight, to intimidate and take vengeance upon the other settlers, to drive from the county all the old citizens and possess their lands. He further averred that they had already committed great violence upon Adam Black by forcing him to sign a paper of a disgraceful character. This affidavit was made in Ray County; and on the 11th day of August a committee of citizens came from that place to Far West to make inquiry of the Saints concerning the charges therein made. It stands as a monument of disproof against the assertions of Peniston, that the citizens of Ray County did not hesitate to place themselves in the power of the "Mormons" and their Prophet—knowing full well, as they did from past experience, that the Saints were full of kind disposition toward all men who would treat them as fellow citizens possessed of equal rights.

In answer to the inquiry of the committee from Ray County, the Saints appointed a delegation of seven men to make a full explanation of the facts and to demonstrate to all fair-minded men their own innocence as well as the wrongs inflicted upon them.

On the 11th of August, 1838, the Prophet went to visit some brethren from Canada who had settled on the banks of the Grand River and remained with them through the succeeding day, which was the Sabbath, offering such counsel as their situation required. On the 13th, while returning to Far West, he was pursued by some of the mobbers but managed to elude them. When within eight miles of Far West, he was met by several of the brethren who had gone out to inform him that a writ had been issued by Judge King for his arrest and that of Lyman Wight, on a complaint made by Peniston. Calmly as one returning to his evening rest from the harvest field, the Prophet went to his home, despite the fears and warnings of his friends. He remained there awaiting the coming of the officers for three days, and all the time being engaged in labor for the prosperity and protection of the community.

On the 16th of August, 1838, the sheriff of Daviess County, accompanied by Judge Morin, appeared and said that he had a writ to take Joseph into Daviess for trial, for the offense of visiting that county on the 7th of August. The sheriff was no doubt surprised to find the Prophet and to serve his writ without molestation, because a report had been spread by the mob that Joseph would not be apprehended by legal process. Joseph informed the sheriff that he always hoped to submit to the law of his country. The sheriff was impressed as well as astonished by the calm action and dignified deportment of the Prophet; and when Joseph expressed a wish to be tried in Caldwell instead of Daviess County, since he thought that the statute of the state gave him that privilege and justice for him in Daviess was out of the question, the sheriff declined to serve the writ and said he would go to Richmond to consult Judge King. Joseph promised to remain at home until the sheriff returned. The pledge was fulfilled; and when the officer got back he told Joseph that Caldwell was out of his jurisdiction and he would not act.

For the greater general prosperity, the Saints in the various parts of Caldwell County now organized, under the Prophet's direction, into agricultural companies, to enclose their lands into large fields. Joseph showed them how this plan would be economical and add facility to the tilling of the soil. So readily could this inspired man turn from the tragic tribulations of life to render to his brethren calm assistance in their daily labors!

On the 28th of August, 1838, Adam Black made oath before a justice of the peace of Daviess County that he had been threatened with instant death by an armed force of more than one hundred and fifty men on the 8th day of August. He named several of the brethren whom he charged with aiding and abetting in the perpetration of the offense, and this was Black's revenge upon the Prophet who had detected him in an attempt to steal back the land which he had sold to the Saints.

The agitation in Daviess County and the perjuries of the foiled mobbers aroused Lilburn W. Boggs, of memory already infamous, who was now governor of the state; and he sent letters to General David R. Atchison and six other generals, ordering them to raise immediately within the limits of their divisions four hundred mounted men armed and equipped as infantry or riflemen.

This act, which was ostensibly for the protection of good order, accomplished its wicked purpose. It aroused intense excitement and inflamed the desire of the mob to find an excuse for an attack upon the Saints, since they knew that the militia would be composed of men who hated the "Mormons" and would be willing to plunder them on the first opportunity.

Joseph saw the tendency of events and wrote at this time in his journal as follows:

> There is great excitement at present among the Missourians, seeking if possible an occasion against us. They are continually chaffing us, and provoking us to anger if possible; one sign of threatening following another. But we do not fear them; for the Lord God, the Eternal Father is our God, and Jesus, the Mediator is our Savior, and in the great I AM is our strength and confidence. We have been driven from time to time, and that without cause, and been smitten again and again, and that without provocation, until we have proved the world with kindness, and the world proved us that we have no design against any man or set of men; that we injure no man; that we are peaceable with all men; minding our own business, and our own business only. We have suffered our rights and our liberties to be taken from us; we have not avenged ourselves for those wrongs. We have appealed to magistrates, to sheriffs, judges, to governors and to the President of the United States, all in vain. Yet we have yielded peaceably to all these things. We have not complained at the great God. We murmured not; but peaceably left all, and retired into the back country, in the broad wild prairie, in the barren and desolate plains, and there commenced anew. We made the desolate places to bud and blossom as the rose; and now the fiend-like race are disposed to give us no rest.

Prophet
on Trial

Angered at the frustration of their plots of force and legal treachery against the Prophet, the mob continued to spread reports in August and September of 1838, that he was defying the law and refusing submission to process of court. This perjured tale received additional credence among the uninformed from the fact that the Daviess County sheriff had failed to arrest him; though, as all should have known, this failure was no fault of Joseph. But the falsehood was bringing renewed menace upon the Saints. Upper Missouri erupted a lava stream of bad men into Daviess, Carroll, Saline and Caldwell Counties. Something must be done to turn aside the overflow or it would sweep over all the dwelling places of the Saints.

To stay the fiery river of hate, the Prophet offered himself as a sacrifice. On the fourth day of September, 1838, he volunteered, through his lawyers, Generals Atchison and Doniphan, to be tried before Judge King, in Daviess County. Lyman Wight, who had been charged with him, followed his example.

It was characteristic of this industrious Prophet, that on the day when he tendered his liberty and his life as a price for the physical and political redemption of his brethren, he began the methodical study of law. The anxiety natural to his position was unfelt. He had looked so often upon danger that its face was no longer terrible. And he knew that such learning as he should ever acquire must be gained in the midst of turmoil. He wanted to know the science upon which statutes were based, and to become learned in the knowledge of his country's Constitution and enactments that he might the better minister temporal salvation to his fellow men, and the hour when prison and even murder menaced him was as propitious as any he might ever see.

The time appointed for the trial in Judge King's court was Thursday, the 6th day of November, 1838. Joseph was there, but the case could not proceed, because the prosecuting witness was absent, and no testimony was forthcoming. The court adjourned for the day, and Joseph returned to his home, but the next morning he was again in attendance and the trial proceeded. Peniston prosecuted and Adam Black swore to everything which Peniston asked. He had been bribed by money, promises or threats, else he was incited by murderous hate, and he told things which manifestly could not have had any existence except in his false mind. He was the only witness against the defendants. In their behalf four reputable men testified, proving incontestably that Black's oaths were perjury and Peniston's complaint was a lie. Judge King admitted in private conversation that nothing had been proved against the Prophet and his companion, and yet he bound them over in bonds of $500. Without a murmur the Prophet and Lyman submitted and gave the necessary bail.

From the trial they were followed to Far West by two gentlemen who stated that they had come from Chariton County as a commission of inquiry in behalf of their fellow citizens. A demand had been made by the mobbers upon the residents of Chariton County for assistance to capture Joseph Smith and Lyman Wight, and a committee had been appointed by the fair-minded people of Chariton to investigate the situation. When these gentlemen saw that the real purpose of the request was to secure ruffian help to impoverish the defenseless Saints and drive them once again into the wilderness, they declared that they had been outrageously imposed upon by the demand of the mob, and they returned to their own county filled with sympathy and friendly feeling for Joseph and his brethren. Their findings they subsequently embodied in an affidavit.

An attack was planned by the mob upon Adam-ondi-Ahman; on the 9th a wagon laden with guns and ammunition in the charge of a party of the murderous rabble was going to that place from Richmond. But it was intercepted by Captain William Allred, who arrested the men in charge, John B. Comer and two others— Miller and McHoney and took possession of the weapons. A letter was addressed to Judge King immediately by the Saints, asking him what should be done with the prisoners and the captured munitions. This coward responded to turn the prisoners loose and let them receive kind treatment. He was the judicial officer who, to satisfy the mob instead of satisfying justice, had placed the Prophet and Lyman Wight under bonds when, by his own confession, not one illegal act could be proved against them. Concerning the guns he was reluctant to give advice, although he promised that they should not be taken from the Saints to be converted and used for illegal purposes.

Under the same date this unjust judge wrote to General Atchison to send two hundred or more men to force the "Mormons" to surrender. He well knew that the Saints were not in a rebellious or unlawful attitude, nor in a position to fight. They had not even the power to resist mobocratic aggression against themselves, to say nothing of being the assailants in any illegal movement.

On the 12th of September, the men who had been arrested while transporting guns to the mob in Daviess County, were held to bail for their appearance at the circuit court.

About the same time a large body of the mob entered De Witt in Carroll County and warned the brethren to leave on pain of death.

William Dryden, justice of the peace in Daviess County, complained falsely to the governor that service of process from his court, issued against Alanson Ripley, George A. Smith and others for threatening Adam Black, had been withstood.

General Atchison called out the militia of Clay and Ray Counties which, under the command of Brigadier-General Doniphan, marched to the timber on Crooked River, while he went with a single aide to Far West, the county seat of Caldwell, to confer with the leading men among the Saints. Here he was the guest of the Prophet.

Doniphan's troops had ostensibly been called into the field to suppress an insurrection and preserve peace. But instead of the military powers being used as a menace to the mob, it was operated as if the long-suffering Saints had been the aggressors. General Doniphan, a friendly, fair, and kindly disposed man, was acting under the governor's orders, and the responsibility of his conduct fell chiefly upon the executive of the state. The mob prisoners were demanded and were set free with no regard for any other law than that which seemed to reign supreme in Missouri— the law of mobocratic will. The arms which had been seized on the way from Richmond into Daviess County were collected and delivered up to the General. From Crooked River General Doniphan brought his troops through Millport in Daviess County to the spot where a mob had congregated to make an attack upon the Saints. When the general read an order of dispersion to the rabble, they declared that their object was solely for defense; and yet they would not even permit the general in command of the state militia to approach them without going through such military formalities as might have greeted a flag of truce from an opposing force, while all the time that he was conferring with them guards were marching in and out, showing that the camp was being kept in a state of activity. Although they promised to obey the order requiring them to withdraw, they failed to do so.

From this place the general proceeded to the spot where the Saints had assembled together for mutual protection under the direction of Lyman Wight. A conference ensued in which the Saints agreed to disband, to surrender up any one of their number accused of crime, on condition that the hostile forces of the mob, only a few miles distant, should be dispersed. The Saints had every wish to comply with the law and to avoid every appearance of resistance, but they knew too well that if they scattered, unless the mobbers were also disbanded, they would be murdered and plundered. General Atchison, also in command of troops, was joined on the 15th at the county seat of Daviess by General Doniphan and his regiments. He found that the mobbers were still under arms and still aggressive, while the Saints were still huddled together for safety. To him the Saints also stated their willingness to yield to any legal requirement, and they would cheerfully submit to any investigation which might be demanded. General Atchison thought that peace might be restored and so wrote to the governor; but immediately Boggs ordered the Booneville guards to be mounted with ten days' provisions and in readiness to march on his arrival; and he also ordered General Lucas to proceed immediately with four hundred mounted men to cooperate with General Atchison. Similar orders were issued to Major Generals Lewis Bolton, John B. Clark and Thomas B. Grant.

While this military movement was taking place, the mob continued to seize prisoners and to send threatening messages, hoping to incite the Saints to some overt act that the whole power of the mob and militia combined might be brought against them to annihilate them. Several times word was brought to the encampment of the Saints that prisoners taken by the mob were being tortured. This was done in the hope to provoke a spirit of retaliation. It seems strange that this situation could have continued for more than a day with such a military force at hand. A little prompt and vigorous action would have dispersed the mob and taught them to respect the power of the law. It would not have been necessary to shed blood, only to let constitutional majesty be asserted; and the Saints might have remained in peace. But this was not the purpose. The troops really had been called out, not to protect the "Mormons," but to answer the lying call of a justice of the peace. This mighty power of war was brought into operation to apprehend two or three men, charged with a petty offense, and who had not resisted any attempt to serve legal papers upon them.

On the 20th of September, General Atchison wrote to the governor that the insurrection was practically ended; all the leading offenders against the law had been arrested and bound over to appear at court. It is noticeable that the people were called offenders, the plundering rabble going scot free. All of the troops, except two companies of the Ray militia under command of Brigadier General Parks, were discharged. In this same letter General Atchison said:

They [the Mormons] appear to be acting on the defensive, and I must further add, gave up the offenders with a good deal of promptness. The arms and prisoners taken by the Mormons were also given up upon demand with seeming cheerfulness.

This candid opinion was reenforced a few days later by a letter from General Parks to the governor, in which he uses the following expressions:

Whatever may have been the disposition of the people called "Mormons" before our arrival here, since we have made our appearance they have shown no disposition to resist the laws, or of hostile intentions. There has been so much prejudice and exaggeration concerned in this matter that I found things entirely different from what I was prepared to expect. When we arrived here we found a large body of men from the counties adjoining, armed and in the field, for the purpose, as I learned, of assisting the people of this county against the "Mormons," without being called out by the proper authorities.

P.S.—Since writing the above, I have received information that if the committee do not agree, the determination of the Daviess County men is to drive the "Mormons" with powder and lead.

Near the same time, General Atchison wrote to Governor Boggs as follows:

Things are not so bad in this county [Daviess] as represented by rumor, and, in fact, from affidavits I have no doubt your Excellency has been deceived by the exaggerated statements of designing or half-crazy men. I have found there is no cause of alarm on account of the "Mormons"; they are not to be feared; they are very much alarmed.

About the 26th day of September, 1838, a committee from the mob met some of the leading brethren at Adam-ondi-Ahman and entered into an agreement whereby the Saints were to purchase lands and possessions of all who desired to sell; but this resulted in nothing, for the mob had other purposes in view.

About fifteen or twenty of the Saints with Lyman Wight were pledged to appear before the court at Gallatin for trial on the 29th of September.

Hundreds of men drawn into the militia service of Generals Atchison, Doniphan, Parks, and Lucas were in personal affiliation with the mob. When the greater part of the forces were disbanded in Daviess County, a general movement took place toward De Witt, in Carroll County. On their way the bandits breathed their murderous intent against the Saints; and before the onslaught, the brethren addressed a humble petition to Lilburn W. Boggs, imploring him to send succor, but he was deaf to the appeal. His ears were always open to the voice of the murderer; never to that of the victim. The mob could not ask him in vain for help; the injured Saints supplicated again and again without a reply. With the opening of October, the mob pressed hard upon the Saints in De Witt, threatening death to men, captivity to children and outrage to women.

CHAPTER 38

Saints
at Far West

Greater love hath no man than this, that a man lay down
his life for his friends. (John 15:13.)

On the 5th day of October, 1838, word came to the Prophet of
the bombardment of the town of De Witt, in Carroll County,
by a mob army with muskets and artillery. The ravenous wretches,
many of whom had been in the militia companies of Atchison,
Doniphan and Parks, foiled for the moment in Daviess and
Caldwell Counties, had concentrated upon the more remote and
defenseless places for the purpose of plundering the Saints and
driving them forth. As soon as Joseph heard the news, he hastened
to the scene of conflict. The rage of the mob naturally fell against
him more heavily than against anyone else; but it was his nature
always to be where danger threatened his brethren.

It was on the 2nd of October that the mob, under the
leadership of Dr. Austin; Major Ashley, a member of the legislature;
and Sashiel Woods, a Presbyterian clergyman, fired first upon the
town of De Witt. They continued during that day and the next,
when they were reinforced by two companies of militia under
the command of Captains Bogart and Houston, who were soon
followed by Brigadier General Parks. It is not wrong to speak for
these troops as a reinforcement of the mob. They were nothing
else. Bogart was a Methodist preacher by profession and only led
the company of militia to De Witt for the purpose of wreaking
the sectarian vengeance of a bigot upon the Saints. Parks himself
confessed that Bogart's men would not be controlled and were
with the mob in feeling; and this was the general's excuse for

allowing the outrages of this time to go unchecked. On the 4th of October, after forty-eight hours of siege, the people of the town, in command of Colonel Hinkle, returned the fire. Parks made no effort to check the mob's plan of organized murder. On the 6th he coolly wrote in his report to Atchison, as follows:

> *The Mormons are at this time too strong* and no attack is expected before Wednesday or Thursday next, at which time Dr. Austin [who with Bogart was leader of the mob] hopes his forces will amount to five hundred men, when he will make a second attempt on the town of De Witt, with small arms and cannon. *In this posture of affairs I can do nothing but negotiate between the parties until further aid is sent me.*

Evidently in this posture of affairs Parks wanted to do nothing. The "Mormons" were too strong. He would wait until Austin's rabble increased to five hundred, and by that time he hoped to have more companies of militia, which in turn would swell the ranks of the plundering besiegers. Parks' conduct indicates his utter lack of conscience; because in the same letter he says: "As yet they, the Mormons, have acted only on the defensive as far as I can learn."

General Lucas had been an observer of the gathering at De Witt and had been informed that a fight had taken place there, in which several persons were killed. Upon this he wrote to the governor that if his information was true it would create excitement in the whole of upper Missouri, "and those base and degraded beings will be exterminated from the face of the earth." He added that if one of the citizens of Carroll should be killed, before five days there would be raised against the "Mormons" five thousand volunteers whom nothing but blood would satisfy. Without attempting to suggest a remedy to Boggs, this cruel and sanguinary Lucas significantly informed his excellency that his troops of the fourth division were only dismissed subject to further order and could be called into the field at an hour's warning. He wanted to share in the work of extermination!

These events had happened before the Prophet reached De Witt. It was a trying journey, in which he had been obliged to travel by unfrequented roads and had put his life in constant jeopardy because mobs guarded every ingress to the town. When Joseph entered the place, he found the brethren only a handful in comparison to their assailants. Their provisions were exhausted, and there was no prospect of obtaining more. The Prophet concluded to send a message to the governor and secured the services of several influential and honest gentlemen who lived in that vicinity and who had been witnesses of the wanton attack upon the Saints. These men were bold as well as honest, for they made affidavit of the outrages which had been perpetrated within their sight, and they accompanied the supplication for redress to the executive office. The answer of the men who had been chosen by the suffrages of his fellow citizens as the chief officer of the state, sworn to uphold its honor, protect its dignity and maintain the supremacy of its laws, was only this:

The quarrel is between the Mormons and the mob, and they may fight it out.

Joseph's presence was a solace and a sustaining power to the Saints. He animated them by the courage of his presence and taught them patience by his own tenacity of endurance. He was not there as a warrior; he did not bear arms; and yet he was a tower of strength to his brethren.

Mobs were gathering in from Ray, Saline, Howard, Livingston, Clinton, Clay, Platte and other parts of the state to reinforce the besiegers. For the combined assailants a man named Jackson was chosen as the leader. The Saints were forbidden to leave the town under penalty of death. It was the purpose to starve them, since even this large crowd of mobbers, outnumbering the Saints ten to one, feared to risk a hand-to-hand contest. Fires were set to some of the houses; the cattle were stolen and roasted; the horses were driven off; while the mob made merry in feasting within sight of the starving people whom they had plundered.

Joseph directed applications for protection to the judges of the circuit court and in other quarters, but without avail; for where aid was given, it consisted of men willing to join and abet the mobs and to share in the spoils. In the town men were perishing for want of food; women and children cried for bread. There was no hope of earthly succor.

In this crisis Henry Root and David Thomas, two men who had been the sole cause of the settlement at De Witt, solicited the Saints to leave the place, claiming that they had assurance from the besiegers that, in such case, no further attack would be made and all the losses would be paid. Yielding to a necessity the Saints agreed to this proposition. A committee of appraisement was appointed from men not connected with the Saints. They placed a meager value on the bare land, and said nothing about the houses and other improvements which were still standing or had been destroyed by the mob, and nothing about the stock and the vehicles which had been run off. It was, however, an unnecessary economy of valuation; because the price, meager as it was, has never been paid.

On the 11th day of October, 1838, the Prophet and the Saints vacated De Witt and started for Caldwell with the small remnants of their possessions that they could gather and hope to convey. They were harassed continually on the journey by the mob which, in violation of its pledge, fired upon the retreating people. Among the exiles men died from fatigue and starvation—for the journey was greatly hurried because of the mobocratic threats; and one poor woman, who had given birth to a child on the very eve of the banishment, died on the journey and was buried in a grave without a coffin.

The experience at De Witt and on the journey from that place to Far West taught the Prophet and the Saints anew that they had no hope of protection, no hope of redress, while they remained in Missouri; and no hope that if they attempted to leave they would not be set upon and massacred by the bloodthirsty mob. Nothing was left them but to organize in some fashion for self-defense, as they came fleeing into Far West from all the surrounding country, leaving their worldly all and glad to escape with their lives.

The tiger spirit of the mob had grown upon its food. As the brethren left De Witt, Sashiel Woods called many of the mobocrats together and invited them to hasten into Daviess County to continue their work there. He said that the land sales were coming on and that if the "Mormons" could be first driven out the mob could get all the land entitled to preemption; besides, they could get back without pay the property already bought from them by the Saints. It was a welcome invitation, and, taking their artillery, this horde, with appetites whetted for their base and cruel work, departed for Adam-ondi-Ahman.

Other mobs were raised in other parts to join in this general movement for rapine, among the rabble being a man named Cornelius Gilliam, who called himself Delaware Chief, with a party of miscreants painted to represent Indians.

When the Prophet arrived in Far West from De Witt, on the 12th day of October, General Doniphan informed him that a mob of eight hundred men was marching against the people in Daviess County. A small party of militia had been on the way and might have intercepted the rabble; but Doniphan ordered them back, knowing well that instead of hindering they would join the mob. He said: "They are damned rotten hearted."

Pursuant to an order made by General Doniphan, a company of militia was raised in the county of Caldwell to act under Colonel Hinkle and to proceed to Adam-ondi-Ahman for the protection of that place. Joseph went with the militia to give counsel to his friends, risking his own life again, and taking with him many who were willing to stand with him in martyrdom if need were.

At Adam-ondi-Ahman the scenes of De Witt were repeated. Houses were burned, cattle were run off, women and children were driven out and exposed to a terrible storm which prevailed on the 17th and 18th of October. In many cases people in ill health were torn from their beds and were refused time to secure comfortable clothing in which to make their flight. Among the fugitives was Agnes Smith, the wife of the Prophet's brother,

Don Carlos, who was absent on a mission to Tennessee. Her house had been burned by the mob, her property seized, and she had fled three miles, wading Grand River and carrying all the way two helpless babes in her arms—glad to escape death and outrage.

Joseph's soul rose in arms at these crimes. The sacrifice had been sufficient. Every possible appeal had been made and denied. Henceforth the Saints must protect themselves, and God arm the right! It was this resolve alone which saved the remaining element of the Church that finally escaped from Missouri. At Adam-ondi-Ahman the mob intended to make a work of extermination; but after the arrival of the troops there, promises were demanded and secured from General Parks for the organization of a militia company to resist the attack and quell the mob. The force was immediately raised and placed under the command of Colonel Lyman Wight who held a commission in the fifty-ninth regiment under General Parks. These troops went out with a determination to drive the mob or die. They no longer fought in the state of Missouri for their rights as American citizens; that day had passed. They fought for life, for home, and for that which was dearer than all, the honor and safety of their wives and daughters who had been threatened with ravishment.

A remembrance of the day at Gallatin, when twelve had put one hundred and fifty to flight, suddenly came upon the mob as they saw the advancing forces of the Saints; and they fled. But fleeing, they resorted to stratagem. They removed everything of value from some of their own old log cabins and then set fire to these structures, afterwards spreading abroad through all the country the declaration that the "Mormons" had plundered and burned the mansions of law-abiding citizens.

An incident of this period shows the Prophet's calmness and self-command in the face of danger, as well as the influence of his presence even upon sworn enemies.

He was sitting in his father's house near the edge of the prairie one day, writing letters, when a large party of armed mobocrats called at the place. Lucy Smith, the Prophet's mother, demanded their business, and they replied that they were on the way to kill "Joseph, the Mormon Prophet." His mother remonstrated with them; and Joseph, having finished his writing and hearing the threats against himself, walked to the door and stood before them with folded arms, bared head and such a look of majesty in his eyes that they quailed before him. Though they were unacquainted with his identity, they knew they were in the presence of greatness; and when his mother introduced him as the man they sought, they started as if they had seen a spectre.

The Prophet invited the leaders into the house, and without alluding to their purpose of murder, he talked to them earnestly with regard to the persecutions against the Saints. When he concluded, so deeply had they been impressed, that they insisted upon giving him an escort to protect him to his home.

As they departed, one of the mob leaders said to another:

Didn't you feel strange when Smith took you by the hand?

And his companion replied:

I could not move. I would not harm a hair of that man's head for the whole world.

It was always so when men would listen to Joseph long enough to let the spirit which animated him assert itself to their reason.

The extent of the unhallowed league against the Saints is shown by the fact that not even the United States mails were safe during this period, for every post was plundered and all letters addressed to the Prophet were opened.

Unable to bear the pressure and to face the terrors of the time, Thomas B. Marsh had apostatized and had joined with McLellin and other evil men to act the part of Judas against the Prophet. The faith of others also failed, and, thinking by apostasy to save themselves from the destruction which seemed impending, they came out against Joseph and the Church and went over to their enemies.

On the 24th of October, eight armed mobbers plundered a house some little distance from Far West and took three of the brethren prisoners, namely, Nathan Pinkham, William Seely and Addison Green. With much exultation, these brigands declared their intention to murder their prisoners that night. Learning of this awful boast, the judge of the county instructed Colonel Hinkle to send out a company to rescue the men and disperse their captors. Seventy-five of the militia, under command of David W. Patten, were directed by Hinkle to fulfill this order. In departing, Captain Patten announced his hope to rescue his unoffending brethren without shedding any blood and to bring them back to Far West. Fifty men of this company marched to the ford on Crooked River, where they came upon an ambuscade of the mob, who fired upon them, mortally wounding a young man named O'Banion. Captain Patten ordered a charge upon the enemy, at the same time shouting the watchword, "Our God and liberty!" The concealed mobocrats fired as the company rushed down upon them. A musket ball pierced the bowels of David W. Patten, fatally wounding him. At the same fire a shower of bullets struck Gideon Carter, who fell to the ground to die after a few moments of agony. So defaced was Carter by his many wounds that later, when his brethren were gathering up their dead and wounded, they failed to recognize his body. Several others among the brethren were wounded. The others, even after the fall of their leader, dashed on in pursuit and put the mob to flight. The prisoners were rescued, but one of them was shot by the mob during the engagement. From them it was learned that Bogart had commanded the marauders and that his forces had been greater than those of the attacking party.

When the affray was over, David W. Patten—still alive, but gasping in mortal extremity—was lifted up by his brethren, and they carried him tenderly to his home.

A courier brought the news to Far West, and Joseph and Hyrum went out to meet the sorrowful cavalcade. Several were with Apostle Patten when he died that night, in the triumph of the faith. He had fulfilled his covenant to yield life rather than to yield the right. As he was departing, he spoke with holy exultation of the eternity opening to his view, and with sorrow of those traitorous apostles and elders who had forsaken the Saints to save their own lives and property. One of his last expressions to his wife was:

Whatever you do else, oh, do not deny the faith.

Thus perished the first apostolic martyr to the cause of Christ in this dispensation. How much better his fate than that of the Judases who helped to bring him to his death!

At the funeral Joseph stood in the presence of the assemblage, and, pointing at the noble form marred by the assassin's bullet, testified:

There lies a man who has fulfilled his word: he has laid down his life for his friends.

CHAPTER 39

Haun's Mill
Massacre

On the day of the martyr Patten's funeral at Far West, Lilburn W. Boggs issued to General John B. Clark an order of extermination against the Saints. His words were:

> The Mormons must be treated as enemies, and must be exterminated or driven from the state, if necessary, for the public good. Their outrages are beyond all description.

The excuse of this tyrant was the encounter between the militia, sent out by Colonel Hinkle under judicial endorsement, and Bogart's mobbers. How quickly Boggs could respond when any of his assassins were checked in their career of massacre and plunder! Before making his order of extermination he had already directed two thousand troops to be raised; and in his edict of death, entrusted to General Clark, he authorized any desired increase of forces. He also directed Major General Wallock and General Doniphan, with one thousand men, to intercept the retreat of the Saints, should they attempt one, by this act proving that the Saints were not to be permitted to leave the state, and that his order of extermination was intended to be construed absolutely and without alternative. He had taken the command from General Atchison and given it to General Clark because the latter was more suitable to his purpose, since he feared that Atchison might have some qualms of conscience. Incensed at this official slight, at a later time, General Atchison declared in a public speech:

If the governor does not restore my commission to me,
I will kill him, so help me God.

To make some show of palliation for this unparalleled act of
atrocity, Boggs published the most infamous lies concerning the
doings and intentions of the "Mormons," making it appear that
they, a little handful of poverty-stricken exiles, were about to
flood the state with a ruinous war. His stories were full of tragedy
and bombast. They would have been too ridiculous to be believed
for an instant, but that the infuriate element for whose incitement
they were addressed were eager as he to plunge the knife into the
heart of innocence.

All the vile characters in that section of the country
soon flocked to the mob organizations. The most diabolical
combinations were formed: one of the worst being under the
direction of Dr. Sampson Avard, one of the apostate spirits, who
formed a band which he called Danites, to aid him in purposes
of plunder and murder, which he intended to attribute to the
Church, and thus furnish an excuse for the attacks upon his
former brethren. But his plot was discovered by the Prophet, and
Avard was publicly excommunicated so that the world might know
that the Church had no part in this infamy. His plan was, by this
prompt action, defeated almost before it had birth.

By the 26th of October, twenty-five hundred of the mob
militia had congregated at Richmond, and from there they took
up their march for Far West, robbing, plundering, shooting, and
threatening ravishment by the way. It was such rare sport, this
outrage of the innocents, that it drew an overwhelming force to
execute the ghastly order of Boggs, the executioner at wholesale.

The executive decree of massacre fell like music upon the ears
of the wicked mob. On Tuesday, the 30th of October, 1838, a party
of two hundred and forty of them fell upon a few families of Saints
at Haun's Mill on Shoal Creek and butchered them. The awful
particulars of that deed must be left, with many others of like
character, for another publication now in course of preparation,
since the scope of this volume will not permit of more than a

general view of events, however important, in which the Prophet had no personal part. But one or two circumstances of that atrocious deed can be detailed to show the unquenchable thirst for blood of Boggs' emissaries. Among the Saints at Haun's Mill was one old man named McBride, who had fought for independence under General Washington. This veteran patriot the mob seized and shot with his own gun, then they slashed him to pieces with a corn cutter. Stalwart Missourians slew and mutilated little children, and afterwards boasted of their deeds. They even robbed the dead.

On the 30th day of October, the mob army beleaguered Far West. Their ranks were constantly augmented, and during the ensuing week six thousand demoniac men had taken part against that city.

On the first day of the siege, a messenger was sent into the town to demand three persons to whom amnesty was to be accorded, as the mob declared their intention to massacre all the rest of the people and lay Far West in ashes. Adam Lightner, John Cleminson and wife were these three persons. When the messengers offered them the chance of life they responded: "If the people must be destroyed, we will die with them."

Elder Charles C. Rich was sent out, bearing a flag of truce, to hold a conference with General Doniphan and others; but when he approached the camp of the besiegers, Bogart, the Methodist preacher, fired upon him.

The defenders of the city threw up a temporary fortification of wagons and timber on the south, for they were in hourly expectation of the attack.

About eight o'clock on the morning of Wednesday, the 31st day of October, a white flag approached the city from the camp of the mobbers.

Colonel George M. Hinkle went out to meet it and accompanied it back to the camp. What he did there ought to have made even a Judas blush. He returned at evening and said to Joseph that hope had arisen for the settlement of the difficulties, and that the presence of the Prophet and some of his leading friends was desired by the officers of the militia. Hinkle pledged his own honor and that of the besieging generals that no harm was intended or would be permitted against the brethren.

Always ready to meet personal danger in a just cause, the Prophet complied and was joined by the men whom Hinkle designated: Sidney Rigdon, Parley P. Pratt, Lyman Wight and George W. Robinson. Led by Colonel Hinkle they proceeded toward the camp and were met by General Lucas with one piece of artillery and the whole army at his heels. At this moment Hinkle earned his thirty pieces of silver, for he said:

These are the prisoners I agreed to deliver up.

Lucas brandished his sword and ordered his men to surround the Prophet and his companions. A fierce and exultant yell burst from the throats of the mob, and horrid blasphemies poured from them in torrents. They would not wait for an order to butcher before assailing the Prophet, so eager were they to take his life; and several of them snapped their guns at him, but he was spared. Arrived at the camp, the prisoners were placed in the charge of a strong guard of obscene and blasphemous wretches, who hour after hour profaned the name of God, mocked at Jesus Christ and boasted of having defiled virgins and wives by force. They demanded a miracle from Joseph, saying:

There is one of your brethren here in camp whom we took prisoner yesterday in his own house, and knocked his brains out with his own rifle, which we found hanging over his own mantel; he lies speechless and dying; speak the word and heal him, and then we will all believe.

Among the people who came to gloat over them was William E. McLellin, the apostate. He taunted them with their impending fate, declaring that there was no hope for them.

When the news reached Far West the people were appalled. They had feared for Joseph and his brethren because they knew that to go out was to enter the lair of a monster; and now they felt that their worst fears were confirmed.

That night the Prophet and his friends lay upon the wet ground, chilled by the rains of dawning November and subject to the most cruel and exasperating insults. The next morning Hyrum Smith and Amasa M. Lyman were dragged from their families in Far West and brought as prisoners into the camp.

On the evening of November 1, 1838, Lucas convened a court-martial, over which he presided. It was composed of seventeen preachers and some of the principal officers of the mob army. Its purpose was to put the Prophet and his friends on trial for their lives, but not one of them was permitted to be present during any part of its deliberations. A few moments were sufficient for the promulgation of its edict, since no testimony was to be heard and no pleas admitted. The sentence was that Joseph and his companions should be shot at eight o'clock the next morning, November 2, 1838, on the public square at Far West in the presence of their helpless wives and little children.

When the sentence was passed, General Doniphan said:

I wash my hands of this thing; it is murder!

Then he ordered his brigade of troops off the ground, for he would not permit them to take part in the assassination. General Graham also resisted the sentence with honor and manliness.

After the adjournment of the court-martial, the Prophet demanded from General Wilson the reason why he should be shot, since he had always been a supporter of the Constitution and the government of his country. Wilson's answer was:

I know it, and that is the reason why I want to kill you.

It was an absurdity to try by court-martial, even if that body had been a legal and just tribunal, a man who had not borne arms nor engaged in warfare nor committed any overt act. Joseph was a licensed minister of the gospel, not a soldier. He belonged to the class recognized always and everywhere as noncombatant. Probably this was the reason why Lucas had seventeen preachers as members of the court, to give the proceedings an ecclesiastical air.

On this same day, November 1, 1838, Lucas required the Caldwell militia to give up their arms. They only numbered five hundred men, all told, while the mob army numbered thousands. But the diabolical purpose which they had in view made it desirable to the attacking horde that no one in the city should have any power of resistance remaining. Lucas gave color to his demand by the fact that Hinkle, the betrayer, who had commanded the forces in Far West, had made a treaty by which the disarmament of the Caldwell militia was conceded.

The brethren were all marched out of the town and their weapons taken from them. Then gangs of miscreants were turned loose in Far West to work their will. They rushed through the streets like wolves, tearing and devouring whatever came in their way. Such deeds were done that day as would make a savage hang his head in shame. Property was seized and carried away without a pretext; houses were fired; the sick and the infantile were insulted and abused; the men were secured as prisoners; and women were outraged in sight of their helpless husbands and fathers.

The Prophet's house was singled out for a special attack; his family was driven out and all his property seized or destroyed.

The brethren who possessed real estate were brought before Lucas, and at the point of the bayonet, were compelled to sign deeds of trust of all their possessions to pay the expenses of the mob.

A more appalling instance of cruelty history does not record. An innocent people are ordered exterminated. But before proceeding to the final act of massacre, the immolators demand their pay in advance from the victims.

It was an awful night at Far West; but more awful it was feared the morrow would be, for the sentence of death pronounced upon the Prophet and his fellow captives was promised to be executed at eight o'clock the next morning.

CHAPTER 40

Prophet's Life Spared

On the morning of Friday, November 2, 1838, in pursuance of the sentence of the secret tribunal of preachers and mobocrats—misnamed a court-martial—the Prophet and his fellow prisoners were marched into the public square at Far West. But the brutal murder which had been decreed did not take place. The failure of Lucas to enforce that part of the sentence was due in part to the manly rebellion of Generals Doniphan and Graham and in part to his own wish to drag the Prophet and his brethren through the country and exhibit them as his captives. General Clark was expected immediately at Far West. He wanted the prisoners delivered to him; and jealousy worked in the mind of Lucas. It was esteemed a high honor to hold Joseph Smith in captivity; and Lucas was determined not to share this glorious trophy of war with another. What the tears of women and children, the innocence of men, and a sense of justice could not accomplish in this bad man's mind, was easily achieved by the base motives of envy and vanity. He wanted to be recognized as a victorious general, and the presence of the captives would add to the pageantry of his march. If greater notoriety could have been achieved or greater admiration for his prowess secured by the murder of these men at Far West, he would not have stayed his hand. It was an opportunity of a lifetime for a militia leader to cover himself with the dishonors of war. Less than a quarter of a century from that time, the state of Missouri and all its citizens had ample occasion to deal with real enemies and to view in every city and village, and every field and every forest, and in every home the misery of fratricidal strife. Men who had thirsted for blood were given more than a glut of it, for hundreds of them weltered in their own gore.

Lucas prepared to continue his triumphal march, intending to take the brethren to Jackson County and expose them as captives at Independence. Before they left, they begged to be permitted to bid their families farewell. This boon, so estimable to them and so trifling to the mob, was ostensibly granted, but under conditions which showed an inhuman desire to torture. Every prisoner was permitted, under a strong guard, to seek out his beloved ones, *but was forbidden to speak to them.* He might gaze on them with tearful eyes and wave them farewell, a long farewell—forever, if he would; but no word from his lips might fall as balm upon their bruised spirits.

Hyrum, the Prophet's beloved brother, who was never very far away from Joseph, was one of the captives. Hyrum's young wife, Mary—for he was again a husband—was prostrated with suffering. When he was dragged before her by his armed captors he would have solaced her agony with a few words of comfort and cheer. He wanted to bid her look up and trust in God; but the mob soldiers threatened to kill him at her feet if he breathed a syllable, and to spare her tortured soul this awful pang he held his peace. Mary saw her husband carried from her, perhaps to death; she gathered the motherless little children of Jerusha about her and sought to comfort them. She did not see her noble husband again until after she had passed through the trial and pain of maternity; for her son, Joseph Fielding Smith, was born eleven days after, and while his father was still a captive in the hands of the mob.

To moan and weep over the captive Prophet came his wife and babes and his aged father and mother. He had begged to have a moment in which to comfort his wife, for she was utterly overpowered with fear for his life. He wanted to reassure her that the sentence of death was not to be executed that morning and to promise her that they should meet again in this life. But the mob guards with their swords rudely thrust his wife and little ones away from Joseph's side and threatened to kill him if he should speak.

Joseph gazed upon the overwhelming scene at Far West as he was being marched forth a captive. He commended the city and its people to the care of that God whose kindness had always followed them into the dark valley of tribulation and who alone could protect them from death and defilement.

That night the Prophet with Hyrum Smith, Sidney Rigdon, Parley P. Pratt, Lyman Wight, Amasa M. Lyman and George W. Robinson, were started for Independence. Under a strong guard, commanded by Generals Lucas and Wilson, they camped at night on Crooked River.

A vision of hope and security came to Joseph that night, and when he arose in the morning he spoke to his brethren in a low and cheerful tone, saying:

> Be of good cheer, my brethren, the word of the Lord came to me last night that our lives should be given us and that whatever else we might suffer during this captivity, not one of us should die.

An express from General Clark demanding the august prisoners reached Lucas at this point. This commanding general had so far achieved little, the triumphs of the cruel contest being with his subordinates. He was therefore determined that the prisoners should be dragged at *his* chariot wheels and that their slaughter should be under *his* personal direction, to show Boggs and the populace that he was worthy of the truculent enterprise entrusted to him. But Lucas was no less determined that, having won the victory, he himself should enjoy the spoils and the plaudits; and with all possible speed he hastened forward with the captives.

Leaving the Prophet and his companions advancing toward their unknown fate, we must return with their anxious thoughts to the proceedings at Far West, as General Clark was marching upon that place, and the prisoners feared for their unprotected families.

Lucas had sent several companies of the mob militia, including Neal Gilliam's band of painted wretches under General Parks, to Adam-ondi-Ahman with instructions to disarm the militia at that place and to take prisoners. By his orders also a large body of troops had been left to guard some eighty brethren held captive at Far West.

General Clark did not arrive at the beleaguered city until the 4th of November, 1838; but on that day he came at the head of two thousand troops. In the interval of two days, the people in the town had been subjected to every possible indignity. Apostates prowled through the streets pointing out to the mob all the men of influence or station in the Church and aiding to put them in irons. At first it had been ordered that all who were not held as prisoners should flee the city on the instant. But finally the mob concluded to keep the people within the town until General Clark's arrival.

It was a joy to the sectarian ministers of the neighborhood to see this work of ruin; and many of them visited Far West to exult over the prisoners and their suffering families.

Many privations and tortures were endured. The captives were kept without food until they were on the verge of starvation. The mob continued their work of ruin, hunting and shooting human beings like wild beasts and ravishing and murdering women.

Upon Clark's arrival at Far West, he selected fifty-six of the leading men and held them under a strong guard for trial, for what offense neither he nor they could tell. He also sent a messenger to the commander of the troops advancing to assault Adam-ondi-Ahman, requiring him to take all of the "Mormon" prisoners and to secure all their property to pay the damages of other citizens.

On the 6th day of November, 1838, Clark assembled the people and delivered an address to them as follows:

> Gentlemen:
>
> You whose names are not attached to this list of names will now have the privilege of going to your fields and of providing corn, wood, etc., for your families. Those who are now taken will go from this to prison, be tried and receive the due demerit of their crimes; but you (except such as charges may hereafter be preferred against), are at

liberty, as soon as the troops are removed that now guard the place, which I shall cause to be done immediately.

It now devolves upon you to fulfill a treaty that you have entered into, the leading items of which I shall now lay before you. The first requires that your leading men be given up to be tried according to law; this you already have complied with. The second is that you deliver up your arms; this has been attended to. The third stipulation is that you sign over your properties to defray the expenses of the war. This you have also done. Another article yet remains for you to comply with—and that is that you leave the state forthwith. And whatever may be your feelings concerning this, or whatever your innocence, it is nothing to me. General Lucas (whose military rank is equal with mine), has made this treaty with you, I approve of it. I should have done the same had I been here. I am therefore determined to see it executed.

The character of this state has suffered almost beyond redemption from the character, conduct, and influence that you have exerted; and we deem it an act of justice to restore her character to its former standing among the states by every proper means. *The orders of the Governor to me were that you should be exterminated and not allowed to remain in the state. And had not your leaders been given up and the terms of the treaty complied with, before this time, you and your families would have been destroyed and your houses in ashes.*

There is a discretionary power vested in my hands, which, considering your circumstances, I shall exercise for a season. You are indebted to me for this clemency. I do not say that you shall go now, but you must not think of staying here another season or of putting in crops; for the moment you do this the citizens will be upon you; and if I am called here again in case of a noncompliance of a treaty made, do not think that I shall do as if I have done now. *You need not expect any mercy, but extermination, for I am determined the Governor's order shall be executed.*

As for your leaders, do not think, do not imagine for a moment, do not let it enter into your minds, that they will be delivered and restored to you again, for their fate is fixed, their dye is cast, their doom is sealed.

I am sorry, gentlemen, to see so many apparently intelligent men found in the situation that you are; and oh! if I could invoke that Great Spirit, the unknown God, to rest upon and deliver you from that awful chain of superstition, and liberate you from those fetters of fanaticism with which you are bound—that you no longer do homage to a man.

I would advise you to scatter abroad, and never again organize yourselves with bishops, presidents, etc., lest you excite the jealousies of the people and subject yourselves to the same calamities that have now come upon you. You have always been the aggressors—you have brought upon yourselves these difficulties by being disaffected and not being subject to rule. And my advice is that you become as other citizens, lest by a recurrence of these events you bring upon yourselves irretrievable ruin.

The prisoners whom he had taken were sent by him to Richmond, in Ray County, for trial.

About this same time Boggs wrote a letter requiring Clark to finish the awful work which had been begun. He directed a movement against the Saints at Adam-ondi-Ahman and said:

My instructions to you are to settle this whole matter completely, if possible, before you disband your forces.

To fulfill this edict, Clark ordered General Wilson with his brigade to Adam-ondi-Ahman, although there were enough mob troops already there to furnish a special guard and a special executioner for every man, woman and child in the place. On the 8th of November a cordon was drawn about Adam-ondi-Ahman.

A court of inquiry was instituted with the notorious Adam Black on the bench and with a man from General Clark's army as prosecuting attorney. Not a thing could be proved against any of the brethren, except that they had been long-suffering victims of senseless hate, and they were acquitted; but not until a military order was prepared requiring them, one and all, to vacate the place in ten days and to be outside of the state as early as the next spring or to be exterminated.

CHAPTER 41

"Majesty in Chains"

Early in the year 1838, while it was more than his life was worth for any Saint to penetrate Jackson County, the Prophet made a public prophecy that some one of the elders would preach a sermon there before the close of the ensuing December.

Lucas crossed the ferry of the Missouri River from Clay into Jackson County with his prisoners on the night of Saturday, the 3rd of November, 1838. His march had been made with great expedition because he feared to be overtaken by a further demand from his superior officer for the captives.

The next morning was the Sabbath; and the people along the road came out in their best attire to view the "Mormon" Prophet, for the news had preceded his advent, and the whole country was aroused. While they were yet in camp on that morning, a number of ladies and gentlemen visited them; and one woman inquired of the guards, "Which of the captives is the Lord worshiped by the Mormons?"

The mobocrat pointed to Joseph with a significant smile and said, "That is he." After gazing upon the Prophet for a moment, the lady candidly asked whether he professed to be the Lord and Savior Jesus Christ. Joseph answered:

> I am only a man, a humble minister of salvation sent
> by the Redeemer to preach His gospel.

Astounded at this reply, so different from what she had been led to expect, the lady pressed question after question upon the Prophet. As he responded, many listeners gathered around, including a company of the wondering soldiers; and there on that

Sabbath morning, with hundreds of spectators and his captors for a congregation, the Prophet preached as impressive a discourse as ever before in his life. He set forth the doctrines of faith in Jesus Christ, repentance, baptism for the remission of sin, with a promise of the gift of the Holy Ghost—as recorded in the Acts of the Apostles. And by this sermon was his own prophecy fulfilled.

His listeners were filled with strange emotions; this man spoke as no other had ever talked in their hearing. The woman who had first asked to see the Prophet was wrought upon by a spirit of conviction. When Joseph finished his remarks, she arose and praised God in solemn tones, and she went away praying that the Lord would protect and deliver His servants.

At ten o'clock of that Sunday morning, the entire brigade having crossed the river, the march was resumed. As they passed along the road, hundreds of people flocked to see them, and General Wilson often halted the cavalcade to introduce his prisoners to the populace, pointing out each one of the captives by name. A few hours later the prisoners entered Independence surrounded by the exultant troops, who blew every instant triumphant blasts upon their bugles to arouse the inhabitants into a frenzy of joy. Rain was falling in torrents, but it could not extinguish the blazing hate and exultation of the mob as they paraded the Prophet through the streets of the city whence his brethren had been once driven from homes and growing wealth.

But soon after their arrival a reaction of feeling set in, and the prisoners began to be treated with some show of compassion. It is true they were badly lodged, closely guarded and exhibited every day as a victorious Roman general might have exhibited his captive kings; but they were fed, partly shielded from the severity of the season and were permitted to plead their cause and proclaim their belief to any interested listener.

The effect of their situation and their teachings was most amazing. Here in this region where they had once met cruelty in its direst shape and whither they had been brought in hourly peril of their lives, they awakened feelings of pity, respect and personal regard.

They were permitted occasionally to walk out in the charge of a guard; and then they visited the spot dedicated for a temple, which had been denuded of its noble forests and now lay desolate, and also the place where had once stood the dwellings of the Saints, but not a vestige of these habitations remained, for they had been consumed by fire or carried away by plunderers.

After four days' imprisonment at Independence, and after repeated demands from Clark for their persons, it was decided to send them to Richmond, Ray County; but the officers, now become somewhat friendly, could not give them any light concerning the charges to be made against them. It was agreed that they were not to be tried by civil process, because none had been served upon them; it was also agreed that they could not be tried by court-martial since they were civilians—amenable to civil law; martial law had not been declared, and they had not committed any military offense.

It was extremely difficult to secure guards to accompany the brethren to Richmond. None would volunteer, and when drafted from the ranks they refused to obey orders. The soldiers, impressed by the personality of the captives and wrought upon by the spirit of mercy, wished the brethren to go at liberty. Hundreds of the men who had fought against them with bitterness now entertained for them the kindest feelings; and, besides, both officers and troops disliked to see General Clark secure the triumph so ardently desired by him. The view entertained by Lucas was shared by his officers and men and was stated to the brethren by General Wilson in the following words:

It was repeatedly insinuated by the other officers and troops that we should hang you prisoners on the first tree we came to on the way to Independence. But I'll be damned if anybody shall hurt you. We just intend to exhibit you in Independence, let the people look at you, and see what a damned set of fine fellows you are. And more particularly to keep you from that G—d damned old bigot of a General Clark and his troops, from down country, who are so stuffed with lies and prejudice that they would shoot you down in a moment.

Finally, three men consented to escort the prisoners to Richmond, and on the morning of Thursday, the 8th day of November, 1838, they started on their journey. What a reflection it is upon the doings of that time that the officers in charge of these captives should entrust seven of them to three guards! Joseph and his brethren had been designated and treated as the most desperate men in the state of Missouri. The mob proved their own assertion to be false when they arranged the journey to Richmond. That afternoon, between Independence and Roy's Ferry, the three guards became drunk. As Joseph and his brethren had no physical restraint upon them, they could easily have killed their guards and escaped; but instead of doing this, they merely secured the arms and the horses, that the intoxicated soldiers might not injure themselves or their prisoners and that the steeds might not stray away.

After crossing the Missouri, they were met by Colonel Sterling Price with a guard of seventy-four men, by whom they were conducted to Richmond and thrown into a vacant house closely watched. A few hours after their arrival General Clark visited them. When they demanded the reason why they had thus been carried from their homes and demanded a statement of the charge made against them, the great General Clark, called an eminent lawyer, answered that he could not then determine what particular offense could be alleged against them, but would think the matter over. Immediately after he had withdrawn, Colonel Price came in with ten armed men and some chains and padlocks. The guards were ordered to stand with muskets ready to fire. Then the windows were nailed down, and a man named John Fulkerson chained the seven brethren together and fastened the manacles with padlocks.

General Clark spent many hours trying to find some definite charge against the prisoners and trying to find some authority to arraign them before a court-martial. The result of his researches is shown in a letter addressed to the governor at that time, in which he says:

> I have detained General White and his field officers here a day or two, for the purpose of holding a court-martial, if necessary. I this day made out charges against the prisoners, and called on Judge King to try them as a committing court; and I am now busily engaged in procuring witnesses and submitting facts. There being no civil officers in Caldwell, I have to use the military to get witnesses from there, which I do without reserve. The most of the prisoners here, I consider guilty of treason; and I believe will be convicted; and the only difficulty in law is, can they be tried in any county but Caldwell? If not, they cannot be there indicted until a change of population. In the event the latter view is taken by the civil courts, I suggest the propriety of trying Joseph Smith and those leaders taken by General Lucas for mutiny. This I am in favor of only as a dernier resort. I would have taken this course with Smith at any rate; but it being doubtful whether court-martial has jurisdiction or not in the present case—that is, whether these people are to be treated as in time of war, and the mutineers as having mutinied in time of war—and I would here ask you to forward to me the Attorney-General's opinion on this point. It will not do to allow these leaders to return to their treasonable work again on account of their not being indicted in Caldwell. They have committed treason, murder, arson, burglary, robbery, larceny and perjury. (Joseph Smith, *History of the Church*, III, 206–207.)

A more helpless state of mind than that of General Clark can scarcely be imagined. The document which has been quoted and which he closes with charges against the brethren of nearly all the offenses under the law—and yet does not know how to substantiate or legally punish a single one of them—proves that he was in a desperate state of mind.

He was determined that they should die and made his preparations for the commission of the murder before he had even decided what charge to bring against the prisoners. While this matter was pending, Brother Jedediah Grant, then a young man, put up at the same tavern with the general at Richmond. He saw Clark select the men to shoot Joseph and his fellow prisoners, and he heard the day of the execution fixed as Monday, November 12, 1838. He saw the men who were selected load their rifles with two bullets each, and after this was done he heard General Clark say to them:

> *Gentlemen, you shall have the honor of shooting the Mormon leaders next Monday morning at eight o'clock.*

Colonel Price, who had immediate charge of the prisoners, permitted all manner of abuse to be heaped upon them. They were kept chained together like wild beasts; left to lie upon the bare floor without any covering. When they might have forgotten their sufferings of body and mind in slumber, the inhuman guards kept them awake by yelling ribald songs and jests and by shrieks of laughter. Parley P. Pratt, who was one of the prisoners confined with Joseph, writes of one of these painful nights as follows:

> In one of those tedious nights we had lain as if in sleep, till the hour of midnight had passed, and our ears and hearts had been pained, while we had listened for hours to the obscene jests, the horrid oaths, the dreadful blasphemies and filthy language of our guards, Colonel Price at their head, as they recounted to each other their deeds of rapine, murder, robbery, etc., which they had committed among the Mormons while at Far West and vicinity. They even boasted of defiling by force wives, daughters and virgins, and of shooting or dashing out the brains of men, women and children.
>
> I had listened till I became so disgusted, shocked, horrified, and so filled with the spirit of indignant justice, that I could scarcely refrain from rising upon my feet and

rebuking the guards, but I had said nothing to Joseph or anyone else, although I lay next to him, and knew he was awake. On a sudden he arose to his feet and spoke in a voice of thunder, or as the roaring lion, uttering, as near as I can recollect, the following words:

"Silence! Ye fiends of the infernal pit! In the name of Jesus Christ I rebuke you, and command you to be still. I will not live another minute and hear such language. Cease such talk, or you or I die this instant!"

He ceased to speak. He stood erect in terrible majesty. Chained, and without a weapon, calm, unruffled, and dignified as an angel, he looked down upon his quailing guards, whose knees smote together, and who, shrinking into a corner, or crouching at his feet, begged his pardon, and remained quiet until an exchange of guards.

I have seen ministers of justice, clothed in ministerial robes, and criminals arraigned before them, while life was suspended upon a breath in the courts of England; I have witnessed a congress in solemn session to give laws to nations; I have tried to conceive of kings, of royal courts, of thrones and crowns; and of emperors assembled to decide the fate of kingdoms; but dignity and majesty have I seen but once, as it stood in chains, at midnight, in a dungeon, in an obscure village of Missouri. (Joseph Smith, *History of the Church*, III, footnote, p. 208.)

More than fifty of the brethren from Far West were also held in captivity at Richmond; failing to find authority or excuse for trying any of these men by court-martial, Clark informed them that the whole party would be turned over to the civil authorities. A court was convened with Austin A. King presiding, and Thomas C. Burch, the state's attorney for the prosecution. The first act of this strange tribunal was to send out a body of mobocratic soldiers, armed with guns instead of civil process, to bring in witnesses, who, when they arrived, were sworn at the point of the bayonet. Nearly forty persons gave evidence for the prosecution.

Though they all swore in a general way monstrous crimes against the accused, not one definite charge was maintained. When the defense were asked for their witnesses they named as many as fifty, any of whom could have disproved the accusations. Captain Bogart, the Methodist preacher, was sent out with a company of soldiers to procure these witnesses, and when he brought them in under arrest, they were thrust into jail and kept there until after the trial, without being accorded an opportunity to testify or to see the defendants.

One day, while the trial was proceeding, a man named Allen, who knew something of the facts and was there as an interested spectator, was called by the defense and sworn. As his testimony was favorable to the Prophet and the other prisoners, the mob set upon him in open court and tried to murder him. When he left the building he was pursued by mobocrats with loaded guns. Observing the outrages inflicted upon people who wanted to tell the truth, the Prophet and his brethren ceased to demand witnesses, preferring themselves to suffer than to involve other people in the toils of mobocratic hate.

The mock investigation continued from day to day until Saturday, November 24, 1838, when all of the brethren were discharged except Joseph Smith, Hyrum Smith, Lyman Wight, Caleb Baldwin, Alexander McRae, Sidney Rigdon, Parley P. Pratt, Morris Phelps, Luman Gibbs, Darwin Chase, and Norman Shearer, who were held for murder and treason.

The judge was a Methodist, and he had been particularly anxious to know whether the defendants believed in the prophecy of Daniel, that:

> In the days of these kings shall the God of heaven set up a kingdom, which shall break in pieces all other kingdoms, and stand forever.

And,

> ... the kingdom and dominion, and the greatness of the kingdom, under the whole heaven, shall be given to the people of the saints of the most High. . . . (Daniel 7:27.)

When it appeared clear that the prisoners believed in the Bible and in this particular part of it, their treason was established. The judge so decided in express terms and he then committed them; and as General Doniphan, who was present, remarked:

> If a cohort of angels were to come down and declare the innocence of the prisoners it would be all the same; for King has determined from the beginning to throw them into prison.

King and Burch, the judge and prosecuting attorney, had sat in Lucas' secret tribunal in Far West that had sentenced the brethren to be shot; and they were anxious to take this new opportunity to wreak their vengeance. In open court the judge stated that there was no law to protect "Mormons" in the state of Missouri, and he was bound to aid the governor's edict of extermination.

The prisoners had been kept in chains during the examination; and in chains they stood to hear the judgment of the court. It was that Joseph Smith, Hyrum Smith, Lyman Wight, Alexander McRae, Caleb Baldwin, and Sidney Rigdon be imprisoned in the jail of Clay County until delivered therefrom by due course of law. The others who were held were retained in Richmond Jail.

Thus was the charge of treason maintained in that day; and upon the same grounds it has been repeated against the Saints down to the present time, for they still continue to believe that the Bible is the word of God.

Joseph and his companions were carried to Liberty, Clay County, in irons. As they entered the town, considerable excitement prevailed among people desirous to view them. Arrived at the jail, they descended from the vehicle and walked up the steps to a landing or platform in front of the entrance of the prison building. Joseph wore a suit of black and had a cloak of dark-colored material hanging on his arm. Hyrum followed him and the others stood close around. The gaze of the spectators was concentrated upon Joseph, and his majestic air made a deep impression upon them. One lady in the crowd cried: "Their Prophet looks like a gentleman!" Another, looking at the group, expressed the opinion: "Well, they are fine looking men if they are Mormons."

It was on the 30th day of November, 1838, that they were incarcerated in Liberty Jail; and at once an order was made to cut off all communication between them and their friends, while every effort was put forth to drive away or frighten any witnesses whose testimony might be desirable for the defendants. And at the same time the threat went out through all that region that if judges or juries or courts of any kind should clear the prisoners, they would be slaughtered.

After a little time the rule concerning communications was relaxed, and Joseph was able to write to his brethren. In one of his letters, dated from Liberty Jail, December 16, 1838, he said:

> But we want you to remember Haman and Mordecai: you know Haman could not be satisfied so long as he saw Mordecai at the king's gate, and he sought the life of Mordecai and the people of the Jews. But the Lord so ordered it, that Haman was hanged upon his own gallows.
>
> So shall it come to pass with poor Haman in the last days. Those who have sought by unbelief and wickedness, and by the principle of mobocracy, to destroy us and the people of God, by killing them and scattering them abroad, and willfully and maliciously delivering us into the hands of murderers, desiring us to be put to death, thereby having us dragged about in chains and cast into prison, and for what cause? It is because we were honest men, and were determined to save the lives of the Saints at the expense of our own. I say unto you, that those who have thus vilely treated us like Haman, shall be hanged on their own gallows; or in other words, shall fall into their own gin and snare, and ditch and trap, which they have prepared for us, and shall go backwards and stumble and fall, and their names shall be blotted out, and God shall reward them according to all their abominations. (Joseph Smith, *History of the Church*, III, p. 227.)

The people were making their preparations to leave the state; but in the meantime they addressed a memorial and petition to the legislature of Missouri, setting forth the wrongs and outrages committed upon them. These appeals were presented, but after an angry discussion they were laid upon the table. At the same time an appropriation of $200,000 was made to the mob to pay them for their crimes against the Saints.

This action was so outrageous that something needed to be done to distract public attention, and the mob element secured the publication of the most enormous falsehoods against the people. In these accounts the wickedness of the mob was disguised or denied. But the Prophet exposed them in the following words:

> But can they hide the Governor's cruel order for banishment or extermination? Can they conceal the facts of the disgraceful treaty of the generals with their own officers and men at Far West? Can they conceal the fact that twelve or fifteen thousand men, women and children have been banished from the state without trial or condemnation? And this at the expense of two hundred thousand dollars—and this sum appropriated by the state legislature in order to pay the troops for this act of lawless outrage? Can they conceal the fact that we have been imprisoned for many months, while our families, friends and witnesses have been driven away? Can they conceal the blood of the murdered husbands and fathers, or stifle the cries of the widow and the fatherless? Nay! The rocks and mountains may cover them in unknown depths, the awful abyss of the fathomless deep may swallow them up—and still their horrid deeds stand forth in the broad light of day, for the wondering gaze of angels and men! They cannot be hid.

The year drew to a close. The Saints were impoverished and scattered. The Prophet and his companions, loaded with chains, were in a noisome dungeon; several times they were poisoned, and, during a period of five days, human flesh was served to them as meat. The guards called it "Mormon beef," and the Prophet warned his companions not to touch it.

The earth was wrapped in gloom for the people of God when the sun sank for the last time upon the year 1838; but beyond and above this sphere was the star of eternal faith, whose light no prison walls could shut out from trusting souls.

CHAPTER 42

To Illinois

With the dawn of 1839, a pledge was given by many of the brethren in Missouri that they would assist each other and assist the poor to escape from the state; and the promise was sacredly redeemed.

But the persecution did not cease. Brigham Young, who had been chosen president of the twelve in place of Thomas B. Marsh, an apostate, was driven out of Far West by mobs that sought his life. He, with other fugitive Saints went to Illinois, and the charitable people of Quincy, Adams County, extended to the persecuted people a hand of kindness.

In January Heber C. Kimball and Alanson Ripley went to Liberty and began to importune at the feet of judges for relief for their suffering Prophet and brethren in prison. One Judge Hughes believed that they were pleading the cause of the innocent and wanted the captives admitted to bail; but his associates were hardened and would not consent. The two supplicants were soon compelled, by mob fury, to desist from their importunities and were driven away from Liberty.

A writ of *habeas corpus* was secured about the close of January to bring the prisoners before Judge Turnham. An examination was held, but it was a farce. Nearly all the officers of the law, if not in league with the mob, were in terror of its power. Sidney Rigdon alone was released at the hearing upon the writ; but he had to return to jail because the rabble swore they would kill him if he was turned loose. A little later Sidney was let out of the prison secretly in the night by a friendly jailor, and he escaped to Quincy.

The families of Joseph, Hyrum and the other captive brethren gathered up to Quincy after undergoing the most appalling privations. It was Stephen Markham who escorted Emma, Joseph's wife, and their children from Far West, through all the dangers of Missouri and to a place of safety. The Saints were arriving there in large numbers during the winter and early spring, but were not decided yet where to settle.

On the 15th day of March the Prophet and the other brethren in Liberty Jail made petitions to the judges of the supreme court for writs of *habeas corpus*, by which they hoped to have the proceedings of their imprisonment examined; but they were obstructed by the hatred against them. It was evident that the purpose of their enemies was to withhold judicial hearing until after the brethren had suffered death in prison. And their efforts from this time on during their captivity were continuous to secure such hearing.

A conference was held at Quincy on the 17th of March, 1839, over which Brigham Young presided as the head of the twelve. Thomas B. Marsh and several other persons of some prominence were excommunicated from the Church.

A gathering place for the Saints was necessary. This the Prophet felt every hour. While he was in prison in Liberty the brethren had friendly communication with one Dr. Isaac Galland upon the subject of settlement by the Saints in Iowa Territory and at Commerce, Illinois. From his dungeon the Prophet pressed the elders to make a close examination of this matter, as the springtime was at hand and the crops for the year must be planted.

In prison Joseph was in constant communion with the heavens, and he received revelations, without which he and his brethren must have been cast down and without hope. He also sent epistles full of instruction and hope to leading men among the Saints. And his cheerful courage under the most trying circumstances of his life was very helpful in animating the banished people to pursue their migration with energy and fortitude.

While the Prophet and companions were still in Liberty Jail, and after having repeatedly and vainly sought release by law, they thought they saw an opportunity to escape. At Hyrum's instance Joseph prayed to the Lord and asked if it was His will that they should depart from prison. The answer came to the Prophet that if they were all agreed in faith and purpose they might escape that night. When this response was made known, all of the brethren except Lyman Wight coincided in the opinion that they should seize their liberty, for they relied implicitly upon the promise given. But Lyman trembled, hesitated; and, as his companions would not resolve to leave him and as the promise of the Lord was based upon their unanimity, they resolved to wait until the next night as Lyman Wight agreed then to accompany them. The delay was fatal; they broke the conditions of the promise and remained in durance. On the night for which the promise was given, the jailor came in alone with their suppers and left the doors wide open, so that they might easily have escaped. The next night he brought a double guard with him and also six visiting brethren. As the jailor was leaving their dungeon, some of them attempted to follow him; but they were foiled. The guards were so enraged at the effort, although it had been a vain one, that they locked up the visiting brethren and made threats against their persons and property. The attempt to escape created great excitement; and the people of the town swarmed around the jail proposing various plans to destroy Joseph and all his companions. But the Prophet told his brethren to have no fear; not a hair of their heads should be harmed, and the brethren who had come in to comfort them should not lose any of their personal belongings—not even a horse or a saddle. He told them that they had risked their lives to bring joy to himself and companions and the Lord would bless them. These promises were fulfilled to the letter.

When the visiting brethren were called for trial, Brother Erastus Snow, who was one of them, pleaded their cause as he had been counseled by Joseph. He did so in such a forcible and eloquent manner that orders of discharge in some cases and orders for bail in the others were immediately entered.

Elder Snow's argument had been so strong and logical in its legal deductions that the lawyers who heard him supposed that he was a trained attorney.

Many enemies of the Prophet were permitted by the guard to visit and insult him in prison. It was their habit to charge him with murder. Several different men accused him of having killed their sons at the battle of Crooked River; several more, who were no kin to each other, charged him with having killed their brothers in the same battle. And this was the texture of the accusations made against him in and out of court. It had been alleged that only one man was killed at the battle of Crooked River, so it was impossible for several different men to lose sons and brothers there; and Joseph was not near the scene of that contest.

On one occasion a company under the leadership of William Bowman made solemn oath that they would never eat or drink more until they had taken the life of Joseph Smith. Bowman himself went to one of the elders and made this boast:

> After I once lay eyes on your Prophet, I will never taste food or drink until I have killed him.

As these men all saw the Prophet soon afterward, and as he lived more than five years from that time, they either broke their oath or endured a long fast.

Before Brigham Young was driven out of Missouri into Illinois, he went with Elders Heber C. Kimball and George A. Smith to see the Prophet in prison. Joseph enjoyed two visits with them; and when they left him they were much affected and were determined to do something further for his release. In the latter part of March, Elders Heber C. Kimball and Theodore Turley, carrying with them the papers in the case, went to see the governor. As Boggs was absent from the capital, the secretary of state reviewed the documents; and he was amazed that any man should be held in custody upon such papers, for they were in every sense illegal, insufficient and absurd. However, nothing was done from the executive office to relieve them; and Elders Kimball and Turley then applied to the supreme court judges for a writ of *habeas corpus* but without avail. When these devoted men returned to Liberty and reported the failure of their mission, the Prophet bade them be of good cheer and said:

> We shall be delivered; but no arm but that of God can save us now. Tell the brethren to be of good cheer and to get the Saints away from Missouri as soon as possible.

On Saturday, the 6th day of April, 1839, Judge King ordered the Prophet and his fellow prisoners off to Gallatin, Daviess County. This judicial autocrat feared a change of venue or some movement from a superior tribunal to secure the release of the prisoners or their removal from his personal power, and he determined to carry them away from Liberty. He sent them under a guard of ten men, promising the brethren that they should be permitted to go through Far West to see their friends, as that place was directly on their route. Instead, however, of fulfilling his promise, the guards carried the captives eighteen miles out of the direct course to avoid the city, dragging them through a dangerous country, apparently in the hope that some of their sworn enemies would fall upon and massacre them.

The journey to Gallatin was very painful, for Joseph and his brethren had been greatly enfeebled by their long confinement and the privations which they had endured while enchained in Liberty dungeon. Before they had started on this journey, some of the captive brethren had desired to have a party of friends to accompany them for protection. But as they never did anything without asking the Prophet, they consulted him upon this point. He responded:

> In the name of the Lord, if we put our trust in Him alone we shall be saved, and no harm shall befall us, and we shall be better treated than ever before since we have been prisoners.

Although this surprised the brethren, it satisfied them. But when they arrived at the place where the court was to be held at Gallatin, they began to think the Prophet had been mistaken for

once, for the rabble rushed out upon them shrieking, "Kill them;
_ _ _ _ _ _ _ them, kill them!" There was apparently no chance for
escape except to fight, and they were unarmed. At this instant the
Prophet rose to his feet and said:

> We are in your hands; if we are guilty, we do not refuse
> to be punished by the law.

Some of the bitterest mobocrats hearing these words and
being impressed by the power with which they were uttered,
warned the bloodthirsty rabble back and quieted the storm.
During the time of their stay in Gallatin, the Prophet's promise
was fulfilled; for they enjoyed all the comforts and some of the
luxuries of life, tendered them by men who sympathized with their
long-suffering and patient endurance. The day after their arrival
at Gallatin, an examination of their case commenced before a
drunken jury. Austin A. King, who acted here as the presiding
judge, was as drunk as the jurymen. The same perjured testimony
was invoked at this time as on previous occasions. Everything
which was prejudicial to the prisoners, even when it was a patent
falsehood, and even when, if true, it could have had no relevancy
to the case, was eagerly seized and applauded. Stephen Markham
desired to testify to some facts which were favorable to the
defendants. He had reached Gallatin on the afternoon of the
9th, having hastened from Far West, swimming several streams
by the way, to bring money and comfort to the Prophet and his
companions. At his request his testimony was received. It did
not suit the mobocratic guards, and they attempted to kill him.
The notorious Colonel William P. Peniston was one of their
number. Judge King and all the members of the grand jury saw the
attack upon Markham, and the threats against his life, but they
took no cognizance of these outrages.

On the 11th of April, 1839, the grand jury brought in a bill
against Joseph Smith, Hyrum Smith, Alexander McRae, Caleb
Baldwin and Lyman Wight for "murder, treason, burglary, arson,
larceny, theft and stealing." All of these counts were embodied in
one indictment, and not one of them was sustained by any specific

statement of circumstances. The language of the bill proves that the grand jury, like General Clark, had failed to find a definite charge which they could substantiate, and so included everything which they could think of. That night Elder Markham stayed with the brethren, and while he slept a vision came to Joseph, showing him that his beloved Brother Markham was in peril of his life, at the same time showing him that his own deliverance, and that of his captive companions, was nigh. The Prophet aroused Stephen and told him to hasten away from Gallatin, because if he waited until broad day—according to his expectation for the purpose of meeting the lawyers—he would be waylaid by a mob which intended to assassinate him. Stephen knew that the warning was from the Lord, and he fled, thereby baffling the mobocrats who, as shown to Joseph in the vision, had really made their plot to kill Stephen. After he was gone, an armed party pursued him a long distance on the road to Far West; but they were unable to overtake him.

Elder Alexander McRae, who was a prisoner with Joseph at this time, says that it was the Prophet's characteristic always to defend his companions no matter how unpopular it might be to speak in their favor. He was much more solicitous for them than for himself. And as an illustration Brother McRae says that while they were at Gallatin, Peniston began to insult one of the captive brethren. Joseph darted a glance of lightning upon the wretch and said in tones of thunder: "Your heart is as black as your whiskers."

Peniston threw his hand over his beard, which was as black as a crow, and rushed from the room, quaking in every limb.

Elder Markham had left with the brethren a recent statute which enabled them to secure a change of venue upon their own affidavit; and after the mock examination in Gallatin the Prophet and his companions procured a change of venue to Boone County, for which place they departed on the 15th day of April, 1839, under charge of a strong guard. On the evening of the 16th, while pursuing their journey, all of the guards became intoxicated. It was a favorable moment for an escape, and the brethren seized the opportunity. The Prophet's reasons for consenting to this escape were stated by him at the time in the following language:

> Knowing the only object of our enemies was our destruction, . . . we thought that [escape] was necessary for us, inasmuch as we love our lives, and did not wish to die by the hands of murderers and assassins; and inasmuch as we love our families and friends. (Joseph Smith, *History of the Church*, III, p. 320.)

By this act the brethren took their change of venue from the state of Missouri to the state of Illinois. After indescribable hardships, traveling by night and suffering all manner of privations, they arrived in Quincy, Illinois, and met the congratulations of their friends and the embraces of their families.

Reviewing the awful experience through which he and his fellow captives had passed, Joseph wrote on the day of his arrival at Quincy as follows :

> We were in their hands, as prisoners, about six months; but notwithstanding their determination to destroy us, . . . and although at three different times (as we were informed) we were sentenced to be shot, without the least shadow of law (as we were not military men) and had the time and place appointed for that purpose, yet through the mercy of God, in answer to the prayers of the Saints, we have been preserved and delivered out of their hands, and can again enjoy the society of our friends and brethren, whom we love and to whom we feel united in bonds that are stronger than death, and in a state where we believe the laws are respected, and whose citizens are humane and charitable.

> During the time we were in the hands of our enemies, we must say that although we felt anxiety respecting our families and friends, who were so inhumanly treated and abused, and who had to mourn the loss of their . . . slain, and, after having been robbed of nearly all that

they possessed, be driven from their homes, and forced to wander as strangers in a strange country, in order that they might save themselves and their little ones from the destruction they were threatened with in Missouri, yet as far as we were concerned, we felt perfectly calm, and resigned to the will of our Heavenly Father. We knew our innocency, as well as that of the Saints, and that we had done nothing to deserve such treatment from the hands of our oppressors. Consequently, we could look to that God who has the hearts of all men in His hands, and who has saved us frequently from the gates of death, for deliverance; and notwithstanding that every avenue of escape seemed to be entirely closed, and death stared us in the face, and that our destruction was determined upon, as far as man was concerned, yet from our first entrance into the camp, we felt an assurance that we, with our families, should be delivered. Yes, that still small voice, which had so often whispered consolation to our souls, in the depths of sorrow and distress, bade us be of good cheer, and promised deliverance, which gave us great comfort. And although the heathen raged, and the people imagined vain things, yet the Lord of Hosts, the God of Jacob, was our refuge, and when we cried unto Him in the day of trouble, He delivered us; for which we call upon our souls to bless and praise His holy name. For although we were troubled on every side, yet not distressed; perplexed, but not in despair; persecuted, but not forsaken; cast down, but not destroyed.

CHAPTER 43

Missouri
Atones

The agony of the exodus from Missouri cannot be described. Many of the brethren had been killed; many more were in prison; and all the rest were pursued with vindictive hate and threats of death. But for the spirit of mutual help which prevailed, the half of the stricken Saints must have perished by massacre or starvation in Missouri. A pitiful picture of some of the trials they endured was drawn by Sister Amanda Smith, a survivor of the Haun's Mill massacre. The mob had killed her husband and one son and had dangerously wounded another of her children.

She says:

> They [the mob] told us we must leave the state forthwith or be killed. It was cold weather, and they had our teams and clothes, our men all dead or wounded. I told them they might kill me and my children and welcome. They sent word to us from time to time, saying that if we did not leave the state they would come and kill us. We had little prayer meetings; they said if we did not stop these, they would kill every man, woman and child. We had spelling schools for our little children; they said if we did not stop these they would kill every man, woman and child. We [the women] had to do our own milking, cut our own wood; no man to help us.
>
> I started on the 1st of February for Illinois without money; mobs on the way; drove our own team; slept out of doors. I had five small children; we suffered hunger, fatigue and cold. (Joseph Smith, *History of the Church*, III, p. 325.)

This is one scene by which the whole Missouri tragedy of that day may be judged.

Some time after the Saints had completed their exodus Hyrum Smith epitomized the awful events in the following words:

> Governor Boggs and Generals Clark, Lucas, Wilson and Gilliam, also Austin A. King, have committed treasonable acts against the citizens of Missouri, and did violate the Constitution of the United States and also the constitution and laws of the state of Missouri, and did exile and expel, at the point of the bayonet, some twelve or fourteen thousand inhabitants of the state, and did murder some three or four hundred of men, women and children in cold blood, in the most horrid and cruel manner possible. And the whole of it was caused by religious bigotry and persecution, and because the Mormons dared to worship Almighty God according to the dictates of their own conscience, and agreeably to His divine will, as revealed in the scriptures of eternal truth.

The Prophet himself bore testimony that the conduct of the Saints under their accumulated wrongs and sufferings was most praiseworthy. He had observed them from within his prison walls, and after the order of exile was fully enforced he wrote:

> The courage of the Saints in defending their brethren from the ravages of the mobs, their attachment to the cause of truth, under circumstances most trying and distressing which humanity can possibly endure; their love to each other; . . . their sacrifice in leaving Missouri and assisting the poor widows and orphans and securing them homes in a more hospitable land; all combine to raise them in the estimation of all good and virtuous men, and has secured them the favor and approbation of Jehovah, and a name as imperishable as eternity. And their virtuous deeds and heroic actions, while in defense of truth and their brethren, will be fresh and

blooming when the names of their oppressors shall be either entirely forgotten, or only remembered for their barbarity and cruelty.

On the 5th day of April, 1839, Captain Bogart, who was now the county judge of Caldwell, with a number of apostates and mobocrats, visited Elder Theodore Turley in Far West and called his attention to the revelation given through Joseph Smith, July 8, 1838, in which the following passage occurs:

> Let them [the twelve] take leave of my saints in the city of Far West, on the 26th day of April next, on the building-spot of my house, saith the Lord. (D&C 118: 5.)

Bogart and his companions said to Elder Turley:

> As a rational man, you must give up the claim that Joseph Smith is a prophet and an inspired man; the Twelve are scattered all over creation; let them come here if they dare: if they do, they will be murdered. As that revelation cannot be fulfilled, you must now give up your faith. This is like all the rest of Joseph Smith's damned prophecies.

Elder Turley rebuked them with such manliness and power of the Spirit that John Whitmer, one of the apostates who was present, hung his head in shame.

But the Lord God Almighty would not permit one jot or tittle of His promise to fail; He had servants with the courage and fidelity to perform His command. At one o'clock in the morning of the 26th day of April, 1839, the day promised in the revelation, seven of the twelve apostles, a majority of the quorum, held a conference on the temple site at Far West; and the master workman laid a cornerstone of the foundation of the Lord's house. After the inspiring services were ended, the twelve took leave of the congregation of the Saints, as had been promised.

It was at this conference that Wilford Woodruff and George A. Smith were ordained to the apostleship. Brigham Young presided over the meeting, and John Taylor was its clerk.

President Brigham Young, in speaking of this matter in his history, details the following incident:

> As the Saints were passing away from the meeting, Brother Turley said to Page and Woodruff, "Stop a bit, while I bid Isaac Russell good-bye"; and knocking at the door called Brother Russell.
>
> His wife answered, "Come in, it is Brother Turley."
>
> Russell replied, "It is not; he left here two weeks ago," and appeared quite alarmed; but on finding it was Turley, asked him to sit down; but he replied, "I cannot; I shall lose my company." "Who is your company?" inquired Russell.
>
> "The Twelve."
>
> *"The Twelve!"*
>
> "Yes. Don't you know that this is the twenty-sixth, and the day the Twelve were to take leave of their friends on the foundation of the Lord's House, to go to the islands of the sea? The revelation is now fulfilled, and I am going with them."
>
> Russell was speechless, and Turley bid him farewell.
>
> Thus was this revelation fulfilled, concerning which our enemies said, if all the other revelations of Joseph Smith were fulfilled, that one should not, as it had day and date to it.

After the fulfillment of this prophecy, none of the Saints had any desire to remain longer in the state of Missouri, and the last remnant, except such as were held in chains and dungeons, hastened away to join their brethren in Illinois and to find a new place of gathering. And a few months later, after undergoing thrice the tortures of death, Parley P. Pratt and the other captives had all been released.

The turbulent spirits in Missouri had conquered, overriding law and justice and trampling humanity into the dust. This is not the place for a review in detail of all the sufferings of the Church of

Jesus Christ in that region; but when the chapter shall be written, it will be as tragic as anything in American history.

The edict of exile was made and enforced, and so far as the Saints were concerned, the deed ended there; but not so with the state of Missouri, for the wrong committed remained to plague and wreak its vengeance upon guilty and innocent alike. The demon conjured into power by the murderous and plundering element of that region would not down. When there were no "Mormons" to persecute, the turbulent spirits of the border at times fell upon each other and at other times fell unitedly upon law-abiding, prosperous citizens. Missouri became deeply involved in the Kansas troubles, in which the lawless, mobocratic element took bloody part; and when the Civil War opened, the government of Missouri, from the executive office down, became a chaos. The man who occupied the place disgraced by Lilburn W. Boggs was a secessionist and fled from his capital to lead the state militia at Booneville against the Union troops. The national power triumphed, and the governor and his forces, among which were many of the old mobocrats, were utterly routed. The offices which had once been disgraced by cowards were now declared vacant by an arbitrary decree of a state convention in sympathy with the Republic, one and indivisible. The state was declared out of the Union by the secessionist governor and then became the theater for a fratricidal strife which deluged it with blood.

On the 31st day of August, 1861, General John C. Fremont, then in command of the western department, declared martial law in the state of Missouri and proclaimed free the slaves of all persons who had taken up arms against the United States. It was a wonderful retribution that Missouri, in which the mob had declared as a pretext for their assaults upon the Saints that the latter were abolitionists, should be the first state in which an edict of manumission went forth. It is also a wonderful retribution that the state in which the civil power had once been helpless to protect law-abiding citizens, should, only five months after the breaking out of the war, have its civil power abrogated and all its people placed under martial rule. Some of the statements

332   Life of Joseph Smith the Prophet

in Fremont's proclamation show with startling significance the
character of that evil population which had been rewarded by the
state for expatriating the Latter-day Saints.

The general says:

> Circumstances in my judgment of sufficient urgency,
> render it necessary that the Commanding General of this
> Department should assume the administrative powers
> of the state. Its disorganized condition, *the helplessness
> of its civil authority, the total insecurity of life, and the
> devastation of property by hands of murderers and
> marauders, who infest nearly every county in the state, and
> avail themselves of the public misfortunes and the vicinity
> of a hostile force to gratify private and neighborhood
> vengeance, and who find an enemy wherever they find
> plunder*—finally demand the severest measures to repress
> the daily increasing crimes and outrages, *which are driving
> off the inhabitants and ruining the state.* In this condition,
> the public safety and the success of our arms require
> unity of purpose: without let or hindrance, to the prompt
> administration of affairs.

> In order, therefore, to suppress disorders, to maintain
> as far as now practicable the public peace, and to give
> security and protection to the persons and property of
> loyal citizens, I do hereby extend, and declare established,
> martial law throughout the state of Missouri. The lines
> of the army of occupation in this state are for the present
> declared to extend from Leavenworth, by way of the posts
> of Jefferson City, Rolla and Ironton, to Cape Girardeau,
> on the Mississippi River.

> All persons who shall be taken with arms in their
> hands within these lines shall be tried by court martial,
> and if found guilty, will be shot.

Upon the subject of the slaves, in the same proclamation, the
general says:

The property, real and personal, of all persons in the state of Missouri who shall take up arms against the United States, and who shall be directly proven to have taken active part with their enemies in the field, is declared to be confiscated to the public use; *and their slaves*, if any they have, *are hereby declared free men.*

And in enforcement of his proclamation to set the Negroes free, he issued deeds of manumission, of one of which we are able to present a copy:

Deed of manumission.—Whereas, T. L. S., of the city and county of St. Louis, Missouri, has been taking active part with the enemies of the United States in the present insurrectionary movement against the government of the United States, Now, therefore, I, John Charles Fremont, Major-General, commanding the Western Department of the Army of the United States, by authority of law, and the power vested in me, as such Commanding-General, declare Frank Lewis, heretofore "held to service" or labor, by said T. L. S. to be free, and forever discharged from the bonds of servitude; giving him full right and authority to have, use and control his own labor or service as to him may seem proper, without any accountability whatever to said T. L. S., or any one to claim by, through or under him. And this Deed of Manumission shall be respected and treated by all persons and in all courts of justice, as the full and complete evidence of the freedom of said Frank Lewis.

In testimony whereof this act is done at St. Louis, Missouri, this 1st day of September, 1861, as is evidenced by the departmental seal hereto affixed by my order.

(Signed) JOHN C. FREMONT.

Horace Greeley, in his *American Conflict*, speaks of "Missouri, betrayed by Jackson" (the governor). Referring to the spectacle of anarchy and treason exhibited by the seceding states, Greeley reaches the culmination with Missouri and uses the following words:

> *We are now to contemplate more directly the spectacle of a state plunged into secession and civil war, not in obedience to, but in defiance of, the action of her convention and the express will of her people—not, even, by any direct act of her legislature, but by the will of her executive alone.* . . . The state school fund, the money provided to pay the July interest on the heavy state debt, and all other available means, amounting in the aggregate to over three millions of dollars, were appropriated to military uses, and placed at the disposal of [Governor] Jackson, under the pretense of arming the state against any emergency. By another act the governor was invested with despotic power—*even verbal opposition to his assumptions of authority being constituted treason*; while every citizen liable to military duty was declared subject to draft into active service at Jackson's will, and an oath of obedience to the state executive exacted.

To support him in his treasonable exercise of power, among the men chosen by Governor Jackson was John B. Clark, the man whom Boggs had selected as a willing tool and whom Jackson now found pliant to his purpose. Another of the mob officers, Sterling Price, was now made by Jackson major general of the state forces.

Poor Missouri atoned with rivers of blood and tears for her sin against herself in permitting the executive to usurp unlawful authority. The precedent of Boggs' exercise of power was handed down. In the day of the persecution of the Saints, a court had decided that belief in the Bible was treason against the government. The idea had moved with terrible momentum; for here we find in 1861 that, "even verbal opposition to the governor's assumption of authority was constituted treason."

It is true that with any kind of population Missouri must have taken part either for or against the Union; but it is also true that the existence within her boundaries of thousands of lawless wretches who loved plunder and rapine largely increased her sufferings. The entire state was punished for permitting the massacre of the Saints to go unchecked and for encouraging the spirit of plunder by rewarding the mobocrats with money from the state treasury. Men learned to live by murder and rapine. It cost Missouri dearly to get rid of the evil, but happily for her much of the bad element was eliminated. Many of the old mobocrats suffered all the tortures which they had inflicted.

But Missouri largely purged herself of the vile element, and after the strife was ended better men and better sentiments came into the ascendency. Some of the men who had been averse to mobocratic violence against the Latter-day Saints believed that retribution would come. They lived to see the day of atonement and to participate in a local reconstruction and a restoration of better things.

The constituency of the mob is thus described by the Prophet in a letter dated at Commerce, Illinois, May 17, 1839:

> We have not at any time thought there was any political party, as such, chargeable with the Missouri barbarities, neither any religious society as such. They were committed by a mob composed of all parties, regardless of all difference of opinion either political or religious. (Joseph Smith, *History of the Church*, III, 355.)

And at a later day in repeating this view, he said:

> We consider that in making these remarks, we express the sentiments of the Church in general as well as our own individually, and also when we say in conclusion, that we feel the fullest confidence, that when the subject of our wrongs has been fully investigated by the authorities of the United States, we shall receive the most perfect justice at their hands; whilst our unfeeling oppressors shall be brought to condign punishment, with the approbation of a free and enlightened people, without respect to sect or party.

CHAPTER 44

Beautiful
Nauvoo

It was a sudden shifting of scenes from Missouri to Illinois in that sad springtime of 1839.

An examination had been made of lands in Iowa, and tracts were eventually secured there; but the beauty of the site of Commerce and the hospitality evinced by the people of Illinois were great attractions and decided the Prophet upon making the location at that place. It was on the 1st day of May that Joseph made the first purchase of lands in that locality. The town consisted of only six houses; the land was covered with trees and brush; and the soil was so wet that teams mired in the streets. The climate was very unhealthful; but the Prophet knew that the blessing of God would make it a fit habitation for His Saints.

It was a magnificent site, overlooking the Mississippi, which swept around it in a half circle, giving the place three fronts upon the noble river. Because of the loveliness of the site the name of Commerce was changed to Nauvoo which means in Hebrew, the fair or beautiful.

The woes of the Saints while in Missouri had been observed with an eye of pity from Illinois. Such monstrous crime against an unoffending people shocked the patriotism and humanity of all who witnessed it, and the people of Illinois wondered how the Missourians could be so lost to all sense of justice and mercy as to commit these acts of murder and pillage. Under date of May 8, 1839, Governor Thomas Garlin, Senator Richard M. Young, and many other prominent citizens of Illinois, wrote a letter to all whom it might concern, in which they spoke of "the sufferings of this unfortunate people [the Saints], stripped as they have been of their all, and now scattered throughout this part of the state. We say to the charitable and benevolent, you need have no fear, but your contributions in aid of humanity will be properly applied if entrusted to the hands of Mr. [John P.] Greene. He is authorized by his church to act in the premises; and we most cordially bear testimony to his piety and worth as a citizen."

It was on the 10th day of May that Joseph arrived with his family at the Commerce purchase, taking up his abode in a small log cabin on the bank of the river, thankful to get even this poor shelter.

Joseph had been as much a sufferer as any among the Saints. He and his family were in a state of utter destitution, as were his brethren and sisters when the location was made at Nauvoo. His own afflictions and poverty showed him what the Saints were enduring, and he ministered among them with the unselfishness and vigor of his life. The people looked to him for counsel and help from day to day; and he found time, in all the multiplicity of the business thrust upon him, to aid and advise each individual according to his needs. It was almost a work of creation from chaos to gather the scattered people and establish the community in one spot, to feed and clothe and house the destitute and afflicted.

The region surrounding Nauvoo had been too sickly for other settlers, and soon after the Saints reached there they suffered greatly from malaria. Joseph had filled his house and tents with the sick, and through his exertions in their behalf and his other labors he was soon prostrated. But on the morning of the 22nd day of July, 1839, the Spirit of the Lord rested powerfully upon him, and he arose from his own bed and commenced to administer to the sick who were at his place. He commanded them in the name of the Lord Jesus Christ to arise and be made whole; and all who heard him in faith were healed. The events of that day of miracles are thus minutely described in the journal of President Wilford Woodruff, which was written at the time:

> Many lay sick along the bank of the river, and Joseph walked alone up to the lower stone house, occupied by

Sidney Rigdon, and he healed all the sick that lay in his
path. Among the number was Henry G. Sherwood, who
was nigh unto death. Joseph stood in the mouth of his
tent and commanded him in the name of Jesus Christ to
arise and come out of his tent, and he obeyed him and
was healed. Brother Benjamin Brown and his family also
lay sick, the former appearing to be in a dying condition.
Joseph healed them in the name of the Lord. After healing
all that lay sick upon the bank of the river as far as the
stone house, he called upon Elder Kimball and some
others to accompany him across the river to visit the sick
at Montrose. Many of the Saints were living at the old
military barracks. Among the number were several of the
Twelve. On his arrival, the first house he visited was that
occupied by Elder Brigham Young, the President of the
Quorum of the Twelve, who lay sick. Joseph healed him,
then he arose and accompanied the Prophet on his visit to
others who were in the same condition. They visited Elder
W. Woodruff, also Elders Orson Pratt and John Taylor, all
of whom were living in Montrose. They also accompanied
him. The next place they visited was the home of Elijah
Fordham, who was supposed to be about breathing his
last. When the company entered the room, the Prophet
of God walked up to the dying man, and took hold of his
right hand and spoke to him; but Brother Fordham was
unable to speak, his eyes were set in his head like glass,
and he seemed entirely unconscious of all around him.
Joseph held his hand and looked into his eyes in silence for
a length of time. A change in the countenance of Brother
Fordham was soon perceptible to all present. His sight
returned, and upon Joseph asking him if he knew him, he,
in a slow whisper, answered, "Yes." Joseph asked him if he
had faith to be healed. He answered, "I fear it is too late;
if you had come sooner I think I could have been healed."
The Prophet said, "Do you not believe in Jesus Christ?"
He answered in a feeble voice, "I do." Joseph then stood

erect, still holding his hand in silence several moments, then he spoke in a very loud voice, saying, "Brother Fordham, I command you in the name of Jesus Christ to arise from this bed and be made whole." His voice was like the voice of God, and not of man. It seemed as though the house shook to its very foundation. Brother Fordham arose from his bed and was immediately made whole. His feet were bound in poultices, which he kicked off, then putting on his clothes he ate a bowl of bread and milk and followed the Prophet into the street. The company next visited Brother Joseph Bates Noble, who lay very sick. He also was healed by the Prophet. By this time the wicked became alarmed, and followed the company into Brother Noble's house. After Brother Noble was healed, all kneeled down to pray. Brother Fordham was mouth, and, while praying, he fell to the floor. The Prophet arose, and looking round, he saw quite a number of unbelievers in the house, whom he ordered out. When the room was cleared of them, Brother Fordham came to and finished his prayer.

After healing the sick in Montrose, all the company followed Joseph to the bank of the river, where he was going to take the boat to return home. While waiting for the boat, a man from the west, who had seen that the sick and dying were healed, asked Joseph if he would not go to his house and heal two of his children, who were very sick. They were twins and were three months old. Joseph told the man he could not go; but he would send some one to heal them. He told Elder Woodruff to go with the man and heal his children. At the same time he took from his pocket a silk bandanna handkerchief, and gave it to Brother Woodruff, telling him to wipe the faces of the children with it and they should be healed; and remarked at the same time: "As long as you keep that handkerchief it shall remain a league between you and me." Elder Woodruff did as he was commanded, and the children were healed, and he keeps the handkerchief to this day.

There were many sick whom Joseph could not visit, so he counseled the twelve to go and visit and heal them, and many were healed under their hands. On the day following that upon which the above described events took place, Joseph sent Elders George A. and Don Carlos Smith up the river to heal the sick. They went up as far as Ebenezer Robinson's—one or two miles, and did as they were commanded, and the sick were healed.

With the summer the building of the city was begun; also settlements were established across the river in Iowa.

Joseph bestowed constant attention upon the spiritual as well as the temporal interests of the people. He gave them many important points of doctrine at this time; and he labored as a missionary among both Saints and strangers throughout the regions surrounding. His efforts and those of his brethren, the apostles, in preaching the gospel bore rich fruit. There were many sincere people who were seeking for light and these soon joined the ranks of the believers.

The material welfare of the Saints increased marvelously; the marshy wilderness on the Mississippi banks soon grew to be a solid resting place for their weary feet. The Twelve, on whom the burden of the exodus from Missouri had fallen, were now preparing for their mission to England; but before they went Joseph uttered the warning sound which was to penetrate to the ends of the earth:

The signs of the coming of the Son of Man are already commenced. One pestilence will desolate after another. We shall soon see war and bloodshed. The moon will be turned into blood. I testify of these things, and that the coming of the Son of Man is nigh, even at your doors. If our souls are not looking forth for Him, we shall be among those to call for the rocks to fall upon us.

I see men hunting the lives of their own sons, and brother murdering brother, women killing their own daughters, and daughters seeking the lives of their mothers. I see armies arrayed against armies. I see blood, fire, desolation. Jesus has said that the mother shall be against the daughter, and the daughter against the mother. These things are at our doors. They will follow the Saints of God from city to city.... I know not how soon these things will take place; and after a view of them, shall I cry peace? No! I will lift up my voice and testify of them.

The apostles shared in his zeal. About the 1st of July, 1839, six of them, all who were there at that point—Brigham Young, Heber C. Kimball, John E. Page, Wilford Woodruff, John Taylor and George A. Smith—addressed a communication to the elders of the Church, to all the branches, and to all the Saints scattered abroad wherever they might be. Their epistle was so pleasing to the Prophet that he embodied it in his personal journal, and from it the following sentiments are selected:

Many of you have been driven from your homes, robbed of your possessions, and deprived of the liberty of conscience. You have been stripped of your clothing, plundered of your furniture, robbed of your horses, your cattle, your sheep, your hogs, and refused the protection of law; you have been subject to insult and abuse, from a set of lawless miscreants; you have had to endure cold, nakedness, peril and sword; your wives and your children have been deprived of the comforts of life; you have been subject to bonds, to imprisonment, to banishment, and many to death, "for the testimony of Jesus, and for the word of God." Many of your brethren, with those whose souls are now beneath the altars, are crying for the vengeance of heaven to rest upon the heads of their devoted murderers, and saying, "How long, O Lord, holy and true, dost Thou not judge and avenge our blood on them that dwell on the earth?" But it was said to them, that they should rest yet for a little season, until their fellow servants also, and their brethren that should be killed as they were, should be fulfilled.

Dear brethren, we should remind you of this thing; and although you have had indignities, insults and injuries heaped upon you, till further suffering would seem to be no longer a virtue: we would say, be patient, dear brethren, for as saith the Apostle, "ye have need of patience, that after being tried you may inherit the promise." You have been tried in the furnace of affliction; the time to exercise patience is now come; and we shall reap, brethren, in due time if we faint not. Do not breathe vengeance upon your oppressors, but leave the case in the hands of God: "for vengeance is mine, saith the Lord, and I will repay."

We would say to the widow and the orphan, to the destitute, and to the diseased, who have been made so through persecution, be patient; you are not forgotten; the God of Jacob has His eye upon you; the heavens have been witness to your sufferings, and they are registered on high; angels have gazed upon the scene, and your tears, your groans, your sorrows, and anguish of heart, are had in remembrance before God; they have entered into the sympathies of that bosom who is "touched with the feelings of our infirmities," who was "tempted in all points like unto you"; they have entered into the ears of the Lord of Sabaoth; be patient then, until the words of God be fulfilled, and His designs accomplished; and then shall He pour out His vengeance upon the devoted heads of your murderers; and then shall they know that He is God, and that you are His people. . . .

We wish to stimulate all the brethren to faithfulness; you have been tried; you are now being tried; and those trials, if you are not watchful, you will corrode upon the mind, and produce unpleasant feelings; but recollect that now is the time of trial; soon the victory will be ours: now may be a day of lamentation—then will be a day of rejoicing; now may be a day of sorrow—but by and by we shall see the Lord; our sorrow will be turned into joy, and our joy no man taketh from us. Be honest; be men of truth and integrity; let your word be your bond; be diligent, be prayerful; pray for and with your families; train up your children in the fear of the Lord; cultivate a meek, a quiet spirit; clothe the naked, feed the hungry, help the destitute, be merciful to the widow and orphan, be merciful to your brethren, and to all men; bear with one another's infirmities, considering your own weakness; bring no railing accusation against your brethren. . . .

We are glad, dear brethren, to see that spirit of enterprise and perseverance which is manifested by you in regard to preaching the gospel; and rejoice to know that neither bonds nor imprisonment, banishment nor exile, poverty nor contempt, nor all the combined powers of earth and hell, hinder you from delivering your testimony to the world, and publishing those glad tidings which have been revealed from heaven by the ministering of angels, by the gift of the Holy Ghost, and by the power of God, for the salvation of the world in these last days. And we would say to you, that the hearts of the Twelve are with you, and they with you are determined to fulfill their mission, to clear their garments of the blood of this generation, to introduce the gospel to foreign nations, and to make known to the world these great things God has developed. They are now on the eve of their departure for England, and will start in a few days. They feel to pray for you, and to solicit an interest in your prayers, and in the prayers of the Church, that God may sustain them in their arduous undertaking, grant them success in their mission, deliver them from the powers of darkness, the stratagem of wicked men, and all the combined powers of earth and hell. And if you unitedly seek after unity of purpose and design; if you are men of humility, and of faithfulness, of integrity and perseverance; if you submit yourselves to the teachings of heaven, and are guided by the Spirit of God;

if you at all times seek the glory of God and the salvation of men, and lay your honor prostrate in the dust, if need be, and are willing to fulfill the purposes of God in all things, the power of the priesthood will rest upon you, and you will become mighty in testimony, the widow and the orphan will be made glad, and the poor among men rejoice in the Holy One of Israel.

The bond between the Prophet and his brethren, the apostles, was close and strong. He relied upon them, confided in them, and showed them all the respect which their nobility of soul deserved. In their exercise of authority during his incarceration in Missouri, he gave them cordial support, subsequently having all their acts ratified by the voice of the general conference. When he escaped from captivity and joined them in Illinois, the love with which he greeted them was like that of brother for brothers. Brigham Young, writing of the meeting, says:

It was one of the most joyful scenes of my life to once more strike hands with the Prophet, and behold him and his companions free from the hands of their enemies. Joseph conversed with us like a man who had just escaped from a thousand oppressions, and was now free in the midst of his children.

Joseph met with the apostles frequently before their departure, praying for them and blessing them for their work. He also attended their farewell meetings and added his voice to the instructions which they gave to the Saints at Nauvoo before departing to engage in the vast work in the Old World. Elder Parley P. Pratt, now freed from prison, and Elder Orson Pratt were with them. In the months of August and September seven of the Twelve departed on their mission to England.

Elders John Taylor and Wilford Woodruff were the first, leaving on the 8th day of August, 1839. Elder Woodruff arose from the bed to which he had been confined for two weeks in order to start on this journey. Both of these devoted men left their no less devoted families at Montrose in sickness and poverty and distress; and yet all relying upon the Lord for preservation and blessing. Elders Taylor and Woodruff started together without purse or scrip.

Elders Parley P. Pratt and Orson Pratt, making all necessary sacrifices, departed from Nauvoo on the 29th of August.

Elders Brigham Young and Heber C. Kimball started together on the 18th of September, 1839. Brigham was so sick that he was unable to walk a few rods down to the river without assistance. He left his wife ill with a babe only ten days old, and all his other children helpless. Heber was in the same plight. His wife and all her children but one were prostrated. After Brigham and Heber had traveled thirteen miles on their journey, they stopped at the residence of a friend and were so feeble as to be unable to carry into the house their trunks, which contained the very few articles of clothing they were able to take with them. In less than a month after their departure, President Brigham Young's father, John Young, died at Quincy, Adams County, Illinois; so when Brigham bade his father farewell to go on this mission, the parting was for the remainder of their earthly lives. John Young was a noble man: he had been a soldier in the Revolution. At his death the Prophet said of him:

> He was a firm believer in the everlasting gospel of Jesus Christ, and fell asleep under the influence of that faith which buoyed up his soul, in the pangs of death, to glorious hope of immortality; fully testifying to all that the religion he enjoyed in life was able to support him in death. He was driven from Missouri with the Saints; . . . he died a martyr to the religion of Jesus; for his death was caused by his sufferings in that cruel persecution.

On the 21st of September, 1839, Elder George A. Smith departed for England. He left his father, mother, sister and brother sick in a log stable, all unable to help themselves or each other. He, himself, was so emaciated that after he was a little way on his journey, he met some men who cried out: "Somebody has been robbing a graveyard of a skeleton."

Three other men started with the apostles: Hiram Clark in company with Parley and Orson, and Theodore Turley and Reuben Hedlock in company with George A. Smith.

This was the sublime missionary movement of the apostles. How like the grain of mustard seed! Leaving the people of God in sickness and in poverty, they themselves being on the verge of the grave, these disciples of Jesus went forth to proclaim the gospel of redemption. If their faith had not been such as not to be shaken, the world never more would have heard of their endeavor. But it was firm and steadfast, and God rewarded it; and the little mustard seed quickened and grew and became a mighty tree. The Prophet said of them:

> Perhaps no men ever undertook such an important mission under such peculiarly distressing, forbidding and unpropitious circumstances. Most of them . . . were worn down with sickness and disease or were taken sick on the road. Several of their families were also afflicted and needed their aid and support. But knowing that they had been called by the God of heaven to preach the gospel to other nations, they conferred not with flesh and blood, but obedient to the heavenly mandate, without purse or scrip, commenced a journey of five thousand miles entirely dependent on the providence of that God who had called them to such a holy calling.

The Twelve faltered not an instant in their appointed labor, and while they spread abroad the tidings of salvation, the Prophet in Nauvoo was directing the gathering Saints that they might build a city whose loveliness and greatness should attract the eye of every beholder.

On the 5th day of October, 1839, a general conference of the Church of Jesus Christ of Latter-day Saints was convened at Nauvoo, at which it was decided to establish there a stake of Zion, and to organize a branch of the Church on the opposite side of the river in Iowa Territory, and officers were appointed to preside and officiate in the stake and over the branch.

At this same conference it was resolved that Joseph Smith, accompanied by Elias Higbee and Sidney Rigdon, should proceed to Washington to lay before the President and Congress of the nation the wrongs which the Saints had endured.

CHAPTER 45

Your Cause
Is Just

The Saints had suffered innocently in Missouri; they had appealed in vain for redress; they were impoverished through the robberies which had been perpetrated upon them; and their old men, delicate women, and little children, even after the gathering to Nauvoo, were dying of privations.

These were material reasons for an application to the national government for succor; and besides these, the Prophet knew that the Lord required this appeal to be made that—upon the answer thereto—the nation's responsibility for the barbarities might be judged.

On Tuesday, the 29th day of October, 1839, Joseph and his companions departed from Nauvoo. At Columbus, Ohio, Joseph was obliged to leave Sidney Rigdon in the care of attendants, as Sidney's frail health made travel slow, and the Prophet's business required expedition; so Joseph went on with Judge Elias Higbee.

Joseph and Judge Higbee traveled in the coach; and on the way while they were passing through the mountains the driver of the stage stopped at a public house to get some liquor. While he was gone the horses took fright and ran down a steep hill, at full speed. The coach was crowded with passengers, some of whom were members of Congress, with two or three ladies. There was very much excitement in the vehicle. Joseph did all he could do to calm his fellow passengers and was able to reassure most of them. But he had to hold one woman to keep her from throwing her infant out of the stage window. As soon as he got the people in the coach under control, he opened the door; and securing his hold on the side, he climbed up into the driver's seat, a feat requiring physical strength, as well as nerve and a cool head, for the stage was pitching and rolling like a boat in a storm. He instantly seized the lines and stopped the maddened steeds. They had run about three miles; but the coach, horses and passengers all escaped without injury—thanks to Joseph's presence of mind and courage. The passengers praised him extravagantly; they thought his conduct most heroic; and the members of Congress even went so far as to suggest that the incident should be mentioned in that body, as such a deed of daring deserved a public recognition. But upon inquiring of Joseph what his name was, in order to mention it as that of the hero who had saved their lives, they found that their deliverer was Joseph Smith, the "Mormon Prophet." The mere mention of the name was sufficient for them; and he heard no more of their praise, gratitude or promises of reward.

Joseph and his companion reached Washington on the 28th day of November, 1839; and secured rooms at the corner of Missouri and Third streets. The Prophet determined that the cause of his people should be vigorously presented. He visited the leading men of the nation, including the President of the United States, Martin Van Buren. He had prepared for presentation to Congress an eloquent memorial in which was plainly stated the crimes of Missouri. Nothing was set down in malice; but the facts were all given in such a straightforward way that they formed apparently an irresistible argument.

The closing paragraphs of this paper must be here presented:

> The above statement will also show, that the Mormons on all occasions submitted to the laws of the land, and yielded to its authority in every extremity, and at every hazard, at the risk of life and property. The above statement will illustrate another truth: that wherever the Mormons made any resistance to the mob, it was in self-defense; and for these acts of self-defense they always had the authority and sanction of the officers of the law for so doing. Yet they, to the number of about fifteen thousand souls, have been driven from their homes in Missouri.

Their property to the amount of two millions of dollars, has been taken from them or destroyed. Some of them have been murdered, beaten, bruised or lamed, and have all been driven forth, wandering over the world without homes, without property.

But the loss of property does not comprise half their sufferings. They were human beings possessed of human feelings and human sympathies. Their agony of soul was the bitterest drop in the cup of their sorrows.

For these wrongs the Mormons ought to have some redress; yet how and where shall they seek and obtain it? Your Constitution guarantees to every citizen, even the humblest, the enjoyment of life, liberty and property. It promises to all, religious freedom, the right to all to worship God beneath their own vine and fig tree, according to the dictates of their conscience. It guarantees to all the citizens of the several states the right to become citizens of any one of the states, and to enjoy all the rights and immunities of the citizens of the state of his adoption. Yet of all these rights have the Mormons been deprived. They have, without a cause, without a trial, been deprived of life, liberty, and property. They have been persecuted for their religious opinions. They have been driven from the state of Missouri, at the point of the bayonet, and prevented from enjoying and exercising the rights of citizens of the state of Missouri. It is the theory of our laws, that for the protection of every legal right, there is provided a legal remedy. What, then, we would respectfully ask, is the remedy of the Mormons? Shall they apply to the legislature of the state of Missouri for redress? They have done so. They have petitioned, and these petitions have been treated with silence and contempt. Shall they apply to the federal courts? They were, at the time of the injury, citizens of the state of Missouri. Shall they apply to the courts of the state of Missouri? Whom shall they sue? The order for their destruction, their extermination, was granted by the Executive of the state of Missouri. Is not this a plea of justification for the loss of individuals, done in pursuance of that order? If not, before whom shall the Mormons institute a trial? Shall they summon a jury of the individuals who composed the mob? An appeal to them were in vain. They dare not go to Missouri to institute a suit; their lives would be in danger.

For ourselves we see no redress, unless it is awarded by the Congress of the United States. And here we make our appeal as *American citizens*, as *Christians*, and as *Men*—believing that the high sense of justice which exists in your honorable bodies, will not allow such oppression to be practiced upon any portion of the citizens of this vast republic with impunity, but that some measures which your wisdom may dictate, may be taken, so that the great body of people who have been thus abused, may have redress for the wrongs which they have suffered. And to your decision they look with confidence, hoping it may be such as shall tend to dry up the tear of the widow and orphan, and again place in situations of peace, those who have been driven from their homes, and had to wade through scenes of sorrow and distress.

And yet the appeal was vain, as far as any practical help was concerned. Some members of Congress showed a great deal of interest in the Prophet, and the cause which he was pleading; but after the most earnest effort, the only result was to receive from Martin Van Buren the famous, almost infamous, reply:

Your cause is just, but I can do nothing for you.

And in the sense of this answer, if not in its words, the Senate and House of Representatives coincided. No arm of national power would be outstretched in behalf of the Saints. As, early in the Missouri trouble, Governor Dunklin—to whom the people appealed—had sent them back to their plunderers for redress and protection; so now the President and Congress of the grandest republic under the sun, told them to apply to Missouri to rectify the wrong. It was as if one who had been robbed and beaten on the public highway, should apply to a magistrate for help and should be sent back to ask the highwayman to restore his purse and pour balm on his wounds.

In one of his interviews with Van Buren the latter coolly told the Prophet: "If I take up for you, I shall lose the votes of Missouri."

This response shocked Joseph in more than a personal sense. He was astounded that the flagrant outrages committed against his people aroused no purpose of redress; but more than this, he felt the insult offered to every American citizen when the chief executive of the nation placed his political aspirations above his sense of right. The Prophet himself was a man whose whole life was unstained by any act of fear. He knew the right and dared all in its accomplishment. Before such a man as he, towering in all his personal majesty and in the grandeur of the cause he represented, how even the President of the United States must have cringed when he confessed to the basest motives which can animate a public man! Joseph could not, upon hearing these words, disguise the contempt which he felt for the occupant of that position to which every American citizen loves to pay honor. The disdain which flashed from his eyes must have made even Martin Van Buren feel small; for it is the universal testimony of enemies and friends alike, that Joseph Smith's righteous scorn was terrible as the lightning flash.

It is a historic picture, this meeting of the two presidents. The subject of their interview was justice for an unpopular people, few in number and poor in earthly influence. The manner in which the negotiation was carried on clearly shows the different natures of the two men.

Van Buren, a truckler to political influence and power, was on this occasion autocratic and insolent. Your sycophant is always, when opportunity offers, a tyrant. Van Buren was no exception to this. The opportunity to display the insolence of office without jeopardizing his own interests was eagerly embraced. He doubtless had received his cut from the traitorous officials who had besmirched the escutcheon of the state of Missouri with their foul crimes against the Constitution, the laws and the principles of justice, or from those who represented them, and deported himself accordingly.

On the other hand, his visitor was but a private citizen in a political sense, and was the religious leader of a mere handful of refugees, exiled from home and all the comforts of this life, and now apparently as helpless in politics as they were weak in numbers and distressed in finances. And yet Joseph stood as an equal, overcoming vain arrogance by natural dignity. Before they finally parted, the advantage was all with the humbler man; he crushed down the insolence of Van Buren by his personal kingliness and his declaration of the principles of truth and justice.

Becoming satisfied that there was little use for him to press further the claims of the Saints, Joseph departed from the nation's capital and returned to Nauvoo, reaching there on the 4th day of March, 1840. While in the east he had preached the gospel at every opportunity, in Washington, Philadelphia and other places, and had met with much success. And this was a partial compensation for the utter failure of his appeal.

After he returned home he wrote:

> I arrived safely at Nauvoo, after a wearisome journey, through alternate snow and mud, having witnessed many vexatious movements in government officers, whose sole object should be the peace and prosperity of the whole people; but I discovered this, that popular clamor and personal aggrandizement are the ruling principles of those in authority; and my heart faints within me when I see by the visions of the Almighty, the end of this nation if she continues to disregard the cries and petitions of her virtuous citizens.

In the Prophet's absence Hyrum had acted as the president at Nauvoo. He had labored assiduously for the temporal as well as the spiritual advancement of the people, to sustain their bodily life and strength through the trying winter and their faith through all the assaults of the adversary. He had also published an account of the Missouri persecutions in the *Times and Seasons*, a semimonthly paper begun at Commerce in November, 1839, by Don Carlos Smith and Ebenezer Robinson.

CHAPTER 46

Missions
to Europe

They "went forth weeping, bearing precious seed"; but they "have returned with rejoicing bearing their sheaves with them."

This is what the Prophet says of the apostles and the other missionaries who first went out from Nauvoo. The details of the sublime work, which then was resumed with such unparalleled vigor and which resulted in such a marvelous increase to the Church, will soon be published in another work of this series. There is only space in this volume for a recognition of the general movement and its success, as Joseph observed it and as it brought many precious souls to restore the numerical strength and the prosperity of the Saints.

We have seen how the apostles went out from the poverty of Nauvoo and Montrose. No man who reads the history of that mission, undertaken at such a time, can doubt that they and their fellow missionaries were inspired; for no mere zealot, without the absolute consciousness of divine direction and divine protection, would have joined the movement.

We shall now see how these men triumphed over that which to human understanding was impossible. Briefly told:

Departing from Nauvoo ill and penniless, they made their way across the country, scattering the seeds of truth on every hand. And before they had reached the seacoast some of the harvest was ready to gather. Their way was miraculously opened to them in this land, that they might have means to pursue their voyage to another. Elders Taylor and Woodruff reached England on the 11th of January, 1840, in company with Elder Theodore Turley. Elders Young, Kimball, Parley P. and Orson Pratt, and George A. Smith, accompanied by Elder Reuben Hedlock, landed at Liverpool on the 6th day of April, 1840, just ten years from the day of the Church's organization. The brethren found there Elder Willard Richards and ordained him to the apostleship in obedience to the revelation. They scattered among the honest in heart, and each of them achieved a quick and lasting victory for the faith. In the name of Jesus Christ they went forth healing the sick, restoring the lame and opening the eyes of the blind. In all their labors they gave evidence of such personal humility, bearing such a strong testimony to the truth of the gospel that the honest in heart flocked by hundreds to the standard which they reared.

Every one among those brethren performed some special labor or occupied some special field. Elder Woodruff made the proclamation of the truth in Staffordshire and afterwards in Herefordshire, which yielded a wonderful harvest of fruit. Elder Taylor organized a large branch of the Church in Liverpool and established the gospel in Ireland and the Isle of Man. Elder Heber C. Kimball, who had been so successful on his previous mission in proclaiming the gospel in Lancashire, opened the work in London; in this labor he was accompanied by Elders Wilford Woodruff and George A. Smith. In this conference the faithful and talented young elder Lorenzo Snow, now an apostle, soon became president. Elder George A. Smith followed Elder Woodruff into Staffordshire, in which field he continued to labor after Elder Woodruff went to Herefordshire. Elder Smith set apart and directed Elder William Barratt for a mission to South Australia; and about the same time William Donaldson, an English convert, was ordained and blessed to perform a mission in the East Indies. Elder Willard Richards labored principally in Lancashire, though he spent some time with Elder Woodruff in Herefordshire. Elder Orson Pratt carried the work to Scotland. Elder Parley P. Pratt, under the direction of President Brigham Young and the other brethren of the Twelve, began the publication of the *Millennial Star*. President Brigham Young directed the printing of the Book of

Mormon, hymn book and other works, and traveled and preached as opportunity offered, being looked up to and sustained by his brother apostles as their president.

As early as the 6th of June, 1840, a company of Saints sailed from England to make their way to Nauvoo. This party consisted of forty-one people, the first to emigrate from a foreign land to join the cause of Jesus Christ in this last dispensation. Three months later the ship *North America* sailed with two hundred Saints. From this time on the work of immigration has been too vast to be followed in the brief space now at command.

The greatness of the work which the brethren were to perform in England was revealed to Joseph by the Spirit, and he was impressed to extend the missionary movement still further. On the 6th day of April, 1840, Elder Orson Hyde, one of the Twelve Apostles, was directed to take a mission to Jerusalem. He left his home in Commerce on the 15th of the month, and in due time he reached his field and offered a prayer to heaven from the Mount of Olives as an introduction to his work.

The preaching of the gospel in the Old World was a marvelous work and a wonder. From the time of the first mission, Elders Joseph Fielding, Willard Richards and William Clayton, with many other faithful brethren, had kept open the source of the stream by their noble efforts; but when the apostles landed there again in obedience to divine revelation, and put forth their hands, the little stream became an on-rushing river bearing triumph for the Church upon its bosom.

From their labor the work spread into every land and has gathered up its tens of thousands of heroic and self-sacrificing souls.

Such a foundation was laid that when the majority of the apostles were called home, the work continued, and it has continued up to the present time.

Joseph's appreciation of their labor is evinced in a letter he addressed to them in October, 1840. He says:

Beloved Brethren:

May grace, mercy and peace rest upon you from God the Father and the Lord Jesus Christ. . . .

Be assured, beloved brethren, that I am no disinterested observer of the things which are transpiring on the face of the whole earth; and amidst the general movements which are in progress, none is of more importance than the glorious work in which you are now engaged; consequently I feel some anxiety on your account, that you may, by your virtue, faith, diligence and charity, commend yourselves to one another, to the Church of Christ, and to your Father who is in heaven; by whose grace you have been called to so holy a calling; and be enabled to perform the great and responsible duties which rest upon you. And I can assure you, from the information I have received, I feel satisfied that you have not been remiss in your duty; but that your diligence and faithfulness have been such as must secure you the smiles of that God whose servants you are, and also the goodwill of the Saints throughout the world. The spread of the gospel throughout England is certainly pleasing. . . .

It is likewise very satisfactory to my mind that there has been such a good understanding between you, and that the Saints have so cheerfully hearkened to counsel, and vied with each other in the labor of love, and in the promotion of truth and righteousness. This is as it should be in the Church of Jesus Christ: unity is strength. "How pleasing it is for brethren to dwell together in unity." Let the Saints of the Most High ever cultivate this principle, and the most glorious blessings must result, not only to them individually, but to the whole Church—the order of the kingdom will be maintained, its officers respected, and its requirements readily and cheerfully obeyed.

Love is one of the chief characteristics of Deity, and ought to be manifested by those who aspire to be the sons of God; A man filled with the love of God is not content with blessing his family alone, but ranges through the whole world, anxious to bless the whole human race. This has been your feeling, and caused you to forego the pleasures of home, that you might be a blessing to others, who are candidates for immortality, but strangers to truth; and for so doing, I pray that heaven's choicest blessings may rest upon you. . . .

Let the Saints remember that great things depend on their individual exertion, and that they are called to be coworkers with the Holy Spirit in accomplishing the great work of the last days; and in consideration of the extent, the blessings and glories of the same, let every selfish feeling be not only buried, but annihilated, and let love to God and man predominate, and reign triumphant in every mind, that their hearts may become like unto Enoch's of old, and comprehend all things, present, past and future, and come behind in no gift, waiting for the coming of the Lord Jesus Christ.

The work in which we are unitedly engaged is one of no ordinary kind. The enemies we have to contend against are subtle and well skilled in maneuvering; it behooves us to be on the alert to concentrate our energies, and that the best feelings should exist in our midst; and then, by the help of the Almighty, we shall go on from victory to victory, and from conquest to conquest; our evil passions will be subdued, our prejudices depart; we shall find no room in our bosoms for hatred, vice will hide its deformed head, and we shall stand approved in the sight of heaven, and be acknowledged the sons of God.

Let us realize that we are not to live to ourselves, but to God; by so doing the greatest blessings will rest upon us, both in time and in eternity.

And to the Saints scattered abroad the Prophet wrote:

Beloved Brethren:

We address a few lines to the Church of Jesus Christ, who have obeyed from the heart that form of doctrine which has been delivered to them by the servants of the Lord, and who are desirous to go forward in the ways of truth and righteousness, and by obedience to the heavenly command, escape the things which are coming on the earth, and secure to themselves an inheritance among the sanctified in the world to come. . . .

The work of the Lord in these last days is one of vast magnitude and almost beyond the comprehension of mortals. Its glories are past description, and its grandeur unsurpassable. It is the theme which has animated the bosom of prophets and righteous men from the creation of this world down through every succeeding generation to the present time; and it is truly the dispensation of the fullness of times, when all things which are in Christ Jesus, whether in heaven or on the earth, shall be gathered together in Him, and when all things shall be restored, as spoken of by all the holy prophets since the world began; for in it will take place the fulfillment of the promises made to the fathers, while the displays of the Most High will be great, glorious and sublime.

The purposes of our God are great. His love unfathomable, His wisdom infinite, and His power unlimited; therefore the Saints have cause to rejoice and be glad, knowing that this God is our God forever and ever, and He will be our Guide until death. Having confidence in the power, wisdom and love of God, the Saints have been enabled to go forward through the most adverse circumstances, and frequently when, to all human appearance, nothing but death presented itself, and destruction inevitable, has the power of God been manifest, His glory revealed and deliverance effected; and the Saints, like the children of Israel, who came out of the land of Egypt and through the Red Sea, have sung an anthem of praise to His holy name. This has not only been the case in former days, but in our days, and within a few months have we seen this fully verified.

Having, through the kindness of our God been delivered from destruction, and secured a location upon which we have again commenced operations for the good of His people, we feel disposed to go forward and suit our energies for the up-building of the kingdom and establishing the Priesthoods in their fullness and glory. The work which has to be accomplished in the last days is one of vast importance and will call into action the energy, skill, talent, and ability of the Saints, so that it may roll forth with that glory and majesty described by the prophets, and will consequently require the concentration of the Saints, to accomplish works of such magnitude and grandeur.

The work of the gathering spoken of in the Scriptures will be necessary to bring about the glories of the last dispensation. It is probably unnecessary to press this subject on the Saints, as we believe the spirit of it is manifest, and its necessity obvious to every considerate mind; and everyone zealous for the promotion of truth and righteousness is equally so for the gathering of the Saints.

Dear brethren, feeling desirous to carry out the purposes of God to which we have been called, and to be workers with Him in this last dispensation, we feel the necessity of having the hearty cooperation of the Saints throughout this land and upon the islands of the sea; and it will be necessary for them to hearken to counsel and turn their attention to the Church, the establishment of the Kingdom, and lay aside every selfish principle— everything low and groveling.

During the remaining years of his life, the subject of missionary work was very near to the Prophet's heart. He desired that all men might have the privilege of hearing the truth. The gospel was proclaimed in many lands, including the distant isles of the sea, during his lifetime; and a plan was laid for the most comprehensive and unselfish system of proselyting since the day when Jesus Christ said to His apostles: "Go ye into all the world, and preach the gospel to every creature." (Mark 16:15.)

Colonel Kane
Visits

A general conference was held at Nauvoo on the 6th day of April, 1840, at which Joseph presided and gave much instruction. Frederick G. Williams came before the congregation and humbly asked forgiveness for his former wrongdoing; he expressed a determination to do the will of God, and the Church forgave him and received him into fellowship.

Commerce was officially recognized as Nauvoo by the Post Office Department on the 21st day of April, 1840. It was growing into the dignity of a town. In a year after the first settlement of the Saints there, two hundred and fifty houses had been built. The region was becoming more healthful; and the Saints were achieving prosperity. It is not the least of the miracles connected with this work that the people have so often and so quickly risen from the ashes of their homes.

On the 27th day of May, 1840, the faithful Bishop Edward Partridge, the first Bishop in the Church, died at Nauvoo, aged forty-six years.

Joseph bore this testimony concerning him:

He lost his life in consequence of the Missouri persecutions; and is one of that number whose blood will be required at the hands of his persecutors.

In June of this year, William W. Phelps made humble confession of his wrongdoing and begged the fellowship of the Prophet and the Saints. This event and the return of Frederick G. Williams were most gratifying to Joseph because Elders Williams and Phelps before their fall had occupied a large place in his affections.

Through the season of 1840, many stakes were organized in different parts of the country.

On the 7th day of July, four brethren, James Allred, Noah Rogers, Alanson Brown and Benjamin Boyce, were kidnapped at Nauvoo by a large party of Missourians and carried over the river. Before they were able to escape, they were almost murdered. After much agony they got loose from their chains and returned home. This event showed that the mobocratic spirit was not dead. No excuse existed for the crime; the men kidnapped were not even accused of any offense by their captors. The barbarous deed was the precursor of a larger movement. A meeting was held immediately at Nauvoo to protest against the renewal of such outrages, and to appeal to the executive of the state of Illinois for redress for this injury and protection from further wrong.

On Monday, the 14th day of September, 1840, Joseph Smith, Sr., Patriarch of the Church of Jesus Christ of Latter-day Saints, and the father of the Prophet, died at Nauvoo from the effect of exposure and privation during the Missouri persecutions.

The Prophet says of him:

> He was the first person who received my testimony after I had seen the angel, and exhorted me to be faithful and diligent to the message I had received. He was baptized April 6th, 1830.
>
> In August, 1830, in company with my brother Don Carlos, he took a mission to St. Lawrence County, New York, touching on his route at several of the Canadian ports, where he distributed a few copies of the Book of Mormon, visited his father, brothers and sister, residing in St. Lawrence County, bore testimony to the truth, which resulted eventually in all the family coming into the Church, except his brother Jesse and sister Susan.
>
> He removed with his family to Kirtland in 1831; was ordained Patriarch and President of the High Priesthood,

under the hands of Oliver Cowdery, Sidney Rigdon, Frederick G. Williams and myself, on the 18th of December, 1833; was a member of the first high council, organized on the 17th of February, 1834 (when he confirmed on me and my brother Samuel H., a father's blessing).

In 1836 he traveled in company with his brother John 2,400 miles in Ohio, New York, Pennsylvania, Vermont and New Hampshire, visiting the branches of the Church in those states, and bestowing patriarchal blessings on several hundred persons, preaching the gospel to all who would hear, and baptizing many. They arrived at Kirtland on the 2nd of October, 1836.

During the persecutions in Kirtland in 1837, he was made a prisoner, but fortunately obtained his liberty, and after a very tedious journey in the spring and summer of 1838, he arrived at Far West, Missouri.

After I and my brother Hyrum were thrown into the Missouri jails by the mob, he fled from under the exterminating order of Governor Lilburn W. Boggs, and made his escape in mid-winter to Quincy, Illinois, from whence he removed to Commerce in the spring of 1839.

The exposures he suffered brought on consumption, of which he died on this 14th day of September, 1840, aged sixty-nine years, two months, and two days. He was six feet, two inches high, was very straight, and remarkably well proportioned. His ordinary weight was about two hundred pounds, and he was very strong and active. In his young days he was famed as a wrestler, and, Jacob-like, he never wrestled with but one man whom he could not throw. He was one of the most benevolent of men, opening his house to all who were destitute. While at Quincy, Illinois, he fed hundreds of the poor Saints who were flying from the Missouri persecutions, although he had arrived there penniless himself.

On the 3rd day of October, 1840, a conference was held at Nauvoo at which it was decided to build a house of the Lord in that city and that the Saints each give every tenth day of labor to the erection of the holy edifice. At the conference an address from the Prophet and his counselors was presented to the Church, in which brief reference is made to the changes within the two years then just past. The communication says:

> We feel rejoiced to meet the Saints at another General Conference, and under circumstances as favorable as the present. Since our settlement in Illinois we have for the most part been treated with courtesy and respect, and a feeling of kindness and of sympathy has generally been manifested by all classes of the community, who, with us deprecate the conduct of those men whose dark and blackening deeds are stamped with everlasting infamy and disgrace. The contrast between our past and present situation is great. Two years ago mobs were threatening, plundering, driving and murdering the Saints. Our burning houses enlightened the canopy of heaven. Our women and children, houseless and destitute, had to wander from place to place to seek a shelter from the rage of persecuting foes. Now we enjoy peace, and can worship the God of heaven and earth without molestation, and expect to be able to go forward and accomplish the great and glorious work to which we have been called.
>
> Under these circumstances we feel to congratulate the Saints of the Most High, on the happy and pleasing change in our circumstances, condition and prospects, and which those who shared in the perils and distresses, undoubtedly appreciate; while prayers and thanksgivings daily ascend to that God who looked upon our distresses and delivered us from danger and death, and whose hand is over us for good.

The Prophet saw a grand city of Nauvoo to rise in the near future; and his vision and hope were fulfilled.

Ascending the upper Mississippi in the autumn, when its waters were low, I was compelled to travel by land past the region of the Rapids. . . . My eye wearied to see everywhere sordid, vagabond and idle settlers, and a country marred, without being improved, by their careless hands. I was descending the last hillside upon my journey when a landscape in delightful contrast broke upon my view. Half encircled by a bend of the river, a beautiful city lay glittering in the fresh morning sun; its bright, new dwellings, set in cool green gardens, ranging up around a stately dome-shaped hill, which was covered by a noble marble edifice, whose high tapering spire was radiant with white and gold. The city appeared to cover several miles; and beyond it, in the background, there rolled off a fair country, chequered by the careful lines of fruitful husbandry. The unmistakable marks of industry, enterprise and educated wealth everywhere, made the scene one of singular and most striking beauty.

This is what Colonel, afterwards Major General, Thomas L. Kane thought of Nauvoo when his eyes rested upon it from a distance in 1846, only seven years after the purchase by the Saints of the marshy ground upon which the city stood. It partially shows how well the Prophet and his fellow laborers had been able to fulfill his high hopes of the city's destiny. For the Prophet did have a definite and exalted plan for Nauvoo. It was his purpose, under the direction of the Almighty, to make this a fit abiding place for the Saints of the Most High; not only a place where they might receive spiritual guidance, but a place where the arts and sciences might be taught and where all the benefits of civilization might be enjoyed. The Prophet understood the gospel which he proclaimed—that it comprehended the material betterment of all mankind; and he aspired to establish in Nauvoo such social conditions as would show the efficacy of gospel teachings in the daily life of the community. He wanted to demonstrate in Nauvoo to the gaze of all the world how nearly perfect community life might become in a free republic, when all men were animated by the same motives of pure religion and unselfish association; how much they might be prospered and how easily they might be governed.

On the 16th day of December, 1840, the charter of the city of Nauvoo, with charters of the Nauvoo Legion and the University of the City of Nauvoo, were signed by Governor Thomas Carlin, having previously passed both houses of the legislative assembly of the state of Illinois. Under the terms of these charters, it would be possible for the Prophet to demonstrate his social problem; but he was not permitted to do it without molestation.

It had been held out to the world by shrewd observers that all the charges made in the state of Missouri against the Prophet and his companions were false and would not bear fair judicial scrutiny; because, after the escape of the brethren, they lived openly at Nauvoo and no effort was made to secure them by the officers of the adjoining state. It seemed very clear that the men who had murdered and plundered the Saints did not want to have their acts reviewed, even though the Prophet's liberty was the price of their inaction. But they were taunted by some of their prominent fellow citizens with this fact, and they decided to answer this disagreeable clamor by renewing the persecutions against the Prophet. The old mob element was determined to have vengeance for this logical exposure of its unjust deeds.

On the 15th day of September, 1840, after a silence of a year and a half, Governor Boggs of Missouri made a demand upon Governor Carlin of Illinois for Joseph Smith, Jr., Sidney Rigdon, Lyman Wight, Parley P. Pratt, Caleb Baldwin and Alanson Brown, as fugitives from justice. Governor Carlin complied with the requisition by issuing an order for the apprehension of these men. When the officer went to serve the papers, the brethren were away from home; and, learning of the movement, they determined to evade the process—not that they feared any righteous inquiry into their conduct, but, having once escaped from Missouri murderers, they declined to give themselves up again to be assassinated.

A leading article from the Quincy, Illinois, *Whig* of that period—written by the editor, who was only an acquaintance of the Prophet and not in affiliation with the Church—presents the situation so clearly that it should be preserved for all time to come:

We repeat, Smith and Rigdon should not be given up. The law requiring the governor of our state to deliver up fugitives from justice is a salutary and a wise one, and should not in ordinary circumstances be disregarded; but as there are occasions when it is not only the privilege but the duty of the governor of the state to refuse to surrender the citizens of his state upon the requisition of the executive of another,—and this we consider is the case of Smith and Rigdon.

The law is made to secure the punishment of the guilty, and not to sacrifice the innocent, and the governor whose paramount duty it is to protect the citizens of his state from lawless violence, whenever he knows that to comply with such requisition he could be delivering the citizens into the hands of a mob as a victim to appease the thirst of the infuriate multitude for blood, without trial and against justice: under such circumstances, we repeat, the governor is bound by the highest of all human laws, to refuse to comply with the requisition; and will Governor Carlin pretend to say that the present is not a case of this kind?

The history of the Mormon difficulties in Missouri is of too recent an origin not to be well known to the governor. A few years since, when they had settled in the Far West, and had gathered around them the comforts and conveniences of life, and were beginning to reap the just reward of their industry and enterprise, a mob attempted to drive them from their homes; as peaceable citizens, enjoying all the rights guaranteed to them by a republican Constitution, they had a right, and did call on the governor of Missouri for protection. Did he, in obedience to the oath which he had taken to support the constitution of the state, respond to the call as a governor should? No! and forever will a stain rest upon the name of Lilburn W. Boggs, and the state of Missouri. Mr. Boggs told the Mormons that they must take care of themselves—in fact denying them the protection of the constitution under whose broad folds they had taken shelter. Thus denied the protection of the state, they prepared to defend their homes, wives and children. Did Mr. Boggs, as the controversy proceeded, remain a neutral spectator, as his first intimation had given the Mormons to understand? Oh, no! when the mob was forced to fly for safety—like cowards as they were—then this wise and oath-bound executive, called on the militia of the state, to aid in expelling—or rather, to use one of the expressions of Mr. Boggs—in "exterminating" the Mormons. Which is as much as to say, if the Mormons cannot be driven from their homes, their possessions, and all else that they hold dear, peaceably, why then, kill, murder, burn, destroy, anything so the Mormons are "exterminated" from the state! Most just, humane, wise, and patriotic Governor Boggs!

Many of them were barbarously butchered, and all shamefully unsettled and cruelly driven from their comfortable firesides at an inclement season of the year; those who escaped secret murder, were inhumanly and savagely treated, their females violated, and their property confiscated and plundered, by the barbarous vandals who were persecuting them even unto death! and to such men and to such people, would Governor Carlin deliver up two of our Mormon citizens for a sacrifice! We oppose this barter and trade in blood, upon higher grounds than the mere forms of law upon which the *Argus* justifies the governor. If we believe that Smith and Rigdon had been guilty of criminal acts in Missouri, and could have a fair trial for such acts, under the laws of that state, we should be among the first to advocate the surrender of those gentlemen. It is not the laws of Missouri, of which we complain, it is of the officers who are appointed to execute and carry out those laws. Their conduct must be forever reprobated—it is a lasting disgrace to the state.

The Mormons have resided in our state since they were driven out of Missouri—behaving as good citizens. Smith and Rigdon in particular, have resided ever since within the limits of our state, undoubtedly with the full knowledge of the authorities of Missouri, but no demand is made till the citizens of Missouri, pursuing them in their new homes in this state, with the same disregard of law that marked their previous conduct, a call is made upon the governor of that state to deliver them over to our authorities to be tried for violating our laws, then the very vigilant governor of Missouri calls for the apprehension of Smith and Rigdon!

It may be that Governors Carlin and Boggs had a private understanding—that a cartel, an exchange of prisoners, may be agreed on between them. If it is so, the governor is trifling with the lives of our citizens—with the lives of those whom he is sworn to protect. Reason, justice and humanity, cry out against the proceeding.

We repeat, that compliance on the part of Governor Carlin, would be to deliver them not to be tried for crime, but to be punished without crime; and that under those circumstances, they had a right to claim protection as citizens of this state.

This was the beginning of a trouble which lasted during the few remaining years of the Prophet's life. While he was upon one hand building up Nauvoo into a beautiful city and spreading abroad the glory of the gospel; upon the other hand, he was himself harassed and driven day and night by the relentless efforts of vindictive enemies incited by bigotry which failed to comprehend the grandeur of his work and the purity of his soul.

From this time on, though his labor was constantly expanding, he himself was being hedged in. And as the events of the remaining four years crowd each other with lightning rapidity, this is the proper time to pause and look at length upon his matured person and character, just as he is about to rise to the zenith of his career and just at the hour when all the forces of the adversary are being united in a movement to drag him down and destroy the cause entrusted to his care.

Manliness
of Joseph

When the Prophet first went to Commerce, he was thirty-three years old; and he was martyred in his thirty-ninth year. Despite the outrages perpetrated upon him and the privations which he had endured, he was, during this period, still a man of great physical beauty and stateliness. He was just six feet in height, standing in his stockings, and was grandly proportioned. In his mature years he weighed about two hundred pounds. His eyes were blue and tender; his hair was brown, plentiful and wavy; he wore no beard, and his complexion was one of transparency so rare as to be remarkable; the exquisite clearness of his skin was never clouded, his face being naturally almost without hair. His carriage was erect and graceful; he moved always with an air of dignity and power which strangers often called kingly. He was full of physical energy and daring. Without any appearance of effort he could perform astonishing feats of strength and agility, and without any apparent thought of fear he met and smiled upon every physical danger. From his boyhood up he was fond of athletics, and in his mature years and at the very zenith of his fame he loved to unbend and wrestle or jump with a friend. The men who could contest with him were very few. When his situation would permit he was as happy as a school boy to join in manly sports.

He showed a sense of gentle humor in his games. On one occasion two sectarian ministers had addressed themselves to him with the boasted purpose of conquering him in argument. His theological strength dumbfounded them; he drove them from one position to another until they were glad to cry for quarter.

Then, as they were about to depart with a crestfallen air, he said to them in a tone of kindness:

> Come, gentlemen, since you withdraw from the contest of logic, let us jump at a mark. I think I can beat you at this.

The preachers hastened away, filled with indignation, and spread all manner of ridiculous reports concerning Joseph Smith because he could condescend at times to run or jump or wrestle like a boy. Probably their defeat in argument had more to do with their indignation than the professed shock to their religious sensitiveness. He was always gentle and good-natured in his sports. Several men are yet living who jumped or tried a fall with the Prophet. They say Joseph did not lose dignity in these sports. His rare physical beauty and grace and his athletic excellence set him far above his fellows and made his condescension seem kingly.

Nearly every one of his commentators, whether friend or foe, speaks of him as a handsome man, of distinguished appearance and possessing a marvelous power of fascination. By his opponents, the inspiration which was over him and upon him— enveloping and permeating him and radiating from his whole being—was attributed to magnetism.

In every association with his fellow beings he was considerate and just. He was always willing to carry his part of the burden and to share in any suffering or deprivation inflicted upon his friends. He was gentle to children and universally won their love. Elder Lyman O. Littlefield, now of Logan, Utah, was a boy thirteen years old with the camp of Zion which went up into Missouri. He narrated an incident of that journey which is characteristic of the Prophet's entire life, for his deeds and words of thoughtfulness were a constantly flowing stream. As we recollect Elder Littlefield's statement, it was this:

> The journey was extremely toilsome for all, and the physical suffering, coupled with the knowledge of the

persecutions endured by our brethren whom we were traveling to succor, caused me to lapse one day into a state of melancholy. As the camp was making ready to depart, I sat tired and brooding by the roadside. The Prophet was the busiest man of the camp; and yet when he saw me, he turned from the great press of other duties to say a word of comfort to a child. Placing his hand upon my head, he said, "Is there no place for you, my boy? If not, we must make one." This circumstance made an impression upon my mind which long lapse of time and cares of riper years have not effaced.

Joseph always sought to help the distressed. A cry of sorrow quickly touched his ear, and its appeal invariably aroused him to helpful action.

When he had become educated and refined as gold in the furnace by his communion with the Holy Spirit, his words were heeded as if they were falling jewels. He never had to beg for listeners; nor had he to ask twice an audience with anyone who had once met him. The great men of the nation, with whom he came in contact, felt the power of his mighty spirit. He was their peer and a philosopher and a statesman. He was more, because he not only knew the past, but he saw the future.

The judgment of a man's friends is always the best judgment, especially when his character and career are such as to excite the jealousy and enmity of the world. But in the case of Joseph the Prophet, while none but his friends could understand the full strength and beauty of that Godlike soul, there were not wanting plenty of nonbelievers who recognize in him a man of amazing power. When a man is dead, he is usually judged by his works, and few characters can bear the judgment of the world pronounced during their lives by their opponents. Joseph Smith was one of the few. In speaking of his opponents, we refer not to the sectarian bigots or to the mobocrats and apostates; but we refer to men of standing and reputation, who were not so foolish as to speak falsely in describing his attributes. We refer to men who recognized in Joseph Smith a social factor and in his work a social movement, even while they denied his inspiration and its divinity.

A writer for the New York *Herald* had visited the Prophet, and in 1842 that paper said:

> Joseph Smith is undoubtedly one of the greatest characters of the age. He indicates as much talent, originality and moral courage as Mahomet, Odin or any of the great spirits that have hitherto produced the revolutions of past ages. In the present infidel, irreligious, ideal, geological, animal-magnetic age of the world, some such singular prophet as Joseph Smith is required to preserve the principle of faith, and to plant some new germs of civilization that may come to maturity in a thousand years. While modern philosophy, which believes in nothing but what you can touch, is overspreading the Atlantic States, Joseph Smith is creating a spiritual system, combined also with morals and industry, that may change the destiny of the race. . . . We certainly want some such prophet to start up, take a big hold of the public mind— and stop the torrent of materialism that is hurrying the world into infidelity, immorality, licentiousness and crime.

The Pittsburg *American* declared that Joseph Smith could not be denied the attributes of greatness. A Cleveland paper responding said that he was without education or genius, and that "he used to live near these 'diggings.'" The Pittsburg *Visitor* then took up the argument, saying:

> *No man was ever a prophet near the edge of his own diggings.* . . . We know that principally from a country which boasts its superior intelligence; where ignorance is supposed to be banished, and every man and woman taught to read and write; he [Joseph Smith] has built up a name, a temple and a city, conquering all opposition, and this both vindictive and powerful, and so entirely unaided

that he can exclaim like the proud and haughty Roman, "Alone I did it!"

If he is advancing the cause of truth, he certainly has claim to our sympathies and respect, as well for its discovery as the bold and determined manner in which he has maintained it. If it is a gross imposture, as you assert, he must be both ingenious and cunning to gloss over its deformities and make them so attractive.

We have nothing to do with his doctrines—we only consider him the most remarkable man among the "diggings."

Probably the most comprehensive view taken of the Prophet by a man not intimate with him was that of Josiah Quincy, who, in company with Hon. Charles Francis Adams, the senior, visited Joseph Smith at Nauvoo on the 15th day of May, 1844, just forty-three days before the Prophet's martyrdom. Among many things descriptive of Joseph, Quincy says:

It is by no means improbable that some future textbook, for the use of generations yet unborn, will contain a question something like this: What historical American of the nineteenth century has exerted the most powerful influence upon the destinies of his countrymen? And it is by no means impossible that the answer to that interrogatory may be thus written: *Joseph Smith, the Mormon Prophet.* And the reply, absurd as it doubtless seems to most men now living, may be an obvious commonplace to their descendants. History deals in surprises and paradoxes quite as startling as this. The man who established a religion in this age of free debate, who was and is today accepted by hundreds of thousands as a direct emissary from the Most High—such a rare human being is not to be disposed of by pelting his memory with unsavory epithets. Fanatic, impostor, charlatan, he may have been; but these hard names furnish no solution to the problem he presents to us. Fanatics and impostors

are living and dying every day, and their memory is
buried with them; but the wonderful influence which
this founder of a religion exerted and still exerts throws
him into relief before us, not as a rogue to be criminated,
but as a phenomenon to be explained. The most vital
questions Americans are asking each other today have
to do with this man and what he has left us. A generation
other than mine must deal with these questions. Burning
questions they are, which must give a prominent place
in the history of the country to that sturdy self-asserter
whom I visited at Nauvoo. Joseph Smith, claiming to be
an inspired teacher, faced adversity such as few men have
been called to meet, enjoyed a brief season of prosperity
such as few men have ever attained, and finally, forty-
three days after I saw him, went cheerfully to a martyr's
death. When he surrendered his person to Governor Ford,
in order to prevent the shedding of blood, the Prophet had
a presentiment of what was before him. "I am going like
a lamb to the slaughter," he is reported to have said; "but
I am as calm as a summer's morning. I have a conscience
void of offense, and shall die innocent." I have no theory
to advance respecting this extraordinary man. I shall
simply give the facts of my intercourse with him. At some
future time they may be found to have some bearing upon
the theories of others who are more competent to make
them. Ten closely written pages of my journal describe my
impressions of Nauvoo, and of its Prophet, mayor, general
and judge. . . .

Preeminent among the stragglers by the door stood
a man of commanding appearance, clad in the costume
of a journeyman carpenter when about his work. He
was a hearty, athletic fellow, with blue eyes standing
prominently out upon his light complexion, a long nose,
and a retreating forehead. He wore striped pantaloons, a
linen jacket which had not lately seen the wash tub, and a
beard of some three days' growth. This was the founder of

the religion which had been preached in every quarter of the earth.

A fine looking man is what the passerby would instinctively have murmured upon meeting this remarkable individual who had fashioned the mould which was to shape the feelings of so many thousands of his fellow mortals. But Smith was more than this, and one could not resist the impression that capacity and resource were natural to his stalwart person. I have already mentioned the resemblance he bore to Elisha R. Potter, of Rhode Island, whom I met in Washington in 1826. The likeness was not such as would be recognized in a picture, but rather one that would be felt in a grave emergency. Of all men that I have met, these two seemed best endowed with that kingly faculty which directs as by intrinsic right, the feeble or confused souls who are looking for guidance. This it is just to say with emphasis; for the reader will find so much that is puerile and even shocking in my report of the Prophet's conversation that he might never suspect the impression of rugged power that was given by the man. . . .

"General Smith," said Dr. Goforth, when we had adjourned to the green in front of the tavern, "I think Mr. Quincy would like to hear you preach." "Then I shall be happy to do so," was the obliging reply; and mounting the broad step which led from the house, the Prophet promptly addressed a sermon to the little group about him. Our numbers were constantly increased from the passers in the street, and a most attentive audience of more than a hundred persons soon hung upon every word of the speaker. The text was Mark 16:15, and the comments, though rambling and disconnected, were delivered with the fluency and fervor of a camp-meeting orator. The discourse was interrupted several times by the Methodist minister before referred to, who thought it incumbent upon him to question the soundness of certain theological positions maintained by the speaker.

One specimen of the sparring which ensued I thought worth setting down. The Prophet is asserting that baptism for the remission of sins is essential for salvation. *Minister:* Stop! What do you say to the case of the penitent thief? *Prophet*: What do you mean by that? *Minister*: You know our Savior said to the thief, "This day shalt thou be with me in Paradise," which shows he could not have been baptized before his admission. *Prophet*: How do you know he wasn't baptized before he became a thief? At this retort the sort of laugh that is provoked by an unexpected hit ran through the audience; but this demonstration of sympathy was rebuked by a severe look from Smith, who went on to say: But that is not the true answer. In the original Greek, as this gentleman [turning to me] will inform you, the word that has been translated paradise means simply a place of departed spirits. To that place the penitent thief was conveyed, and there, doubtless, he received the baptism necessary for his admission to the heavenly kingdom. The other objections of his antagonist were parried with a similar adroitness, and in about fifteen minutes the Prophet concluded a sermon which it was evident that his disciples had heard with the heartiest satisfaction. . . .

In the afternoon we drove to visit the farms upon the prairie which this enterprising people had enclosed and were cultivating with every appearance of success. On returning we stopped in a beautiful grove where there were seats and a platform for speaking. "When the weather permits," said Smith, "we hold our services in this place; but shall cease to do so when the temple is finished." "I suppose none but Mormon preachers are allowed in Nauvoo," said the Methodist minister, who had accompanied our expedition. "On the contrary," replied the Prophet, "I shall be very happy to have you address my people next Sunday, and I will insure you a most attentive congregation." "What! do you mean that I may

say anything I please, and that you will make no reply?"
"You may certainly say anything you please; but I must
reserve the right of adding a word or two, if I judge best.
I promise to speak of you in the most respectful manner."
As we rode back, there was much dispute between the
minister and Smith. "Come," said the latter, suddenly
slapping his antagonist on the knee, to emphasize the
production of a triumphant text, "if you can't argue better
than that, you shall say all you want to say to my people,
and I will promise to hold my tongue, for there's not a
Mormon among them that will need my assistance to
answer you." Some back-thrust was evidently required to
pay for this; and the minister, soon after, having occasion
to allude to some erroneous doctrine which I forgot,
suddenly exclaimed, "Why, I told my congregation the
other Sunday that they might as well believe Joe Smith
as such theology as that." "Did you say Joe Smith in a
sermon?" inquired the person to whom the title had been
applied. "Of course I did. Why not?" The Prophet's reply
was given with a quiet superiority that was overwhelming:
"Considering only the day and the place, it would have
been more respectful to have said Lieutenant General
Joseph Smith." Clearly the worthy minister was no match
for the head of the Mormon Church.

I have quoted enough [from letters of converts] to
show what really good material Smith managed to draw
into his net. Were such fish to be caught with Spaulding's
tedious romance and a puerile fable of undecipherable
gold plates and gigantic spectacles? Not these cheap and
wretched properties, but some mastering force of the man
who handled them, inspired the devoted missionaries who
worked such wonders. The remaining letters [picked up
from Joseph's waste basket by Quincy] both written a year
previous to my visit, came from a certain Chicago attorney,
who seems to have been the personal friend as well as the
legal adviser of the Prophet. With the legal advice come

warnings of plots which enemies are preparing, and
of the probability that a seizure of his person by secret
ambush is contemplated. "They hate you"; writes this
friendly lawyer, "because they have done evil unto you. . . .
My advice to you is, not to sleep in your own house, but
to have some place to sleep strongly guarded by your
own friends, so that you can resist any sudden attempt
that might be made to kidnap you in the night. When the
Missourians come on this side and burn houses, depend
upon it they will not hesitate to make the attempt to
carry you away by force. Let me again caution you to be
every moment upon your guard." The man to whom this
letter was addressed had long been familiar with perils.
For fourteen years he was surrounded by vindictive
enemies, who lost no opportunity to harass him. He was
in danger even when we saw him at the summit of his
prosperity, and he was soon to seal his testimony—or,
if you will, to expiate his imposture—by death at the
hands of dastardly assassins. If these letters go little way
toward interpreting the man, they suggest that any hasty
interpretation of him is inadequate. . . .

I asked him to test his [prophetic] powers by naming
the successful candidate in the approaching presidential
election. "Well, I will prophesy that John Tyler will not be
the next President, for some things are possible and some
things are probable; but Tyler's election is neither the one
nor the other." We then went on to talk of politics. Smith
recognized the curse and iniquity of slavery, though he
opposed the methods of the abolitionists. His plan was
for the nation to pay for the slaves from the sale of the
public lands. "Congress," he said, "should be compelled to
take this course, by petitions from all parts of the country;
but the petitioners must disclaim all alliance with those
who would disturb the rights of property recognized by
the Constitution and foment insurrection." It may be
worth while to remark that Smith's plan was publicly

advocated eleven years later, by one who has mixed so much practical shrewdness with his lofty philosophy. In 1855, when men's minds had been moved to their depths on the question of slavery, Mr. Ralph Waldo Emerson declared that it should be met in accordance "with the interest of the South and with the settled conscience of the North. It is not really a great task, a great fight for this country to accomplish, to buy that property of the planter, as the British nation bought the West Indian slaves." He further says that the "United States will be brought to give every inch of their public lands for a purpose like this." We who can look back upon the terrible cost of the fratricidal war which put an end to slavery, now say that such a solution of the difficulty would have been worthy a Christian statesman. But if the retired scholar was in advance of his time when he advocated this disposition of the public property in 1855, what shall I say of the political and religious leader who had committed himself, in print, as well as in conversation, to the same course in 1844? If the atmosphere of men's opinions was stirred by such a proposition when war clouds were discernible in the sky, was it not a statesmanlike word eleven years earlier, when the heavens looked tranquil and beneficent?

General Smith proceeded to unfold still further his views upon politics. He denounced the Missouri Compromise as an unjustifiable concession for the benefit of slavery. It was Henry Clay's bid for the presidency. Dr. Goforth might have spared himself the trouble of coming to Nauvoo to electioneer for a duellist who would fire at John Randolph, but was not brave enough to protect the Saints in their rights as American citizens. Clay had told his people to go to the wilds of Oregon and set up a government of their own. Oh, yes, the Saints might go into the wilderness and obtain justice of the Indians, which imbecile, time-serving politicians would not give them in a land of freedom and equality. The Prophet then talked of the details of government. He thought that the number of members admitted to the lower house of the National Legislature should be reduced. A crowd only darkened counsel and impeded business. A member to every half million of population would be ample. The powers of the President should be increased. He should have authority to put down rebellion in a state, without waiting for the request of any governor; for it might happen that the governor himself would be the leader of the rebels. It is needless to remark how later events showed the executive weakness that Smith pointed out,—a weakness which cost thousands of valuable lives and millions of treasure; but the man mingled Utopian fallacies with his shrewd suggestions. He talked as from a strong mind utterly unenlightened by the teachings of history. Finally, he told us what he would do, were he President of the United States, and went on to mention that he might one day so hold the balance between parties as to render his election to that office by no means unlikely. . . .

Who can wonder that the chair of the National Executive had its place among the visions of this self-reliant man? He had already traversed the roughest part of the way to that coveted position. Born in the lowest ranks of poverty, without book-learning and with the homeliest of all human names, he had made himself at the age of thirty-nine a power upon earth. Of the multitudinous family of Smith, from Adam down (Adam of the "Wealth of Nations," I mean), none had so won human hearts and shaped human lives as this Joseph. His influence, whether for good or for evil, is potent today, and the end is not yet.

I have endeavored to give the details of my visit to the Mormon Prophet with absolute accuracy. If the reader does not know just what to make of Joseph Smith, I cannot help him out of the difficulty. I myself stand helpless before the puzzle.

A member of Congress wrote to his wife after meeting Joseph in Washington:

> Everything he says is said in a manner to leave an impression that he is sincere. There is no levity, no fanaticism, no want of dignity in his deportment. He is apparently from forty to forty-five years of age, rather above the middle stature, and what the ladies would call a very good-looking man. In his garb there are no peculiarities, his dress being that of a plain, unpretending citizen. He is by profession a farmer, but is evidently well read. . . . Throughout his whole address he displayed strongly a spirit of charity and forbearance.

The Masonic Grand Master, in the state of Illinois, wrote of Joseph to the *Advocate*:

> Having recently had occasion to visit the city of Nauvoo I cannot permit the opportunity to pass without expressing the agreeable disappointment that awaited me there. I had supposed, from what I had previously heard, that I should witness an impoverished, ignorant and bigoted population, completely priest-ridden and tyrannized over by Joseph Smith, the great Prophet of these people.
>
> On the contrary, to my surprise, I saw a people apparently happy, prosperous and intelligent. Every man appeared to be employed in some business or occupation. I saw no idleness, no intemperance, no noise, no riot; all appeared to be contented, with no desire to trouble themselves with anything except their own affairs. With the religion of this people I have nothing to do; if they can be satisfied with the doctrines of their new revelation, they have a right to be so. The Constitution of the country guarantees to them the right of worshiping God according to the dictates of their own conscience, and if they can be

so easily satisfied, why should we, who differ with them, complain? . . .

During my stay of three days I became well acquainted with their principal men, and more particularly with their Prophet. I found them hospitable, polite, well informed and liberal. With Joseph Smith, the hospitality of whose house I kindly received, I was well pleased. Of course, on the subject of religion we widely differed, but he appeared to be quite as willing to permit me to enjoy my right of opinion as I think we all ought to be to let the Mormons enjoy theirs. But instead of the ignorant and tyrannical upstart, judge my surprise at finding him a sensible, intelligent companion and gentlemanly man. In frequent conversations with him he gave me every information that I desired, and appeared to be only pleased at being able to do so. He appears to be much respected by all the people about him, and has their entire confidence. He is a fine-looking man, about thirty-six years of age, and has an interesting family.

An officer of the United States artillery who visited Nauvoo in September, 1842, said:

The Smiths are not without talent, and are said to be as brave as lions. Joseph, the chief, is a noble-looking fellow, a Mahomet every inch of him. . . . The city of Nauvoo contains about ten thousand souls, and is rapidly increasing. It is well laid out, and the municipal affairs appear to be well conducted. The adjoining country is a beautiful prairie. Who will say that the "Mormon" Prophet is not among the great spirits of the age?

In 1842 or 1843 a Methodist preacher by the name of Prior visited Nauvoo and on the Sabbath day attended religious services for the purpose of hearing a sermon by the Prophet. He published the following description of Joseph's appearance and words:

I will not attempt to describe the various feelings of my bosom as I took my seat in a conspicuous place in the congregation, who were waiting in breathless silence for his appearance. While he tarried, I had plenty of time to revolve in my mind the character and common report of that truly singular personage. I fancied that I should behold a countenance sad and sorrowful, yet containing the fiery marks of rage and exasperation. I supposed that I should be enabled to discover in him some of those thoughtful and reserved features, those mystic and sarcastic glances, which I had fancied the ancient sages to possess. I expected to see that fearful, faltering look of conscious shame which, from what I had heard of him, he might be expected to evince. He appeared at last; but how was I disappointed when instead of the heads and horns of the beast and false prophet, I beheld only the appearance of a common man, of tolerably large proportions. I was sadly disappointed, and thought that, although his appearance could not be wrested to indicate anything against him, yet he would manifest all I had heard of him when he began to preach. I sat uneasily, and watched him closely. He commenced preaching, not from the Book of Mormon, however, but from the Bible; the first chapter of the first of Peter was his text. He commenced calmly, and continued dispassionately to pursue his subject, while I sat in breathless silence, waiting to hear that foul aspersion of the other sect, that diabolical disposition of revenge, and to hear rancorous denunciation of every individual but a Mormon; I waited in vain; I listened with surprise; I sat uneasy in my seat, and could hardly persuade myself but that he had been apprised of my presence, and so ordered his discourse on my account, that I might not be able to find fault with it; for instead of a jumbled jargon of half-connected sentences, and a volley of imprecations, and diabolical and malignant denunciations, heaped upon the heads of all who differed from him, and the dreadful twisting and wresting of the Scriptures to suit his own peculiar views, and attempt to weave a web of dark and mystic sophistry around the gospel truths, which I had anticipated, he glided along through a very interesting and elaborate discourse with all the care and happy facility of one who was well aware of his important station and his duty to God and man.

In 1843 an English traveler wrote a letter which appeared in most of the American newspapers concerning a visit to Nauvoo. He first recites many of the awful tales which he had heard concerning the Prophet and the Saints, and describes the fears of his own life which were entertained by his friends should he put himself in the Prophet's power, evidently taking much credit to himself for his "chivalric" and "foolhardy" enterprise. But when he reaches Nauvoo, he finds all his fears and adventurous calculations dispelled; so he sits calmly down to make a dispassionate review of the city and its founder. A portion of his letter is as follows:

The city is of great dimensions, laid out in beautiful order; the streets are wide, and cross each other at right angles, which will add greatly to its order and magnificence when finished. The city rises on a gentle incline from the rolling Mississippi, and as you stand near the temple, you may gaze on the picturesque scenery around; at your side is the temple, the wonder of the world; round about, and beneath, you may behold handsome stores, large mansions, and fine cottages, interspersed with varied scenery; at the foot of the town rolls the noble Mississippi, bearing upon its bosom the numerous seaships which are conveying the Mormons from all parts of the world to their home. I have seen them landed, and I have beheld them welcomed to their homes with the tear of joy and the gladdening smile, to share the embrace of all around. I have heard them exclaim, How happy to live here! how happy to die here! and then how happy to rise here in the resurrection! It is their happiness; then why disturb the Mormons so long as they are happy and peaceable, and are willing to live so with all men? I would say, "Let them live."

The inhabitants seem to be a wonderfully enterprising people. The walls of the temple have been raised considerably this summer; it is calculated, when finished, to be the glory of Illinois. They are endeavoring to establish manufactories in the city. They have enclosed large farms on the prairie ground, on which they have raised corn, wheat, hemp, etc.; and all this they have accomplished within the short space of four years. I do not believe that there is another people in existence who could have made such improvements in the same length of time, under the same circumstances. And here allow me to remark, that there are some here who have lately emigrated to this place, who have built themselves large and convenient houses in the town; others on their farms on the prairie, who, if they had remained at home, might have continued to live in rented houses all their days, and never once have entertained the idea of building one for themselves at their own expense.

Joseph Smith, the Mormon Prophet, is a singular character; he lives at the "Nauvoo Mansion House," which is, I understand, intended to become a home for the stranger and traveler; and I think, from my own personal observation, that it will be deserving of the name. The Prophet is a kind, cheerful, sociable companion. I believe that he has the goodwill of the community at large, and that he is ever ready to stand by and defend them in any extremity; and as I saw the Prophet and his brother Hyrum conversing together one day, I thought I beheld two of the greatest men of the nineteenth century. I have witnessed the Mormons in their assemblies on a Sunday, and I know not where a similar scene could be effected or produced. With respect to the teachings of the Prophet, I must say that there are some things hard to be understood; but he invariably supports himself from our good old Bible. Peace and harmony reign in the city. The drunkard is scarcely ever seen, as in other cities, neither does the awful imprecation or profane oath strike upon your ear; but, while all is storm, and tempest, and confusion abroad respecting the Mormons, all is peace and harmony at home.

In June, 1851, a work appeared entitled "The Mormons" published by a journalist connected with the *Morning Chronicle*, London, England. The author had made some close personal researches into the question, and the volume was the candid expression of his matured views. Being skeptical, and having little sympathy for a religious movement of this character, naturally his conclusions were colored by his prejudices. But he says:

> Joseph Smith was indeed a remarkable man: and, in summing up his character, it is extremely difficult to decide, whether he were indeed the vulgar impostor which it has been the fashion to consider him, or whether he were a sincere fanatic who believed what he taught. But whether an impostor, who, for the purposes of his ambition, concocted the fraud of the *Book of Mormon*, or a fanatic who believed and promulgated a fraud originally concocted by some other person, it must be admitted that he displayed no little zeal and courage; that his tact was great, that his talents for governing men were of no mean order, and that, however glaring his deficiencies in early life may have been, he manifested, as he grew older, an ability both as an orator and a writer, which showed that he possessed strong natural gifts, only requiring cultivation to have raised him to a high reputation among better educated men. There are many incidents in his life which favor the supposition that he was guilty of a deliberate fraud in pretending to have revelations from heaven, and in palming off upon the

world his new Bible: but, at the same time, there is much in his later career which seems to prove that he really believed what he asserted—that he imagined himself to be in reality what he pretended—the chosen medium to convey a new gospel to the world—the inspired of heaven, the dreamer of divine dreams, and the companion of angels. If he were an impostor, deliberately and coolly inventing, and pertinaciously propagating a falsehood, there is this much to be said, that never was an impostor more cruelly punished than he was, from the first moment of his appearance as a prophet to the last. Joseph Smith, in consequence of his pretensions to be a seer and prophet of God, lived a life of continual misery and persecution. He endured every kind of hardship, contumely and suffering. He was derided, assaulted and imprisoned. His life was one long scene of peril and distress, scarcely brightened by the brief beam of comparative repose which he enjoyed in his own city of Nauvoo. In the contempt showered upon his head his whole family shared. Father and mother, and brothers, wife and friends, were alike involved in the ignominy of his pretensions, and the sufferings that resulted. He lived for fourteen years amid vindictive enemies, who never missed an opportunity to vilify, to harass, and to destroy him; and he died at last an untimely and miserable death, involving in his fate a brother to whom he was tenderly attached. *If anything can tend to encourage the supposition that Joseph Smith was a sincere enthusiast* maddened with religious frenzies, as many have been before and will be after him—*and that he had strong and invincible faith in his own high pretensions and divine missions, it is the notability that unless supported by such feelings, he would have renounced the unprofitable and ungrateful task, and sought refuge from persecution and misery in private life and honorable industry.* But whether knave or lunatic, whether a liar or a true man, *it can not be denied that he was one of the most*

extraordinary persons of his time, a man of rude genius,
who accomplished a much greater work than he knew; and
whose name, whatever he may have been whilst living, will
take its place among the notabilities of the world.

A writer in Chamber's *Encyclopedia* speaking of the Prophet
says:

> From his early years he was regarded as a visionary
> and a fanatic; a fact which is of the utmost importance as
> affording a clue to his real character, and an explanation
> of that otherwise unaccountable tenacity of purpose
> and moral heroism displayed in the midst of fiercest
> persecution. A *mere* impostor . . . would have broken down
> under such a tempest of opposition and hate as Smith's
> preaching excited.

The foregoing opinions quoted from the Prophet's contemporaries and observers—his opponents, candid though
they were—are as favorable as could be looked for in a skeptical,
materialistic age. They prove all that can be asserted of the
Prophet by his believers, except the essential feature of his
inspiration. This could not be testified to by any except a believer.
His reviewers, whom we have quoted, judge entirely from external
evidence. They saw the phenomenon presented by his life and
work, and recorded it, excluding entirely from their consideration
of his character and deeds all thought of the superhuman.
And yet such candid judgment of these men is worthy of
preservation; it reinforces to the world the idea expressed of
him by those who accepted the faith which he taught. If some
of these opposing writers could have known him as intimately
as his brethren knew him, the same sincerity which prompted
their favorable testimony concerning his remarkable character
must have compelled them to speak of those finer qualities which
endeared him to the Saints. The Prophet was only a man; but he
was a good man, an inspired man, a better man than he could
have been without the inspiration of his master, Christ. In all his

actions he was fearless as an angel of light. Not in all that has ever been written or said of him by friend or foe is there one word to impugn the magnificent physical bravery and moral courage of Joseph Smith. Withal he was as meek and gentle as a little child. Disciplined by the Spirit of God, which was his constant monitor, he put away from him alike the fear of men and the ambitions of the world. These were things which a remote or casual observer would not be likely to discover.

It cannot be expected that any nonbeliever will testify to the prophetic power of Joseph Smith. To admit it is to believe. And yet this power, too, can be proved by external evidence. Of his predictions not one word has failed. His inspiration may also be proved by eternal evidence. It is now admitted by every student of his life and work that the Book of Mormon came from or through him. This work could not have been originated by any other man in the nineteenth century.

But the best evidence of the divine inspiration which had descended upon him is not external. It is like faith in Christ. It is the whisper of the Spirit. During Joseph Smith's lifetime many thousands of people bore solemn testimony that they knew he was a Prophet of God. Since his death many more thousands have declared the same knowledge. Such proof may be insufficient for the world, but it is enough for the Saints. The world says that men who knew him were deceived by his personal magnetism. But what shall be said of men who believe and yet never saw him? Very few of the Latter-day Saints living today ever met the Prophet. Magnetism has a limited circle and a limited duration. Inspiration is infinite and eternal. The men who never saw Jesus Christ believe on Him because the Holy Spirit inspires belief; the men who never saw Joseph Smith believe in him because the Holy Spirit inspires belief. The Jews were witnesses to the miracles of our Savior. Their great historian Josephus says:

Now there was about this time Jesus, a wise man, if it be lawful to call him a man: *for he was a doer of wonderful works*, a teacher of such men as received the truth with pleasure. He drew over to him both many of the Jews and many of the Gentiles. He was Christ. And when Pilate at the suggestion of the principal men amongst us, condemned him to the cross, those that loved him at the first did not forsake him; for he appeared to them alive again the third day; as the divine prophets had foretold these and ten thousand other wonderful things concerning him. And a tribe of Christians, so named from him, are not extinct at this day.

But Josephus remained a Jew, and very few of his race accepted the Redeemer, despite their knowledge of His works; they had only the external testimony which is insufficient; they hardened their hearts against the internal testimony which is all-convincing. Josephus' testimony of Jesus Christ is no stronger considering the time in which he lived, than is the testimony of some of Joseph Smith's unbelieving commentators, considering the age in which they lived. If Christians were dependent today solely upon the history of Christ's work, their faith might be insecure; but they have that testimony of the Spirit which gives to the sincere seeker after truth a conviction so firm as to be unassailable by all the power of Satan. It is this same Spirit which convinces the Saints of latter days that as truly as Christ lived, God's Only Begotten Son, as truly as He performed a divine mission upon earth, as truly as He died upon Calvary a martyr to redeem a fallen world; just so truly was Joseph Smith ordained and inspired of God to reveal his truths and lead men back out of the darkness of ages, into communion with the heavens. The physical strength and the mental power of an unbelieving world may be arrayed against the followers of this Prophet of latter days, as these same powers were arrayed against the early Christians. But prisons and crosses and swords and bullets cannot undo a fact. They may operate upon the fears of men and they may induce recantation; but they cannot destroy absolute knowledge.

As the years pass away the recognition of Joseph Smith's wonderful career grows more widespread. The day is near, even if it has not already come, when the world of thinking but unbelieving men must accept him as a marvel. They confess the mystery of his power and the unaccountable grandeur of his deeds, even while they dispute all claim to inspiration. They say he "was a doer of wonderful works." They confess their special amaze that an unlearned farmer lad, dwelling in the backwoods in the early part of this century, should have conceived of his own mind, a system of theology and a purpose of church organization, a plan of social redemption, so vast, so extraordinary; and that he should have held to his work with such heroic tenacity, through all the ills of life and unto the final scene of martyrdom. No words of a believer can of themselves convince an unbeliever. There is but one power of demonstration, and that is to seek by humble prayer for the voice of the Holy Spirit. So surely as man prays in faith and meekness, so surely will the answer come. This answer is the testimony of Jesus Christ; it is the testimony to His servant Joseph Smith.

The world will not put this to the test. Only here and there an honest, humble soul, struggling to the light will bow before the eternal throne and make sincere petition for guidance.

By this testimony will the age be judged. We declare unto all to whom these words shall come that Joseph Smith was a Prophet of God. Flesh and blood have not revealed it unto us, but our Father which is in heaven: and this holy revelation is the gift, exclusively, to no man and no class of men. It is free to all who will seek for it in obedience and sincere humility.

CHAPTER 49

Nauvoo
Temple

With the establishment of Nauvoo as a city, Dr. John C. Bennett came into prominent association with the Church. He was a quartermaster general of the state of Illinois, and a man of extensive acquirements and many ambitions. At the time of the Prophet's imprisonment in Missouri, he had offered his services to secure Joseph's release, by force, if necessary, but the tender was not accepted. His expressed sympathy was no doubt sincere. He saw the sufferings of the people and was drawn toward them. He saw the grandeur of the Prophet's character and was attracted by it. When the people moved into Illinois, he made a closer examination of their faith, and accepted it. No doubt he was still sincere at this time; and if he had been willing to heed the Prophet's warning and to be humble and pure, he might have been a blessing to the Church for many years, and might have lived and died a happy man, with a full assurance of eternal salvation.

On Sunday, the 24th day of January, 1841, Hyrum Smith received the office of Patriarch to the Church, to succeed his deceased father; he was also by revelation sustained as a prophet and revelator to the Church. The vacancy in the quorum of the First Presidency, thus occasioned, was filled by the selection of William Law to be second counselor to Joseph.

On the 30th day of January a special conference was held at Nauvoo at which Joseph was elected sole trustee-in-trust for the Church, to hold the office during his life, his successor to be of the First Presidency of the Church. This action was taken in pursuance of the provisions of an act of the Illinois Legislature concerning religious societies.

The charter of the city of Nauvoo was devised by Joseph, as he says "on principles so broad that any honest man might dwell secure under its protective influence without distinction of sect or party." It was comprehensive, and in some respects unusual, but its provisions were purely republican and the end designed by its framer was insured. It was signed by Thomas Carlin, governor, and was certified by Stephen A. Douglas, secretary of state.

On the 1st day of February, 1841, the charter for the city of Nauvoo took effect. On the same day an election was held for mayor and members of the city council. John C. Bennett was elected mayor; with William Marks, Samuel H. Smith, Daniel H. Wells and Newel K. Whitney for aldermen; and Joseph Smith, Hyrum Smith, Sidney Rigdon, Charles C. Rich, John T. Barnett, Wilson Law, Don Carlos Smith, John P. Greene and Vinson Knight for councilors.

The twenty-fourth section of the charter of the city of Nauvoo was as follows:

> The city council may establish and organize an institution of learning within the limits of the city, for the teachings of the arts, sciences and learned professions, to be called the "University of the City of Nauvoo," which institution shall be under the control and management of a Board of Trustees, consisting of a Chancellor, Registrar and twenty-three Regents, which Board shall thereafter be a body corporate and politic, with perpetual successors by the name of the "Chancellor and Regents of the University of the City of Nauvoo," and shall have full power to pass, ordain, establish and execute all such laws and ordinances as they may consider necessary for the welfare and prosperity of said University, its officers and students; provided that the said laws and ordinances shall not be repugnant to the Constitution of the United States, or of this state; and provided, also, that the Trustees shall at all times be appointed by the city council, and shall have all the powers and privileges for the advancement of the

cause of education which appertain to the Trustees of any other college or university of this state.

In pursuance of this provision, at the first meeting of the city council, Joseph Smith presented an ordinance organizing the university and appointed a board of trustees.

The purpose of this institution of learning was to give the Saints and all others who loved learning an opportunity to gain a knowledge of the arts and sciences; for Joseph was ever desirous to bring his brethren and friends into close acquaintance with all that was best in the experience of the world. One of the trustees of the university was Daniel H. Wells, who also had been elected an alderman of the city. He was not then a member of the Church, but he was a young man of such manifest fairness and integrity that the Prophet was glad of his assistance.

The twenty-fifth section of the city charter was as follows:

The city council may organize the inhabitants of said city, subject to military duty, into a body of independent military men, to be called the "Nauvoo Legion," the court-martial of which shall be composed of the commissioned officers of said legion, and constitute the law-making department, with full powers and authority to make, ordain, establish and execute all such laws and ordinances as may be considered necessary for the benefit, government and regulation of said Legion; provided said court-martial shall pass no law or act, repugnant to, or inconsistent with, the Constitution of the United States, or of this state; and provided also that the officers of the Legion shall be commissioned by the governor of the state. The said Legion shall perform the same amount of military duty as is now or may be hereafter required of the regular militia of the state, and shall be at the disposal of the mayor in executing the laws and ordinances of the city corporation, and the laws of the state, and at the disposal of the governor for the public defense, and the execution of the laws of the state or of the United States, and shall be entitled to their proportion of the public arms; and provided also, that said Legion shall be exempt from all other military duty.

In pursuance of the provisions of the charter, the Nauvoo Legion was organized on the 4th day of February, 1841. Subsequently citizens of Hancock County enrolled themselves in the legion, and at the election Joseph Smith was chosen as lieutenant general and John C. Bennett major general, with Wilson Law and Don Carlos Smith as brigadier generals of the two cohorts of the legion.

Speaking of the university and the legion in a letter written at this time, the Prophet describes their purpose in these words:

The "Nauvoo Legion" embraces all our military power, and will enable us to perform our military duty by ourselves, and thus afford us the power and privilege of avoiding one of the most fruitful sources of strife, oppression and collision with the world. It will enable us to show our attachment to the state and nation, as a people, whenever the public service requires our aid, thus proving ourselves obedient to the paramount laws of the land, and ready at all times to sustain and execute them.

The "University of the City of Nauvoo" will enable us to teach our children wisdom, to instruct them in all knowledge and learning, in the arts, sciences and learned professions. We hope to make this institution one of the great lights of the world, and by and through it to diffuse that kind of knowledge which will be of practical utility, and for the public good, and also for private and individual happiness. The Regents of the University will take the general supervision of all matters appertaining to education, from common schools up to the highest branches of a most liberal collegiate course. They will establish a regular system of education, and hand over the pupil from teacher to professor, until the regular gradation is consummated and the education finished.

At a session of the city council held on the 8th day of February, 1841, Joseph reported a bill for an ordinance to prohibit the sale of liquor at retail, which was subsequently passed and put into effect under the title "An ordinance in relation to temperance." The purpose of this measure was to prevent dram drinking, and the event proved that it was wisely and safely drawn, for Nauvoo, under the strict enforcement of this provision, was able to get rid of the low and the depraved. In the discussion of the bill, the Prophet spoke at some length on the use of liquors, showing that they operated as a poison upon the system and demonstrating that even in medicine other and harmless things might take their place.

The part taken by Joseph Smith indicates his willingness to join in any practical labor for the advancement of his fellow men and for the welfare of his country. He consented to act as a member of the city council because he desired to assist in the promotion of a wholesome municipal government. His inspiration was not entirely among the clouds. It prompted him to those practical works without which no community can hope to achieve happiness and prosperity. He became a trustee of the university because no man of his time loved knowledge more than he, and he wished to assist the institution to present the wisdom of past and present times to the rising generation. He consented to act as lieutenant general of the Nauvoo Legion— not that he loved military powers or expected to go to war, but that he recognized the duty of every citizen to be prepared to give his arm to his country's service. His conduct in this respect is a reminder that, notwithstanding his divine appointment, he held himself amenable to every law and every regulation of his country.

On the 1st day of March, Councilor Joseph Smith presented bills for ordinances providing for the freedom of all religious sects and denominations, and the freedom of all peaceable public meetings within the city of Nauvoo. The ordinances were passed in accordance with the provisions of his bills. His purpose was not to secure freedom for the Saints within the municipality; but this was made certain by their numerical preponderance and by the fact that nearly all the officials were of their number. But it was always Joseph's plan to encourage further discussion and consideration of religious matters, and he desired that no insult or injury should be offered by any of the people of Nauvoo to any minister or to any other person who might desire to present views not in accordance with the opinions of the majority. He and his associates had suffered so much at the hands of a bigoted majority in the past that he determined to prevent any such offense against justice and against heaven by the citizens of Nauvoo.

On the 10th day of March, Governor Thomas Carlin issued a commission to Joseph Smith as "lieutenant general, Nauvoo Legion, of the militia of the state of Illinois."

The spiritual welfare of the people was never neglected by him, and during this busy period he was still able to impart religious instruction from time to time as the needs of the people made such instruction necessary. A revelation was received on the 19th day of January, 1841, concerning the building of the Nauvoo Temple and the order and authority of the priesthood; also making proclamation to all the world to give heed to the light and glory of Zion. In March of the same year, the Saints were commanded by revelation to build a city in Iowa, across the river from Nauvoo, to be called Zarahemla.

The building of the Nauvoo House was directed by revelation that it should be an abiding place for the weary traveler who might seek health and safety and the opportunity to contemplate the word of the Lord. The Prophet and his brethren went forward to fulfill this commandment.

The site selected for a temple at Nauvoo was most beautiful for situation. The city of Nauvoo was partly built on a level plain and on a noble hill which rose boldly to a height which gave from its summit a commanding view of the surrounding country. The site of the temple was at the summit and in the foreground of this hill. The Mississippi River swept in a half circle around the lower level of the city, and a number of the north and south terminations of the streets in that part were on the river. The temple could be seen from up and down the river for many miles, and was the most conspicuous building in all that region. The view from its roof and tower was very grand—embracing an extensive view of the river and a wide stretch of forest and improved lands on both the Illinois and Iowa sides of the "Father of Waters."

On the 6th day of April, 1841, the first day of the twelfth year of the existence of the Church of Jesus Christ in this last dispensation, a general conference was convened in the city of Nauvoo. At the same time conferences were being held in England under the direction of Brigham Young and the other apostles, nine of that quorum being in that land and at Philadelphia under the direction of Hyrum Smith.

At Nauvoo the first step was to lay the cornerstone of the temple as directed by revelation from the Lord. On the morning of the 6th, a vast procession was formed, which proceeded to the grounds selected for a site. A hollow square of people was formed around the spot, and the officers of the Nauvoo Legion, with the architect of the building, the speakers and others, were conducted to the stand at the principal cornerstone—the southeast. After an address by Sidney Rigdon, followed by hymns and prayer, the architect, by direction of the Prophet, lowered the southeast cornerstone to its place, and Joseph Smith pronounced the benediction, saying:

> The principal cornerstone, in representation of the First Presidency, is now duly laid in honor of the great God; and may it there remain until the whole fabric is completed; and may the same be accomplished speedily; that the Saints may have a place to worship God, and the Son of Man have where to lay His head.

After an adjournment for one hour, the people again assembled, and the southwest cornerstone was laid by direction of Don Carlos Smith and his counselors, presiding over the High Priesthood. The northeast cornerstone was laid under the direction of the high council; and the northeast cornerstone was put in place under the direction of Bishop Newel K. Whitney and other officers of the Aaronic Priesthood. As each stone was placed in its position a prayer was offered, and blessings were invoked upon it by the priesthood of the quorum officiating.

This occasion was a time of much rejoicing for Joseph and the Saints. After all their sufferings from mobocracy, they had at last reached a place where they could rest for a season and commence the erection of a house of the Lord.

The Lord had a great endowment in store for His Saints. A suitable house was necessary in which to bestow this endowment—a place where the holy ordinances of the gospel could be administered. The foundation stones were now laid, and many and fervent were the prayers which were offered up that the Saints might be permitted to complete it. Joseph was eager to push the work ahead. The people were sick and poor, and it seemed like a very heavy undertaking for so few people as there were there to attempt the erection of such a house. But God had commanded, and they stepped forth cheerfully to obey.

Joseph, in alluding to the proper manner of laying the foundation stones of temples, said:

> If the strict order of the priesthood were carried out in the building of temples, the first stone would be laid at the southeast corner by the First Presidency of the Church. The southwest corner should be laid next. The third or northwest corner next; and the fourth or northeast corner last. The First Presidency should lay the southeast cornerstone and dictate who are the proper persons to lay the other cornerstones. If a temple is built at a distance, and the First Presidency are not present, then the Quorum of the Twelve Apostles are the persons to dictate an order for that temple; and in the absence of the Twelve Apostles, then the Presidency of the Stake will lay the southeast cornerstone, the Melchizedek Priesthood laying the cornerstones on the east side of the temple, and the Lesser Priesthood those on the west side.

At a later time President Young explained concerning the laying of the cornerstones of the Salt Lake temple:

The First Presidency, who are Apostles, started on the southeast corner; then the second Priesthood laid the second stone; we bring them into our ranks at the third stone, which the High Priests and Elders laid; we take them under our wing to the northeast cornerstone which the Twelve and the Seventies laid; and there again joined the Apostleship. It circumscribes every other Priesthood, for it is the Priesthood of Melchizedek, which is after the order of the Son of God.

The conference at Nauvoo continued five days, and the time was a happy one for the Saints. In an address to the people on the second day, the Prophet said:

The Presidency of the Church of Jesus Christ of Latter-day Saints feel great pleasure in assembling with the Saints at another general conference, under circumstances so auspicious and cheering; and with grateful hearts to Almighty God for His providential regard, they cordially unite with the Saints, on this occasion, in ascribing honor, glory and blessing to His holy name.

It is with unfeigned pleasure that they have to make known the steady and rapid increase of the Church in this state, the United States and Europe. The anxiety to become acquainted with the principles of the gospel, on every hand, is intense, and the cry of "Come over and help us" is reaching the Elders on the wings of every wind; while thousands who have heard the Gospel have become obedient thereto, and are rejoicing in its gifts and blessings. Prejudice, with its attendant train of evils, is giving way before the force of truth, whose benign rays are penetrating the nations afar off.

The reports from the Twelve Apostles in Europe are very satisfactory, and state that the work continues to

progress with unparalleled rapidity, and that the harvest
is truly great.

In the eastern states the faithful laborers are
successful, and many are flocking to the standard of truth.
Nor is the south keeping back. Churches have been raised
up in the southern and western states, and a very pressing
invitation has been received from New Orleans for some of
the Elders to visit that city, which has been complied with.
In our own state and immediate neighborhood, many are
avowing their attachment to the principles of our holy
religion and have become obedient to the faith.

Peace and prosperity attend us, and we have favor in
the sight of God and virtuous men. The time was when
we were looked upon as deceivers and that Mormonism
would soon pass away, come to nought and be forgotten.
But the time has gone by when it was looked upon as a
transient matter, or a bubble on the wave, and it is now
taking a deep hold in the hearts and affections of all those
who are noble-minded enough to lay aside the prejudice
of education and investigate the subject with candor and
honesty. The truth, like the sturdy oak, has stood unhurt
amid the contending elements which have beat upon
it with tremendous force. The floods have rolled, wave
after wave, in quick succession, and have not swallowed
it up. "They have lifted up their voice, O Lord, the floods
have lifted up their voice; but the Lord of Hosts is mightier
than the mighty waves of the sea, nor have the flames of
persecution, with all the influence of mobs, been able to
destroy it; but, like Moses' bush, it has stood unconsumed,
and now at this moment presents an important spectacle
both to men and angels. Where can we turn our eyes
to behold such another? We contemplate a people who
have embraced a system of religion, unpopular, and the
adherence to which has brought upon them repeated
persecutions. A people who, for their love to God and
attachment to His cause, have suffered hunger, nakedness,

perils, and almost every privation. A people who, for the sake of their religion, have had to mourn the premature deaths of parents, husbands, wives and children. A people who have preferred death to slavery and hypocrisy, and have honorably maintained their characters and stood firm and immovable in times that have tried men's souls. Stand fast, ye Saints of God, hold on a little longer, and the storm of life will be past, and you will be rewarded by that God whose servants you are, and who will duly appreciate all your toils and afflictions for Christ's sake and the gospel's. Your names will be handed down to posterity as Saints of God and virtuous men.

On the third day of the conference, the Prophet stated to the assembled Saints that the presidents of the different quorums would be presented before them for their acceptance or rejection. He declared the rule of acceptance or rejection to be by a majority in each quorum; and he exhorted them to deliberation, faith and prayer, that they might be strict and impartial in their examinations. Objection was made to Elder John E. Page, one of the twelve apostles, and his case was laid over to be tried before his quorum. Elder Page had been called to accompany Apostle Orson Hyde upon his mission to Jerusalem, but had felt the sacrifice demanded was too great for him, and had delayed until this time.

On this same day Lyman Wight was chosen as an apostle to fill the vacancy occasioned by the death of Elder David W. Patten.

About the 1st of May, 1841, Joseph received a visit at Nauvoo from the Honorable Stephen A. Douglas, of the Supreme Court of the state of Illinois. On this occasion Douglas was accompanied by his political opponent Cyrus Walker, Esq. "The Little Giant" had not yet entered upon the greatness of his career in politics; but the Prophet recognized in him a master spirit among men. Douglas himself was so deeply impressed by the grandeur of the Prophet's character that he sought him out with deference.

On the 24th of May, the Prophet directed a call to all the Saints to gather to the counties of Lee in Iowa and Hancock in Illinois; and directed the discontinuance of all stakes of Zion outside of these two.

Under date of June 1, 1841, the Prophet records that Elder Sidney Rigdon had been ordained a prophet, seer and revelator. This ordination was probably attended to in the month of May.

CHAPTER 50

Prophet
Aids Sheriff

On the 1st day of June, 1841, the Prophet accompanied his brother Hyrum and William Law as far as Quincy, Illinois, on their mission to the east. While at Quincy he called upon Governor Carlin at the latter's residence and was treated with marked respect and kindness. In the lengthy conversation which Joseph had with Carlin, nothing was said concerning the requisition formerly issued by the state of Missouri and endorsed by Carlin for the arrest of the Prophet. This requisition had been returned, not served; all excitement concerning it had died away; and the absurd character of the demand made for Joseph's person was supposed to be understood by Carlin and all the other officials of the state.

After enjoying the hospitality of the governor, Joseph withdrew and had only proceeded a little distance on his homeward journey, when Carlin sent Thomas King, sheriff of Adams County, Thomas Jasper, constable of Quincy, and several others, as a posse, with an officer from Missouri to apprehend the Prophet and deliver him up to the emissaries of Boggs. This large party pursued Joseph and on the 5th day of June overtook and arrested him at Heberline's Hotel, Beer Creek, about twenty-eight miles south of Nauvoo. With the formal act of arrest, the offense charged against the Prophet was made known, that he was "a fugitive from justice"; but as the fact of his persecution in Missouri was well known to the posse, and as the officer from Missouri did not conceal the vindictive hate with which he viewed his prisoner nor smother his threats, many of the party left in disgust and returned to their homes, declaring that they would have nothing to do with such outrageous proceedings. Their action had a salutary effect upon the officers who remained. Joseph was taken back to Quincy and there obtained a writ of *habeas corpus* from Charles A. Warren, master in chancery. Judge Stephen A. Douglas arrived at Quincy that night and appointed a hearing on the writ for Tuesday, the 8th day of June, in Monmouth, Warren County, where the court for the fifth judicial circuit for Illinois would then commence the regular term. On the morning after the arrest, Sheriff King and the Missouri officer, with their aides, went to Nauvoo with their prisoner in charge. In the meantime considerable excitement had prevailed in the city, as news of the Prophet's arrest had been conveyed there, and his brethren well knew that for him to return to Missouri was to return to assassination. A party of his friends, including Hosea Stout, Tarleton Lewis, John S. Higbee, and others, had come by the river to find him at Quincy but had missed him on the way, as he came to Nauvoo by land.

Sheriff King was suffering greatly from ill health; and, after leaving Quincy, was seized with violent illness. At Nauvoo the Prophet took the sheriff to his own house and nursed him like a brother, and continued this assiduous care for his captor during the four days intervening until after the arrival at Monmouth.

On Monday, the 7th day of June, the Prophet departed very early in the morning for the appointed place, which was seventy-five miles distant. He was accompanied by Charles C. Rich, Amasa Lyman, Shadrach Roundy, Reynolds Cahoon, Charles Hopkins, Alfred Randall, Elias Higbee, Morris Phelps, John P. Greene, Henry G. Sherwood, Joseph Younger, Darwin Chase, Ira Miles, Joel S. Miles, Lucien Woodworth, Vinson Knight, Robert B. Thompson, George Miller and others. They traveled all day and until very late, making their camp about midnight in the road.

On Tuesday morning, June 8th, they reached Monmouth, where great excitement prevailed. A multitude of citizens had gathered, filled with curiosity to obtain a sight of the Prophet, whom they expected and hoped to see loaded down with chains. A mob incited by sectarian bigotry attempted to seize his person; but the sheriff, whose health had been partially restored through

Joseph's careful nursing, declared that he would protect his prisoner at all hazards, and after much difficulty the mob was repulsed by the sheriff and the friends of order.

An effort was made to have the hearing on the writ immediately, but the state's attorney objected and secured a postponement until the next morning. On that day the citizens were kept in a state of ferment. The sectarian enemies of the Prophet hoped they saw an opportunity to injure him, and they employed a great array of counsel to assist in overthrowing the writ and remanding the Prophet back to his old and bloodthirsty enemies. Others there were not so vindictive, who besought him to preach to the populace that night. They crowded around the prison and flocked to the window to get a peep at him, but the confinement was too close to permit of his addressing them even through the bars, further than to promise them that Elder Amasa Lyman should give them a sermon on the succeeding evening.

At an early hour on Wednesday, the court at Monmouth was filled with spectators anxious to witness the proceedings. The counsel in behalf of the Prophet were Charles A. Warren, Sidney H. Little, O. H. Browning, James H. Ralston, Cyrus Walker and Archibald Williams. On behalf of the prosecution, there were not only the state's attorneys, but also a large number of prominent lawyers employed by Joseph's opponents, and there were also some volunteer prosecutors who thought to get some fame or notoriety out of this case. Threats of the most awful character were uttered against the Prophet's advocates; and even the conservative element warned them that they might expect no further political favors from that county if they persisted in defending a man so repugnant to the sectarian religious element. They were not to be frightened by any such means, and they pursued their course vigorously. Two points were raised for the Prophet. One was that the writ was void, having once been returned to the executive by the sheriff of Hancock County; and the other was that the whole proceeding on the part of Missouri was illegal and that the indictment upon which the requisition was based had been obtained through fraud, bribery and corruption.

A young lawyer from Missouri was among the volunteers to plead against Joseph. While uttering his tirade in court, he was stricken by such pains that he ceased to talk and rushed from the courthouse. Many of the people who had been amused by his antics shouted after him as they saw his pale face and the contortions of his stomach: "Now we know why they call the people of Missouri *Pukes.*"

O. H. Browning made the principal speech for the Prophet. This Mr. Browning afterward became a member of President Johnson's cabinet as secretary of the interior. He was a man of great courage and possessed vigor and eloquence in speech. After covering the points of law involved, he recited many of the indignities which had been perpetrated upon the Prophet in Missouri and ridiculed the idea of his going back to be tried by his sworn murderers. Mr. Browning had been a witness to much of the distress of the Saints. He stated the circumstances of the exile from Missouri and feelingly and emphatically pointed out the impossibility of Joseph's obtaining justice there. He said that the very men who would be called as witnesses for the defense in the Prophet's case, if it were to be tried in Missouri, were actually forbidden by executive decree under the penalty of death, to enter upon the soil of that bloodstained state. He recounted the cruelties which had been practiced upon the Saints until the streams of Missouri had run with sanguinary hues; and declared that he himself had seen women and children destitute and defenseless, crossing the Mississippi to seek refuge from ruthless mobs. After saying that to send Joseph Smith back to Missouri for trial was but adding insult to injury, he concluded:

> Great God! Have I not seen it? Yes, mine eyes have beheld the blood-stained traces of innocent women and children, in the drear winter, who had traveled hundreds of miles barefoot through frost and snow, to seek a refuge from their savage pursuers. It was a scene of horror,

sufficient to enlist sympathy from an adamantine heart. And shall this unfortunate man, whom their fury has seen proper to select for sacrifice, be driven into such a savage land, and none dare to enlist in the cause of justice? If there was no other voice under heaven ever to be heard in this cause, gladly would I stand alone and proudly spend my latest breath in defense of an oppressed American citizen.

So effective was Browning's address that many of the officers and spectators of the court wept for the woes of the Prophet and his persecuted people.

The case was then adjourned until the next morning. In the meantime, Elder Amasa M. Lyman preached a sermon to which a large congregation listened attentively. His address was marked by such power and spirit that a total revulsion in sentiment took place; and when the court next day decreed the discharge of the prisoner, the populace could no longer be incited by jealous priests into a demonstration against Joseph.

The opinion of Judge Douglas in releasing the Prophet was recorded as follows:

That the writ being once returned to the Executive by the sheriff of Hancock County was dead, and stood in the same relationship as any other writ which might issue from the circuit court; and consequently, the defendant could not be held in custody on that writ. The other point, whether evidence in the case was admissible or not, he would not at that time decide, as it involved great and important considerations relative to the future conduct of the different states. There being no precedent, as far as they have access to authorities, to guide them; but he would endeavor to examine the subject and avail himself of all the authorities which could be obtained on the subject before he would decide that point. But on the other, the defendant must be liberated.

About 2 P.M. on Thursday, June 10th, the Prophet and his company started upon their return to Nauvoo where they arrived at 4 P.M. on the 11th and were greeted by the joyous acclamations of the Saints.

Some of the so-called religious publications made this trial a pretext for all manner of false and senseless utterances against Joseph and the people. Their purpose was very apparent. The ministers who preached for hire and divined for money feared to see their craft in danger; the growth of the Saints was too rapid; the influence of Joseph was too great. It did not matter to these enemies of the work that the Saints were law-abiding and industrious, and that the Prophet exercised no unrighteous authority, but labored in love and charity among his brethren and all people. They were determined to spread their lies abroad that a feeling of hatred might be incited against Joseph and the people of Nauvoo; and they were successful, for prejudice continued to enlarge its circle from that time. All these evil reports were colored by statements of the Missouri officials who, to screen themselves gave out the *ex parte* testimony of mobocrats as being truthful statements of the Missouri persecutions. A few papers had the courage and truth to examine carefully before committing themselves; and were led to protest against the unhallowed warfare waged by the bloodthirsty mob against Joseph and his law-abiding an order-loving brethren in Nauvoo. Among articles of this character was one which appeared in the *Joliet Courier*, written to the editor of that journal by a spectator of the trial at Monmouth, from which the following is an excerpt:

> Before this reaches you, I have no doubt you will have heard of the trial of Joseph Smith, familiarly known as the Mormon Prophet. As some misrepresentations have already gone abroad in relation to Judge Douglas's decision, and the merits of the question decided by the judge, permit me to say, the only question decided, though many were debated, was the validity of the executive writ which had once been sent out, I think in Sept., 1840, and a

return on it that Mr. Smith could not be found. The same writ was issued in June, 1841. There can really be no great difficulty about this matter, under this state of facts.

The judge acquitted himself handsomely, and silenced clamors that had been raised against the defendant.

Since the trial I have been at Nauvoo, on the Mississippi, in Hancock County, Illinois, and have seen the manner in which things are conducted among the Mormons. In the first place, I cannot help noticing the plain hospitality of the Prophet Smith to all strangers visiting the town, aided as he is in making the stranger comfortable by his excellent wife, a woman of superior ability. The people of the town appear to be honest and industrious, engaged in their usual avocations of building up a town and making all things around them comfortable. On Sunday I attended one of their meetings, in front of the temple now building and one of the largest buildings in the state. There could not have been less than 2,500 people present, and as well appearing as any number that could be found in this or any state. Mr. Smith preached in the morning, and one could have readily learned, then, the magic by which he has built up this society, because, as we say in Illinois, "they believe in him," and in his honesty. It has been a matter of astonishment to me, after seeing the Prophet, as he is called, Elder Rigdon and many other gentlemanly men anyone may see at Nauvoo who will visit there, why it is that so many professing Christianity, and so many professing to reverence the sacred principles of our Constitution (which gives free religious toleration to all), have slandered a persecuted this sect of Christians.

In the month of July, 1841, the apostles began to return to Nauvoo from their missions to Europe, and their coming was a great comfort to the Prophet in his hour of affliction. At a special conference which was held at Nauvoo on the 16th of August, 1841, shortly after the return of the twelve, Joseph stated to the people there assembled that the time had come when the apostles must stand in their places next to the First Presidency. They had been faithful and had borne the burden and heat of the day, giving the gospel triumph in the nations of the earth, and it was right that they should now remain at home and perform duty in Zion. At the same conference the Twelve selected a number of elders to go on missions, and Joseph stated to the congregation that it was desirable to build up the cities in Hancock County, Illinois, and Lee County, Iowa.

In addition to the woes wrought by his enemies upon the Prophet, he had cause to mourn in August. His infant child Don Carlos died, bringing great distress upon the household. Also his youngest brother, Don Carlos Smith, departed this life on the seventh day of August, 1841. This was a great blow to the Prophet and the family. Don Carlos was but twenty-five years of age at the time of his death. He was a young man of considerable promise and had been very active and zealous in the work from the commencement. He was one of the first to receive the testimony of Joseph respecting the gospel. The evening after the plates of the Book of Mormon were shown to the eight witnesses, a meeting was held at which all the witnesses bore testimony of the truth of the latter-day dispensation. Don Carlos was present at this meeting, and also bore the same testimony. He was ordained to the priesthood when only fourteen years old, and at that age accompanied his father on a mission to his grandfather and relatives in St. Lawrence County, New York. While on this mission he was the means of convincing a Baptist minister of the truth of the work of God. After this he took several missions, and was very active in the ministry at home, being one of the twenty-four elders who laid the cornerstones of the Kirtland Temple. Before he was quite twenty years old he was ordained president of the high priests' quorum, in which capacity he acted until the time of his death. He and his counselors laid the southwest cornerstone of the temple at Nauvoo. He was a printer, having learned the business in the office of Oliver Cowdery at Kirtland, and when the *Elders' Journal* was published there he took charge of the establishment.

After the Saints removed to Nauvoo, he commenced making preparations for the publishing of the *Times and Seasons*. To get the paper issued at an early date he was under the necessity of cleaning out a cellar, through which a spring was constantly flowing, that being the only place where he could put up the press. He caught cold at this labor, and this, with administering to the sick, impaired his health, which he never fully recovered again. At the time of his death, he was brigadier general of the first cohort of the Nauvoo Legion, and a member of the city council of Nauvoo.

Like Joseph and his other brothers, he was a splendidly formed man physically, being six feet, four inches high, very straight and well made, and strong and active. He was much beloved by all who knew him; for he was wise beyond his years, and he appeared to have a great future before him.

On the 12th day of this month, Nauvoo was visited by a band of Sac and Fox Indians, under Chiefs Keokuk and Kiskukosh and Appenose. The party consisted of about one hundred chiefs and braves with their families, and they had come to Nauvoo to see the Prophet. At the landing they were met by Joseph and Hyrum and escorted to the meeting ground in the grove, where the Prophet proceeded to address them upon their origin and the promises of God concerning them. His remarks were interpreted to them and gave them great delight. Then he advised them to cease killing each other and warring with other tribes and besought them to keep peace with the whites. In reply to this Keokuk said he had a Book of Mormon which the Prophet had given him years before. Said he to Joseph:

> I believe you are a great and good man. I look rough, but I also am a son of the Great Spirit. I have heard your advice; we intend to quit fighting and follow the good advice you have given us.

On the 27th day of August, 1841, Elder Robert Blashel Thompson died at his residence in Nauvoo in the thirtieth year of his age. He had been Joseph's scribe and trusted friend, and the

Prophet mourned him sincerely. On the 13th day of September, 1841, Willard Richards was appointed to be his successor.

On the 13th day of September, 1841, Edward Hunter visited Nauvoo and made the acquaintance of the Prophet. This noble man had journeyed from Chester County in Pennsylvania, in answer to the gospel call; and he brought his substance with him. Being a man of wealth, he proved a blessing to the people and city.

Brigadier General Swazey and the colonel of the militia of Lee County, Iowa, invited Joseph and Hyrum with John C. Bennett, to view a military parade at Montrose on the 14th of September, 1841. They accepted the invitation and were very courteously received by the general and the officers, and every mark of respect was extended to them by the militia. A foolish fellow named D. W. Kilbourn, a merchant, took umbrage at the presence of the Prophet and his party and attempted to raise a riot. During the noon hour, when the militia were resting from their exercises, he gathered a large crowd around his store and read to them the following quotation:

> Citizens of Iowa:—The laws of Iowa do not require you to muster under or be reviewed by Joseph Smith or General Bennett, and should they have the impudence to attempt it, it is hoped that every person having a proper respect for himself will at once leave the ranks.

Neither the Prophet nor his brother was in military costume, being there entirely in the capacity of private citizens, and the ridiculous insult was so apparent that even Kilbourn's friends resented it. After the exercises were over, the Prophet was escorted to the river landing by a large party, which bade him farewell with every manifestation of respect and friendship.

At the general conference which was held in the grove at Nauvoo on the 2nd, 3rd and 4th days of October, 1841, many matters of Church welfare were transacted. At the request of the Twelve, Joseph gave instruction on the subject of baptism for the dead.[1] His remarks were a revelation of comfort to the

---

[1] See Note 4, Appendix.

Saints who had sorrowed that their ancestry had been deprived of the privilege of hearing the gospel truth. Among other things which the Prophet uttered on this memorable occasion were the following sentiments:

The only way to obtain truth and wisdom, is not to ask it from books, but to go to God in prayer, and obtain divine teaching. It is no more incredible that God should save the dead than that he should raise the dead.

There is never a time when the spirit is too old to approach God. All are within the reach of pardoning mercy, who have not committed the unpardonable sin, which hath no forgiveness, neither in this world, nor in the world to come. There is a way to release the spirit of the dead; that is by the power and authority of the priesthood—by binding and loosing on earth. This doctrine appears glorious, inasmuch as it exhibits the greatness of divine compassion and benevolence in the extent of the plan of human salvation.

This glorious truth is well calculated to enlarge the understanding, and to sustain the soul under troubles, difficulties and distresses. For illustration: suppose the case of two men, brothers, equally intelligent, learned, virtuous and lovely, walking in uprightness and in all good conscience, so far as they had been able to discern duty from the muddy stream of tradition, or from the blotted pages of the book of nature.

One dies and is buried, having never heard the Gospel of reconciliation; to the other the message of salvation is sent, he hears and embraces it, and is made the heir of eternal life. Shall the one become a partaker of glory, and the other be consigned to hopeless perdition? Is there no chance for his escape? Sectarianism answers, None! none!! none!!! Such an idea is worse than atheism. The truth shall break down and dash in pieces all such bigoted Pharisaism; the sects shall be sifted, the honest in heart brought out, and their priests left in the midst of their corruption.

At this conference the Prophet announced:

> There shall be no more baptisms for the dead until the ordinance can be attended to in the font of the Lord's house, and the Church shall not hold another general conference until they can meet in said house. For thus saith the Lord!

The conference had begun under discouraging circumstances. The weather was unpropitious, and there was some ill health. But before its conclusion a vast number of Saints and visitors from abroad had gathered, and at the last day, when the weather became more favorable, the congregation was a multitude. There was much occasion at this conference for congratulations. The work was prospering at home and abroad. Unanimity prevailed among the Saints in the stakes of Zion; and the missionary elders were constantly sending up reports of their success among the honest in heart.

As the brethren of the Twelve had taken upon their own shoulders many of the burdens which the Prophet had borne in their absence, he was enabled to perform greater labors in the way of general instruction than ever before. Under his direction the temporal interests of the people in Nauvoo prospered greatly. He also read the proofs of the Book of Mormon previous to its being stereotyped.

On the 8th day of November, 1841, the baptismal font in the Lord's house was dedicated, President Brigham Young being spokesman.

The falsehoods concerning the Saints bore evil fruit. Bad men gathered in Hancock and Lee and made depredations upon the property of the Saints and other citizens alike. The thefts perpetrated upon other citizens were attributed to the followers of the Prophet; and the thieves themselves circulated the report secretly that these evil deeds were committed under the direction of Joseph and Hyrum. So industriously were these bad reports scattered and so generally were they believed that in November of 1841 the Prophet and Hyrum gave out to the world their innocence of these deeds, stating that they did not sanction any evil practice in any person whatever, and they warned all people of Nauvoo and the surrounding country against being made the dupes of thieves, plunderers and falsifiers. They declared that the Church would purge itself of all persons connected with any such crime.

CHAPTER 51

The Relief Society

U pon one occasion, when the power of persecution was descending upon the people, a threat of the mobocrats was carried to the Prophet. It was this: "We are going to drive the Mormons to hell, this time, sure."

With an entrancing mildness of look and sweetness of voice, Joseph replied:

Never mind, my brethren, if they drive us to hell, we'll turn the devil out and make a heaven of it.

This sentiment is at once a sermon upon unity and an epitome of the history of the Latter-day Saints. By their union and system of mutual help they have again and again redeemed wildernesses; every time demonstrating that the Prophet's view of the power of human harmony was correct—for where the love of truth and the concord of the Saints exist there is no room for Satan, and hell itself must be transformed into a region of bliss.

Joseph was putting these principles into practice at Nauvoo, and a beautiful city was growing out of a marsh; and institutions for human liberty and human advancement were growing out of the most adverse conditions.

Near the opening of 1842 the Prophet, with President Brigham Young and Bishop Newel K. Whitney, began to devise a plan by which a cheap and expeditious conveyance of the Saints from the Old World to Nauvoo might be secured through a united effort; and the mercantile interests of the people might be made to serve the general welfare and protect and help the poor. The Prophet himself did not hesitate to engage in mercantile and industrial pursuits; the gospel which he preached was one of temporal salvation as well as spiritual exaltation; and he was willing to perform his share of the practical labor. This he did with no thought of personal gain, for in opening the store at Nauvoo he said:

> I rejoice that we have been enabled to do as well as we have, for the hearts of many of the poor brethren and sisters will be made glad with these comforts which are now within their reach.

In a letter to Brother Edward Hunter, under date of January 5, 1842, the Prophet shows his humility and the love of his heart in these words:

> The store has been filled to overflowing and I have stood behind the counter all day, distributing goods as steadily as any clerk you ever saw, to oblige those who were compelled to go without their Christmas and New Year's dinners for the want of a little sugar, molasses, raisins, etc.; and to please myself also, for I love to wait upon the Saints and to be a servant to all, hoping that I may be exalted in the due time of the Lord.

What a picture is presented here! A man chosen by the Lord to lay the foundation of His Church and to be its Prophet and President, takes joy and pride in waiting upon his brethren and sisters like a servant. The self-elected ministers of Christ in the world are forever jealous of their dignity and fearful of showing disrespect to their cloth; but Joseph never saw the day when he did not feel that he was serving God and obtaining favor in the sight of Jesus Christ by showing kindness and attention "even unto the least of these."

One Tom Sharp, editor of the Warsaw *Signal*, was devoting the greater part of his time and the greater part of his paper's space to slanders and misrepresentations of the Saints. The Prophet's comment upon this man, who afterward became a prominent factor in the persecutions against the people, was: "Let Sharp publish what he pleases: the faster he prints his lies the sooner he will get through."

There were signs of prosperity for the Saints, and although they were not yet surrounded by comforts, they began to give freely of their substance to rear the temple, anxiously looking forward to its completion as a thing of mighty importance to the living and to the dead. With the rapid increase of their numbers, the politicians of the state sought their favor. The Prophet took occasion, during the gubernatorial contest of 1842, to announce that he would support without regard to their political predilections, the men who were devoted to humanity and equal rights—the cause of liberty and the law. And this was his text in every political campaign in which the people took part.

John Wentworth, proprietor of the Chicago *Democrat*, wrote to the Prophet early in 1842, asking for a sketch of the Church and its founder, stating that he desired the data for a Mr. Barstow who was writing the history of New Hampshire. Joseph very willingly complied with this request and gave a succinct history of the founding of the Church, its progress and persecutions; with a statement of the faith of the Latter-day Saints. The Prophet's own words cannot fail to be of intense interest to students of his life; and as his account shows masterly condensation and completeness, it is here presented in full:

> I was born in the town of Sharon, Windsor County, Vermont, on the 23rd of December, A. D. 1805. When ten years old my parents removed to Palmyra, New York, where we resided about four years, and from thence we removed to the town of Manchester. My father was a farmer and taught me the art of husbandry. When about fourteen years of age I began to reflect upon the importance of being prepared for a future state, and upon inquiring upon the plan of salvation, I found that there was a great clash in religious sentiment; if I went to one society they referred me to one plan, and another to another; each one pointing to his own particular creed

as the *summum bonum* of perfection; considering that all could not be right; and that God could not be the author of so much confusion, I determined to investigate the subject more fully, believing that if God had a church it would not be split up into factions, and that if He taught one society to worship one way, and administer in one set of ordinances, He would not teach another principles that were diametrically opposed.

Believing the word of God, I had confidence in the declaration of James—"If any man lack wisdom, let him ask of God, who giveth to all men liberally and upbraideth not, and it shall be given him." I retired to a secret place in a grove, and began to call upon the Lord; while fervently engaged in supplication, my mind was taken away from the objects with which I was surrounded, and I was enwrapped in a heavenly vision, and saw two glorious personages, who exactly resembled each other in features and likeness, surrounded with a brilliant light which eclipsed the sun at noonday. They told me that all the religious denominations were believing in incorrect doctrines, and that none of them was acknowledged of God as His Church and kingdom; and I was expressly commanded to "go not after them"; at the same time receiving a promise that the fullness of the gospel should at some future time be made known unto me.

On the evening of the 21st of September, A.D. 1813, while I was praying unto God, and endeavoring to exercise faith in the precious promises of scripture, on a sudden a light like that of day, only of a far purer and more glorious appearance and brightness, burst into the room; indeed the first sight was as though the house was filled with consuming fire. The appearance produced a shock that affected the whole body. In a moment a personage stood before me surrounded with a glory yet greater than that with which I was already surrounded. This messenger proclaimed himself to be an angel of God, sent to bring the joyful tidings, that the covenant which God made with ancient Israel was at hand to be fulfilled, that the preparatory work for the second coming of the Messiah was speedily to commence; that the time was at hand for the gospel, in all its fullness to be preached in power unto all nations that a people might be prepared for the millennial reign.

I was informed that I was chosen to be an instrument in the hands of God to bring about some of His purposes in this glorious dispensation.

I was also informed concerning the aboriginal inhabitants of this country, and shown who they were and from whence they came; a brief sketch of their origin, progress, civilization, laws, governments, of their righteousness and their iniquity, and the blessings of God being finally withdrawn from them as a people, was made known unto me. I was also told where there were deposited some plates on which were engraven an abridgement of the records of the ancient prophets that had existed on this continent. The angel appeared to me three times the same night, and unfolded the same things. After having received many visits from the angels of God, unfolding the majesty and glory of the events that should transpire in the last days, on the morning of the 22nd of September, A.D. 1827, the angel of the Lord delivered the records into my hands.

These records were engraven on plates which had the appearance of gold. Each plate was six inches wide and eight long, and not quite so thick as common tin. They were filled with engravings in Egyptian characters, and bound together in a volume as the leaves of a book, with three rings running through the whole. The volume was something near six inches in thickness, a part of which was sealed. The characters on the unsealed part were small and beautifully engraved. The whole book exhibited many marks of antiquity in its construction and much skill in the art of engraving. With the records was found a curious instrument, which the ancients called "Urim and Thummim," which consisted of two transparent stones set in the rim of a bow fastened to a breastplate.

Through the medium of the Urim and Thummim I translated the record, by the gift and power of God.

In this important and interesting book the history of ancient America is unfolded, from its first settlement by a colony that came from the tower of Babel at the confusion of languages, to the beginning of the fifth century of the Christian era. We are informed by these records that America in ancient times had been inhabited by two distinct races of people. The first were called Jaredites, and came directly from the tower of Babel. The second race came directly from the city of Jerusalem about six hundred years before Christ. They were principally Israelites of the descendants of Joseph. The Jaredites were destroyed about the time the Israelites came from Jerusalem, who succeeded them in the inheritance of the country. The principal nation of the second race fell in battle towards the close of the fourth century. The remnant are the Indians that now inhabit this country. This book also tells us that our Savior made His appearance upon this continent after His resurrection, that He planted the gospel here in all its fullness, and richness, and power, and blessing; that they had apostles, prophets, pastors, teachers and evangelists; the same order, the same Priesthood, the same ordinances, gifts, powers and blessings as were enjoyed on the eastern continent; that the people were cut off in consequence of their transgressions; that the last of their prophets who existed among them was commanded to write an abridgement of their prophecies, history, etc., and to hide it up in the earth, and that it should come forth and be united with the Bible for the accomplishment of the purpose of God in the last days. For a more particular account I would refer to the Book of Mormon.

As soon as the news of this discovery was made known, false reports, misrepresentations and slander flew as on the wings of the wind in every direction; the house was frequently beset by mobs and evil-designing persons. Several times I was shot at and very narrowly escaped, and every device was made use of to get the plates away from me, but the power and blessing of God attended me, and several began to believe my testimony.

On the 6th of April, 1830, the Church of Jesus Christ of Latter-day Saints was organized in the town of Fayette, Seneca County, state of New York. Some few were called and ordained by the spirit of revelation and prophecy, and began to preach as the Spirit gave them utterance, and, though weak, they were strengthened by the power of God, and many were brought to repentance, were immersed in the water, and were filled with the Holy Ghost by the laying on of hands. They saw visions and prophesied, devils were cast out, and the sick healed by the laying on of hands. From that time the work rolled forth with astonishing rapidity, and churches were soon formed in the state of New York, Pennsylvania, Ohio, Indiana, Illinois and Missouri; in the last named state a considerable settlement was formed in Jackson County; numbers joined the Church, and we were increasing rapidly; we made large purchases of land, our farms teemed with plenty, and peace and happiness were enjoyed in our domestic circles and throughout our neighborhoods; but as we could not associate with our neighbors—who were, many of them, the basest of men, and had fled from the face of civilized society to the frontier country to escape the hand of justice—in their midnight revels, in their Sabbath breaking, horse racing and gambling, they commenced at first to ridicule, then to persecute, and, finally, an organized mob assembled and burned our houses, tarred

and feathered, and whipped many of our brethren, and
finally drove them from their habitations, who, houseless
and homeless, contrary to law, justice and humanity, had
to wander on the bleak prairies till the children left the
tracks of their blood on the prairie. This took place in the
month of November, and they had no other covering but
the canopy of heaven, in this inclement season of the year.
This proceeding was winked at by the government, and
although we had warranty deeds for our land, and had
violated no law, we could obtain no redress.

There were many sick, who were thus inhumanly
driven from their houses, and had to endure all this abuse,
and to seek homes where they could be found. The result
was, that a great many of them, being deprived of the
comforts of life and the necessary attendance, died; many
children were left orphans, wives widows, and husbands
widowers. Our farms were taken possession of by the mob,
many thousands of cattle, sheep, horses and hogs were
taken, and our household goods, store goods, and printing
press and type were broken, taken or otherwise destroyed.

Many of our brethren removed to Clay, where they
continued until 1836, three years; there was no violence
offered, but there were threatenings of violence. But in
the summer of 1836 these threatenings began to assume
a more serious form; from threats, public meetings
were called, resolutions were passed, vengeance and
destruction were threatened, and affairs again assumed a
fearful attitude. Jackson County was a sufficient precedent,
and as the authorities in that county did not interfere,
they boasted that they would not in this, which, upon
application to the authorities, we found to be too true, and
later much violence, privation and loss of property, we
were again driven from our homes.

We next settled in Caldwell and Daviess counties,
where we made large and extensive settlements, thinking
to free ourselves from the power of oppression by settling

in new counties with very few inhabitants in them; but here we were not allowed to live in peace, for in 1838 we were again attacked by mobs; an exterminating order was issued by Governor Boggs, and under the sanction of law organized banditti ranged through the country, robbed us of our cattle, sheep, horses, hogs, etc. Many of our people were murdered in cold blood, the chastity of our women was violated, and we were forced to sign away our property at the point of the sword; and after enduring every indignity that could be heaped upon us by an inhuman, ungodly band of marauders, from twelve to fifteen thousand souls—men, women and children—were driven from their own firesides, and from lands that they had warranty deeds of, houseless, friendless and homeless, in the depth of winter, to wander as exiles on the earth, or to seek an asylum in a more genial clime and among a less barbarous people.

Many sickened and died in consequence of the cold and hardships they had to endure; many wives were left widows, and children orphans and destitute. It would take more time than is allotted me here to describe the injustice, the wrongs, the murders, the bloodshed, the theft, misery and woe that have been caused by the barbarous, inhuman and lawless proceedings of the state of Missouri.

In the situation before alluded to, we arrived in the state of Illinois in 1839, when we found a hospitable people and a friendly home; a people who were willing to be governed by the principles of law and humanity. We have commenced to build a city called "Nauvoo," in Hancock County. We number from six to eight thousand here, besides vast numbers in the county around, and in almost every county of the state. We have a city charter granted us, and a charter for a legion, the troops of which now number 1,500. We have also a charter for a university, for an agricultural and manufacturing society, have our own laws and administrators, and possess all the privileges that other free and enlightened citizens enjoy.

Persecution has not stopped the progress of truth, but has only added fuel to the flame, it has spread with increasing rapidity: proud of the cause which they have espoused, and conscious of their innocence, and of the truth of their system, amidst calumny and reproach, have the Elders of this Church gone forth, and planted the gospel in almost every state in the Union; it has penetrated our cities, it has spread over our villages, and has caused thousands of our intelligent, noble and patriotic citizens to obey its divine mandates, and be governed by its sacred truths. It has also spread into England, Ireland, Scotland and Wales; in the year 1840, where a few of our missionaries were sent, over five thousand joined the Standard of Truth; there are numbers now joining in every land.

Our missionaries are going forth to different nations, and in Germany, Palestine, New Holland, the East Indies and other places, the Standard of Truth has been erected; no unhallowed hand can stop the work from progressing, persecutions may rage, mobs may combine, armies may assemble, calumny may defame, but the truth of God will go forth boldly, nobly, independently, till it has penetrated every continent, visited every clime, swept every country, and sounded in every ear, till the purposes of God shall be accomplished, and the great Jehovah shall say the work is done.

We believe in God the Eternal Father, and in His Son Jesus Christ, and in the Holy Ghost.

We believe that men will be punished for their sins, and not for Adam's transgression.

We believe that through the atonement of Christ all mankind may be saved by obedience to the laws and ordinances of the gospel.

We believe that these ordinances are 1st: Faith in the Lord Jesus Christ; 2nd, Repentance; 3rd, Baptism by immersion for the remission of sins; 4th, Laying on of hands for the gift of the Holy Ghost.

We believe that a man must be called of God by "prophecy and by laying on of hands" by those who are in authority, to preach the gospel and administer in the ordinances thereof.

We believe in the same organization that existed in the primitive church, namely, Apostles, Prophets, Pastors, Teachers, Evangelists, etc.

We believe in the gift of tongues, prophecy, revelations, visions, healing, interpretations of tongues, etc.

We believe the Bible to be the word of God as far as it is translated correctly; we also believe the Book of Mormon to be the word of God.

We believe all that God has revealed, all that He does now reveal, and we believe that He will yet reveal many great and important things pertaining to the kingdom of God.

We believe in the literal gathering of Israel and in the restoration of the Ten Tribes; that Zion will be built upon this continent; that Christ will reign personally upon the earth, and that the earth will be renewed and receive its paradisiacal glory.

We claim the privilege of worshiping Almighty God according to the dictates of our own conscience, and allow all men the same privilege, let them worship how, where or what they may.

We believe in being subject to kings, presidents, rulers and magistrates, in obeying, honoring and sustaining the law.

We believe in being honest, true, chaste, benevolent, virtuous, and in doing good to *all men*; indeed we may say that we follow the admonition of Paul "we believe all things, we hope all things," we have endured many things, and hope to be able to endure all things. If there is anything virtuous, lovely or of good report, or praiseworthy, we seek after these things.

Respectfully, etc.,

JOSEPH SMITH

In February of 1842, Joseph became the editor of the *Times and Seasons*, assisted by Apostle John Taylor. The Prophet continued to carry this responsibility for nearly a year when a press of other business, combined with the persecution of his enemies, compelled him to relinquish the task into the hands of his assistant, Elder Taylor, who was then formally announced as the editor. During 1842 Joseph gave many instructions of precious truth through that periodical to the Saints, and published, with engravings made by Elder Reuben Hedlock, his translation of the Book of Abraham.

In the issue of the *Times and Seasons* for March 1, 1842, appears the Prophet's first editorial article. It is significant and strong:

"HONOR AMONG THIEVES"

We extract the following from the New York Tribune:

The paymaster of the Missouri militia, called out to put down the Mormons some two years since, was supplied with money some time since and started for western Missouri, but has not yet arrived there. It is feared that he has taken the saline slope.

We are not surprised that persons who could wantonly, barbarously and without the shadow of law, drive fifteen thousand men, women and children from their homes, should have among them a man who was so lost to every sense of justice, as to run away with the wages for this infamous deed; it is not very difficult for men, who can blow out the brains of children; who can shoot down and hew to pieces our ancient veterans that fought in the defense of our country and delivered it from the oppressor's grasp; who could deliberately, and in cold blood, murder men, and rob them of their boots, watches, etc., and whilst they were yet weltering in their blood and grappling with death, and then proceed to rob their widowed houses. Men who can deliberately do this, and steal nearly all the horses, cattle, sheep, hogs and property of a whole community, and drive them from their homes *en masse*, in an inclement season of the year, will not find many qualms of conscience in stealing the pay of his brother thieves, and taking the saline slope.

The very idea of government paying these men for their bloody deeds, must cause the sons of liberty to blush, and to hang their harps upon the willow; and make the blood of every patriot run chill. The proceedings of that state have been so barbarous and inhuman that our indignation is aroused when we reflect upon the scene.

We are here reminded of one of the patriotic deeds of the government of that state, which, after it had robbed us of everything we had in the world, and taken from us many hundred thousand dollars worth of property, had its sympathies so far touched (*alias,* its good name,) that it voted two thousand dollars for the relief of the "suffering Mormons," and choosing two or three of the state's noblest sons to carry the heavenly boon, these angels of salvation came in the plenitude of their mercy, and in the dignity of their office, to Far West. To do what? To feed their hungry, and clothe their naked with the $2,000? Verily nay! but to go into Daviess County and steal the Mormons' hogs (which they, [the Mormons] themselves, were prohibited from obtaining, under penalty of death) to distribute among the destitute, and to sell where they could obtain the money. These hogs, thus obtained, were shot down in their blood, and not otherwise bled; they were filthy to a degree. These, the Mormons' own hogs, and a very few goods, the sweepings of an old store in Liberty, were what these patriotic and noble-minded men gave to the "poor Mormons," and then circulated to the world how sympathetic, benevolent, kind and merciful the legislature of the state of Missouri was in giving two thousand dollars to the "suffering Mormons." Surely, "the tender mercies of the wicked are cruel."

The organization of the Female Relief Society at Nauvoo began under the Prophet's direction on the 17th of March, 1842, and was completed on the 24th day of that month. The purpose of the society was to comfort the poor and relieve the destitute and sustain the widow and the orphan. The sisters among the Saints had always been signalized for their acts of kindness; but the cruel usage they had received in Missouri had prevented their extending the hand of charity as they desired. Yet even in the midst of their persecution, when the bread was torn from the mouths of their offspring by the oppressors, they had always been willing to open their doors to the weary travelers and to divide their pittance with the stranger. With the growing prosperity of the Church, the Prophet felt sure that the sisters would concentrate their efforts to ameliorate the condition of the suffering stranger, to pour oil and wine into the wounded heart of the distressed, to dry up the tears of the orphan, and make the widow's heart to rejoice.

On the 20th day of March, 1842, after a sermon in the grove near the temple, the Prophet went down to the river and baptized eighty persons for the remission of their sins. Fifty of this number received their confirmation under his hands later in the day. One week afterward he baptized one hundred and seven people in the Mississippi.

At the conference of the Church held at the city of Nauvoo on the 6th day of April, 1842, the twelfth anniversary of its organization, Apostle Page made explanation of the delays through which he failed to accompany Elder Orson Hyde to Jerusalem.

The Prophet decided that Elder Page should be restored to his fellowship; he took the occasion to instruct the elders that when they went forth as companions they were to adhere to each other as Elisha and Elijah of old.

During this conference two hundred and seventy-five elders were ordained under the hands of the apostles.

On Saturday, the 9th day of April, 1842, the Prophet attended the funeral of Ephraim Marks, a son of William Marks, president of the Nauvoo Stake. President Wilford Woodruff's journal of that date records that Joseph addressed the funeral assemblage, and in the course of his remarks said:

> Some of the Saints have supposed that "Brother Joseph" could not die; but this is a mistake. It is true that there have been times when I have had the promise of my life to accomplish certain things; but, having now done these things, I have no longer any lease of my life. I am as liable to die as other men.

This sermon is like a premonition of his own fate. At the time it was uttered his surroundings had never been so propitious since the day when he first received the plates from the Hill Cumorah. But soon after he made this declaration, his enemies began again to pursue him vindictively, and they continued until his death a little more than two years after he delivered that sermon.

In the spring of 1842, the Nauvoo Legion of the Illinois state militia consisted of twenty-six companies, comprising about two thousand troops. On the 7th day of May, the staff of the Legion dined at the house of the commander-in-chief. Other guests were there, including Judge Stephen A. Douglas, who had adjourned the circuit court, then in session at Carthage, that he and the lawyers might visit Nauvoo and witness the parade of the Legion. A sham battle between the two cohorts under Brigadier Generals Wilson Law and Charles C. Rich was a feature of the day. The battle and the parade were brilliant; and the visitors expressed their admiration of the energy and the patriotism of the Prophet and his brethren who had organized and trained this large body of loyal troops to be in readiness for their country's call.

It was during the sham battle of this day that the Prophet became assured that John C. Bennett was a wicked man—impure and traitorous. The proper place for the lieutenant general commanding was upon an eminence where, surrounded by his staff, and the ladies and distinguished visitors, he could review the contest between his cohorts. But Bennett made several endeavors to draw Joseph down into the battle; failing in that, to get him separated from his staff and party and in the rear of one of his forces. Joseph might have yielded to some of these requests, but the Spirit whispered him that treachery was meditated. A little later the purpose of Bennett was made manifest. He had intended to get Joseph into such a position that he could be killed by a shot, and no one be able to identify the assassin. Bennett no doubt had accomplices in this plot, and his plans were shrewdly laid; but this was not the hour nor this the method for the Prophet's death.

In recording the events of this day in his journal, Joseph develops Bennett's treachery and predicts that the wicked doing of the traitor will soon be made manifest before the world. The prophecy was fulfilled.

CHAPTER 52

Traitors Within

Insidious as was the attempt of Bennett upon the Prophet's life during the sham battle of the Legion on the 7th of May, 1842, it was not so cowardly as the stab which Bennett sought to inflict very soon after that. The first blow aimed solely at the Prophet's life; the second intended to slay his reputation and then to have him killed with a dishonorable stain upon his name. Bennett was lustful in his nature, though he had brought that disposition into subjection, or at least concealment, for a little time after his arrival at Nauvoo. But he soon gave way to the whisper of the tempter. And to make his purpose successful, and to cloak himself with protection, he taught secretly to men and women that the Prophet countenanced sin between the sexes. Bennett's prominence, and the intimacy that he represented as existing between the Prophet and himself, deceived a few, and he found some followers in the city of Nauvoo. Men and women professing to accept his teachings as having emanated from the Prophet, gave themselves up to profligacy. They excused themselves to their own souls and their fellow beings by the pretense that the Prophet of God justified these immoralities. Bennett's converts were few; and these were only among the ignorant or the depraved, for everyone who was himself pure in soul and blessed with reasonable intelligence knew that nothing was more abhorrent to the Prophet than sexual impurity. Joseph's teachings upon this point were emphatic and frequent. He regarded and taught that virtue in man or woman was dearer than life, and that adultery was a sin second only to the shedding of innocent blood.

But Bennett worked secretly and prevailed over several to yield to his desires, and induced a few men to engage in his awful course, securing concealment by the most adroit and outrageous falsehoods.

Among the persons addressed by Bennett were some pure minded brethren and sisters, who knew in an instant that his teachings were corrupt, and knew by the Spirit of the Lord that the Prophet was no party to such an atrocious crime.

Bennett's sins were not long hidden from Joseph's knowledge. The Prophet acted promptly as was his wont. He charged the sins of falsehood and seduction upon Bennett, and the latter was forced to confess. He humbled himself and with many tears begged for pardon. Of his own volition he went before Alderman Daniel H. Wells and made oath that Joseph Smith had never taught him "anything contrary to the strictest principles of the gospel, or of virtue, or of the laws of God or man, under any circumstance, or upon any occasion, either directly or indirectly in word or in deed." These sentiments he reiterated in public assemblages, declaring that so far as he knew and believed, Joseph's life was unspotted by one act or word of immorality. On the 17th of May he resigned the office of mayor, being terrified by the indignation of insulted men and abused women. The council accepted his resignation and appointed Joseph to fill the vacancy.

On the 25th of May, notice was given to John C. Bennett that his fellowship had been withdrawn from him and that notice must be given through the press to warn the public against his evil doings. Weeping, he fell upon his knees, acknowledged his licentious conduct toward women in Nauvoo, confessed that he was worthy of the severest chastisement; but supplicated the brethren to spare him for his poor old mother's sake, promising that he would sin no more and would endeavor to atone for his wrongdoing. Joseph, who had been deeply injured, was the one to plead for mercy for Bennett, and at his especial solicitation the public notice was temporarily withdrawn. But the tears were hypocritical, for Bennett renewed his machinations; and it became necessary to warn all people against him as a dangerous man, a liar and a seducer. Some of the persons who had lent a willing ear to his corrupt counsels were also excommunicated. Evil reports soon began to come in from other places concerning Bennett, and it was discovered that he had pursued on former occasions the same sinful line of conduct which caused his fall at Nauvoo.

In June Bennett withdrew from Nauvoo and circulated lying publications against the truth and the Prophet and endeavored to incite a mob to march up against Nauvoo. The hideous character of this man is fully shown by one circumstance: Shortly after the Saints settled in Nauvoo he began to publish a series of letters over the *nom de plume* of "Joab, General in Israel," in which he recounted many of the atrocities of the Missouri persecutions. His articles breathed a spirit of resentment against the mobocrats and their official supporters, but these views belonged to Bennett personally and were not shared by anyone else. When he fled from Nauvoo after the exposure of his evil deeds, he called attention through the public prints to the sanguinary utterances of his own letters attributing them to the Saints and attempting by their sentiments to show that Joseph and his people were disposed to violence. Such an act of duplicity is almost unparalleled.

Bennett published a book filled with dark falsehoods about the Prophet and the Saints. It created a momentary excitement; but its author was despised by everybody and soon sank into obscurity and distress. He lived some years in agony, being wrecked in mind and body and died in poverty and distress.

On the 6th day of May, 1842, ex-Governor Lilburn W. Boggs was shot and dangerously wounded in his house at Independence, Jackson County, Missouri. His little boy had found him lying near an open window, weltering in blood, with three buckshot in his head. Outside of the window were footprints and a smoking pistol. The case was clearly one of attempted assassination. At first no hope was entertained that Boggs would recover; but he subsequently took a favorable turn and his life was saved. A rumor at once went forth charging the affair upon the "Mormons," although there was not the slightest circumstance to connect them with the deed. Boggs had plenty of enemies of a desperate character; he had shown the utmost disregard for law, and had glutted his vengeful spirit by murder and excitement to murder. What more natural than that he who had invoked massacre should fall by the hand of a ruffian taught by the example of Boggs himself to hold human life in light esteem! At first the charge against the Saints was a general one. It was safer to say that "Mormons did it," than to designate the particular hand which fired the shot.

It was stated that the Prophet had predicted a violent death for Boggs; and this rumor was circulated by his enemies to confirm suspicion against the Saints. But he promptly denied having expressed any such idea.

While this falsehood was being spread through that region, John C. Bennett and David and Edward Kilbourn conspired to kidnap Joseph and get him into Missouri. All the evil forces and powers of persecution united themselves at this hour.

Under the Prophet's direction Governor Reynolds of Missouri and Governor Carlin of Illinois were informed of the efforts which were being made in both states to precipitate mobocratic attacks upon the Saints; Joseph being determined that the officials should not permit this movement to gain head except by their willful acquiescence or neglect.

About the 1st of July, 1842, the first "Anti-Mormon" political convention was held in Hancock County, Illinois. Its resolutions read like a page out of recent Utah history.

The complete set of candidates were pledged to a man to receive no support from and to yield no quarter to the "Mormons"; and then the ticket was *commended to the suffrage of all the citizens of Hancock County.* The Prophet punctured the bubble by a vigorous exposure of the hypocrisy, intolerance and stupidity of such a campaign.

On Sunday, the 3rd day of July, eight thousand people assembled in the grove to hear the Prophet and his brother Hyrum preach. Joseph addressed the vast assemblage in the morning and Hyrum in the afternoon.

In the Prophet's journal, under date of July 11, 1842, he records the fact that he bought a horse of Harmon T. Wilson, which he afterwards named Joe Duncan. This was the famous and beautiful steed which Lieutenant General Smith afterwards rode at the head of the Nauvoo Legion. The Prophet had a great fondness for animals. His horse Charley was widely known among the people, and with the boys of Nauvoo he was a great favorite. Speaking of the horse, Charley brings to mind an occurrence which created considerable amusement at the time. A boy named Wesley Cowle was flying a kite in one of the streets of Nauvoo. One or two strangers came up to him and asked him where the Prophet could be found. At that time officers were said to be coming from Carthage for the purpose of serving papers upon Joseph and arresting him. "Wes" Cowle did not know but the strangers were officers. He said the Prophet was not in the city. He and Hyrum had gone to heaven on "old Charley" and he was flying his kite to send them their dinner.

On Saturday, the 6th day of August, 1842, while Joseph was conversing with several of his brethren at Montrose, Iowa, he uttered a remarkable prophecy which, like every other prediction from his lips, has been literally fulfilled. He declared that the Saints would continue to suffer much affliction and would finally be driven to the Rocky Mountains. Many would apostatize; others would be put to death by their persecutors or lose their lives in consequence of their exile; and many of those who listened to him would live to assist in building cities and to see the Saints become a mighty people in the tops of the Rocky Mountains.

That prophecy was uttered publicly and was placed on record at the time.

CHAPTER 53

Appeals
to Governor

Independence was hundreds of miles from Nauvoo. The vast stretch of country lying between the two cities was inhabited by a people who had sworn death to any "Mormon" daring to set foot on Missouri soil. The county of Jackson was the place from which the Saints had first been driven in the state, with the loss of all their possessions; and from which the Prophet and his companions, in 1839, had barely escaped with their lives. On the day when Lilburn W. Boggs was shot at Independence, Jackson County, Missouri, Joseph Smith attended the officers' drill at Nauvoo. The day before the attempt on Boggs' life General Adams of Springfield had been with the Prophet; the day following the attempt, Judge Stephen A. Douglas and many lawyers of his court, with twelve thousand other people, saw Joseph Smith reviewing the Legion at Nauvoo.

And yet Lilburn W. Boggs went before a justice of the peace for Jackson County, one Samuel Weston, and swore to a complaint charging Joseph Smith with "being an accessory before the fact, to an assault with intent to kill made by one Orrin P. Rockwell on Lilburn W. Boggs, on the night of the 6th of May, 1842." This affidavit was not made until the latter part of July; and, during the interval, Boggs and his friends had ample time to ascertain that no "Mormon" could possibly have been connected with the assault—even if they had not been able to secure the actual assassin. They had investigated the subject, for their kidnappers were constantly hovering around the Prophet's person. If they could have secured him by force, Boggs would not have committed this perjury. But they must get him at all hazards.

It would not do to charge him as principal in the commission of the deed because hundreds of prominent men in the state of Illinois could have testified to an alibi. They must select some person comparatively obscure, upon whom to charge the deed itself. As this victim they chose Orrin Porter Rockwell, although he had spent the spring and summer of 1842 in Illinois; and they charged the Prophet as being accessory, without taking the pains to trace any connection between Rockwell and the deed, or between the Prophet and Rockwell.

Boggs, having been governor of Missouri, found it easy to secure a requisition from Governor Reynolds for the persons of Joseph Smith and Orrin P. Rockwell; and upon this manifestly absurd and unconstitutional demand, Governor Carlin issued his warrant for their apprehension.

On the 8th day of August, 1842, the deputy sheriff of Adams County, with two assistants, arrested Joseph Smith and Orrin P. Rockwell, at Nauvoo, by virtue of the warrant from Carlin upon the requisition of the governor of Missouri.

The monstrous character of the charge and the proceedings was clearly apparent, but neither Joseph nor his fellow prisoner made any attempt to use force in the evasion of the illegal process. They succeeded in getting a writ of *habeas corpus*; but the officers refused to comply with its demands for the bodies of Smith and Rockwell and returned their original writ to Governor Carlin for further instruction. No doubt they were aware of the character of the duty entrusted to them: they were to arrest as fugitives from the justice of Missouri men who had not been in that state during or since the commission of the crime charged, men who were as palpably innocent of the offense as the officers themselves. Under these circumstances it is no cause for wonder that they should have sought renewed orders.

When the officers were gone from Nauvoo, Joseph and Orrin absented themselves pending preparations for a legal defense against this unlawful seizure. The sheriff returned with his aides to Nauvoo on Wednesday, the 10th of August. Failing to find his prey, he sought to terrify Emma and others into a disclosure of the

Prophet's whereabouts—making violent threats to be executed in case of their refusal. William Law contended in argument with the officers, pronouncing the whole proceedings to be illegal and ridiculous. So closely did he press the point that the deputy sheriff acknowledged his own belief that Joseph was entirely innocent, and that Governor Carlin's course was unjustifiable and unconstitutional.

Rockwell, to escape from the Missouri kidnappers, took a journey to the eastern states where he remained some months.

Joseph left Nauvoo and spent a little time at his Uncle John Smith's in Zarahemla. On the night of Thursday, the 11th of August, he went in a skiff with Brother Erastus H. Derby to an island in the Mississippi between Nauvoo and Montrose, where they were met by Emma, Hyrum, William Law, Newel K. Whitney, George Miller, William Clayton and Dimick B. Huntington. Joseph's visitors stated to him the current report that the governor of Iowa had issued a warrant for his apprehension and that the sheriff of Lee County was expected at any hour to execute it. The situation was critical; and Joseph's immediate removal from his Uncle John's seemed necessary. It was decided that the Prophet should proceed to the house of Edward Sayers in Nauvoo, and abide there for a time. The next day William Walker crossed the river from Nauvoo into Iowa, riding the Prophet's well-known horse Joe Duncan, to lead the gathered officers and kidnappers away from the idea that Joseph was on the Nauvoo side of the river.

On Saturday, the 13th, a letter was received by Hyrum from Elder Hollister at Quincy, stating that Governor Carlin admitted the proceedings to be illegal and declared that he would not pursue them further. Ford, the agent appointed to receive Joseph from the hands of the sheriff and carry him to Missouri, now announced his conclusion to take the first boat for home, as it was useless to wait longer. These announcements of Carlin and Ford were but part of a plan to lead the Prophet from his hiding place and get him into the hands of his enemies. It was learned that Ford had declared his purpose to have a large force brought from Missouri, and already companies of marauders were making search in Montrose, Nashville, Keokuk and other places for Joseph, to win the reward of $1,300 which was offered for his capture. William Walker's ruse had been successful, and most of the efforts were directed to the Iowa side of the river; but the officers of Illinois, who were also eager to gain the reward, were determined, if possible, to have him delivered to them at Nauvoo. They said they would stay in the city a month but that they would find him, and if he were not then forthcoming, they would lay Nauvoo in ashes.

Emma had followed Joseph to the house of Edward Sayers to nurse him as he was in ill health.

On the 14th of August Joseph wrote to Wilson Law, who had been elected major general of the Nauvoo Legion, concerning the threats of Missouri mobocrats and Illinois kidnappers against the welfare of Nauvoo and the liberty of her citizens. He said:

> We will take every measure in our power, and make every sacrifice that God or man can require at our hands, to preserve the peace and safety of the people without collision. And if sacrificing my own liberty for months and years were necessary I would bow to my fate with cheerfulness, and with a due consideration for the lives, safety and welfare of others. But if this policy cannot accomplish the desired object . . . we will defend ourselves to the best advantage we can and to the very last.

The entire sentiment of this letter indicates the wish of the Prophet for peace and the supremacy of the law, and also his courageous intention of submitting supinely no more to mobocratic violence—murder and plunder.

The answer of Wilson Law is important in a personal sense. He says:

> I do respond with my whole heart to every sentiment you have so nobly and feelingly expressed; and while my heart beats or this hand which now writes is able to draw and yield a sword, you may depend on its being at your

service in the glorious cause of liberty and truth, ready at a moment's warning to defend the rights of men, both civil and religious.

Brave words these; but they were not sustained by subsequent deeds. Wilson Law was the Benedict Arnold of Nauvoo. In less than two years after he wrote that letter, filled with sentiments of intense affection, he aided to bring the Prophet to his death.

Joseph had considered, during a brief time after the service of this writ, the advisability of taking his family and traveling into the distant northwest, to remain for a season, in order that persecution might be drawn away from Nauvoo and the people there be spared the horrors which had attended the Saints in Missouri. But when he found that the hatred of his opponents was extended to the city and people of Nauvoo, he abandoned all thought of retreating from the scene. If his absence could have preserved his brethren and sisters, he would have cheerfully banished himself into the wilderness; but since the danger which menaced them was a common danger he would remain and share it.

On the night of the 15th of August, Hyrum Smith and several others came to Joseph's hiding place and informed him that the officers had threatened to bring a great force against the city and that the Prophet would be safer at a distance. The brethren who brought this message and advice labored under great excitement and fear for Joseph; but he took occasion to calmly reprove them for their agitation, and he advised them to maintain an even and undaunted mind. Their courage was renewed with this exhibition of his fortitude, and they gladly remained with him in serenity and joy, listening to his salutary counsels until two o'clock in the morning.

From his retreat he issued on the 15th an editorial article for the *Times and Seasons* under the title of "Persecution," in which he analyzes this movement against himself and the Saints, and demonstrated the ridiculous illegality and insufficiency of the process.

Emma had declared her willingness to share her husband's exile and self-imposed banishment if necessary. As that plan was abandoned, she offered to visit Governor Carlin and lay Joseph's case before that functionary. In answer to this proposition the Prophet wrote to her:

> The governor is a fool; the more we flatter him the more eager he will be for our destruction. You may write to him whatever you see proper; but to go and see him I do not give my consent.

With this permission to write, Emma addressed a dignified and able communication to Carlin in which she called upon him, by virtue of his position as an officer and by every sense of manliness, to spare Joseph and the people of Nauvoo from unjust persecution. This letter alone is sufficient to demonstrate that Emma was a woman of superior ability, and that she had an exalted appreciation and love for her great husband. She says:

> Was my cause the interest of an individual, or of a number of individuals, then, perhaps, I might be justified in remaining silent. But it is not. Nor is it the pecuniary interest of a whole community alone that prompts me again to appeal to your excellency. But, dear sir, it is for the peace and safety of hundreds, I may safely say, of this community, who are not guilty of any offense against the laws of the country; and also the life of my husband, who has not committed any crime whatever, neither has he transgressed any of the laws, or any part of the Constitution of the United States; neither has he at any time infringed upon the rights of any man, or of any class of men, or community of any description. Need I say, he is not guilty of the crime alleged against him by Governor Boggs? Indeed, it does seem entirely superfluous for me, or any one of his friends in this place, to testify to his innocence of that crime, when so many of the citizens of your place, and of many other places in this state, as well

as in the territory, do know positively that the statement of Governor Boggs is without the least shadow of truth; and we do know, and so do many others, that the prosecution against him has been conducted in an illegal manner; and every act demonstrates the fact, that all the design of the prosecution is to throw him into the power of his enemies, without the least ray of hope that he would ever be allowed to obtain a fair trial, and that he would be inhumanly and ferociously murdered, no person having a knowledge of the existing circumstances, has one remaining doubt; and your honor will recollect that you said to me, that you would not advise Mr. Smith ever to trust himself in Missouri.

And, dear sir, you cannot for one moment indulge one unfriendly feeling towards him, if he abides by your counsel. Then, sir, why is it that he should be so cruelly pursued? Why not give him the privilege of the laws of this state? When I reflect upon the many cruel and illegal operations of Lilburn W. Boggs, and the consequent suffering of myself and family, and the incalculable losses and sufferings of many hundreds who survived, and many precious lives that were lost—all the effect of unjust prejudice and misguided ambition, produced by misrepresentations and calumny, my bosom heaves with unutterable anguish. And who, that is as well acquainted with the facts as the people of the city of Quincy, would censure me if I should say that my heart burned with just indignation towards our calumniators as well as the perpetrators of those horrid crimes?

But happy would I now be to pour out my heart in gratitude to Governor Boggs if he had arose with the dignity and authority of the chief executive of the state and put down every illegal transaction and protected the peaceable citizens and enterprising emigrants from the violence of plundering outlaws who have ever been a disgrace to the state and always will so long as they go unpunished. Yes, I say, how happy would I be to render him not only the gratitude of my own heart but the cheering effusion of the joyous souls of fathers and mothers, of brothers and sisters, widows and orphans, whom he might have saved by such a course, from now dropping under the withering hand of adversity, brought upon them by the persecutions of wicked and corrupt men.

And now may I entreat your Excellency to lighten the hand of oppression and persecution which is now laid upon me and my family, which materially affect the peace and welfare of this whole community; for let me assure you that there are many whole families that are entirely dependent upon the prosecution and success of Mr. Smith's temporal business for their support; and if he is prevented from attending to the common avocations of life, who will employ those innocent, industrious, poor people, and provide for their wants?

But, my dear sir, when I recollect the interesting interview I and my friends had with you, when at your place, and the warm assurances you gave us of your friendship and legal protection, I cannot doubt for a moment your honorable sincerity, but do still expect you to consider our claims upon your protection from every encroachment upon our legal rights as loyal citizens, as we always have been, still are, and are determined always to be a law-abiding people; and I still assure myself, that when you are fully acquainted with the illegal proceedings practiced against us in the suit of Governor Boggs, you will recall those writs which have been issued against Messrs. Smith and Rockwell, as you must be aware that Mr. Smith was not in Missouri, and of course could not have left there, with many other considerations, which, if duly considered, will justify Mr. Smith in the course he has taken.

And now I appeal to your Excellency, as I would unto a father, who is not only able but willing to shield me and mine from every unjust prosecution. I appeal to your sympathies, and beg you to spare me and my helpless children. I beg you to spare my innocent children the heart-rending sorrow of again seeing their father unjustly dragged to prison or to death; I appeal to your affections as a son and beg you to spare our aged mother—the only surviving parent we have left—the unsupportable affliction of seeing her son, whom she knows to be innocent of the crimes laid to his charge, thrown again into the hands of his enemies, who have so long sought for his life; in whose life and prosperity she only looks for the few remaining comforts she can enjoy. I entreat your Excellency to spare us these afflictions and many sufferings which cannot be uttered, and secure to yourself the pleasure of doing good, and vastly increasing human happiness—secure to yourself the benediction of the aged, and the gratitude of the young, and the blessing and veneration of the rising generation.

The tone of the foregoing also proves that Emma shared the Prophet's humanitarian views, and it proves that the sentiments Joseph breathed at home were the sentiments he uttered abroad, prophetic and noble. William Clayton carried this letter to Governor Carlin at Quincy and delivered it to him in the presence of Judge Ralston. Carlin read the communication with great attention and expressed astonishment and admiration at its character. He first proceeded to announce his certainty that there was no excitement anywhere but in Nauvoo and among the "Mormons" themselves: that elsewhere all was quiet and there was no apprehension of trouble. However, before Elder Clayton departed, the governor so far forgot his falsehood as to say that persons were offering their services every day either in person or by letter to fight the "Mormons"; and that these warlike volunteers held themselves in readiness to come up against Nauvoo whenever he should call upon them. He had the effrontery to suggest that Joseph should give himself up to the sheriff, despite the fact that all the proceedings were notoriously illegal, and despite the fact that the Prophet's enemies had sworn to kill him in case he should be acquitted of the charge made against him. Carlin could not even say that if Joseph gave himself up his protection from the mob, in traveling to and from court, would be guaranteed.

On the 18th of August, the pursuers had pressed so closely upon the Prophet's retreat that he departed from Brother Sayers' house and went to the residence of Carlos Granger in the northeast part of the city.

On the 19th of August, Joseph concluded to go to his own home and remain for a time.

The next day, Saturday, August 20, 1842, the apostles met in council and ordained Amasa M. Lyman to be one of the Twelve. Amasa had been ordained an elder under Joseph's hands in Hiram, Portage County, Ohio, in 1832, and had been one of the Prophet's fellow prisoners chained to him with the same manacles, in Richmond Jail, Missouri.

On Monday, the 29th day of August, 1842, the Prophet had been absent from the congregation of the Saints three weeks—hiding from his enemies. On that day the conference was assembled in the grove near the temple, when Joseph suddenly appeared upon the stand. The Saints were delighted to see him and showed great animation and cheerfulness. He addressed them with all his wonted fire, and advised them concerning all the exigencies of their situation. He reminded the people that the lies of John C. Bennett were being scattered over the land and called for elders to go abroad to declare the truth and refute the slanders which the enemies of the Prophet and the Church were circulating. While he talked, an indescribable transport of joy was manifested by the assembly; and when he concluded, three hundred and eighty elders volunteered to go immediately into the east upon the proposed mission of enlightenment.

C H A P T E R   5 4

Joseph
in Hiding

The interposition of Providence saved Joseph from the hands of his enemies on the 3rd day of September, 1842.

A considerable party of mobocrats, joined with some officers of the law, left Quincy on the 2nd of the month, intending to reach Nauvoo in the night, surround the Prophet's house and seize him in his bed. Although their road lay plainly before them, and to lose it would seem impossible, yet they wandered from the track and were many hours late in reaching their destination. About noon on the 3rd, Deputy Sheriff Pitman, with two other men, came stealthily upon Joseph's residence and entered it while he was at dinner with his family. Before they reached the room where the Prophet was, they met John Boynton and demanded that he should reveal Joseph's hiding place. While Boynton was making some evasive answer, the Prophet walked out through a rear door of the mansion, and entering a patch of tall corn in the garden, passed serenely through to the residence of Newel K. Whitney.

In the meantime the officers proceeded to search the house. Emma demanded a sight of the warrant under which they were proceeding. Pitman said he had none authorizing him to search, but insisted upon going through the house. After Emma felt sure that Joseph had escaped, she permitted them to hunt through the building.

Again that night two parties made another search of the residence but failed to discover him whom they wished to make their prey.

About nine o'clock in the evening, the Prophet went to the house of Edward Hunter, where he received a joyous welcome and where it was believed that he could be kept safe from the hands of his enemies. News was brought that the Missourians were again moving in force to obtain his person, and two requisitions were issued, one upon the governor of Illinois and the other upon the governor of Iowa.

From his retirement the Prophet sent out comforting epistles to the Saints. In one letter, written from the residence of Elder Hunter under date of September 6, 1842, the Prophet said:

> ... It is sufficient to know, in this case, that the earth will be smitten with a curse, unless there is a welding link of some kind or other between the fathers and the children, upon some subject or other: and behold, what is the subject? It is baptism for the dead. For we without them cannot be made perfect; neither can they without us be made perfect. Neither can they or we be made perfect without those who have died in the gospel also; for it is necessary in the ushering in of the dispensation of the fullness of times, which dispensation is now beginning to usher in, that a whole, and complete and perfect union, and welding together of dispensations, and keys, and powers, and glories should take place, and be revealed, from the days of Adam even to the present time; and not only this, but those things which have never been revealed from the foundation of the world, but have been kept hid from the wise and prudent, shall be revealed unto babes and sucklings in this the dispensation of the fullness of times.
>
> Now, what do we hear in the gospel which we have received? A voice of gladness! A voice of mercy from heaven, and a voice of truth out of the earth; glad tidings for the dead; a voice of gladness for the living and the dead; glad tidings of great joy. How beautiful upon the mountains are the feet of those that bring glad tidings of good things, and that say unto Zion, Behold! thy God

reigneth. As the dews of Carmel, so shall the knowledge of God descend upon them!...

Brethren, shall we not go on in so great a cause? Go forward, and not backward. Courage, brethren, and on, on, to victory! Let your hearts rejoice, and be exceeding glad. Let the earth break forth into singing. Let the dead speak forth anthems of eternal praise to the King Immanuel, who hath ordained before the world was, that which would enable us to redeem them out of their prisons; for the prisoners shall go free.

Let the mountains shout for joy, and all ye valleys cry aloud; and all ye seas and dry lands tell the wonders of your eternal King. And ye rivers and brooks and rills flow down with gladness. Let the woods and all the trees of the field praise the Lord; and ye solid rocks weep for joy. And let the sun, moon and the morning stars sing together, and let all the sons of God shout for joy. And let the eternal creations declare His name for ever and ever. And again I say, how glorious is the voice we hear from heaven, proclaiming in our ears, glory, and salvation and honor, and immortality and eternal life, kingdoms, principalities and powers!

Behold the great day of the Lord is at hand; and who can abide the day of His coming, and who can stand when He appeareth?

The brethren constantly visited him in his retirement, and he gave them instructions and counsels to suit every need.

On the 10th day of September, the Prophet returned to his home, believing that he would be as safe there as anywhere else, since his enemies would no longer expect him to take such a risk.

About the 1st of October, Governor Carlin issued a proclamation offering a reward of two hundred dollars each for the persons of Joseph Smith and Orrin P. Rockwell. At the same time Governor Reynolds of Missouri promised an additional price for the same purpose. On the day when this news was brought to the Prophet, his wife Emma was dangerously sick. She continued to grow worse until the 5th, when fear of her death was entertained. The Prophet had her baptized twice in the river; and she began to mend, and on the day following, hope was restored to the family.

Sidney Rigdon and Elias Higbee reported at Nauvoo that the Missourians were gathering to unite with the militia of Illinois to secure the Prophet's person. They had learned that Carlin had intentionally issued an illegal writ, expecting thereby to draw Joseph to Carthage where he would be discharged under *habeas corpus* proceedings and fall at once into the hands of his waiting enemies, who were to be there in numbers to seize and carry him away to Missouri without further ceremony. Sidney Rigdon was told by Stephen A. Douglas that the governor's proclamation, offering a reward to any man or set of men to secure Joseph's person, would give as much authority as a legal warrant could to an officer.

It seemed likely that a general search would be instituted in Nauvoo, and Joseph concluded to leave his home once more and go into more remote retirement. On the night of Friday, the 7th of October, 1842, he started away from Nauvoo, in company with Elders John Taylor, Wilson Law and John D. Parker, traveling through that night and a part of the next day when, greatly wearied, they arrived at Father Taylor's house. Elder John Taylor was very dangerously ill at this time, being prostrated with fever. The message from the Prophet that he desired Elder Taylor to accompany him as a guide to Father Taylor's came to him when he was in bed and too weak to be capable of much exertion. It was a task utterly beyond his strength, and to human appearance it might cost him his life if he attempted it. But Joseph had sent him word that the Lord would strengthen him and heal him, and he would be able to perform the journey. Elder Taylor believed him and prepared to start. He was so weak that he had to be lifted on his horse. The night was dark, and he was not very familiar with the road, and they lost their way; but the promise of the servant of the Lord to Elder Taylor was fulfilled. He endured the fatigue of the journey excellently and they reached his father's house safely.

The Prophet remained away until Thursday, the 20th of October, when he returned to his family and the brethren who needed his presence and advice.

In this same month a written opinion was received from Justin Butterfield, United States attorney for the district of Illinois, in which he proved the illegality of the requisition made by the governor of Missouri upon the governor of Illinois for the surrender of the Prophet. In the same document he showed in a very lucid manner what were the rights and privileges of the people of Nauvoo, pertaining to writs of *habeas corpus* issued from their municipal court, and the full power and authority of the city council. This opinion removes at once and forever all shadow of suspicion that the Prophet was acting in a disrespectful manner toward the laws of his country.

After one day at Nauvoo, Joseph returned to Father Taylor's; but in a week he was called home to find Emma worse. With his presence her health was soon renewed.

On Sunday, the 30th of October, the Saints met in worship upon a temporary floor in the temple. The Prophet was expected to address them, but on that day he was so ill as to be unable to be present. Two days later, while driving out with his three children and William Clayton, the carriage was upset on the hillside. Joseph was thrown some distance, but all of the little ones were pinioned under the shattered vehicle. As soon as he could rise, he rushed to rescue his boys and found them unhurt. The escape was marvelous, and he thanked his Maker therefor.

The multiplicity of other business upon his hands made it impossible for Joseph to continue as editor of the *Times and Seasons*. On the 15th day of November, 1842, he appointed Apostle John Taylor to that position.

Carlin's term as governor closed in 1842, and on the 8th day of December of that year Thomas Ford, his successor, delivered an inaugural address to the Senate and House of Representatives of the state in which he declared that the charters granted to the people of Nauvoo were objectionable to other citizens of the state, and that these charters should be modified and restricted.

On the next day, the 9th, Hyrum Smith started for Springfield, with a number of other brethren, to present testimony to the governor that Joseph was in Illinois at the time Boggs was shot, and consequently could not have been a fugitive from the justice of Missouri. It was hoped by this means, to procure a recall by Governor Ford of the writs and proclamations issued by Carlin. On the day of the departure of these brethren, the Prophet began personally to haul and cut wood for the poor of Nauvoo; and this labor of love and charity was continued vigorously and cheerfully as opportunity permitted. About this same time he began to read German in company with Apostle Orson Hyde.

The friends of the Prophet called upon Governor Ford at Springfield on Wednesday, the 14th day of December, 1842, accompanied by Mr. Butterfield, United States district attorney. Butterfield read to the governor several papers in the case—including the affidavit of Boggs, the writs and proclamation of Carlin, the petition of the Prophet, and also his own written opinion upon the question at issue. In reply, the governor stated that he believed the writ issued by Carlin was illegal, but he hesitated to interfere with the act of his predecessor. Ford on the 17th of December, directed the following letter to Joseph:

> Your petition requesting me to rescind Governor Carlin's proclamation and recall the writ issued against you has been received and duly considered. I submitted your case and all the papers relating thereto to the judges of the Supreme Court, or at least to six of them who happened to be present. They were unanimous in the opinion that the requisition from Missouri was illegal and insufficient to cause your arrest, but were equally divided as to the propriety and justice of my interference with the acts of Governor Carlin. It being, therefore, a case of great doubt as to my power, and I not wishing even in an official station, to assume the exercise of doubtful

powers, and inasmuch as you have a sure and effectual remedy in the courts, I have decided to decline interfering. I can only advise that you submit to the laws and have a judicial investigation of your rights. If it should become necessary, for this purpose, to repair to Springfield, I do not believe that there will be any disposition to use illegal violence towards you, and I would feel it my duty in your case, as in the case of any other person, to protect you with any necessary amount of force from mob violence whilst asserting your rights before the courts, going to and returning.

This advice was repeated in communications of the same date from Justin Butterfield and General Adams to the Prophet; as these gentlemen thought that he would be certain of discharge and protection.

Joseph, after a few days of deliberation and prayer, concluded to pursue the course suggested. He allowed himself to be arrested under the governor's proclamation, on the 26th day of December by General Wilson Law. In custody of Law, and accompanied by Hyrum Smith, Willard Richards, John Taylor and others, the Prophet departed for Springfield on Tuesday, the 27th day of December.

Joseph and his party arrived at Springfield on the afternoon of Friday, December 30th; and the next morning under direction of his attorney, Butterfield, he signed a petition to Judge Pope for a writ of *habeas corpus*. Upon the brief and vigorous showing made by the lawyer, the writ was granted at once; and, the Prophet being there, it was served and returned to the court in one minute. Bail was granted and General James Adams and General Wilson Law signed the bonds for the Prophet, in the sum of $2,000 each, Monday the 2nd day of January being set for the trial. While these preliminaries were being arranged, a vast crowd was gathering in the court room curious to see the famous Prophet. As Joseph and his friends were passing through the building, one of the multitude observed:

There goes Smith the Prophet, and a good-looking man he is.

Another said:

Every one that takes his part is as damned a rascal as he is.

A riot would have ensued and a mob would have been raised to do violence upon the Prophet and his friends, but for the vigorous exertion of Marshal Prentice.

After the crowd was dispersed so that the Prophet could get clear of the building, he walked for some distance between living walls of staring people. In company with his attorney, Mr. Butterfield, and Elder Willard Richards, he went to the American House to see Governor Ford, who was sick. In the course of their conversation, Ford remarked: "I am not religiously minded."

Joseph responded: "I have no narrow creed to circumscribe my mind; therefore the sectarians do not like me.

When the visit closed the governor said: "Well, from reports, I had reason to think that the Mormons were a peculiar people, different from other people, having horns or something of the kind; but I found that they looked like other people; indeed, I think Mr. Smith a very good-looking man."

The interest and curiosity concerning the Prophet grew more intense throughout the day, after the news of his presence became generally circulated. In the afternoon a team ran away, dashing past the state house. Someone raised the cry:

Joseph Smith, the Mormon Prophet, is running away!

So great was the excitement occasioned by this announcement that the House of Representatives adjourned on the instant, to give the members an opportunity to get into the street and participate in the supposed sensation.

The next morning was Sunday, the 1st day of January, 1843; when the speaker of the house visited the Prophet and tendered the hall of representatives for religious service. Joseph appointed Apostles Orson Hyde and John Taylor to preach to the people; and a large congregation gathered to hear the sermons and feast their eyes upon Joseph Smith.

On Monday, before going to court, Joseph prophesied in the presence of Judge Adams that, in the name of the Lord, he would not go to Missouri dead or alive.

A postponement was had of the case at the request of the attorney general of the state until the morning of Wednesday, January 4th. During the intervening two days, the Prophet made many friends. He was invited to the houses of the most distinguished people and received as much deferential attention as would have been accorded by faithful Catholics to a prince of the church of Rome.

At nine o'clock on the morning of the day set for the trial, Judge Pope appeared upon the bench with ten ladies by his side, who had been attracted by the novelty of the case and the fame of the petitioner. This Judge Pope was the father of Major General Pope who, in the War of the Rebellion, became so distinguished for his gallant services. An effort was made by Josiah Lamborn, attorney general of the state of Illinois, to have the proceedings dismissed, and the prisoner remanded to the custody of the Missouri officers on the ground that the court lacked jurisdiction. After the motion of Lamborn had been resolutely and eloquently resisted by Butterfield, the court decided that it had jurisdiction.

Mr. Butterfield then made a strong plea for the discharge of the defendant, and proceeded to recount the enormities of these attempts upon the Prophet's liberty. He said that Governor Reynolds had subscribed to a lie in making his demand for the Prophet, as appeared from the papers, and he averred that Governor Carlin would not have given up his dog on such a requisition. That an attempt should be made to deliver up a man who had not been out of the state during or since the commission of the offense, was a blow at the sacred liberty of the citizen and the strength of our institutions. After reminding the court that, if the Prophet's rights were wantonly trampled upon under color

of law, the fate visited upon him might in turn fall upon others—
even upon the judge—for the precedent would be followed;
he concluded by saying:

> I do not think that the defendant ought, under any
> circumstances, be given up to Missouri. It is a matter
> of history that he and his people have been murdered
> or driven from that state. If he goes there it is only to be
> assassinated, and he had better be sent to the gallows
> here. *He is an innocent and unoffending man.*

The opinion of Judge Pope in deciding the case was very
lengthy and comprehensive. It announced the discharge of the
Prophet, and completely annihilated the pretended grounds upon
which the requisition was made from Missouri and the warrant
and proclamation issued in Illinois. In conclusion his Honor said:

> No case can arise demanding a more searching
> scrutiny into the evidence than in cases arising under this
> part of the Constitution of the United States. It is proposed
> to deprive a freeman of his liberty; to deliver him into the
> custody of strangers; to be transported to a foreign state;
> to be arraigned for trial before a foreign tribunal, governed
> by laws unknown to him; separated from his friends, his
> family, and his witnesses, unknown and unknowing.
> Had he an immaculate character, it would not avail him
> with strangers. Such a spectacle is appalling enough to
> challenge the strictest analysis.
>
> The framers of the Constitution were not insensible
> of the importance of courts possessing the confidence
> of the parties. They therefore provided that citizens of
> different states might resort to the Federal Courts in civil
> causes. How much more important that the criminal
> have confidence in his judge and jury. Therefore, before
> the capias is issued, the officers should see that the
> case is made out to warrant it. Again, Boggs was shot on
> the 6th of May. The affidavit was made on the 25th of

July following. Here was time for enquiry, which would confirm into certainty, or dissipate his suspicions. He had time to collect facts to be had before a grand jury, or be incorporated in his affidavit.

The court is bound to assume that this would have been the course of Mr. Boggs but that his suspicions were light and unsatisfactory. The affidavit is insufficient. First, because it is not positive; second, because it charges no crime; third, because it charges no crime committed in the state of Missouri. Therefore he did not flee from the justice of the state of Missouri, nor has he taken refuge in the state of Illinois.

The proceedings in this affair, from the affidavit to the arrest, afford a lesson to governors and judges whose action may hereafter be invoked in cases of this character. The affidavit simply says that the affiant was shot with intent to kill; and he believes that Smith was accessory before the fact to the intended murder, and is a citizen or resident of the state of Illinois. It is not said who shot him, or that the person was unknown. The governor of Missouri, in his demand, calls Smith a fugitive from justice, charged with being accessory before the fact to an assault, with intent to kill, made by one O. P. Rockwell, on Lilburn W. Boggs, in this state (Missouri). This governor expressly refers to the affidavit as his authority for that statement.

Boggs, in his affidavit, does not call Smith a fugitive from justice, nor does he state a fact from which the governor had a right to infer it. Neither does the name of O. P. Rockwell appear in the affidavit, nor does Boggs say Smith fled. Yet the governor says he has fled to the state of Illinois. But Boggs only says he is a citizen or resident of the state of Illinois. The governor of Illinois, responding to the demand of the Executive of Missouri for the arrest of Smith, issues his warrant for the arrest of Smith, reciting that "whereas Joseph Smith stands charged by the affidavit of Lilburn W. Boggs with being accessory before the fact to an assault, with intent to kill, made by one O. P. Rockwell, on Lilburn W. Boggs, on the night of the 6th day of May, 1842, at the county of Jackson, in said state of Missouri; and that the said Joseph Smith has fled from the justice of said state, and taken refuge in the state of Illinois."

Those facts do not appear by the affidavit of Boggs. On the contrary, it does not assert that Smith was accessory to O. P. Rockwell, nor that he had fled from the justice of the state of Missouri, and taken refuge in the state of Illinois.

The Court can alone regard the facts set forth in the affidavit of Boggs as having any legal existence. The mis-recitals and overstatements in the requisition and warrant are not supported by oath, and cannot be received as evidence to deprive a citizen of his liberty and transport him to a foreign state for trial. For these reasons Smith must be discharged.

Thereupon Governor Ford certified that there was no further cause for the arrest or detention of Joseph Smith by virtue of any proclamation or warrant issued by the Executive of Illinois; and that, since the judgment of the circuit court, all such proclamations and warrants were inoperative and void.

After the conclusion of these proceedings and the settlement of matters attendant, the Prophet returned to Nauvoo on the afternoon of the 10th of January. The Saints were delighted to welcome him safe home, and the Twelve Apostles issued an epistle to the Saints, appointing Tuesday, the 17th day of January, 1843, as a day of humiliation, fasting, praise, prayer and thanksgiving before the great God for His mercies, and supplicating for a continued outpouring of His Holy Spirit upon the Prophet and Saints.

The promised joy of this festival was marred by the threats of a traitor. On the 15th of January, Sidney Rigdon received the following letter from John C. Bennett:

Springfield, Illinois, January 10, 1843

Mr. Sidney Rigdon and Orson Pratt:

Dear Friends:—It is a long time since I have written to you, and I should now much desire to see you, but I leave tonight for Missouri, to meet the messenger charged with the arrest of Joseph Smith, Hyrum Smith, Lyman Wight and others, for murder, burglary, treason, etc., etc., who will be demanded in a few days, on new indictments, found by the grand jury of a called court on the original evidence, and in relation to which a *nolle prosequi* was entered by the district attorney.

New proceedings have been gotten up on the old charges, and no *habeas corpus* can save them. We shall try Smith on the Boggs case, when we get him into Missouri. The war goes bravely on; and, although Smith thinks he is now safe, the enemy is near, even at the door. He has awakened the wrong passenger. The Governor will relinquish Joseph at once on the new requisition. There is but one opinion on the case, and that is, nothing can save Joseph on a new requisition and demand predicated on the old charges on the institution of new writs. He must go to Missouri; but he shall not be harmed, if he is not guilty; but he is a murderer, and must suffer the penalty of the law. Enough on this subject.

I hope that both your kind and amiable families are well, and you will please to give them all my best respects. I hope to see you all soon. When the officer arrives, I shall be near at hand. I shall see you all again. Please to write me at Independence immediately.

Yours respectfully,
JOHN C. BENNETT.

Sidney perused the cowardly missive, and instead of warning the Prophet, he gave the communication to Orson Pratt, but the latter at once presented it to the Prophet, that he might know of the further plot against his life. Orson Pratt wanted no correspondence with Bennett, the traitor, and had no fellowship with his works of darkness.

On Wednesday, the 18th day of January, 1843, Joseph and Emma entertained a large company of brethren and sisters at their house to celebrate the fifteenth anniversary of their wedding.

CHAPTER 55

Prophecies

One of the very few seasons of peace in Joseph's life now dawned upon him. It was none the less appreciated because it was brief.

The early part of 1843 is one of the marked epochs in the theological history of the Church. The Prophet, having his unrestrained liberty, was enabled to give to the Saints in writings, sermons and in personal conversations, many prophecies and principles for spiritual and temporal guidance.

Joseph must have known that this was but the lull which precedes the fiercer outburst of the tempest, for in January, 1843, outlining some work which he designed that the Twelve should perform very soon thereafter, he promised his assistance and leadership to them, with this very significant condition, upon which he placed emphasis:

If I live.

A few days later, on Sunday, the 22nd day of January, he preached from the stand which had been erected inside the temple walls, a temporary floor having been put in that building for the purpose of holding meetings there. President Wilford Woodruff made a synopsis of the sermon, in which occurs the following:

God Almighty is my shield; and what can man do if God is my friend? *I shall not be sacrificed until my time comes; then I shall be offered freely.*

The Prophet recorded this same prophecy concerning his own fate in his journal, showing thereby that he recognized its weight and foresaw its fulfillment.

Among the many prophecies of this period was one concerning Orrin P. Rockwell, who had been captured, imprisoned and maltreated in Missouri. There seemed no human possibility of Porter Rockwell's deliverance; his murder was decreed before his arrest; and no one of the brethren would be permitted to enter Missouri to assist him with advice or bail, under penalty of death. And yet on the 15th day of March the Prophet publicly declared:

> In the name of the Lord Jesus Christ I prophecy that Orrin P. Rockwell will get away honorably from the Missourians.

In the same month of March, Joseph, in company with Elders Willard Richards and Wilford Woodruff, discovered in the early evening a stream of light in the southwest quarter of the heavens. Its rays were in the form of a broad sword with the hilt downward; the blade was raised, pointing from the west to the southwest, at an angle of forty-five degrees, and extended nearly to the zenith. As they beheld this marvel in the sky Joseph said:

> As sure as there is a God who sits enthroned in the heavens, and as sure as He ever spoke by me, so sure will there be a bloody war; and the flaming sword in the heavens is the certain sign thereof.

Two or three weeks later, he prophesied in the presence of Elder Orson Hyde and others that a struggle in which much blood would flow would begin in South Carolina, and would probably arise through the slave question. This was a repetition of the revelation which he had received and announced more than ten years earlier.

A delegation of young men from New York came to see Joseph at Nauvoo in February, 1843, and with great respect solicited his views concerning Millerism and the coming of Christ, and the day of judgment, which Miller had fixed for April 3, 1843. The Prophet warned them that Miller was in error; that before Christ should come the prophecies must all be fulfilled, the sun be darkened and the moon turned to blood. A Chicago paper of that time published a certificate of one Hyrum Reading, of Ogle County, Illinois, stating that he had seen the sign of the Son of Man; and the editor of the paper declares that Joseph Smith had met his match. The Prophet responded that Mr. Reading had not seen the sign of the Son of Man, as foretold by Jesus, neither had any man nor will any man, until after the fulfillment of the prophecies; and he declared:

Hear this, oh earth! the Lord will not come to reign over the righteous in this world in 1843, nor until everything for the bridegroom is ready.

Joseph was once praying very earnestly to know the time of the coming of the Savior, when he heard a voice saying:

Joseph, my son, if thou livest until thou art eighty-five years old, thou shalt see the face of the Son of Man. Therefore let this suffice and trouble me no more.

In recording this divine utterance, the Prophet says that he was left thus without being able to decide whether this coming referred to the millennium or to some previous appearing, or whether he should die and thus see the face of Christ. Joseph would have been eighty-five years old on the 23rd day of December, 1890; and he says:

I believe the coming of the Son of Man will not be any sooner than that time.

The question was proposed at a lyceum which Joseph attended whether the kingdom of God was set up before the day of Pentecost or not till then? The Prophet's answer was recorded at some length by Apostle Wilford Woodruff, from whose synopsis the following paragraphs are taken:

Some say the kingdom of God was not set up until the day of Pentecost, and that John did not preach the baptism of repentance for the remission of sins; but I say, in the name of the Lord, that the kingdom of God was set up on the earth from the days of Adam to the present time.

Whenever there has been a righteous man on earth unto whom God revealed His word and gave power and authority to administer in His name, and where there is a priest of God—a minister who has power and authority from God to administer in the ordinances of the gospel and officiate in the Priesthood of God, there is the kingdom of God; and, in consequence of rejecting the gospel of Jesus Christ and the Prophets whom God has sent, the judgments of God have rested upon people, cities and nations, in various ages of the world, which was the case with the cities of Sodom and Gomorrah, which were destroyed for rejecting the prophets.

Now I will give my testimony. I care not for man. I speak boldly and faithfully, and with authority. How is it with the kingdom of God? Where did the kingdom of God begin? Where there is no kingdom of God, there is no salvation. What constitutes the kingdom of God? Where there is a prophet, a priest or a righteous man unto whom God gives His oracles, there is the kingdom of God; and where the oracles of God are not, there the kingdom of God is not.

In these remarks, I have no allusion to the kingdoms of the earth. We will keep the laws of the land; we do not speak against them; we never have spoken against them; though we can scarcely mention the state of Missouri and our persecutions there, but that the cry goes forth that we are guilty of treason, which is false. We speak of the kingdom of God on the earth; not the kingdoms of men.

These emphatic statements show the loyal position which the Prophet maintained toward his country, and the view he had concerning governments in general.

The Prophet gave his brethren three grand keys whereby to know whether any supernatural visitor was from God or from Satan.

When a messenger comes, saying he has a message from God, offer him your hand, and request him to shake hands with you. If he be an angel, he will do so, and you will feel his hand. If he be the spirit of a just man made perfect, he will come in his glory; for that is the only way he can appear. Ask him to shake hands with you, but he will not move, because it is contrary to the order of heaven for a just man to deceive; but he will still deliver his message. If it be the devil as an angel of light, when you ask him to shake hands, he will offer you his hand, and you will not feel anything: you may therefore detect him.

In the midst of these exalted labors, Joseph took great delight in mingling with the brethren in manly sports. On Saturday, the 28th day of January, 1843, he played a fine game of ball at Nauvoo with his brethren. During the same winter some of his friends saw him teaching his little son Frederick to slide upon the ice; and the Prophet enjoyed the exhilaration and was as merry as a boy. On Monday, the 13th day of March, 1843, Joseph met William Wall, the most expert wrestler of Ramus, Illinois, and had a friendly bout with him. He easily conquered Wall, who up to that time had been a champion. About the same time he had a contest at pulling sticks with Justus A. Morse, reputed to be the strongest man in that region. The Prophet used but one hand and easily defeated Morse.

One evening in March twenty-seven children were brought to a meeting to be blessed. Joseph took great joy in laying his hands upon the heads of the innocent little ones, and he blessed nineteen of them himself with great fervency. He turned pale and lost his strength, and was compelled to retire, leaving the meeting and its duties to his brethren. Elder Jedediah M. Grant inquired of him the next day concerning the cause of the strange manifestation. The Prophet replied that as he blessed the little ones, it was made known to him that Lucifer would exert an influence to destroy them, and he strove with all his faith to seal upon them security of their lives and virtue upon earth. So much power emanated from him into the children that he became weak. Joseph referred to the case of the woman who touched the hem of the garment of Jesus, by which her issue of blood was staunched, and the Savior said: "Somebody hath touched me; for I perceive that virtue has gone out of me."

Joseph told Elder Grant that the virtue referred to by the Savior was the spirit of life; and men who exercised great faith in administering to the sick, blessing little children, and making confirmations were liable to become weakened.

On Monday, the 6th day of February, 1843, the Prophet was elected mayor of Nauvoo by unanimous vote; at the same time Orson Spencer, Daniel H. Wells, George A. Smith and Stephen Markham were elected aldermen; and Hyrum Smith, John Taylor, Orson Hyde, Orson Pratt, Sylvester Emmons, Heber C. Kimball, Benjamin Warrington, Daniel Spencer and Brigham Young were elected councilors.

Joseph put his accustomed vigor into his duties as chief officer of the municipality. At the first meeting of the council after the election, Joseph urged the necessity of relieving the city of unnecessary expenses and burdens, and warned the members against demanding pay for every little service rendered. At the same meeting it was resolved to establish markets in the city; and the Prophet spoke earnestly about the regulation of prices, so that the poor should not be oppressed; that, while the farmer should have fair compensation for his products, the mechanic should also have justice in purchasing the necessaries of life.

If the principles of official integrity and economy, and the principles of fair dealing and mutual protection between producers and dealers, which the Prophet taught at this time, could have general acceptance and obedience throughout the world, what a wonderful stride would be taken toward the social redemption of the human race! Politics would be purified—for only men of integrity and nobility of character could or would hold office. Pauperism, that fruitful source of crime, would be practically unknown. Public economy and private prosperity would go hand in hand.

On the 2nd day of March, 1843, the House of Representatives of the Illinois Legislature took up a bill to repeal a part of the Nauvoo city charter. There was a determination on the part of the majority to push the bill to its passage; and all the protests of a few fair-minded and courageous men availed nothing. Representative Thomas B. Owen compared the charter of Nauvoo with those of other cities and showed that this bill proposed to repeal the same powers in the Nauvoo charter which existed in every other charter in the state. He declared positively of his own knowledge that good order and industry characterized the "Mormons," and he made no doubt that they were much abused. He protested against such a malicious and contemptible course of cowardice as that which was proposed. Next day the bill was put upon its passage; and William Smith of Nauvoo, who was a representative in the Assembly, moved an amendment to the title of the measure so that it would read—"A bill for an act to humbug the citizens of Nauvoo." The motion created great sensation, in the midst of which William declared that he considered the amendment perfectly described the contents of the bill, and he was anxious that things should be called by their right names. Naturally the chair decided that such an amendment, "not being respectful," was not in order, and the bill with its original title was then passed. On the 4th of March the Senate considered this same measure and refused to pass it.

Hyrum brought information to the mayor on the evening of the 25th of March, 1843, upon which Joseph issued a proclamation as follows:

> Whereas it is reported that there now exists a band of desperadoes, bound by oaths of secrecy, under severe penalties in case any member of the combination divulges their plans of stealing and conveying properties from station to station, up and down the Mississippi and other routes: And

Whereas it is reported that the fear of the execution
of the pains and penalties of their secret oath on their
persons prevents some members of said secret association
(who have, through falsehood and deceit, been drawn
into their snares), from divulging the same to the legally
constituted authorities of the land:

Know ye, therefore, that I, Joseph Smith, Mayor of the
City of Nauvoo, will grant and insure protection against
all personal mob violence to each and every citizen of this
city who will come before me and truly make known the
names of all such abominable characters as are engaged
in said secret combination for stealing, or are accessory
thereto, in any manner. And I respectfully solicit the
cooperation of all ministers of justice in this and the
neighboring states to ferret out a band of thievish outlaws
from our midst.

Joseph was determined to protect Nauvoo from plunderers
without, and from thieves within, and this determination
expressed in the document just quoted was so vigorously enforced
that the bad elements, in self protection, combined against him.
This league was one of the factors in the culminating persecutions
of his life.

In the beginning of April the Prophet went to Ramus,
accompanied by Apostle Orson Hyde and William Clayton, to
preach to the Saints there. Among many important utterances
contained in his sermons of that time are these:

When the Savior shall appear, we shall see Him as
He is. We shall see that He is a man like ourselves; and
that same sociality which exists among us here will exist
among us there, only it will be coupled with eternal
glory, which glory we do not now enjoy. (John 14:2, 3.)
The appearing of the Father and the Son, in that verse, is a
personal appearance; and the idea that the Father and the
Son dwell in a man's heart is an old sectarian notion, and
is false.

In answer to the question, "Is not the reckoning of God's time, angel's time, prophet's time, and man's time according to the planet on which they reside?" I answer, yes. But there are no angels who minister to this earth but those who do belong or have belonged to it. The angels do not reside on a planet like this earth; but they reside in the presence of God, on a globe like a sea of glass and fire, where all things for their glory are manifest—past, present and future, and are continually before the Lord. The place where God resides is a great Urim and Thummim. This earth, in its sanctified and immortal state, will be made like unto crystal and will be a Urim and Thummim to the inhabitants who dwell thereon, whereby all things pertaining to an inferior kingdom, or all kingdoms of a lower order, will be manifest to those who dwell on it; and this earth will be Christ's. Then the white stone mentioned in Revelation 2:17, will become a Urim and Thummim to each individual who receives one, whereby things pertaining to a higher order of kingdoms, even all kingdoms, will be made known; and a white stone is given to each of those who come into the celestial kingdom, whereon is a new name written, which no man knoweth save he that receiveth it. The new name is the key word. . . .

Whatever principle of intelligence we attain unto in this life, it will rise with us in the resurrection; and if a person gains more knowledge and intelligence in this life through his diligence and obedience than another, he will have so much the advantage in the world to come. There is a law, irrevocably decreed in heaven before the foundations of this world, upon which all blessings are predicated; and when we obtain any blessing from God, it is by obedience to that law upon which it is predicated.

The Father has a body of flesh and bones as tangible as man's; the Son also: but the Holy Ghost has not a body of flesh and bones, but is a personage of spirit. Were it not so, the Holy Ghost could not dwell in us. A man may receive the Holy Ghost and it may descend upon him and not tarry with him.

In May, while returning through Carthage from his mission to Ramus, Joseph dined with Stephen A. Douglas, who was there holding court. After dinner the Prophet, at the request of Douglas, gave a minute history of the persecutions of the Saints in Missouri. The judge listened attentively and pronounced unstinted condemnation upon the conduct of Boggs and the other mobocrats of Missouri and declared that they ought to be punished. Joseph concluded by saying that this wholesale plunder and extermination was a foul and corroding blot upon the fair fame of the Republic, the very thought of which would have caused the patriotic framers of the Constitution to hide their faces in sorrow and shame. He prophesied to Douglas:

> Judge, you will aspire to the presidency of the United States, and if you ever turn your hand against the Latter-day Saints, you will feel the weight of the hand of the Almighty upon you; and you will live to see and know that I have testified the truth to you, for the conversation of this day will be with you through life.

These words of the Prophet to Judge Douglas have been fulfilled to the very letter. Douglas did aspire to the presidency of the United States; he did use his influence against the Latter-day Saints thinking he could gain popularity by so doing; and he miserably failed. He was deserted by his own friends and died a disappointed man.

Commencing on the first day of the fourteenth year of the Church of Jesus Christ of Latter-day Saints, a special conference was held on the floor of the temple at Nauvoo. In presenting the authorities of the Church, the Prophet asked the people if they were satisfied with the First Presidency. "If," said he, "I have done anything to injure my standing or dishonor our religion in the sight of angels, or men, or women, I am sorry for it. I do not know that I have done anything of the kind; but if I have, come forward and tell me of it."

Joseph wanted the Saints to feel that every officer of the Church, from the President down to the least in authority, was responsible to the body of the Saints, as well as to God, for his conduct; and thereby established a rule which was of great help at a later time.

Brigham Young made the motion to sustain Joseph Smith as President of the whole Church, and one vast sea of hands was presented, carrying the motion unanimously.

At this conference Apostle Orson Pratt remarked that a man's body changes every seven years; and Joseph replied:

There is no fundamental principle belonging to a human system that ever goes into another in this world or in the world to come; I care not what the theories of men are. We have the testimony that God will raise us up, and He has the power to do it. If anyone supposes that any part of our bodies, that is, the fundamental parts thereof, ever goes into another body, he is mistaken.

A special conference of the elders was convened on the 10th day of April, 1843, to ordain missionaries to go forth into the vineyards and build up churches; and one hundred and fifteen appointments were made by the united voice of the conference.

On the 12th of April, two large parties of Saints landed at Nauvoo under the charge of Elders Lorenzo Snow, Parley P. Pratt and Levi Richards. On the day following, the emigrants and a great multitude of others assembled at the temple to listen to an address from the Prophet to the newcomers. He advised them concerning their temporal welfare, their means of life; and pronounced the blessings of heaven and earth upon them, inasmuch as they should keep the commandments of God.

The lull in the active persecution against the Prophet was soon at an end. His enemies never for an instant contemplated the relinquishment of their purpose to carry him into Missouri to be assassinated. Threats came to him from time to time, the low mutterings which precede the crash of a thunderbolt. He applied to the governor of Iowa to recall the writs issued against him upon requisitions from Missouri, so that he might visit the Saints in Zarahemla, basing his request upon the action taken by Judge Pope at Springfield, which substantiated the illegality of Missouri's demand. But his request was in vain, and he was obliged to risk his liberty and his life whenever duty called him to the Iowa side of the river.

CHAPTER 56

Eternal
Marriage

Every woman has the right to virtuous wifehood and maternity. This was the omnipotent design in her creation. Yet how shall it be fulfilled under modern systems? Clearly, the Creator can make known.

"When they are out of the world they neither marry nor are given in marriage," saith the revelation; therefore the tie of conjugal relation must be made here, and to endure beyond the gates of death it must be fixed by an eternal covenant with the divine sanction.

Joseph Smith's mission was all comprehending. From the Church organization, it expanded until it made known a code of moral law by which the modern world, under the light of Christian truth, may achieve social redemption and be forever purified.

The decree of the Lord making known to the Prophet the eternity and plurality of marriage was a part of this sublime plan. It came to him little by little, as he was enabled to bear the dazzling light of celestial glory: and when eventually the full view of the holy order was permitted to him, he saw the principles of eternal progression, the laws by which the universe is filled with shining and inhabited spheres to make the infinite glory of our God. The exaltation of these visions was all that mortal man could bear; and the Prophet felt that the dull, selfish world would refuse to understand the purity and promise, would refuse to undergo the earthly trials to secure the heavenly blessing, and would seek the death of such humble disciples of the Savior as should embrace this principle of eternal life.

Even after that portion of the revelation now recorded in the Doctrine and Covenants was made known to him, Joseph did not write it for a time, although he obeyed its commands and taught it to Hyrum and other faithful men, who, in prayer and humility before God, accepted and fulfilled its requirements.

The revelation therefore remained the *unwritten law* of God, established in the hearts and obeyed in the lives of some of His faithful servants, until the 12th day of July, 1843, when it was recorded, that it might remain a comfort and guide to the people after Joseph and Hyrum should pass away. On that day, under the Prophet's dictation, and in the presence of Hyrum, the revelation was written by William Clayton. A copy of it was taken the next day by Joseph C. Kingsbury for Bishop Newel K. Whitney.

On the 12th day of August, 1843, the revelation was read before the high council and presidency of the stake of Nauvoo. There were present Hyrum Smith, who presented the principle; William Marks, Charles C. Rich, and Austin Cowles, the stake presidency; and Samuel Bent, William Huntington, Alpheus Cutler, Thomas Grover, Lewis D. Wilson, David Fullmer, Aaron Johnson, Newel Knight, Leonard Sobey, Isaac Alfred, Henry G. Sherwood, and Samuel Smith, the high council.

After reading the revelation, Hyrum promised his brethren that they who accepted it should be blessed and sustained in the Church by the Spirit of God and the confidence of the Saints, and they who rejected it should fall away in their faith and power; and it was even so.

To promulgate this commandment and to obey it was probably the Prophet's greatest earthly trial. Emma did not at first accept it; but later she became convinced of its truth and gave good women to her husband to wife as Sarah of old administered to Abraham.

Some of the Prophet's brethren caused him great sorrow by teaching impurity of life under the guise of this holy principle; but their wickedness was uncovered and the Church was purged of their presence.

The teaching of the revelation has been a test of personal holiness. The men who have seen in this commandment a holy and exalted duty and who obeyed in meekness and purity, have lived by their faith and have come off triumphant; while those who have sought to minister to evil passions have sunk and been cast out.

There is not one word in the revelation, nor was there one word in the Prophet's teaching other than purity and self sacrifice.

The Lord said:

> I am the Lord thy God; and I give unto you this commandment—that no man shall come unto the Father but by me or by my word, which is my law, saith the Lord.
>
> And everything that is in the world, whether it be ordained of men, by thrones, or principalities, or powers, or things of name, whatsoever they may be, that are not by me or by my word, saith the Lord, shall be thrown down, and shall not remain after men are dead, neither in nor after the resurrection, saith the Lord your God.
>
> For whatsoever things remain are by me; and whatsoever things are not by me shall be shaken and destroyed.
>
> Therefore, if a man marry him a wife in the world, and he marry her not by me nor by my word, and he covenant with her so long as he is in the world and she with him, their covenant and marriage are not of force when they are dead, and when they are out of the world; therefore, they are not bound by any law when they are out of the world.
>
> Therefore, when they are out of the world they neither marry nor are given in marriage; but are appointed angels in heaven, which angels are ministering servants, to minister for those who are worthy of a far more, and an exceeding, and an eternal weight of glory.
>
> For these angels did not abide my law; therefore they cannot be enlarged, but remain separately and singly, without exaltation, in their saved condition, to all eternity; and from henceforth are not gods, but are angels of God forever and ever.

And again, verily I say unto you, if a man marry a wife, and make a covenant with her for time and for all eternity, if that covenant is not by me or by my word, which is my law, and is not sealed by the Holy Spirit of promise, through him whom I have anointed and appointed unto this power, then it is not valid neither of force when they are out of the world, because they are not joined by me, saith the Lord, neither by my word; when they are out of the world it cannot be received there, because the angels and the gods are appointed there, by whom they cannot pass; they cannot, therefore, inherit my glory; for my house is a house of order, saith the Lord God.

And again, verily I say unto you, if a man marry a wife by my word, which is my law, and by the new and everlasting covenant, and it is sealed unto them by the Holy Spirit of promise, by him who is anointed, unto whom I have appointed this power, and the keys of this priesthood; and it shall be said unto them—Ye shall come forth in the first resurrection; and if it be after the first resurrection, in the next resurrection; and shall inherit thrones, kingdoms, principalities, and powers, dominions, all heights and depths—then shall it be written in the Lamb's Book of Life, that he shall commit no murder whereby to shed innocent blood, and if ye abide in my covenant, and commit no murder whereby to shed innocent blood, it shall be done unto them in all things whatsoever my servant hath put upon them, in time, and through all eternity; and shall be of full force when they are out of the world; and they shall pass by the angels, and the gods, which are set there, to their exaltation and glory in all things, as hath been sealed upon their heads, which glory shall be a fullness and a continuation of the seeds forever and ever.

Then shall they be gods, because they have no end; therefore shall they be from everlasting to everlasting, because they continue; then shall they be above all, because all things are subject unto them. Then shall they be gods, because they have all power, and the angels are subject unto them.

Verily, verily, I say unto you, except ye abide my law, ye cannot attain to this glory.

For strait is the gate, and narrow the way that leadeth unto the exaltation and continuation of the lives, and few there be that find it, because ye receive me not in the world neither do ye know me.

But if ye receive me in the world, then shall ye know me, and shall receive your exaltation, that where I am ye shall be also.

This is eternal lives, to know the only wise and true God, and Jesus Christ, whom he hath sent. I am he. Receive ye, therefore, my law....

And again, as pertaining to the law of the priesthood— if any man espouse a virgin, and desire to espouse another, and the first give her consent, and if he espouse the second, and they are virgins, and have vowed to no other man, then is he justified; he cannot commit adultery, for they are given unto him; ... for he cannot commit adultery with that that belongeth unto him and to no one else....

And now, as pertaining to this law, verily, verily, I say unto you, I will reveal more unto you hereafter; ... (D&C 132: 12–24, 61, 66)

CHAPTER 57

Joseph's Homecoming

A pitiable yielding to murderous hate was exhibited in the conduct in June, 1843, of Reynolds and Ford, the governors respectively of the great states of Missouri and Illinois. The adviser of Reynolds was John C. Bennett, the corrupt traitor; the adviser of Ford was Sam C. Owens, one of the leaders of the Jackson mob.

On the 13th day of June, Thomas Reynolds, governor of the state of Missouri, made a requisition upon the state of Illinois for the person of Joseph Smith, charged with treason, on the ground that he was a fugitive from justice. To show the close communion of the quartette, Reynolds, Bennett, Ford and Owens, it is well to note that Bennett and Owens, before any papers were issued, made their boasts that the governors of the two states would comply with their demands, and that Joseph Smith would be delivered to death at the hands of his old enemies in Missouri. And on the 10th of June, three days before the requisition was issued, Sam Owens and John C. Bennett had informed Governor Ford by letter that Joseph Reynolds, sheriff of Jackson County, (although the alleged offense of treason had been committed in Daviess County) would be appointed by Governor Reynolds of Missouri to receive the person of Joseph Smith from the officials of Illinois; and they, in the same letter, instructed Governor Ford to appoint Harmon T. Wilson of Hancock County, to serve the writ which they demanded Ford to issue. Their reason for wanting Reynolds of Jackson County is clear; he was known to be in sympathy with the mob there, while the officers of Daviess County might have an abhorrence of murder and might refuse to be so pliant as the assassins desired. While their reason for demanding the appointment of Harmon T. Wilson was stated in a letter to Ford by Sam C. Owens in the following words:

> Dr. Bennett further writes me that he has _made an arrangement_ with Harmon T. Wilson, of Hancock County, (Carthage, seat of justice), in whose hands he wishes the writ that shall be issued by you to be put.

The plan as dictated to the governors by these villains was executed.

On the same day that the governor of Missouri appointed Reynolds to go to Illinois after the person of the Prophet, Joseph started with Emma and their children to see her sister Mrs. Wasson, who lived near Dixon, Lee County, Illinois. Five days later, on the 18th of June, a message was received at Nauvoo from Judge James Adams, of Springfield, from which it was learned that Ford had issued the writ for Joseph and that it was on the way. Hyrum Smith immediately sent Stephen Markham and William Clayton on horseback, William riding Joe Duncan, to find and warn the Prophet. These devoted men traveled two hundred and twelve miles in sixty-six hours, and found Joseph between the town of Dixon and Wasson's place. When they told him of the danger, he said:

> Do not be alarmed, I have no fear, and shall not flee.
> I will find friends, and the Missourians cannot slay me,
> I tell you in the name of Israel's God.

Wilson and Reynolds had disguised themselves and proposed to be "Mormon" elders, following Joseph to Wasson's. On the 23rd of June they reached that place while the family were at dinner and said: "We want to see Brother Joseph."

They seized him the instant they found him and presented cocked pistols to his breast, without showing any writ or serving any process. Joseph inquired: "What is the meaning of this?"

And Reynolds replied: "God damn you, be still, or I'll shoot you, by God."

Wilson joined in this awful profanity and threat, and they both struck the Prophet with their pistols. He only said:

Kill me if you will, I am not afraid to die; and I have endured so much oppression that I am weary of life. But I am a strong man, and I could cast both of you down, if I would. If you have any legal process to serve, present it, for I am at all times subject to law and shall not offer resistance.

At this time Stephen Markham walked toward them, and the kidnappers swore they would kill him; but he paid no attention to their threats. Still bruising the Prophet with their pistols and threatening every instant to kill him if he spoke, they dragged him to a wagon without, and would have driven away not permitting him to say one word to his family or to obtain his hat and coat, but Stephen Markham interposed. He boldly seized the horses by the bits, and would not let them go until Emma could run from the house with the Prophet's clothing.

Stephen mounted a horse and started to Dixon, where the kidnappers also proceeded at full speed without even allowing Joseph to speak to his wife or little children. The wretches had not shown any writ, nor had they told the Prophet what was the charge against him. During the whole journey of eight miles to Dixon, they continued to strike his sides with their pistols and to swear that they would have his life. So brutal were their blows that he almost fainted, and each side was turned black and blue for a circumference of eighteen inches.

At Dixon they thrust him into a room at the tavern and guarded him there, while ordering fresh horses to be ready in five minutes. As Stephen Markham had raised an alarm at Dixon and proposed to get a lawyer, Reynolds once more declared his intention to shoot the Prophet.

Joseph said: "Why do you make this threat so often? If you want to shoot me, do so. I am not afraid."

The continued calmness and the undaunted heroism of the Prophet had their effect upon his captors; and at last they

desisted from their threats, although they continued their abuse.
No doubt they would have killed him but they were too cowardly.
They wanted to get him into Missouri where the murder could be
consummated without any danger to them. The lawyers whom
Stephen secured for the Prophet were not permitted by Reynolds
and Wilson to consult their client; but the effect of this high-
handed proceeding was to arouse the indignation of the landlord
and his friends. They gathered around the hotel and told Reynolds
that this might be the Missouri way, but it would not do for Dixon,
where the people were law-abiding and would not permit any man
to be kidnapped and dragged away without knowing the charge
against him and without an opportunity for judicial examination.
As a large crowd had gathered by this time, and as they threatened
to take summary action against the brigands, Reynolds and
Wilson concluded to permit a consultation with the lawyers.
As soon as he could get speech with the attorneys, Joseph told
them that he had been taken prisoner without process, had been
insulted, bruised and threatened; and that he wanted to sue out a
writ of *habeas corpus*. At this Reynolds swore that he would only
wait half an hour. A Mr. Dixon, who had opposed Reynolds and
Wilson in their outrageous doings, immediately sent messengers
to the master in chancery and to Lawyer Walker to have them
come to Dixon to get out a writ of *habeas corpus*.

The next morning the writ was issued, returnable before Judge
Caton of the ninth judicial circuit at Ottawa and duly served upon
Reynolds and Wilson.

Writs were also obtained against them for threatening the
life of Stephen Markham, for assaults upon Joseph and for false
imprisonment; and these villains were soon placed in the custody
of the sheriff of Lee County, whereupon their demeanor became
as craven as it had before been bold and threatening.

In the meantime Joseph had sent William Clayton to Nauvoo
to inform Hyrum of what was being done.

The Prophet, still in captivity to Reynolds and Wilson, who
in turn were in custody of Sheriff Campbell, proceeded that
night to Pawpaw grove, thirty-two miles on the road to Ottawa.

Here Reynolds and Wilson again began to abuse their captive; but Campbell came to his assistance and slept by his side that night to protect him from further assault.

Early the next morning the hotel was filled with citizens who wanted to see the Prophet and hear him preach. Fearing the effect of an address from Joseph, Sheriff Reynolds yelled: "I want you to understand that this man is my legal prisoner, and you must disperse."

This was false. No writ or other process had been served upon Joseph, and he was nobody's legal prisoner. But without waiting to discuss the legal question, an old man named David Town, who was lame and carried a large hickory walking stick, advanced upon Reynolds and said:

> You damned infernal puke, we'll learn you to come here and interrupt gentlemen. Sit down there, [pointing to a very low chair] and sit still. Don't you open your head till General Smith gets through talking. If you never learned manners in Missouri, we'll teach you that gentlemen are not to be imposed upon by a nigger-driver. You cannot kidnap men here. There's a committee in this grove that will sit on your case; and, sir, it is the highest tribunal in the United States, as *from its decision there is no appeal.*

Reynolds was made aware that Mr. Town was the head of a committee, just then assembled to deal with some land speculators who had attempted to impose upon honest settlers, and he obeyed with great meekness.

The Prophet talked an hour and a half on the subject of marriage, which was the topic selected for him by his congregation. From that hour on his freedom commenced.

Learning at Pawpaw grove that Judge Caton was absent in New York, the party turned back to Dixon, arriving there about 4 o'clock in the afternoon of June 25th. A return of the writ of *habeas corpus* was made to the master in chancery, with the endorsement that the judge was absent; whereupon a new writ was issued, returnable before the nearest tribunal in the fifth judicial district authorized to hear and determine writs of *habeas corpus*, and Mr. Campbell, the sheriff of Lee County, at once served it upon Wilson and Reynolds. Arrangements were then made to go before Judge Stephen A. Douglas at Quincy, a distance of two hundred and sixty miles; and in the meantime, anticipating treachery, Stephen Markham started with a letter to the Prophet's friends informing them further of his movements. This action was deemed necessary; for the whole country seemed to be swarming with men anxious to carry Joseph into Missouri, where, according to the free boasts of Reynolds, Wilson and others, his death was certain.

The party in charge of the Prophet proceeded toward Quincy. On Tuesday, the 27th of June, shortly after crossing Fox River, they met seven of the Prophet's friends. The brethren burst into tears at sight of Joseph; and as they embraced him he spoke to his captors who, it must be remembered, had not yet shown any writ or other process and were therefore kidnappers:

"I think I will not go to Missouri this time, gentlemen. These are my boys."

Then he mounted his favorite horse, Joe Duncan; and the entire company proceeded to a farmhouse and made a halt. This party of the Prophet's friends was under the leadership of Thomas Grover, and from them it was learned that Elders Charles C. Rich and Wilson Law, with other and larger parties, were seeking the Prophet, to prevent his murder and abduction.

Reynolds and Wilson shook with fear. Peter W. Cownover, one of the Prophet's friends, said to Wilson: "What is the matter with you? Have you got the ague?"

Wilson managed to stammer, "No."

Reynolds asked, "Is Jem Flack in the crowd?"

Someone answered: "He is not now, but you will see him tomorrow about this time."

"Then," said Reynolds, "I am a dead man; for I know him of old."

Cownover told the foolish fellow not to be frightened, for no one intended to injure him.

Stephen Markham had turned back when he met this party and was with them. He walked up to Reynolds and offered his hand, when the bandit cried out: "Do you meet me as a friend? I expected to be a dead man when I met you again."

Markham replied: "We are friends, except in law; that must have its course."

At Andover that night Reynolds and Wilson gathered a party and held a consultation. They intended to raise a company, take the Prophet by force, escape from their own arrest, and run with him to the mouth of Rock River, on the Mississippi, where they said they had a company of men all ready to drag him into Missouri and wreak vengeance upon him. But for Stephen Markham's vigilance they would have executed this plan, but he foiled them by putting the Sheriff of Lee County on his guard.

On Wednesday, the 28th of June, they encamped in a little grove at the head of Elleston Creek. While the animals were feeding, Reynolds said: "No, we will go from here to the mouth of Rock River and take steamboat to Quincy."

Markham replied: "No; for we are prepared to travel and will go by land."

Wilson and Reynolds both yelled out: "No, by God, we won't; we will never go by Nauvoo alive."

Both drew their pistols upon Markham, who turned to Sheriff Campbell saying: "When these men took Joseph a prisoner, they took even his pocket knife. They are now prisoners of yours and I demand that their arms be seized."

Reynolds and Wilson refused to yield their weapons; but when the sheriff threatened to call for assistance, they submitted.

While on this journey and resting in a little grove of timber where the ground was well sodded, one of the lawyers for Reynolds and Wilson began to boast of his prowess as a wrestler. He offered to wager any sum that he could throw any man in the state of Illinois at side-hold. Stephen Markham, a side-hold wrestler, told the lawyer that he would not contest for money but would try a bout for fun. They grappled, and the man threw Markham, when a great shout arose from Joseph's enemies, and they began to taunt the Prophet and his friends.

Joseph turned to Brother Philemon C. Merrill, a young man from Nauvoo, subsequently adjutant in the Mormon Battalion, and later a resident of St. David, Arizona, and said: "Get up and throw that man."

Merrill was about to say that side-hold was not his game; but before he could speak the Prophet commanded him in such a way that his tongue was silenced. He arose to his feet filled with the strength of a Samson. Merrill lifted his arms and said to the lawyer: "Take your choice of sides."

The man took the left side with his right arm under; when the company all declared that this was not fair, as he had a double advantage. Merrill felt such confidence in the word of the Prophet that it made no difference to him how much advantage his opponent took, and he allowed the hold. As they grappled Joseph said: "Philemon, when I count three, *throw him!*"

On the instant after the word dropped from Joseph's lips, Merrill, with the strength of a giant, threw the lawyer over his left shoulder, and he fell striking his head upon the earth.

Awe fell upon the opponents of the Prophet when they saw this, and there were no more challenges to wrestle during the journey.

While they were lodged at a farmhouse near Monmouth, one night Reynolds and Wilson again plotted to raise a mob and seize Joseph; but Peter Cownover detected them, and Sheriff Campbell put them under restraint, feeling that they were no longer to be trusted. On Thursday, the 29th of June, another party of the Prophet's friends joined him. He called James Flack to his side and told him he must not injure Reynolds, whatever the provocation might have been; for the Prophet had pledged himself to protect the Missouri sheriff.

The lawyers and Sheriff Campbell, with other civil officers, decided that the hearing upon the writ of *habeas corpus* might lawfully be held in Nauvoo, and they desired to go there rather than to Quincy; so the party turned in that direction. This occasioned great joy to Joseph. His bruises were forgotten, and that night when they reached the house of Michael Crane, on Honey Creek, he sprang from the buggy, walked up to the fence, and leaped over without touching it.

A messenger had carried the news of the homecoming to Nauvoo, and on Friday, June the 30th, a joyous cavalcade went out to meet the Prophet. The meeting between Joseph and Hyrum was most touching. Joseph had just passed through one of the many perils of his life, but one of the few which Hyrum did not share; and his return caused Hyrum to weep for joy as he took the Prophet in his arms. The spectacle of the entry into Nauvoo was most imposing, for the delighted people sang for joy and made such demonstration of love and gladness in Joseph's behalf, that the lawyers and officers from Dixon were charmed and deeply impressed.

After they were within the city, the multitude seemed unwilling to disperse, but Joseph said to them:

> I am out of the power of the Missourians again, thank God; and thank you all for your kindness and love. I bless you in the name of Jesus Christ. I shall address you in the grove, near the temple, at 4 o'clock this afternoon.

A feast had been prepared at Joseph's house, and there he went—still in the hands of his captors, Reynolds and Wilson, who were the prisoners of Sheriff Campbell of Lee County; and all of these with about fifty of the Prophet's friends sat at his table. The place of honor was given to Reynolds and Wilson, who were waited upon by Emma with as much courtesy as could have been bestowed upon a beloved guest. This kindness heaped coals of fire on their heads, for they remembered the time when they had dragged the Prophet from the side of his wife and little ones and had refused to permit him to say farewell.

Under advice of the lawyers, Joseph with his captors was brought before the municipal court at Nauvoo, and all the writs and other papers were filed there. The case was heard upon its merits, and the Prophet was discharged. The lawyers concurred that in all the transactions since the day of his arrest Joseph had held himself amendable to the law and its officers; and that the decision of the municipal court of Nauvoo was not only legal and just but was within the power of this tribunal under the city charter.

But before the actual hearing began in the municipal court, Reynolds and Wilson in company with Lawyer Davis, of Carthage, started for that place threatening to raise a mob with which to drag Joseph from Nauvoo. Desiring a larger force than they could readily command at Carthage, they applied to Governor Ford for the state militia. But the governor sent a trusted messenger to Nauvoo to obtain evidence concerning the seizure of the Prophet and his discharge on the writ of *habeas corpus*; and this gentleman secured a copy of all the papers and evidence in the case. Prominent citizens of Lee County added their affidavits; and several gentlemen went up to Springfield to represent the matter fairly to his Excellency. Whatever Ford's motive may have been—whether a desire to make political capital for his party with influential men who took the side of the Saints in this question, or whether he had fear that he would lose his personal prestige by precipitating the unlawful strife—he took the only proper course; and after long consideration, and upon the presentation of his trusted messenger, he refused to order out the militia, and so reported to Sheriff Reynolds and Governor Reynolds of Missouri. The position which Ford assumed was that no resistance had been made to any writ issued by the state of Illinois, and therefore that Illinois had neither right nor interest in the matter.

On the 2nd and 3rd days of July, parties returned who had been out from Nauvoo searching for the Prophet. One party had gone up the river on the little steamer *Maid of Iowa*, under command of Dan Jones, and had passed through a very adventurous voyage. This company was accompanied by Apostle John Taylor. Another party, under the leadership of General Charles C. Rich, had traveled five hundred miles on horseback in seven days. They were all delighted to find the Prophet safe at home; and he blessed them for their love and devotion to him.

At a special conference on Monday, the 3rd day of July, a large number of elders were called to go into the different counties of Illinois, to preach the gospel and convey correct information to the people of the state concerning the Prophet's arrest and his discharge from custody.

On the 4th day of July, about fifteen thousand people congregated at the grove near the temple, among them being about one thousand ladies and gentlemen from St. Louis, Quincy and Burlington, who listened attentively to orations and speeches. In the course of the address which he delivered, the Prophet spoke a few words in relation to his own arrest, in which he defended himself to the satisfaction of the vast multitude, both Saints and visitors:

> I never spent more than six months in Missouri, except while in prison. While I was free in that state, I was at work for the support of my family. I was never a prisoner of war during my stay, for I had nothing to do with war. I never took a pistol, gun, or sword; and the most that has been said on this subject by the Missourians is false. I have been willing to go before any governor, judge or tribunal where justice would be done, and have the subject investigated. I could not have committed treason in that state while I resided there, for treason against Missouri consists in levying war against the state or adhering to her enemies. Missouri was at peace, and had no enemy that I could adhere to, had I been disposed; and I did not make war, and no command or authority, either civil or military, but only in spiritual matters as a minister of the Gospel.

CHAPTER 58

Sidney Rigdon
Defects

When the Prophet once more saw one hour of security in Nauvoo, he recorded the fact that he had been subjected in his time to thirty-eight suits against his person and property. Not one of these was just. They were all incited for the purpose of vexing and despoiling him, and by the satanic power that had sought to shed the blood of prophets and holy men through all ages.

But he was compensated and filled with joy to see the progress of Nauvoo. From the states in this country and from the lands across the sea, faithful Saints were gathering by tens, and hundreds, and thousands. Homes were being built and factories were projected; the walls of the temple were rising in grandeur, uplifting the souls of the Saints with hope that they would soon minister in the holy ordinances for their living and their dead; and all that was wanted to insure the dominion of peace was the cessation of the wicked assaults upon the Prophet and his friends.

On the last of August, Joseph and his family moved into the Nauvoo Mansion. It was his intention to support this place as a home for all visitors who should come up to Zion seeking to know the glory of God. Such hospitality was no new thing for the Prophet to bestow. His home, whenever he had one, had always been open to Saints and to strangers. It had been a resting place for thousands; and many times his family had gone without food, after giving their last morsel to the poor wayfarers. The mansion was a place in which such hospitality as the Prophet loved could well be extended. With these facilities to entertain company, Joseph soon found his resources exhausted. But for the persecutions and robberies which he had suffered he might have continued to dispense his bounties with generous hand; but now he was compelled to have the mansion opened as a hotel, at first under his own direction, but a little later it was leased for that purpose to Ebenezer Robinson, the Prophet only retaining two or three rooms for his personal use. Joseph's mother lived with him at this time.

Among the saddest afflictions of the Prophet's closing hours was the recreancy of Sidney Rigdon. As early as August, 1843, Joseph had solemnly withdrawn his fellowship from Sidney, and had refused to acknowledge him longer as a counselor—unless the charge could satisfactorily be refuted that he was in league with the Prophet's enemies to betray him and give him up to death in Missouri. This was not the only ground for complaint. Sidney was charged with an alliance with dishonest persons to deal fraudulently against the innocent and unwary. At a special conference begun in Nauvoo on the 6th of October, examination was made of the statements against President Rigdon. The Prophet recalled the many times that he had borne with Sidney's failings, having forgiven him again and again; and that now Sidney had ceased altogether to be useful and devoted, and Joseph lacked entire confidence in his integrity. Filled with mercy, Hyrum desired that one more trial should be given to Elder Rigdon, and upon his motion Sidney was sustained. The Prophet arose and said:

> I have thrown him off my shoulders, and you have again put him on me. You may carry him, but I will not.

Subsequent events clearly showed how truly the Prophet had judged of the man who was once his friend and counselor, but had now lost faith and power in the gospel.

Assaults from without were threatened, with violence constantly augmenting. In August some of the brethren who were elected to county offices went to Carthage to give bonds and take the official oath. While these men were before the court, a rabble consisting of Constable Harmon T. Wilson and about fifteen others came in armed with hickory clubs, knives and pistols, and swore that the bonds should not be approved nor the men from Nauvoo inducted into office; if they were, blood would be spilled; and the mob pledged their words, honor and reputation, not only to keep these men out of office, but to put clown the "Mormons." After some delay, the rabble withdrew to convene a mob meeting, and the bonds were approved by the court. This mob secured a convention at the courthouse on the 19th of August and appointed a committee to draft resolutions concerning the Saints; and at an adjourned meeting held on the 6th of September, 1843, a most vindictive tirade, filled with lies and threats, was presented and accepted under the name of preamble and resolutions. These mobocrats pledged themselves in the most determined manner to give aid in the capture of Joseph if he were demanded again, and threatened signal and summary vengeance upon the Saints in case of a collision. All the office-seekers were warned that the influence of the mobocrats would be withdrawn from them if they sought support at Nauvoo.

This action was designed to comfort the Missourians and to incite them to further efforts; and also to warn the office-holders and office-seekers of the state of Illinois not to extend any help to Joseph and his people in case of an attack upon them. The sole causes of the movements, in addition to the falsehoods of Reynolds and Wilson, who felt chagrined at their failure to drag the Prophet to his death as they had threatened, was that the people were increasing, Nauvoo was becoming a beautiful city, and Joseph Smith, the Prophet of God and head of the community, was the object of sectarian and apostate jealousy and political hate. Joseph wrote to the governor concerning the threatened movements against the Saints, but received no satisfaction.

The promise of the Hancock County mob and the quiescence of the governor of Illinois gave license and promise of support to the people of Missouri in the commission of further outrages. In November Daniel Avery and his son Philander were kidnapped from Hancock County by a company of Missourians and imprisoned and threatened with death for the purpose of extorting false statements from them upon which prosecutions could be based against the citizens of Nauvoo. A man named Elliot of Carthage, who had assisted the kidnappers, was arrested and brought before a court at Nauvoo for examination. No attempt was made to inflict punishment upon him; the evidence clearly showed his guilt, and he was bound over to the circuit court at Carthage. This same Elliot had sworn to have the Prophet's life, and complaint was lodged against him for threatening to kill. Elliot was alone and defenseless; and when the Prophet saw the man's fear and helplessness, he obtained a withdrawal of the charge, paid the costs himself, and invited Elliot to his own home to be fed and lodged.

Writs for the other persons engaged in the Avery kidnapping were issued, but an armed mob congregated to prevent the service of process. A party of the mob went to the house of David Holman, near Ramus, and in his absence plundered it of provisions and then burned it to the ground, leaving himself and family shelterless in the bleak winter.

An attack was threatened upon Nauvoo by gathering mobs from Missouri and Illinois; and in view of this danger the Nauvoo Legion was ordered to be kept in readiness to repel unlawful assaults.

The vindictive and lawless character of the mob which menaced the city is shown by the statement of Amos Chase, who heard the following conversation between a spectator and the rabble:

"What will you do if the governor refuses to sanction your course?"

"Damn the governor! If he opens his head, we will punch a hole through him! He dare not speak! We will serve him the same sauce we will the Mormons."

And their cowardly character is shown by the experience of Nelson Judd. A man called on Brother Judd at Nauvoo and said he wanted to sell him some wood at a little distance down the river. Nelson went with the man, and when they came into the woods two men on horseback attempted to kidnap him. He avoided them and they drew their pistols and fired, but without effect. Judd then coolly said: "Now it is my turn."

Putting his hand into his pocket as though to draw a pistol, he looked fiercely at the bandits, and they fled shrieking with terror. Nelson had no weapon with him except his bravery and innocence, and he walked home laughing at the ruffians.

At a meeting of the city council in December, 1843, the subject of the menace to the city and the mayor was under consideration, and Joseph said among other things:

> I am exposed to far greater danger from traitors among ourselves than from enemies without, although my life has been sought for many years by the civil and military authorities, priests and people of Missouri; and if I can escape from the ungrateful treachery of assassins, I can live as *Caesar might have lived, were it not for a right-hand Brutus.* I have had pretended friends betray me. All the enemies upon the face of the earth may roar and exert all their power to bring about my death, but they can accomplish nothing, unless some who are among us, who have enjoyed our society, have been with us in our councils, participated in our confidence, taken us by the hand, called us brother, saluted us with a kiss, join with our enemies, turn our virtues into faults, and, by falsehood and deceit, stir up their wrath and indignation against us, and bring their united vengeance upon our heads. All the hue and cry of the chief priests and elders against the Savior could not bring down the wrath of the Jewish nation upon his head, and thereby cause the crucifixion of the Son of God, until Judas said unto them: "Whomsoever I shall kiss he is the man: hold him fast." Judas was one of the Twelve Apostles, even their treasurer, and dipped with their Master in the dish, and through his treachery the crucifixion was brought about; and *we have a Judas in our midst.*

James Arlington Bennett, a lawyer, journalist and politician of New York, had been attracted by the Prophet's fame and character. Mr. Bennett had ambition to run for office in the state of Illinois, and he wrote a very complimentary letter to Joseph, in which he spoke of the boldness of the Prophet's plans and measures; and that he, Bennett, would yet run for high office in Illinois, and would give the Prophet his best services; intimated that he would like to become Joseph's right-hand man, since "Mahomet had his right-hand man"; and he declared that his mind was of so mathematical and philosophical a cast that divinity made an impression upon him.

To this bombastic letter the Prophet replied with such incisive vigor that must have taught Mr. Bennett a lesson:

You say, "The boldness of my plans and measures, together with their unparalleled success so far, are calculated to throw a charm over my whole being, and to point me out as the most extraordinary man of the present age." *The boldness of my plans and measures* can readily be tested by the touchstone of all schemes, systems, projects and adventures—*truth*, for truth is a matter of fact; and the fact is, that by the power of God I translated the Book of Mormon from hieroglyphics, the knowledge of which was lost to the world; in which wonderful event I stood alone, an unlearned youth, to combat the worldly wisdom and multiplied ignorance of eighteen centuries with a new revelation, which (if they would receive the everlasting Gospel) would open the eyes of more than eight hundred millions of people, and make "plain the old paths," wherein, if a man walk in all the ordinances of God blameless, he shall inherit eternal life; and Jesus Christ, who was, and is, and is to come, has borne me safely over every snare and plan, laid in secret or openly, through priestly hypocrisy, sectarian prejudice, popular philosophy, executive power, or law-defying mobocracy, to destroy me.

If, then, the hand of God, in all these things that I have accomplished towards the salvation of a priest-ridden generation, in the short space of twelve years through the boldness of the plan of preaching the Gospel, and the boldness of the means of declaring repentance and baptism for the remission of sins, and a reception of the Holy Ghost, by laying on of the hands, agreeably to the authority of the Priesthood, and the still more bold measures of receiving direct revelation from God, through the Comforter, as promised, and by which means all holy men, from ancient times till now, have spoken and revealed the will of God to men, with the consequent "success" of the gathering of the Saints, throws any "charm" around my being, and "points me out as the most extraordinary man of the age," it demonstrates the fact, that truth is mighty, and must prevail; and that one man empowered from Jehovah has more influence with the children of the kingdom than eight hundred millions led by the precepts of men. God exalts the humble and debases the haughty. . . .

The summit of your future fame seems to be hid in the political policy of a "mathematical problem" for the chief magistracy of this state, which, I suppose, might be solved by "double position," where the *errors* of the *supposition* are used to produce a true answer.

But, sir, when I leave the dignity and honor I received from heaven to hoist a man into power through the aid of my friends where the evil and designing, after the object has been accomplished, can look up the clemency intended as a reciprocation for such favors, and where the wicked and unprincipled, as a matter of course, would seize the opportunity to flintify the hearts of the nation against me for dabbling at a sly game in politics; verily, I say, when I leave the dignity and honor of heaven to gratify the ambition and vanity of man or men, may my power cease, like the strength of Samson, when he was shorn of his locks, while asleep in the lap of Delilah! Truly said the Savior, "Cast not your pearls before swine, lest they trample them under their feet, and turn again and rend you."

Shall I, who have witnessed the visions of eternity, and beheld the glories of the mansions of bliss, and the regions and misery of the damned, shall I turn to be a Judas? Shall I, who have heard the voice of God, and communed with angels, and spake, as moved by the Holy Ghost, for the renewal of the everlasting covenant and for the gathering of Israel in the last days, shall I worm myself into a political hypocrite? Shall I who hold the keys of the last kingdom, in which is the dispensation of the fullness of all things spoken by the mouths of all the holy prophets since the world began, under the sealing power of the Melchizedek Priesthood—shall I stoop from the sublime authority of Almighty God to be handled as a monkey's cat's-paw, and pettify myself into a clown to act the farce of political demagoguery? No, verily no! The whole earth shall bear me witness, that I, like the towering rock in the midst of the ocean, which has withstood the mighty surges of the warring waves for centuries, *am impregnable*, and am a faithful friend to virtue, and a fearless foe to vice; no odds, whether the former was sold as a pearl in Asia or hid as a gem in America, and the latter dazzles in palaces or glitters among the tombs.

I combat the errors of ages; I meet the violence of mobs; I cope with illegal proceedings from executive authority; I cut the Gordian knot of powers; and I solve mathematical problems of universities *with truth— diamond truth; and God is my "right-hand man."*

In December memorials were prepared and sent to Congress supplicating for a redress of the wrongs inflicted upon the Saints in Missouri and for protection against further plundering.

This seemed necessary, for the governor of Illinois had practically confessed the helplessness of the state to prevent the infliction of additional wrongs upon this long-suffering people. The memorials were signed by the citizens of Hancock County and the city council of Nauvoo; they were truthful and eloquent; and they were of as little avail as other appeals for justice made by the people of God in this and other ages. Several of the elders wrote addresses to their native states, setting forth with the vigor of truth the wrongs and oppressions which had been inflicted upon them by Missouri. Joseph wrote a stirring appeal to the people—the Green Mountain boys—of his native state of Vermont. After sketching the great wrongs which the people had endured, the Prophet says:

Must we, because we believe in the fullness of the Gospel of Jesus Christ, the administration of angels and the communion of the Holy Ghost, like the prophets and apostles of old,—must we be mobbed with impunity, be exiled from our habitations and property without remedy, murdered without mercy, and government find the weapons and pay the vagabonds for doing the jobs, and give them the plunder into the bargain? Must we, because we believe in enjoying the constitutional privilege and right of worshiping Almighty God according to the dictates of our own consciences, and because we believe in repentance, and baptism for the remission of sins, the gift of the Holy Ghost by the laying on of hands, the resurrection of the dead, the millennium, the day of judgment and the Book of Mormon as the history of the aborigines of this continent,—must we be expelled from the institutions of our country, the rights of citizenship, and the graves of our friends and brethren, and the government lock the gate of humanity and shut the door of redress against us? If so, farewell freedom! adieu to personal safety! and let the red hot wrath of an offended God purify the nation of such sinks of corruption; for that realm is hurrying to ruin where vice has the power to expel virtue.

My father, who stood several times in the battles of the American Revolution, till his companions in arms had been shot dead at his feet, was forced from his home in Far West, Missouri, by those civilized or satanized savages, in the dreary season of winter, to seek a shelter in another state; and the vicissitudes and sufferings consequent to his flight brought his honored gray head to the grave a few months after. . . .

I appeal to the "Green Mountain Boys" of my native state to rise in the majesty of virtuous freemen, and by all honorable means help to bring Missouri to the bar of justice. If there is one whisper from the spirit of an Ethan Allen, or a gleam from the shade of a General Stark, let it mingle with our sense of honor and fire our bosoms for the cause of suffering innocence, for the reputation of our disgraced country, and for the glory of God; and may all the earth bear me witness, if Missouri—blood-stained Missouri, escapes the due demerit of her crimes—the vengeance she so justly deserves, that Vermont is a hypocrite, a coward, and this nation the hotbed of political demagogues.

I make this appeal to the sons of liberty of my native state for help to frustrate the wicked designs of sinful men. I make it to hush the violence of mobs. I make it to cope with the unhallowed influence of wicked men in high places. I make it to resent the insult and injury made to an innocent, unoffending people, by a lawless ruffian state. I make it to obtain justice where law is put at defiance. I make it to wipe off the stain of blood from our nation's escutcheon. I make it to show presidents, governors and rulers prudence. I make it to fill honorable men with discretion. I make it to teach senators wisdom. I make it to teach judges justice. I make it to point clergymen to the path of virtue. And I make it to turn the hearts of this nation to the truth and realities of pure and undefiled religion, that they may escape the perdition of ungodly men: and Jesus Christ, the Son of God, is my great counselor.

On Christmas morning, 1843, Joseph and Hyrum were roused from their slumbers by the hymn of a choir singing, "Mortals, Awake! with Angels Join." The choir was composed of a widow named Lettice Rushton and her children and neighbors; and their sweet voices and the noble sentiments of the hymn thrilled the souls of the Prophet and Patriarch into gladness and thanksgiving. Joseph blessed the singers and thanked his Heavenly Father for the visit. Hyrum said that he thought at first that a cohort of angels had descended, for the music had such a heavenly effect upon his soul. It was the last Christmas carol that Joseph and Hyrum heard in this life. Before another year had passed these two grand mortals had passed into the slumber of death, to awake with immortality upon them and to join with the choir invisible.

On the night of the same day another joy came to Joseph. He was entertaining a company of friends at his house when the festivities were interrupted by a man who came unbidden to the feast. His hair was long and fell over his face and upon his shoulders. He seemed a stranger to all and yet acted boldly and confidently as if at home. The company thought he was a Missourian and he would have been ejected, but the Prophet came and looked him fairly in the face and discovered to his great joy that it was his long-tried and persecuted friend Orrin Porter Rockwell who, in fulfillment of the prediction of Joseph, had come away honorably from Missouri.

Orrin was gladly welcomed then to the banquet, and the Prophet listened to the recital of his adventures. After going to the East in 1842 and remaining some months, Rockwell determined to return to his home in Nauvoo, not desiring perpetual exile. At St. Louis he was captured and thrown into jail. Iron hobbles and manacles were fastened upon him and he was carried to

Independence. He was dragged from place to place, from court to court, tortured, threatened, starved, and all without any legal or just charge against him. Not the remotest connection could be traced between him and the attempt upon Boggs' life. He had not been seen in the entire state of Missouri during the year in which that event took place. No court from very shame could hold him on this monstrous charge, but when it failed others were concocted; and in the meantime several mob parties attempted to take his life as he was dragged to and fro in custody. After repeated solicitations he induced Joseph Reynolds, the sheriff of Jackson, to write to Bishop Whitney at Nauvoo, and this is the communication which that officer of law forwarded:

Independence, Missouri April 7th, 1843

Sir:—At the request of Orrin Porter Rockwell, who is now confined in our jail, I write you a few lines concerning his affairs. He is held to bail in the sum of $5,000, and wishes some of his friends to bail him out. He also wishes some friend to bring his clothes to him. He is in good health and pretty good spirits. My own opinion is, after conversing with several persons here, that it would not be safe for any of Mr. Rockwell's friends to come here, notwithstanding I have written the above at his request; neither do I think bail would be taken (unless it was some responsible person well known here as a resident of this state). Any letter to Mr. Rockwell, (post paid) with authority expressed on the back for me to open it, will be handed to him without delay. In the meantime he will be humanely treated and dealt with kindly, until discharged by due course of law.

Yours, etc.,

J. H. REYNOLDS

From Orrin's own narrative of his experience the following paragraphs are taken:

When I was put in Independence jail, I was again ironed hand and foot, and put in the dungeon, in which condition I remained about two months. During this time, Joseph H. Reynolds, the sheriff, told me he was going to arrest Joseph Smith, and they had received letters from Nauvoo which satisfied them that Joseph Smith had unlimited confidence in me, that I was capable of toling him in a carriage or on horseback anywhere that I pleased; and if I would only tole him out by riding or any other way, so that they could apprehend him, I might please myself whether I stayed in Illinois or came back to Missouri; they would protect me, and any pile that I would name the citizens of Jackson County would donate, club together and raise, and that I should never suffer for want afterwards: "you only deliver Joe Smith into our hands, and name your pile." I replied—"I will see you all damned first, and then I won't."

About the time that Joseph was arrested by Reynolds at Dixon, 1 knowing that they were after him, and no means under heaven of giving him any information, my anxiety became so intense upon the subject, knowing their determination to kill him, that my flesh twitched on my bones. I could not help it; twitch it would. While undergoing this sensation, I heard a dove alight on the window in the upper room of the jail, and commence cooing, and then went off. In a short time he came back to the window, where a pane was broken; he crept through the bars of iron, which were about two and a half inches apart. I saw it fly round the trapdoor several times; it did not alight, but continued cooing until it crept through the bars again, and flew out through the broken window.

I relate this, as it was the only occurrence of the kind that happened during my long and weary imprisonment; but it proved a comfort to me; the twitching of my flesh ceased, and I was fully satisfied from that moment that they would not get Joseph into Missouri, and that I should regain my freedom. From the best estimates that can be made, it was at the time when Joseph was in the custody of Reynolds.

In a few days afterwards, Sheriff Reynolds came into the jail and told me that he had made a failure in the arrest of Joseph.

At last, finding that no charge could be maintained against the prisoner, and that he could not be bribed or cajoled, or driven into a traitorous act, he was turned loose to find his way on foot across the state of Missouri, which swarmed with enemies. He was marvelously preserved from dangers which encompassed his path, and reached Nauvoo as much to Joseph's joy as to his own.

The Prophet must have compared the fidelity of this unpretending but loyal man with the selfish and traitorous action of some men upon whom benefits and confidences had been showered.

CHAPTER 59

Political
Foresight

For President of the United States: Joseph Smith, of
Illinois.

This was the announcement made to the world in the opening
of 1844, from Nauvoo. At a political meeting held there on the
29th day of January, Joseph was nominated, and on the 17th day of
May, at a state convention held in the same place, the nomination
was sustained.

Such a candidacy was not assumed at such a time without
careful and lengthy deliberation. Its purpose was less to secure
political fame or elevation for the Prophet, than to bring his
patriotic and statesmanlike ideas before the world, and to force
the sufferings of the Saints upon the attention of the thinking men
throughout the land.

Joseph's views of government, its powers and duties, his
knowledge of the steps by which the nation could retrace its way
from the gulf into which it was being plunged, were far in advance
of his time. The recreancy and the moral cowardice of many of
the public men in the republic who were aspirants for that high
station called for some rebuke; for many of them were deliberately
precipitating the evils which soon deluged the land with blood,
and others through fear were skulking from the face of this danger.
It was time for a declaration of truth from a man who not only had
the prophetic foresight but who had the courage to declare for
justice. Viewed from the standpoint of politicians, the candidacy
of the Prophet was hopeless in 1844. What it might have been if he
had lived and it had been renewed at a later time, when the best

minds of the nation could have grasped and advocated the noble principles which he enunciated, and thinking men throughout the length and breadth of the land could have seen that this was the way of all others for escape from war, let the student of history decide. Certain it is, that had Joseph Smith been elected President of the United States and been sustained by Congress in his policy, this land would have been spared the desolating woe which filled its hamlets and fields with carnage and its homes with sobbing widows and orphans.

From this same state of Illinois, a backwoodsman came sixteen years later to settle the national dispute and save the Union by the stern arbitrament of the sword, for by this time the paltering politicians of the schools were by the mighty voice of the people set aside. This man, raised up by Providence for the task, and with the courage to do, was the nation's support and rescuer in 1861–65. But had the nation accepted Joseph Smith, with the views which he proclaimed and with the divine prescience upon him, he would have proved, in 1845–49, the republic's savior. Peaceful methods would have prevailed, and Columbia would have been spared the most bloody and costly civil war of which profane history gives any account.

Looking back upon that time of the war after nearly a generation has past, men are prone to think less of the agonies of the strife; they begin to feel that it was necessary; to feel that the republic is stronger because cemented by the blood of brother who fell under brother's hand and by the tears of the widow and the fatherless. To sense the full beneficence which Joseph Smith might have wrought, let the patriot project his mind into the future and think if peril impended today how much better to save the country and the Constitution by heroic statesmanship than by military valor.

The sentiment which permitted the persecutions in Missouri and Illinois to go unchecked and unredressed was rapidly ripening for the greater strife. Joseph saw this. When he permitted his name to be used he said to his friends:

I would not have suffered my name to have been used by my friends on anywise as President of the United States or candidate for that office, if I and my friends could have had the privilege of enjoying our religious and civil rights as American citizens, even those rights which the Constitution guarantees unto all her citizens alike. But this we as a people have been denied from the beginning. Persecution has rolled upon our heads from time to time from portions of the United States, like peals of thunder, because of our religion; and no portion of the government as yet has stepped forward for our relief. And under view of these things, I feel it to be my right and privilege to obtain what influence and power I can, lawfully, in the United States, for the protection of injured innocence; and if I lose my life in a good cause, I am willing to be sacrificed on the altar of virtue, righteousness and truth, in maintaining the laws and Constitution of the United States, if need be, for the general good of mankind.

Joseph had not allowed this candidacy to be announced until every effort had been made to impress the leading politicians of the day with a sense of national peril and with recognition of the means by which overhanging disaster might be dissipated. Late in 1843 and in the opening of 1844, he held correspondence with Clay, Calhoun, Van Buren, Cass and others, in which his own courage and exalted ideas of government come in contradistinction to the sycophantic and excessive caution of time-serving politicians.

He hit Calhoun, the champion of states rights, on a tender spot, and used the woes of the Saints for an illustration when he said:

Your second paragraph leaves you naked before yourself, like a likeness in a mirror, when you say that "according to your *view*, the Federal Government is one of limited and specific powers," and has no jurisdiction in the case of the Mormons. So then a state can at any time expel any portion of her citizens with impunity, and, in the language of Mr. Van Buren, frosted over with your

gracious *"views of the case,"* though the cause is ever so
just, government can do nothing for them, because it has
no power.

Go on, then, Missouri, after another set of inhabitants
(as the Latter-day Saints did) have entered some two or
three hundred thousand dollars' worth of land, and made
extensive improvements thereon; go on, then, I say, banish
the occupants or owners, or kill them, as the mobbers did
many of the Latter-day Saints, and take their land and
property as spoil; and let the legislature, as in the case of
the Mormons, appropriate a couple of hundred thousand
dollars to pay the mob for doing that job; for the renowned
senator from South Carolina, Mr. J. C. Calhoun, says the
powers of the Federal Government are *so specific and
limited that it has no jurisdiction of the case!* O ye people
who groan under the oppression of tyrants! ye exiled Poles,
who have felt the iron hand of Russian grasp!—ye poor and
unfortunate among all nations! come to the asylum of the
oppressed; buy ye lands of the general government; pay in
your money to the treasury to strengthen the army and the
navy; worship God according to the dictates of your own
consciences; pay in your taxes to support the great heads
of a glorious nation; but remember, a *"sovereign state"*
is so much more powerful than the United States, the
parent government, that it can exile you at pleasure, mob
you with impunity, confiscate your lands and property,
have the legislature sanction it,—yea, even murder you
as an edict of an emperor, *and it does no wrong*; for the
noble senator of South Carolina says the power of the
Federal Government is *so limited and specific, that it has
no jurisdiction of the case.* What think ye of *Imperium in
imperio?*

And to Clay he said:

True greatness never wavers; but when the Missouri compromise was entered into by you for the benefit of slavery, there was a shrinkage of western honor.

Soon after his nomination was promulgated, he wrote an address to the American people containing his views of the powers and policy of the government of the United States. It was something new in the way of political platforms. Ignoring the evasions and the platitudes with which the scheming and shifting talk of the day was burdened, he uttered burning words of patriotism and statesmanship upon the issues which were then paramount in the land. With the acceptance of his plans, the slave question might have been settled without the effusion of blood and at an expense infinitely less than that of war; and rebellion in any state might have been instantly crushed under the national heel. The following paragraphs are from his address:

Born in a land of liberty, and breathing an air uncorrupted with the sirocco of barbarous climes, I ever feel a double anxiety for the happiness of all men, both in time and in eternity.

My cogitations, like Daniel's, have for a long time troubled me, when I viewed the condition of men throughout the world, and more especially in this boasted realm, where the Declaration of Independence "holds these truths to be self-evident, that all men are created equal; that they are endowed by their Creator with certain unalienable rights; that among these are life, liberty, and the pursuit of happiness"; but at the same time some two or three millions of people are held as slaves for life, because the spirit of them is covered with a darker skin than ours; and hundreds of our own kindred for an infraction, or supposed infraction, of some overwise statute, have to be incarcerated in dungeon glooms, or suffer the more moral penitentiary gravitation of mercy in a nutshell, while the duelist, the debauchee, and the defaulter for millions and other criminals, take the uppermost rooms at feasts, or, like the bird of passage, find a more congenial clime by flight.

The wisdom which ought to characterize the freest, wisest and most noble nation of the nineteenth century, should, like the sun in its meridian splendor, warm every object beneath its rays; and in main efforts of her officers, who are nothing more or less than the servants of the people, ought to be directed to ameliorate the condition of all, black or white, bond or free; for the best of books says, God "hath made of one blood all nations of men for to dwell on all the face of the earth."

Our common country presents to all men the same advantages, the same facilities, the same prospects, the same honors, and the same rewards; and without hypocrisy, the Constitution, when it says, *"We, the people* of the United States in order to form a more perfect union, establish justice, ensure domestic tranquility, provide for the common defense, promote the general welfare, and secure the blessings of liberty to ourselves and our posterity, do ordain and establish this constitution for the United States of America," meant just what it said without reference to color or condition, *ad infinitum.*

The aspirations and expectations of a virtuous people, environed with so wise, so liberal, so deep, so broad, and so high a character of *equal rights* as appears in said Constitution, ought to be treated by those to whom the administration of the laws is entrusted with as much sanctity as the prayers of the Saints are treated in heaven, that love, confidence and union, like the sun, moon and stars, should bear witness,

(For ever singing as they shine.)
The hand that made us is divine!

Unity is power; and when I reflect on the importance of it to the stability of all governments, I am astounded at the silly moves of persons and parties to foment discord in order to ride into power on the current of popular excitement; nor am I less surprised at the stretches of power or restrictions of right which too often appear as acts of legislators to pave the way to some favorite political scheme as destitute of intrinsic merit as a wolf's heart is of the milk of human kindness. . . .

Now, O people! people! turn unto the Lord and live, and reform this nation. Frustrate the designs of wicked men. Reduce Congress at least two-thirds. Two senators from a state and two members to a million of population will do more business than the army that now occupy the halls of the national legislature. Pay them two dollars and their board per diem (except Sundays). That is more than the farmer gets, and he lives honestly. Curtail the officers of the government in pay, number and power; for the Philistine lords have shorn our nation of its goodly locks in the lap of Delilah. . . .

Advise your legislators, when they make laws for larceny, burglary, or any felony, to make the penalty applicable to work upon roads, public works, or any place where the culprit can be taught more wisdom and more virtue, and become more enlightened. Rigor and seclusion will never do as much to reform the propensities of men as reason and friendship. Murder only can claim confinement or death. Let the penitentiaries be turned into seminaries of learning, where intelligence, like the angels of heaven, would banish such fragments of barbarism. Imprisonment for debt is a meaner practice than the savage tolerates, with all his ferocity. *Amor vincit omnia.*

Petition, also, ye goodly inhabitants of the slave states, your legislators to abolish slavery by the year 1850, or now, and save the abolitionist, from reproach and ruin, infamy and shame.

Pray Congress to pay every man a reasonable price for his slaves out of the surplus revenue arising from the sale of public lands and from the deduction of pay from the members of Congress.

Break off the shackles from the poor black man, and hire him to labor like other human beings; for "an hour of virtuous liberty on earth is worth a whole eternity of bondage." Abolish the practice in the army and navy of trying men by court-martial for desertion. If a soldier or marine runs away, send him his wages, with this instruction, *that his country will never trust him again; he has forfeited his honor.*

Make *honor* the standard with all men. Be sure that good is rendered for evil in all cases, and the whole nation, like a kingdom of kings and priests, will rise up in righteousness, and be respected as wise and worthy on earth, and as just and holy for heaven, by Jehovah, the author of perfection.

More economy in the national and state governments would make less taxes among the people; more equality through the cities, towns and country, would make less distinction among the people; and more honesty and familiarity in societies, would make less hypocrisy and flattery in all branches of the community; and open, frank, candid decorum to all men, in this boasted land of liberty, would beget esteem, confidence, union and love; and the neighbor from any state, or from any country, of whatever color, clime or tongue, could rejoice when he put his foot on the sacred soil of freedom, and exclaim, the very name of *"American"* is fraught with *friendship.* Oh, then, create confidence! restore freedom! break down slavery! banish imprisonment for debt, be in love, fellowship and peace, with all the world! Remember that honesty is not subject to law: the law was made for transgressors. . . .

Give every man his constitutional freedom, and the President full power to send an army to suppress mobs, and the state authority to repel and impugn that relic of folly which makes it necessary for the governor of a state to make the demand of the President for troops, in case of invasion or rebellion.

The governor himself may be a mobber; and instead of being punished, as he should be, for murder or treason, he may destroy the very lives, rights and property he should protect. . . .

As to the contiguous territories of the United States, wisdom would direct no tangling alliance. Oregon belongs to this government honorably; and when we have the red man's consent, let the Union spread from the east to the west sea; and if Texas petitions Congress to be adopted among the sons of liberty, give her the right hand of fellowship, and refuse not the same friendly grip to Canada and Mexico. And when the right arm of freemen is stretched out in the character of a navy for the protection of rights, commerce and honor, let the iron eyes of power watch from Maine to Mexico, and from California to Columbia. Thus may union be stretched, and foreign speculation prevented from opposing broadside to broadside.

Seventy years have done much for this goodly land. They have burst the chains of oppression and monarchy, and multiplied its inhabitants from two to twenty millions, with a proportionate share of knowledge keen enough to circumnavigate the globe, draw the lightning from the clouds, and cope with all the crowned heads of the world.

The southern people are hospitable and noble. They will help to rid so *free* a country of every vestige of slavery, whenever they are assured of an equivalent for their property. . . .

We have had Democratic presidents, Whig presidents, a pseudo-Democratic-Whig president, and now it is time to have a *President of the United States*: and let the people of the whole Union, like the inflexible Romans, whenever they find a *promise* made by a candidate that is not *practiced* as an officer, hurl the miserable sycophant from his exaltation as God did Nebuchadnezzar, to crop the grass of the field with a beast's heart among the cattle. . . .

In the United States the people are the government, and their united voice is the only sovereign that should rule, the only power that should be obeyed, and the only gentlemen that should be honored at home and abroad, on the land and on the sea. Wherefore, were I the president of the United States by the voice of a virtuous people, I would honor the old paths of the venerated fathers of freedom. I would walk in the tracks of the illustrious patriots who carried the ark of the government upon their shoulders with an eye single to the glory of the people; and when that people petitioned to abolish slavery in the slave states, I would use all honorable means to have their prayers granted, and give liberty to the captive by paying the southern gentlemen a reasonable equivalent for his property, that the whole nation might be free indeed! . . .

And when the people petitioned to possess the territory of Oregon, or any other contiguous territory, I would bend the influence of a chief magistrate to grant so reasonable a request, that they might extend the mighty efforts and enterprise of a free people from the east to the west sea, and make the wilderness blossom as the rose. And when a neighboring realm petitioned to join the union of the sons of liberty, my voice would be, *Come*— yea, come, Texas; come, Mexico; come, Canada; and come, all the world; let us be brethren, let us be one great family, and let there be a universal peace.

Abolish the cruel customs of prisons (except in certain cases), penitentiaries, court-martials for desertion; and let reason and friendship reign over the ruins of ignorance and barbarity; yea, I would, as the universal friend of man, open the prisons, open the eyes, open the ears, and open the hearts of all people, to behold and enjoy freedom— unadulterated freedom; and God, who once cleansed the violence of the earth with a flood, whose Son laid down His life for the salvation of all His Father gave Him out of the world, and who has promised that He will come and purify the world again with fire in the last days, should be supplicated by me for the good of all people.[1]

To enunciate the Prophet's views for the salvation of the republic, the Twelve Apostles and other leading elders were sent throughout the land. It was a long parting with Joseph for most of the Twelve. One of their number, Wilford Woodruff, says:

Joseph looked upon me long and mournfully. I shall never forget his look. It was as though he was bidding us an eternal farewell.

---

[1] See Note 5, Appendix.

CHAPTER 60

Judases Abroad

Joseph had endeavored by every means in his power to create pacific feelings between the Saints and the other citizens of Illinois. He addressed many communications to the public, in which he counseled for good sense and good order.

One of his appeals for peace was written on the 17th of February, 1844. That same day an anti-Mormon convention was held at Carthage, the object being to devise ways and means for expelling the Saints from the state as they had been driven from Missouri. Among the resolutions adopted by the meeting was one appointing the 9th day of March following *as a day of fasting and prayer*, whereon the pious of all the sectarians were to supplicate heaven to aid their efforts against the Prophet and his people. The inciters of this convention purposed that it should inaugurate a massacre; and yet they were so blasphemous as to pretend to ask the aid of the Almighty! Their real supplication, however, was addressed—not to the realms of light, but to the prince of darkness.

On Sunday, the 25th day of February, in a meeting at the assembly room of the Saints in Nauvoo, Joseph prophesied that in five years the Saints would be out of the power of their old enemies, whether apostates or of the world, and he asked the brethren to record the prediction.

About this time he was inspired to direct the glance of the apostles to the western slope where he said the people of God might establish themselves anew, worship after their own sincere convictions, and work out the grand social problems of modern life. This subject was present in his mind and often upon his lips during the brief remainder of his earthly existence. Frequent councils were held, and he directed the organization of an exploring expedition to venture beyond the Rocky Mountains, to seek a home for a righteous people denied every right of citizenship within the boundaries of the United States then existing. His purpose was not to sever the Saints from this sublime republic by any emigration; he saw that this country's domain must soon stretch from ocean to ocean. The entire land of North and South America was the Zion of the Lord, and the people might settle in any spot where peace could be enjoyed, always remembering that in the due time of the Almighty the center stake must be built up.

Work was stopped on the Nauvoo House by the Prophet's direction, and every effort concentrated upon the temple. He determined that the structure should be fitted to receive the worshiping Saints of the Most High before they should go into voluntary exile or submit to expatriation. And though he did not live to see the consummation of this purpose, it was literally fulfilled. And though he did not live to see the exodus of the Saints nor to send out the first pioneer party of explorers, his inspired suggestion was carried out, and through it his prediction was fulfilled that the Saints in five years should be beyond the power of their old enemies.

In March the Prophet addressed a memorial to Congress, asking for the passage of an ordinance to protect citizens of the United States emigrating into the western regions. His purpose was to advance, under national authority, beyond the western boundary of the United States and establish American citizens in this vast domain preparatory to the hour when it should become annexed to our country. He drafted the ordinance, and in its provisions he betrayed his usual grandeur of purpose.

A special conference was held, beginning on the 6th day of April, 1844, at which Joseph addressed a congregation of twenty thousand people. He chose for his subject the death of Elder King Follett, who had died a few days before, and he uplifted the souls of the congregation to a higher comprehension of the glory which comes after death to the faithful. His address ceased to be a mere eulogy of an individual, and became a revelation of eternal truths concerning the glories of immortality. The address occupied three hours and a half in delivery, and the multitude were held spellbound by its power. The Prophet seemed to rise above the world. It was as if the light of heaven already encircled his physical being. In a few weeks he was to pass through the portals of the tomb into the radiance beyond, and he wanted his brethren to grasp some of the sublimities comprehended by his own inspired soul. Those who heard that sermon never forgot its power. Those who read it today think of it as an exhibition of superhuman power and eloquence.

The Judas spirit manifested itself in Nauvoo in the spring of 1844. Alarmed by the Prophet's declaration that there was a right-hand Brutus near him, some of the men who were willing to betray him feared that their machinations were discovered and that vengeance might be wreaked upon them. William Law and William Marks both feared or affected to fear for their lives. They made complaint which reached the ears of the Prophet, and he ordered an investigation in which they were allowed the fullest license to examine witnesses. The result was to show to them how utterly groundless was their fear; but further it showed to all the Saints that these men were not faithful. The people said:

> Is it possible that Brother Law or Brother Marks is a traitor and would deliver Joseph into the hands of his enemies in Missouri? If not, what can be the meaning of this? The righteous are as bold as a lion.

Joseph merely quoted:

> The wicked flee when no man pursueth.

But from this time on he knew from what quarter to expect the kiss of Judas. Jealousy of the Prophet and their personal impurity led several leading men to apostasy and to a thirst for Joseph's blood. Among them were William Law, Wilson Law, Chauncey L. Higbee, Francis M. Higbee and Robert D. Foster. They became his avowed enemies; but in secret sympathy with them were Sidney Rigdon, William Marks and Austin A. Cowles.

William Law was the leader of the movement. He declared that Joseph was a fallen Prophet, and he attempted to set up a church of his own. The apostates sought by every means in their power to precipitate bloodshed in Nauvoo. They flagrantly violated the law; insulted, abused and threatened the officers; usurped official prerogatives; attempted to shoot Joseph; and spread throughout the country, and even beyond its confines, the most wicked misrepresentations and complaints concerning Joseph and the municipal administration of Nauvoo.

The Prophet had long known of their treachery and had warned the Saints that Judases were in their midst, without naming the individuals. He knew that in a little time the traitors would betray themselves. When this expectation of the Prophet was realized and the Saints were enabled to see the perfidy of these men, they were excommunicated.

After this it seemed as if Satan was turned loose in their souls. Having no longer any profit in concealment, they blazoned forth their hatred for the Prophet and their own iniquities. Some of them confessed that they knew that their sins were finding them out and that they would soon have no reputation to lose anyhow, and therefore they would persecute the Prophet and try to drag him down with them. At this time anonymous letters threatening the lives of Joseph and Hyrum were received, and every conceivable annoyance was perpetrated upon them.

The missionary labor had not slackened. While Satan was moving the powers of earth and the infernal regions to slay the Prophet, despoil the city and break the growing strength of righteousness, missionaries were being sent into every field. Under date of Friday, May 17, 1844, the Prophet records, among other similar events, that Elder Franklin D. Richards, then a faithful youth and later a renowned apostle of the Church, was ordained a high priest and set apart to go on a mission to England.

On Saturday, the 25th day of May, 1844, the Prophet was informed that he had been indicted at Carthage for the alleged offenses of polygamy and perjury on the testimony of William Law and others. Two days later, learning that warrants were out for him from the circuit court upon these indictments, he determined to proceed to Carthage and give himself up. He had a double purpose to serve in this action. He desired as usual to show his respect for law and legal process; and he wanted to avoid having a Carthage mob come into Nauvoo to serve the writs. At Carthage he was informed by Charles Foster and other apostates, who repented their purpose for the moment, that a plot had been laid for his death and that it was determined that he should not leave that place alive. He secured lawyers and endeavored to have his case brought forward for trial; but the prosecution insisted upon delay and secured a postponement until the next term. In the meantime Joseph was to be released on bail satisfactory to the sheriff; and that officer told him to go his way without bonds until called upon.

His friends gathered around him when he prepared to depart for home, and by this means his life was saved, for armed men threatened him and tried by force and stratagem to detain him in Carthage until after dark that they might the better accomplish the assassination. But he knew their plot and departed, riding Joe Duncan and accompanied by Hyrum and others, and reached home at 9 o'clock that evening.

CHAPTER 61

Acquittal

The publishers deem it a sacred duty they owe to their
country and their fellow citizens to advocate, through the
columns of the *Expositor,* the unconditional repeal of the
Nauvoo city charter.

This was one of the statements in the prospectus for a
newspaper to be issued at Nauvoo by the Laws, Higbees
and Fosters. These men had been excommunicated from the
Church for their personal impurity and for plotting murder.
With their wickedness exposed to the gaze of the world, they had
no longer any reputation at stake; they associated with gamblers,
counterfeiters and thieves; and their great desire was, by every
means in their power, fair or foul, to injure their former brethren.

The charter of a city is inestimable to the citizens. Without
it rapid advancement is difficult, if not impossible. Nauvoo
had grown into prominence and gave promise of becoming an
important commercial and industrial center. The apostates knew
well the vital point at which to direct their blow. Not only would
they paralyze every industry by securing the repeal of the charter,
but they would turn the city over to the dictation of hostile county
and state officials; so that financial ruin and personal distress
would be inflicted upon many of the people. To this end, they
leagued themselves with kindred spirits whose evil efforts they
could rely upon. The class of allies which they secured is shown by
the fact that one of their associates was known to them, and was
afterwards proved, to be a fugitive murderer.

Among the minor purposes avowed in this prospectus for the issuance of the newspaper, was the advocacy of the pure principles of morality. This was a high sounding pretense to create favor abroad. The Laws, the Higbees and the Fosters cared nothing for morality, except to abuse it. With them it was but a cloak. They had become accustomed to use it for a covering for vile purposes. This was not the first time nor this the last, when evil men—cast out by the Church for sexual sin—made great pretense in print of their morality and sought to charge offenses upon men faithful and pure.

They announced that they would exercise "the freedom of speech in Nauvoo, independent of the ordinances abridging the same"; and that the end would justify the means. The only restriction upon speech in Nauvoo was the forbidding of slander and immorality, and unless these men had intended to work evil with their paper they need not have promised to transgress the law.

But their purpose was not to convince the people of Nauvoo; it was to create sentiment abroad and to this end slander and falsehood were necessary. They were not the first men shrewd enough to see that the publication, within any city, of statements adverse to the community would be accepted abroad as current fact. Their plan was devised with satanic ingenuity: If the *Expositor* were allowed to print its defamations and falsehoods unchecked, the world would believe that all they said was true, and overwhelming sentiment would be created against Nauvoo and its people; if their press was stayed in its crime, they would cry that freedom of speech was assailed—and nothing appeals more quickly to the sympathy of Americans than this same cry, whether it is uttered sincerely or only by wretches who want license to traduce and defame innocence.

There was no disposition to restrain these publishers from printing their paper in Nauvoo. Their announcement was made on the 10th of May, 1844; they brought press and materials into the city and began their work with as much protection and safety as any other publisher there. On the 7th of June next, they were prepared to put forth the first number of the paper. All at once a fear came upon them. They knew the man whom they wished to make their chief victim—Joseph Smith; they knew his truth, dignity and strength; they knew that he would not supinely submit to the ruin of the city and the defamation of its good men and women by such wretches as these publishers were known to be; they knew that if they committed crime they would be called to answer for it if the Prophet lived. So on the very day that the paper was to come forth burdened with lies, Robert D. Foster went to the mansion and demanded a private interview with Joseph. He asked the Prophet to go away with him alone, pretending that he wished to return to the Church and wanted to confer upon that subject. Joseph refused to talk except in the presence of witnesses, for this man Foster had often before misrepresented the Prophet's words. Joseph said to him that there was but one condition upon which he might return and that was to repent and to make restitution as far as possible.

While they stood talking, Joseph put his hand upon Foster's vest and said: "What have you concealed there?"

Foster stammered in reply: "It's my pistol."

He would have lied, but under that piercing glance his bravado deserted him, and he was compelled to acknowledge the fact.

The reason of his visit was soon made plain, and it was made plainer at a later time by the testimony of unimpeachable witnesses, Saints and strangers alike. He had not come to seek forgiveness and restoration of fellowship; he had not come to make amends. He had come to lure Joseph away to his death. His party had sworn to slay the Prophet, and every attempt up to this time had failed. The situation was desperate for the plotters. They were about to commit a flagrant violation of the law, and the one man whom they most feared as the defender and executor of law was the mayor of the city. If they could have taken Joseph away where his assassination could have been accomplished without the instant capture of his murderer, they believed that safe refuge could be found in the bosom of the waiting mob at Carthage and other places.

Joseph only smiled upon the craven wretch, and told him to bring his witnesses, if he desired, and they would confer concerning his restoration to fellowship. This, Foster willingly promised and left the mansion, saying that he would return with his friends immediately. He never came back. His answer was to send forth the *Expositor*, edited by Sylvester Emmons, reeking with libel and fulfilling its promise to override the law in its determination to deal a death blow at the city of Nauvoo. Naturally the inhabitants were enraged. Citizens said:

> If these men do not like Nauvoo, why do they continue to reside here? The repeal of the charter means the financial and social ruin of the city. This would despoil us without benefiting these men, except by the gratification of vengeful hate.

It would have been easy in that state of public feeling to incite an attack upon the paper or its publishers. But the leading men remained cool and counseled strict observance of law. Let this be remembered; for it shows that Joseph was never willing to meet evil with evil; that he would rather suffer wrong than to do wrong; and that his appeal was always made to law and justice instead of passion. And let it be remembered that not only then but afterward through all the difficulties which followed closely upon the publication of the *Expositor*, the lives of the Laws, the Higbees and the Fosters were as safe in Nauvoo as they would have been in Carthage, Springfield or Washington.

Three days later, June 10, at a meeting of the city council the *Expositor* was declared a public nuisance and was ordered to be abated. Under the resolution to this effect, the marshal was ordered to proceed as he would for the removal of any other nuisance—he was to eradicate it. If a vile odor assail the nostrils of decent people, the only effectual remedy is to abolish the cause; and such was the course pursued in this case. Marshal John P. Greene, with his assistants, proceeded to the office of the *Expositor* and destroyed the press and pied the type.

This was summary action; but it was legal. It was the only remedy for any public or private wrong inflicted by the *Expositor.* Its publishers were impecunious. Suits for private redress or fines for public recompense would have been unavailing; while the imprisonment of the publishers would have been heralded as a still greater wrong against the freedom of the press than was the destruction of the offending materials.

Immediate events showed that the league to ruin Nauvoo by newspaper lies was widely extended, for mobocratic excitement outside of Nauvoo arose on the instant, and wholesale and indiscriminate vengeance was threatened.

And yet the destruction of an offending press was not new in Illinois. Thomas Ford was governor at this time, and in the awful crimes which closely followed he was the responsible participant. It is interesting, therefore, to note what he said of a similar destruction of an unpopular press and type, at another time and in another community. In the history of Illinois, published after his death to get bread for his destitute children, he details the proceedings of the Alton mob. In 1837 Reverend Elijah P. Lovejoy, of the Presbyterian church, published the Alton, Illinois, *Observer* as a religious paper, in which slavery was opposed. Abolitionism was not popular there, and to quote Ford's words: "The people assembled and quietly took the press and type and threw them into the Mississippi. It now became manifest to all rational men that the Alton *Observer* could no longer be published in Alton as an abolition paper. The more reasonable of the abolitionists themselves thought it would be useless to try it again. However, a few of them, who *were most violent* seemed to think that the salvation of the black race depended upon continuing the publication at Alton." Certain members of the Presbyterian church determined to continue this paper. One of the principal men engaged in the movement to reestablish the *Observer* was Reverend Beecher, president of Illinois college; and of him Ford says: "Mr. Beecher was a man of great learning and decided talents; but he belonged to the class of reformers who disregard all considerations of policy and expediency. *He believed slavery to be a sin and a great evil, and his indignant and impatient soul could not await God's own good time to overthrow it, by acts of His providence working continual change and revolution in the affairs of men."* A new press was bought, and it was determined that Lovejoy, who was very objectionable to the rabble, should continue as editor. After the arrival of the press, it was guarded in a warehouse; but the mob gathered and demanded its possession. Ford speaks of the protectors of the press as being converted into *demons of obstinacy.* A fight occurred, the mob being the first assailants. Lovejoy and one of the mobocrats were killed; other men were wounded. The press was seized and, like the other, it was thrown into the river—although not a single copy of the paper had yet been printed with these materials. No man was punished for this crime of abolishing a free press at the expense of murder. Thus it will be seen that the will of a community, in other parts of Illinois, was considered sufficient without legal process to secure the extinction of an obnoxious paper and the perpetual silence of its editor—the silence of death by assassination. In Nauvoo no such high-handed course was pursued: no man was injured in his person; and the destroying of the press was in pursuance of a municipal order. At Alton the unpopular publishers advocated merely a national reform, in the highest interest of human liberty and morality; at Nauvoo the publishers attacked the most vital local well-being and assailed the character of the community for the purpose of advancing an immoral purpose and gratifying the revenge of lustful men. At Nauvoo the publishers had practically avowed their intention to incite a mob to come upon the city; and the matter printed in the first and only issue of their paper was manifestly of a character to aid the sanguinary plot.

There had not been the slightest excitement or unnecessary noise in the act of removing the nuisance, and this done the people of the city drew a breath of relief. The *Expositor* had been an invitation to the gathering mobs of Hancock County to descend upon Nauvoo and injure its people and property. It had been calculated to inflame the worst passions of lawless men and to produce murder. In its suppression the people felt that only ordinary prudence and official vigor had been shown. To allay any possible excitement, the mayor issued a proclamation in which he detailed the destruction by municipal order of the *Expositor* press and type, and called upon every citizen to keep the peace by being cool, considerate, virtuous, unoffending, manly and patriotic. The villains who had published the paper threatened everything in the city with destruction. One of their sympathizers declared that he would wade to his knees in blood; others said that the city should be wiped out before "ten suns had set." They sent runners out in all directions to bring the mob upon Nauvoo.

A little after noon on the 12th day of June, Constable David Bettisworth came to Nauvoo from Carthage with a warrant for the arrest of Joseph Smith, Samuel Bennett, John Taylor, William W. Phelps, Hyrum Smith, John P. Greene, Stephen Perry, Dimick B. Huntington, Jonathan Dunham, Stephen Markham, William Edwards, Jonathan Harmon, Jesse P. Harmon, John Lytle, Joseph W. Coolidge, Harvey D. Redfield, Porter Rockwell and Levi Richards, upon a complaint sworn to by Francis M. Higbee charging the parties named with committing a riot. The writ was issued by Thomas Morrison, justice of the peace at Carthage, and commanded the officer to bring the parties named before Morrison or *some other justice of the peace* within the county. Bettisworth immediately upon arriving at Nauvoo served this warrant upon Joseph and afterwards upon the others named therein. Joseph called his attention to the clause in the writ, "before me or some other justice of the peace of said county," and demanded to be taken before Esquire Johnson or some other justice of the peace in Nauvoo. Hyrum made the same demand. Many people were present, and Joseph and Hyrum called upon them to witness that they offered themselves in answer to the writ to go forth before the nearest justice of the peace. This was strictly in accordance with law; but it did not answer the purpose of the mobocrats either at Nauvoo or Carthage, and Bettisworth said: "I will be damned but I will carry you before Justice Morrison at Carthage."

As he still held them in custody and was determined to drag them away from Nauvoo, Joseph sued out a writ of *habeas corpus* in the municipal court, and upon the full showing there he was discharged. Later all the other brethren named in the writ took the same course and secured their release.

On the 14th of June, the mayor addressed a letter of explanation to Governor Ford, in which the entire proceedings against the *Expositor* were fairly detailed. Joseph stated to the governor that if Ford was not satisfied that the whole transaction had been in accordance with the strictest principles of law and the requirements of good order, he would only have to write his wishes and the mayor and all persons participating in the suppression of the *Expositor* would go before Judge Pope or any legal tribunal at the capital and submit to judicial investigation. They would not even trouble his Excellency to send a writ or an officer, but would respond promptly to any letter advising them of his wish. Other men in Nauvoo, some of them prominent visitors there, wrote to Ford at the same time, declaring that no excitement had prevailed, that the proceedings had been calmly and legally taken, and that the action of the municipality in ridding itself of such a menace to peace and life was entirely commendable.

On the 16th day of June, Judge Jesse B. Thomas came to Nauvoo and advised the mayor and the other men named in Morrison's warrant to go before some justice of the peace in the county and be examined upon the charge named therein. Judge Thomas said that if they would do this and should be acquitted or bound over, all excitement would be allayed, the mob would be left without a pretext, and he himself would be bound to compel the mobocrats to keep the peace. Joseph and his brethren expressed their readiness to submit to any fair investigation. The next day, upon the complaint of W. G. Ware, they were arrested by Constable Joel S. Miles on a writ issued by Daniel H. Wells for a riot in destroying the Nauvoo *Expositor* press. They all submitted to this process and went before Justice Wells, who, at this time, it must be remembered, was not a member of the Church. After a long and close examination, it appeared to the court that they had not proceeded illegally, and they were discharged.

As mobs in various parts of the county continued to menace Nauvoo, the Prophet sent several letters and messengers to keep the governor informed. Samuel James went to Springfield on the 15th of June, and Edward Hunter, with Philip B. Lewis and John Bills, went on the 17th. To Elder Edward Hunter, Joseph said as he was leaving: "I charge you solemnly to tell the governor everything you know concerning me, good or bad."

The most outrageous falsehoods were being circulated to inflame the people against Nauvoo. Upon this point Governor Ford, in his history of Illinois, says:

> A system of excitement and agitation was artfully planned [by the mob leaders] and executed with tact. It consisted in spreading reports and rumors of the most fearful character. As examples:—On the morning before my arrival at Carthage, I was awakened at an early hour by the frightful report, which was asserted with confidence and apparent consternation, that the Mormons had already commenced the work of burning, destruction and murder; and that every man capable of bearing arms was instantly wanted at Carthage for the protection of the country. We lost no time in starting; but when we arrived at Carthage we could hear no more concerning this story. Again: During the few days that the militia were encamped at Carthage, frequent applications were made to me to send a force here and a force there, and a force all about the country, to prevent murders, robberies and larcenies, which, it was said, were threatened by the Mormons. No such forces were sent, nor were any such offenses committed at that time, except the stealing of some provisions, and there was never the least proof that this was done by a Mormon. Again: On my late visit to Hancock County, I was informed, by some of their violent enemies, that the larcenies of the Mormons had become

unusually numerous and insufferable. They indeed admitted that but little had been done in this way in their immediate vicinity, but they insisted that sixteen horses had been stolen by the Mormons in one night, near Lima, in the county of Adams. At the close of the expedition, I called at this same town of Lima, and upon inquiry was told that no horses had been stolen in that neighborhood, but that sixteen horses had been stolen in one night in Hancock County. The last informant being told of the Hancock story, again changed the venue to another distant settlement in the northern edge of Adams. . . .

Occasional threats came to my ears of destroying the city and murdering or expelling the inhabitants. . . .

Frequent appeals had been made to me to make a clean and thorough work of the matter by exterminating the Mormons.

The Warsaw *Signal*, edited by an infamous man by the name of Thomas Sharp, took a prominent and diabolical part in arousing the spirit of murder. It published the minutes of mob meetings and resolutions adopted there, in which the most fiendish threats were made. Some of them are as follows:

We therefore declare that we will sustain our press and the editor at all hazards; that we will take full vengeance, terrible vengeance, should the lives of any of our citizens be lost in the effort; that we hold ourselves at all times in readiness to co-operate with our fellow-citizens in this state, Missouri and Iowa, to *exterminate, utterly exterminate the wicked and abominable Mormon leaders*, the authors of our troubles:

Resolved, That a committee of five be appointed forthwith to notify all persons in our township *suspected* of being the tools of the Prophet to leave immediately on pain of *instant vengeance. And we do recommend the inhabitants of the adjacent townships to do the same, hereby pledging ourselves to render all the assistance they may require.*

Resolved, That the time, in our opinion, has arrived when the adherents of Smith, as a body, should be driven from the surrounding settlements into Nauvoo. That the Prophet and his miscreant adherents should then be demanded at their hands; and, if not surrendered, *a war of extermination should be waged, to the entire destruction,* if necessary for our protection, *of his adherents.* And we do hereby recommend this resolution to the consideration of the several townships, to the mass convention to be held at Carthage, hereby pledging ourselves to aid to the utmost the complete consummation of the object in view, that we may thereby be utterly relieved of the alarm, anxiety, and trouble to which we are now subjected.

Resolved, That every citizen arm himself to be prepared to sustain the resolutions herein contained.

It was further resolved that a deputation be sent to Springfield to solicit executive help, but the intention was expressed not to allow the mob movements to be retarded by this action. The mobs at Warsaw and Carthage pretended to believe that the destruction of the Warsaw *Signal* office had been threatened by Hyrum Smith. The statement to this effect was of a piece with the lies told to the governor. No threat had been made against the *Signal* office or the editor, and the mob well knew that any attack from the citizens of Nauvoo upon anybody in Carthage or Warsaw was out of the question.

The mail communications of the Saints were cut off with the connivance of officials.

A company of the mob, numbering three hundred, began training at Carthage on the 13th day of June. Arms were brought to Warsaw and Carthage from Quincy and other places. On the 17th of June, fifteen hundred Missourians were reported to have crossed the river and joined the rabble at Warsaw. Five pieces of artillery had already been brought to the latter place. From

Warsaw the mob forces were to proceed to Carthage and join the Quincy Grays and other companies from Adams County. Scattering from here, it was their purpose to seize the arms of all the Saints in Hancock County, outside of Nauvoo, and compel them to recant their faith or be exterminated. They declared that they would take Joseph and Hyrum and the city council from Nauvoo on Thursday, the 20th of June, and deliver them up to sacrifice. If any resistance were offered, the city would be shelled and all the inhabitants slaughtered or driven away. One of the mob leaders was Levi Williams, a colonel of militia and a Baptist preacher, and to such as he was due the attempt to make the Saints recant.

No word came from the governor. Was the city to be left to massacre, pillage, ravishment, like Far West! Forbid it, Heaven!

Under these circumstances, nothing remained but to prepare for resistance—not attack, only defense. The mayor, on the 18th of June, 1844, declared the city of Nauvoo under martial law, and called out the Legion to protect the city from rapine and its people from massacre by the mob.

Greater Love

Events were now hurrying on to the last awful scene. Joseph saw the sacrificial cup prepared for him and knew that he must drink its bitter draught. As he draws nearer to the final hour, clearer and clearer becomes his mind, more nearly divine are his works, and more closely do we see the likeness to the sacred Master of whom Joseph deemed himself but the humblest follower. It is no mere accidental similarity, this betrayal of the modern Prophet by the modern Judas and this sacrifice of a holy name to glut the hate of Pharisees. The Prophet's work is almost done. More plainly, as the supreme moment draws on, he tells his followers of the fate awaiting him. At first they scarcely understand, so used are they to see him in the midst of peril. It may be that the vision of the end is opened to Hyrum's view, for he will not leave his brother's side. They have loved in life, the elder brother living by the other's prophetic words, and in death they shall not be separated. Joseph says: "Hyrum, take your family on the next boat to Cincinnati. I want you to live to avenge me." Hyrum replies: "Joseph, I will not leave you." It is not a vengeance of blood that the Prophet means: it is the triumph of the work over all murderous mobs, a triumph in which he wants his faithful brother to share in the flesh.

After the traitors had gone out from Nauvoo to join with the Pharisees in raising a mob, the Prophet related a dream to his brethren, assembled in meeting. He said that he thought that he was riding in a carriage, and his guardian angel was with him. They saw two serpents in the road firmly locked together, and the angel told him that these were two of his traitorous enemies, Robert Foster and Chauncey Higbee, so fast bound to each other that of themselves they could not harm him. Then Joseph rode on farther, but his angel was no longer by his side; and William Law and Wilson Law came out upon him, dragged him from his carriage, tied his hands and threw him into a deep pit. After a time he partly loosened his hands and climbed to the edge of the pit and looked out. He saw Wilson Law attacked by ferocious beasts and William Law expiring in the coils of a poisonous snake. They cried for him:

Oh, Brother Joseph! Brother Joseph! save us or we perish!

But he responded that they themselves had deprived him of the power to aid them. Then, after a little time, his angel came once more and said: "Joseph, why are you here?"

And he responded: "Mine enemies fell upon me, bound me, and threw me into this pit."

The angel took him by the hand and drew him up, and they went away together.

Impressive as was the recital of this dream, his brethren failed to comprehend its full significance; but scores of them recalled it at a later time and preserved it as a sacred remembrance.

On Sunday, the 16th day of June, 1844, Joseph preached in the grove east of the temple to the assembled Saints. The rain fell heavily, but the people would not disperse while the Prophet spoke. Nor would he be stayed by all these tears of nature, for it was one of his last opportunities to advise the people for whom he was willing to give his life. Often before the Prophet had counseled his brethren that it was not necessary yet to preach from the revelations of St. John the Divine; that the plain principles of the gospel should first be taught. But now, with the consciousness of his approaching death upon him, he read to the people the third chapter of Revelation. It was to be a message of comfort to the Saints when he was gone. He then turned to the first chapter and read:

And from Jesus Christ, who is the faithful witness, and the first begotten of the dead, and the prince of the kings of the earth. Unto him that loved us, and washed us from our sins in his own blood,

And hath made us kings and priests unto God and his Father; to him be glory and dominion for ever and ever. Amen. (Revelation 1:5-6.)

He carried the Saints into a profounder depth of revealed theology than ever before. He talked of the plurality of Gods and the different glories of the eternal realm. He said:

Go and read the vision in the Book of Covenants. There is clearly illustrated glory upon glory—one glory of the sun, another glory of the moon, and a glory of the stars; and as one star differeth from another star in glory, even so do they of the telestial world differ in glory, and every man who reigns in the celestial glory is a God to his dominion. . . .

It is in the order of heavenly things that God should always send a new dispensation into the world when men have apostatized from the truth and lost the Priesthood; but when men build without authority from God, and when the floods come and the winds blow, their whole fabric will crumble. . . .

Oh thou God who art King of kings and Lord of lords!

After the city had been declared under martial law, the Legion was drawn up in front of the mansion to be addressed by the Prophet. He stood upon the frame of a building opposite his house, dressed in his full uniform as lieutenant general.

William W. Phelps read from an extra issue of the Warsaw *Signal* of the day before, calling upon all the old citizens to assist the mob in exterminating the leaders of the Saints and driving the people into exile.

Joseph then recounted the doings of the time at Nauvoo and demonstrated that he and his brethren had been willing and were still as willing as ever to submit to the authority of law; that they had not transgressed the statutes; that the effort making against them was the device of Satan. He told them that a pretext had been sought by their enemies in order that a band of infuriated mob men might be congregated to fall upon Nauvoo, to murder, plunder, and ravish the innocent. He said:

We are American citizens. We live upon a soil, for the liberties of which our fathers periled their lives and spilt their blood upon the battlefield. Those rights, so dearly purchased, shall not be disgracefully trodden under foot by lawless marauders without at least a noble effort on our part to sustain our liberties.

Will you stand by me to the death, and sustain, at the peril of your lives, the laws of our country, and the liberties and privileges which our fathers have transmitted unto us, sealed with their sacred blood? ["Aye," shouted thousands.] It is well. If you have not done it, I would have gone out there, [pointing to the west], and would have raised up a mightier people.

I call all men, from Maine to the Rocky Mountains, and from Mexico to British America, whose hearts thrill with horror to behold the rights of free men trampled under foot, to come to the deliverance of this people from the cruel hand of oppression, cruelty, anarchy and misrule to which they have long been made subject. Come, all ye lovers of liberty, break the oppressor's rod, loose the iron grasp of mobocracy, and bring to condign punishment all those who trample under foot the glorious principles of our Constitution and the people's rights [Drawing his sword and presenting it to heaven.] I call God and angels to witness that I have unsheathed my sword with a firm and unalterable determination that this people shall have their legal rights, and be protected from mob violence, or my blood shall be spilt upon the ground like water, and my body consigned to the silent tomb. While I live, I will never tamely submit to the dominion of accursed mobocracy. I would welcome death rather than submit to this oppression; and it would be sweet, oh, sweet to rest in the grave, rather than submit to this oppression, confusion and alarm upon alarm any longer. . . .

Peace shall be taken from the land which permits these crimes against the Saints to go unavenged.

I call upon all friends of truth and liberty to come to our assistance; and may the thunders of the Almighty, and the forked lightnings of heaven, and pestilence, and war, and bloodshed come down on those ungodly men who seek to destroy my life and the lives of this innocent people.

I do not regard my own life. I am ready to be offered a sacrifice for this people; for what can our enemies do? Only kill the body, and their power is then at an end. Stand firm, my friends; never flinch. Do not seek to save your lives, for he that is afraid to die for the truth will lose eternal life. Hold out to the end, and we shall be resurrected, and become like Gods and reign in celestial kingdoms, principalities and eternal dominions, while this mob will sink to the portion of all those who shed innocent blood.

God has tried you. You are a good people; therefore I love you with all my heart. Greater love hath no man than that he should lay down his life for his friends. You have stood by me in the hour of trouble, and I am willing to sacrifice my life for your preservation.

May the Lord God of Israel bless you forever and ever. I say this in the name of Jesus of Nazareth, and in the authority of the Holy Priesthood, which He hath conferred upon me.

And all the people cried Amen!

The vast assemblage had listened to his words with breathless attention, for he spoke with a power transcending anything that the Saints had ever before heard, even from him whose speech was always soul-touching. Had he expressed a wish to fight, his people would have followed him with joy to the contest. It is no wonder that his words sank deep into their hearts; it is no wonder that to their sight he appeared grander than mortal. It was the last time for many of them in the flesh that they were to listen to the music of his voice or to feel the spell of his mighty inspiration. It was his last public address! In a few short days, that Godlike form, so perfect in its manly beauty, was to be locked in the embrace of the tomb; and that voice, whose angelic sweetness had comforted them in the hour of darkest woe, was to be hushed in death.

On the 20th of June, he wrote to all the apostles who were absent on missions to come home immediately. Only two of the Twelve were with him, Apostles John Taylor and Willard Richards. He had often stated to the Twelve that upon them would devolve the work when he was gone, and he knew that their presence would soon be needed.

His consciousness of his impending fate and his fortitude were divine. His last deeds and his last thoughts were for the cause and the people whom he loved.

CHAPTER 63

Joseph
at Carthage

On the 21st day of June, 1844, Thomas Ford, governor of the state of Illinois, arrived at Carthage. What Pontius Pilate was to the divine atonement on Calvary, this man Ford was to the sealing martyrdom at Carthage.[1]

He was a politician, a friend to the masses, right or wrong. He submitted himself at Carthage to the direction of the mob leaders. From the moment of his arrival there until the deed was done, he interposed no hand to stay the awful deed. He could not

---

[1] Sixteen years after Ford had acquiesced in the murder of Joseph and Hyrum Smith, he said in his history of Illinois:

The Christian world, which has hitherto regarded Mormonism with silent contempt, unhappily may yet have cause to fear its rapid increase. Modern society is full of material for such a religion. At the death of the Prophet, fourteen years after the first Mormon Church was organized, the Mormons in all the world numbered about two hundred thousand souls (one-half million according to their statistics) ; a number equal, perhaps to the number of Christians when the Christian Church was of the same age. It is to be feared that, in the course of a century, some gifted man like Paul, some splendid orator, who will be able by his eloquence to attract crowds of the thousands who are ever ready to hear, and be carried away by the sounding brass and tinkling cymbal of sparkling oratory, may command a hearing, may succeed in breathing a new life into this modern Mahometanism, and make the name of the martyred Joseph ring as loud, and stir the souls of men as much, as the mighty name of Christ itself. Sharon, Palmyra, Manchester, Kirtland, Far West, Adam-ondi-Ahman, Ramus, Nauvoo and the Carthage Jail may become holy and venerable names, places of classic interest, in another age: like Jerusalem, the Garden of Gethsemane, the Mount of Olives, and Mount Calvary to the Christian, and Mecca and Medina to the Turk. And in that event, the author of this history feels degraded by the reflection, *that the humble governor of an obscure state, who would otherwise be forgotten in a few years, stands a fair chance, like Pilate and Herod, by their official connection with the true religion, of being dragged down to posterity with an immortal name,* hitched on to the memory of a miserable impostor. There may be those whose ambition would lead them to desire an immortal name in history, even in those humbling terms. I am not one of that number.

have been so blind as to fail in seeing that murder impended for the Prophet and Patriarch; and that extermination threatened the Saints. A statesman and a true and brave patriot could have put forth his power and dissipated the evils at a stroke; but Ford was not of such mettle. He affected to view Joseph and his brethren as rebels and the mob as law-abiding citizens—at best, he classed them all together. How he must have cringed when the Prophet asked him:

> Sir, is it not an easy matter to distinguish between those who have pledged themselves to exterminate innocent men, women and children, and those who have only stood in their own defense, and in defense of their innocent families, and that, too, in accordance with the Constitution and laws of the country as required by the oaths, and as good and law-abiding citizens?

On the 21st Ford wrote to Joseph asking for a conference at Carthage with discreet representatives from Nauvoo. Apostle John Taylor and Dr. John M. Bernhisel went at once, in obedience to this request, carrying with them a full account of the situation and the circumstances which had led to it, and a score of affidavits from trustworthy men—some of whom were not connected with the Prophet or his people—showing clearly the purpose of the mob to commit murder. The next day Lucien Woodworth was sent to him from Nauvoo, with further documents and with a letter from the Prophet. When Apostle Taylor and Dr. Bernhisel reached Carthage, they found that the governor had taken the entire mob into his service; that he had passed judicially upon the municipal ordinances and proceedings at Nauvoo; and that, without hearing from them, he had decided upon his course. He received them coolly, and as he read their communications aloud, he was surrounded by mobocrats who interrupted him at every sentence with a torrent of profanity and threats. He could listen to no argument and weigh no justice, for the cry was in his ears, "Crucify! Crucify!" By the hands of these brethren he sent a communication back to Nauvoo to require "all who are or shall be accused, to submit themselves to arrest by the same constable, by virtue of the same warrant, to be tried by the same magistrate whose authority had heretofore been resisted."

He asked that martial law should be abolished. He sent the constable with a guard to Nauvoo to secure Joseph and his friends. Of this circumstance Ford himself says:

> Upon the arrival of the constable and guard [at Nauvoo], the mayor and common council at once signified their willingness to surrender, and stated their readiness to proceed to Carthage next morning at 8 o'clock. Martial law had previously been abolished. The hour of 8 o'clock came, and the accused failed to make their appearance. The constable and his escort returned. The constable made no effort to arrest any of them, or would he or the guard delay their departure one minute beyond the time to see whether an arrest could be made. Upon their return, they reported that they had been informed that the accused had fled and could not be found.
>
> I immediately proposed to a council of officers to march into Nauvoo with a small force then under my command, but the officers were of opinion that it was too small, and many of them insisted upon a further call of the militia. Upon reflection, I was of opinion that the officers were right in the estimate of our force, and the project for immediate action was abandoned. I was soon informed, however, of the conduct of the constable and guard, and then I was perfectly satisfied that a most base fraud had been attempted; that, in fact, it was feared that the Mormons would submit and thereby entitle themselves to the protection of the law. It was very apparent that many of the bustling, active spirits were afraid that there would be no occasion for calling out an overwhelming militia force, for marching it into Nauvoo, for probable mutiny when there, and for the extermination of the Mormon race. It appeared that the constable and the escort were

fully in the secret, and acted well their part to promote the conspiracy.

Informed of all the plots against him and seeing the executive weakness or connivance with the mob, the Prophet determined to make one final effort to draw the menace from Nauvoo. He addressed a letter to the governor, in which he exposed the fallacy and cowardice of Ford's official proceedings and personal position. Then, after dark on the night of the 22nd of June, he called Hyrum, Willard Richards, John Taylor, W. W. Phelps, A. C. Hodge, John L. Butler, Alpheus Cutler and some others into his house and read to them the letter from the governor, merely remarking: "There is no mercy—no mercy here!"

Hyrum said: "No: as sure as we fall into their hands, we are dead men."

Joseph then told the brethren that if he and Hyrum should leave Nauvoo the attention of the mob would be attracted away from the Saints and in pursuit of the Prophet and Patriarch; and if the people would go quietly about their business none of them would be harmed. With this purpose he prepared to cross the river and go into the west. That night they bade farewell to their families. As they departed, it was seen that Joseph's tears were falling fast, and he uttered not a word while they walked down to the bank of the river. Joseph, Hyrum and Willard, rowed by Orrin P. Rockwell, crossed the Mississippi in a leaky skiff, bailing out the water with their boots and shoes to keep the frail boat from sinking. They found refuge on the Iowa side at the house of Brother William Jordan and made immediate preparations to depart toward the Rocky Mountains. But while they were packing their provisions, on the 23rd day of June, messengers came from Emma and others in Nauvoo, entreating the Prophet to return and by innuendo accusing him of cowardice in thus leaving the city. It was a fatal blindness on the part of these professed friends. They seemed to fear that the governor, failing to find Joseph and Hyrum, would fall upon Nauvoo with the militia. The Prophet knew better, that Ford would not dare such a thing as this—he might consent to the murder of individuals, but he dare not lead an army against an unoffending city. It is pitiable to think that the Saints could have so misjudged their leader as to suspect him of cowardice. But it is often so, that men placed in responsible stations, who act by the light of heaven and for the benefit of their brethren, without one thought of personal safety or advantage, are condemned by the unthinking.

"We are going back to be butchered," said Joseph; "If we live or die we will be reconciled to our fate," said Hyrum; as they moved down to the river to cross to Nauvoo on that 23rd day of June. While they walked, Joseph fell behind, deep in thought. Someone shouted to him to quicken his steps, and he remarked: "There is time enough for the slaughter."

That night, Sunday, June 23rd, 1844, Joseph sent a letter to the governor informing him that he would go to Carthage the next morning to meet his trial. He asked that the governor send a posse to meet him near the Mound, outside of Carthage, about two o'clock on the afternoon of the 24th. Seeing the determination of Joseph, the very friends who had induced him to return would now have interposed; but he was firm. To remain in Nauvoo would be to draw the vengeance of the mob upon that city. The next morning Elder Jedediah M. Grant and Theodore Turley, who had carried Joseph's communication to the governor, returned to Nauvoo and reported their mission. Ford had at first agreed to send a posse to escort Joseph in safety to Carthage, but some of the mobocrats and apostates made bitter speeches to him, and he rescinded his promise. He refused to send or allow an escort for Joseph, "as it was an honor not given to any other citizen." He would not even allow Elders Grant and Turley to remain in Carthage that night, but sent them out with a demand that Joseph should appear unaccompanied at Carthage the next morning. The messengers told the Prophet that intense excitement existed at Carthage; but he would not heed their warning.

On the morning of Monday, the 24th of June, 1844, Joseph and the seventeen other men named in the old writ from Morrison, started from Nauvoo. When they reached the temple, the Prophet looked upon it with a long and wistful gaze, and then turned his eyes upon the city, saying: "This is the loveliest place and these are the best people under the heavens. Little do they know the trials that await them."

As they passed out of the city, the Prophet said to Daniel H. Wells: "Squire Wells, I wish you to cherish my memory, and not think me the worst man in the world, either."

On the way out they met Captain Dunn, coming from Carthage with about sixty mounted men. Joseph said: "Do not be alarmed, brethren, for they cannot do more to you than the enemies of truth did to the ancient Saints—they can only kill the body."

Dunn presented to Joseph an order from Governor Ford for all the state arms in the possession of the Nauvoo Legion. Joseph immediately countersigned the order. Then he turned to the company and spoke these memorable words:

> I AM GOING LIKE A LAMB TO THE SLAUGHTER, BUT I AM CALM AS A SUMMER'S MORNING. I HAVE A CONSCIENCE VOID OF OFFENSE TOWARD GOD AND TOWARD ALL MEN.

Again, he said: "If they take my life, I shall die an innocent man, *and my blood shall cry from the ground for vengeance*, and it shall yet be said of me, 'He was murdered in cold blood.'"

Joseph sent Henry G. Sherwood back to Nauvoo to get the arms ready for Captain Dunn and to have all things done with good order and regularity. But Dunn feared that the governor's demands, coming at such a time, would excite resistance, and he requested Joseph and the brethren to return with him to the city under a pledge of mutual protection. He preferred to depend upon the well-known integrity of Joseph rather than to risk the wounded feelings of a much abused people. When the order for the state arms was made known in Nauvoo, many of the brethren regarded this as a preparation for another Far West tragedy;but they heeded the Prophet's word and unresistingly yielded obedience to the requirement.

It was an outrage to ask these arms under the circumstances; they were borne by men who were on the defensive, not the offensive—men who carried them for the protection of home and virtue, and who had not set foot outside the limits of their own city. Ford's action in this matter was atrocious; the compliance of the Prophet and the Saints was noble.

Joseph again bade farewell to his family, and looked again and again upon the fair domain which his mortal eyes were beholding for the last time. His face was white and luminous, yet upon it and in his eyes was a look of anguish. His friends would even now have detained him, be the consequences what they might; but he told them he must either yield himself to his sworn murderers or the city would be given up to massacre and pillage under the sanction of the governor.

Shortly after leaving Nauvoo, they met Brother A. C. Hodge coming from Carthage, who told them that a minister—whom Joseph had previously treated with great kindness—warned him that so sure as Joseph and Hyrum came to Carthage they would be killed. He also said that Hamilton, the innkeeper at Carthage, had pointed to the Carthage Greys, saying: "Hodge, there are the boys that will settle you Mormons."

A little farther on the way, the Prophet received letters from attorneys at Carthage to whom the governor had pledged his own honor and the honor of the state of Illinois that the prisoners should be protected from all harm. This pledge Ford reiterated often; and upon the strength of it many of the Prophet's friends felt that he was safe.

It was not until a little before midnight that the party reached Carthage, but they found the mob up and expecting them with great anxiety. As they passed the public square, many troops, especially the Carthage Greys, gave way to a frenzy of joy.

Some of them shouted, "God damn you, old Joe Smith, we have got you now." Others cried, "Where is the damned Prophet!" "Stand away, you McDonough boys, and let us shoot the damned Mormons." "Clear the way and let us have a view of Joe Smith, the

Prophet of God. He has seen the last of Nauvoo. We'll use him up now, and kill all the damned Mormons."

The profanity of the mob was an avalanche. Such ravings and cursings were scarcely ever before heard from civilized men. The governor was an ear witness to it all and leaned from his tavern window to say in a fawning voice to the rabble:

> Gentlemen, I know your great anxiety to see Mr. Smith, which is natural enough, but it is quite too late tonight for you to have that opportunity; but I assure you, gentlemen, you shall have that privilege tomorrow morning, as I will cause him to pass before the troops upon the square, and I now wish you, with this assurance, quietly and peaceably to return to your quarters.

At this there was a hurrah for Tom Ford, and the mob obeyed his wish.

The prisoners were quartered at the tavern of Hamilton, who had threatened Brother Hodge that the Carthage Greys would settle the "Mormons." At the same inn was a party of apostates. One of them, John A. Hicks, formerly president of the elders' quorum, stated to Brother Cyrus H. Wheelock that it was determined to shed the blood of Joseph Smith, whether he was cleared by the law or not. Hicks talked freely and unreservedly upon the subject, as if he were discoursing upon the most common occurrence of life; and boldly declared that the Laws, the Higbees and the Fosters were all agreed upon this course.

Elder Wheelock carried this information to Governor Ford, but that craven wretch treated it with perfect indifference and suffered Hicks and his associates to go on with their plans for murder.

A few hours later the most prominent enemies of the Prophet at Carthage declared:

> *There is nothing against these men; the law cannot reach them, but powder and ball shall. They will never get out of Carthage alive.*

CHAPTER 64

Charge
of Treason

When the morning came on the 25th of June, 1844, Joseph and his brethren voluntarily presented themselves to Constable Bettisworth, who had held the original writ against them. They sought and had an interview with the governor at his headquarters; and he then and there pledged his own faith and that of the state of Illinois that Joseph and Hyrum and the other prisoners should be protected from personal violence and should have a fair and impartial trial.

A few moments after 8 o'clock A.M., Joseph and Hyrum were arrested upon warrants issued by Justice Robert F. Smith of Carthage, charging them with treason, upon the affidavits of Augustus Spencer and Henry O. Norton.

After making an inflammable speech to the rabble army, the governor led the brothers before the troops, as the mob had requested to have a clear view of Joseph and Hyrum. As they passed in front of the lines, Ford introduced the Prophet and Patriarch as Generals Joseph and Hyrum Smith. The Carthage Greys refused to receive them by that introduction, and some of the officers threw up their hats, drew their swords and said: "We will introduce ourselves to the damned Mormons in a different style." The Governor quieted them by saying:

You shall have full satisfaction.

An hour later the Carthage Greys revolted and were put under guard; they could not be content to wait another hour for the murder. But they were soon released.

Joseph had asked a private interview with Ford, but it had been refused. In declining, the governor looked down with shame.

In the afternoon several officers of the mob militia called upon Joseph at the tavern. They gazed upon him with much curiosity, and he asked them if he appeared like a desperate character. They replied that his outward appearance seemed to indicate exactly the opposite, but they could not tell what was in his heart. To this Joseph responded:

> Very true, gentlemen, you cannot see what is in my heart, and you are therefore unable to judge me or my intentions; but I can see what is in your hearts, and will tell you what I see. I can see you thirst for blood, and nothing but my blood will satisfy you. It is not for crime of any description that I and my brethren are thus continually persecuted and harassed by our enemies, but there are other motives, and some of them I have expressed, so far as relates to myself; and inasmuch as you and the people thirst for blood, I prophesy, in the name of the Lord, that you shall witness scenes of blood and sorrow to your entire satisfaction. Your souls shall be perfectly satiated with blood, and many of you who are now present shall have an opportunity to face the cannon's mouth from sources you think not of; and those people that desire this great evil upon me and my brethren, shall be filled with regret and sorrow because of the scenes of desolation and distress that await them. They shall seek for peace, and shall not be able to find it. Gentlemen, you will find what I have told you to be true.

At 4 o'clock Joseph and Hyrum and thirteen other brethren were taken before Robert F. Smith, justice of the peace and captain of the Carthage Greys, on a charge of riot in destroying the printing press of the *Expositor.* Robert Smith took the place of Morrison, by the direction of the mob and with the connivance of the governor, although Ford had stated that the hearing must be had before the same justice who issued the original writ.

But he had only made this assertion in order to justify himself in overlooking the proceedings in Justice Wells' court.

Now that he had the brethren at Carthage, he was willing that the mob should have them tried before the most vindictive man to be found exercising judicial functions. Upon this hearing before Robert F. Smith, the fifteen brethren were admitted to bail in the sum of $7,500, and John S. Fullmer, Edward Hunter, Dan Jones, John Benbow, and others as sureties. Then the court was adjourned without calling on Joseph and Hyrum to answer to the charge of treason, or even intimating to them or their counsel that an examination of this charge was to be made.

About dark that night the constable appeared with a *mittimus* from Justice Smith and demanded that Joseph and Hyrum go to jail upon the charge of treason. This *mittimus* falsely alleged that the trial for treason had been begun and had been postponed. Joseph and his counsel, Messrs. Woods and Reid, exposed this tyrannical proceeding, showing clearly that the law did not permit the justice to send them to jail by *mittimus* without having them first brought before him for examination, and appealed to the governor. He refused assistance. A little later Captain and Justice Robert F. Smith applied to him to know how he should enforce the illegal *mittimus,* and the governor said significantly: "You have the Carthage Greys at your command." The mob captain took the hint and dragged the prisoners violently to jail.

Apostles John Taylor and Willard Richards, along with John P. Greene, Stephen Markham, Dan Jones, John S. Fullmer, Dr. Southwick, and Lorenzo D. Wasson, accompanied the Prophet and Patriarch to prison; and it is well that they did so. Stephen Markham and Dan Jones walked one on either side of Joseph and Hyrum, keeping off the drunken rabble which several times broke through the ranks of the file of soldiers guarding the brethren on their way to prison.

They made their dungeon seem a heaven that night by their prayers and by their faith.

After spending the night in Carthage Jail, Joseph wrote on the morning of June 26, 1844, soliciting an interview with Ford.

The governor sent back a favorable reply, and to the messengers he spoke apologetically of his failure to interfere the previous night. Apostle John Taylor had been to him in the meantime and had made him feel his falseness and cowardice. About 9:30 A.M. the governor came to the prison and had a lengthy interview with Joseph. President Taylor was present and made an extensive report of the conversation. Joseph charged Governor Ford with absolute knowledge that the enemies of the Saints had first commenced these difficulties; that Joseph and his people had not transgressed the law; and that the Nauvoo Legion had only been ordered out in pursuance of orders received by Joseph from the governor requiring him to assemble the Legion for the protection of Nauvoo against armed bands of marauders.

As they parted, the governor reiterated his promise, pledging his faith, the honor of his officers, and the good name of the state of Illinois that the brethren would be protected. He said that he might go to Nauvoo that day or he next, and if so he would take Joseph with him.

After Ford left the prison, he went to Hamilton's Hotel and began to converse with a mob soldier standing there. Alfred Randall, a man of approved veracity, testified that he heard the mobocrat saying to Ford, "The soldiers are determined to see Joe Smith dead before they leave here"; and heard Ford reply, "If you know of any such thing keep it to yourself." It was common conversation that day on the camping ground and in the dining room of the hotel in the presence of Governor Ford: "The law is too short for these men, but they must not be suffered to go at large." "No; if the law will not reach them, powder and ball must."

Most of the afternoon of the 26th was spent by Dan Jones and Stephen Markham in hewing the warped door of the cell in which the brethren were confined with a penknife so that it would fasten in the frame.

The brethren preached by turns to the guards, several of whom were relieved before their watch was out because they admitted that they were convinced of the innocence of the prisoners.

One of them said: "We have been imposed upon; these men are guiltless."

Another said: "Let us go home, boys, for I will not fight any longer against these men."

During the day Hyrum vainly attempted to lead Joseph into a belief that his life would be saved. To his brethren Joseph said: "Could my brother Hyrum but be liberated it would not matter so much about me."

Then he said: "Poor Rigdon, I am glad he has gone to Pittsburgh out of the way. Were he to preside he would lead the Church to destruction in less than five years."

At half past two that afternoon, Constable Bettisworth demanded the persons of the prisoners from the jailor upon an order signed by Justice Robert F. Smith. The jailor refused, as the prisoners had been committed to his charge to be held by him until released from his custody by due course of law. The justice then inquired of the governor what he should do, and Ford once more responded: "There are the Carthage Greys under your command, bring them out; we have plenty of troops."

Again taking the significant hint, the mob captain and justice used his willing rabble of soldiers to drag Joseph and Hyrum illegally away. He had them brought before him, Robert F. Smith, captain of the Carthage Greys, at the courthouse. The grave charge against them was treason, and when they asked for time in which to get witnesses, they were vehemently opposed. Finally, at five o'clock in the afternoon, the court adjourned until noon of the next day to give the defendants opportunity to send to Nauvoo, twenty miles distant, and obtain their witnesses. Subsequently, without any notification to the prisoners or their counsel, the mob justice and captain postponed the trial until the 29th of June.

Patriarch John Smith, father of Apostle George A. Smith, came from Macedonia to see his nephews Joseph and Hyrum in jail. He narrowly escaped with his life from mobbers on the way. It was with difficulty that he secured admission to the prison. After remaining an hour, he left the jail to carry a message to Almon W. Babbitt, requesting his assistance as attorney for the Prophet at the expected trial. Patriarch John Smith found Babbitt but learned from him that he could not comply with Joseph's request.

That night in prison Hyrum read from the Book of Mormon concerning the sufferings and deliverance of the servants of God from the hands of their enemies. Joseph arose and bore a powerful testimony to the guards to the divinity of the book; he declared that the gospel had been restored and that the kingdom of God was again established on the earth for the sake of which he was then incarcerated in prison, and not because he had violated any law of God or man. They retired to rest very late. In the room with the Prophet and Patriarch were Apostles John Taylor and Willard Richards and Elders John S. Fullmer, Stephen Markham and Dan Jones.

In the night Joseph whispered to Dan Jones, "Are you afraid to die?"

Brother Jones answered: "Has that time come, think you? Engaged in such a cause I do not think that death would have many terrors."

Joseph replied: "You will yet see Wales and fulfill the mission appointed you, before you die."[1]

In the morning Dan Jones went down, at the Prophet's request, to learn the cause of a disturbance of the night, and Frank Worrell, the officer of the guard of Carthage Greys, said to Dan:

> We have had too much trouble to bring old Joe here to let him ever escape alive, and unless you want to die with him, you had better leave before sundown; and you are not a damned bit better than him for taking his part, and you'll see that I can prophesy better than old Joe, for neither he nor his brother, nor anyone who will remain with them, will see the sun set today.

Brother Jones started to find the governor and on the way saw an assemblage of the mob, and heard one of them who was making a speech say:

---

[1] This prediction was gloriously fulfilled.

Our troops will be discharged this morning in obedience to order, and for a sham we will leave the town; but when the governor and the McDonough troops have left for Nauvoo this forenoon, we will return and kill these men, if we have to tear the jail down.

When Dan found the governor, and related the threats, Ford only sneered at him. Ford was actually preparing to go to Nauvoo. He had disbanded some of the troops, and in his hearing they declared that they would return and kill Joseph and Hyrum as soon as he was far enough away from town.

Ford refused permits for the Prophet's friends to pass in and out of the prison. This deprived Joseph and Hyrum of the society of all but Apostles Taylor and Richards, who remained constantly with them.

The governor held consultation with the officers of the mob army. A Dr. Southwick who was there afterward declared that the purpose of the meeting was to consider the best way of stopping Joseph Smith's career, as his views on the government were being widely circulated and they took like wildfire. The mobocrats said that if he did not get into the presidential chair this election he would be sure to next time; and if Illinois and Missouri would join together and kill him, they would not be brought to justice for it.

As the governor continued his preparations to depart from Carthage to Nauvoo, and as it was clear that he intended to break his solemn promise by failing to take Joseph with him, Cyrus H. Wheelock, Dan Jones and John P. Greene went in town to him and protested with all possible solemnity against his deed. He professed to reassure them; and then he took with him Captain Dunn and his company—of all the militia the least vindictive against the Prophet; and left as a guard the Carthage Greys—of all the mob the most bloodthirsty. These Carthage Greys had but two days before been under arrest for insulting the commanding general; their conduct had shown them to be notoriously hostile to the prisoners; and they had often in the governor's hearing threatened the lives of Joseph and Hyrum. Of the disbanded

troops, the governor permitted two or three hundred under
Colonel Levi Williams, a sectarian preacher and a sworn enemy to
Joseph, to remain encamped in the vicinity of Carthage, awaiting
the hour when they might safely descend upon the jail.

Cyrus H. Wheelock was permitted to enter the prison, and
during his visit he slipped a small revolver, of the kind known
in those days as the "pepper-box" revolver, into Joseph's pocket.
Cyrus was going to Nauvoo with messages from the brethren
in prison. They were so numerous that Dr. Richards proposed
to write them down feeling that Wheelock might forget, but
Hyrum fastened his eye upon the messenger, and with a look of
penetration, said:

> Brother Wheelock will remember all that we tell him,
> and he will never forget the occurrences of this day.

CHAPTER 65

Not of
the World

B efore recounting the final act which closed this great life, we
may pause to glance at some of the work of the Prophet and
some of the difficulties which beset his path and wrought the
martyrdom.

During the winter of 1843–4, superhuman power rested
upon the Prophet in his teachings and administrations. He was
impelled to constant labor in his ministry as if he had the briefest
possible time in which to accomplish his work. Perhaps he was not
fully aware how little there was of mortal life left to him, yet many
of his expressions at this time were recalled by the apostles and
others afterwards as foreshadowing the nearness of his departure.
He bestowed upon the faithful apostles and other chosen ones the
endowments and gave them the keys of the priesthood in their
fullness as he had received them. He also taught and administered
to them the sealing ordinances, explaining in great plainness and
power the manner in which husbands and wives, parents and
children are to be united by eternal ties, and the whole human
family, back to Father Adam, be linked together in indissoluble
bonds. In imparting these glorious principles and bestowing these
keys and powers upon his fellow apostles, the Prophet was filled
with Godlike power. More important doctrines and ordinances
were never imparted unto man. The spirit which rested upon
Joseph in teaching and upon the people in listening to them (for
he dwelt much upon these principles in his public discourses) will
never be forgotten by those who heard him. It was to the deep and
abiding effect of these teachings upon the minds of the Saints that

the extraordinary exertions which were made after his death in completing the temple may chiefly be attributed.

The perusal of the history of the Church during the lifetime of Joseph the Prophet suggests many reflections and to many minds prompts many inquiries. One cannot fail to be struck with the unceasing opposition with which he had to contend. From the day that he received the first communication from heaven, up to the day of his martyrdom, his pathway was beset with difficulties, his liberty and life were constantly menaced. Had he been an ordinary man he would have been crushed in spirit and sunk in despair under the relentless attacks which were made upon him. To find a parallel to his case, we must go back to the days of our Savior and His apostles and the prophets who preceded them. Joseph's life was sought for with satanic hate. The thirst for his blood was unappeasable. Had there not been a special providence exercised in his behalf to preserve him until his mission should be fulfilled, he would have been slain by murderous hands long before the dreadful day at Carthage.

To the inexperienced reader it seems unaccountable that any generation of men could have been so blind to everything Godlike, so dead to every humane sentiment, so utterly cruel and barbarous, as not to recognize in the teachings, works and life of God's beloved Son the divinity with which He was clothed and to nail Him upon a cross between two thieves. Also that His chosen apostles, filled with angelic power, preaching so pure a doctrine and laboring with such self-denial and unselfish zeal for the salvation of mankind, should have been slain by the very people whose benefactors they sought to be.

But in our own age the same scenes are reenacted. Joseph Smith, a Prophet of God, called by the Almighty to receive the everlasting priesthood to lay the foundation of the Church of Christ, and to preach the ancient pure gospel, performs the mission to which he was divinely appointed, and is pursued with vindictive hate through his life, and is finally barbarously slain. The explanation of all this is given by the Lord Himself in His words to His disciples: "If ye were of the world, the world would love his own; but because ye are not of the world, but I have chosen you out of the world, therefore the world hateth you." (John 15:19.)

According to the predictions, this is the dispensation of the fullness of times—the crowning dispensation of all. To leave the world without excuse and to prepare the way for the second coming of the Lord, the Holy Priesthood, the pure gospel and the true Church of Christ are restored to earth through the ministration of angels. Satan, fully conscious that if these prevail his dominion will be overthrown, arrays all his forces against the servants and work of God. He resorts to his old tactics to accomplish his purposes. He was a liar and a murderer from the beginning. Lies and murder are the agencies he depends upon. Many, being free agents and having power to choose whom they will serve, become the instruments of hate, and the earth is drenched with the blood of innocence. The Prophet Joseph, while he lived, was the conspicuous object of his vengeance. Like Paul, he could have recounted a long list of perils which he had to encounter, not the least of which, as in the case of Paul, were "perils among false brethren." Of all the evils with which this great Prophet had to contend, none were so grievous or so hard to be borne as the defection and treason of "false brethren." The most deadly wounds he ever received were from those who, Judas-like, had been his companions. When, through their transgressions, they lost the Spirit of God and turned away from the truth, the spirit of murder took possession of them, they became fit instruments for Satan's service, and to this class more than to any others, can the foul murders of the 27th of June, 1844, be charged.

The great bulk of those who composed the mobs which attacked the Saints in Missouri and Illinois were ignorant men. Their passions were easily aroused. A few cunning and unscrupulous leaders were able to use them to accomplish their ends. Seeing the increase of the Saints, they were easily persuaded that, if left to themselves, they would soon outnumber the old settlers, they would outvote them, take possession of the offices, and drive them out of the country. By such representations and artifices as these, appealing to the lowest and basest of motives, they were able to inflame the minds of ignorant and unprincipled men. Envious of the prosperity of the Saints, coveting their possessions, they thought to profit in driving them from their homes. Apostates had personal vengeance and hates to gratify; politicians saw a growing power that they could not control and whose union made it formidable in county and state affairs; the clergy saw a system of religion which they could not controvert; and the rabble had their cupidity excited at the prospect of plunder, which might fall to them through the abandonment of lands and improvements and stock by the people whom they were driving away.

CHAPTER 66

The Final Hour

Governor Ford went to Nauvoo on the morning of the 27th of June, 1844, accompanied by a body of troops. When he arrived there, he made a public speech before thousands of the Saints, in which he used this expression: "A great crime has been done by destroying the *Expositor* press and placing the city under martial law, and a *severe atonement must be made, so prepare your minds for the emergency.*

Whether Ford was fully cognizant of the plot to murder the Prophet during his absence from Carthage is not altogether clear. He was unquestionably aware of the murderous feeling which existed among the Carthage Greys and the men who were associated with Levi Williams and the Laws, Higbees, Fosters, and others at Carthage. It has been stated upon good authority, and it has never been disputed, that he was informed of the intentions of the mob. But he ventured into Nauvoo. Would a cowardly man as he was have dared to risk himself in such a manner at such a time if he was fully advised of the time the massacre was to take place? The presumption is that he was indifferent as to the fate which would befall the Prophet and his companions; but that he did not know, as some of his officers did, that the bloody deed was to be consummated while he was absent at Nauvoo. If Ford had been a man of greater daring, it might with certainty be assured that his visit to Nauvoo was a part of the conspiracy, and that he went there to avoid the appearance of complicity in the murder. This is certain, that while Ford was addressing the people, a sound like the distant firing of a cannon, or the slight sound of distant rumbling thunder, was heard by many in the audience and by some of Ford's aides who stood near him, and that they whispered something to him, and without loss of time and in the greatest haste, he and his escort rode out of Nauvoo. Their departure was more like a flight than the decorous leave-taking of the executive of the state accompanied by a command of troops. A cannon was fired at a certain point distant from Carthage as a signal that the massacre had been accomplished; but it was never known whether or not this was the sound which attracted attention at Nauvoo. Governor Ford's hasty flight at that time has always been deemed conclusive evidence that he had been informed by some of his companions—if he had not been fully advised of the plot and its details before—that Joseph Smith and his companions had been murdered.

Ford and his aides occupied a room in the Nauvoo Mansion that day. Orrin P. Rockwell heard one of them at three o'clock say: *"The deed is done before this time."*

The governor and his company went to the temple. Some of the officers broke the horns from the oxen supporting the baptismal font, while Ford made rare sport of the sacred edifice.

One of his attendants remarked: "This temple is a curious piece of workmanship; and it was a damned shame that they did not let Joe Smith finish it."

Another said: "But he is dead by this time, and he will never see this temple again."

Brother William G. Sterrett stood by and replied: "They cannot kill him until he has finished his work."

At this Ford gave a significant smile and one of his aides standing by said: "Whether he has finished his work or not, by God, he will not see this place again, for he is finished before this time."

At Carthage, after the governor left, the external situation was this: The guarding of the jail had been left to General Deming, who had the Carthage Greys under his command; but Deming retired during the day for fear of his life, as he saw the determination of the troops to connive at murder. The main body of the company was stationed in the public square, one hundred and fifty yards from the jail, while eight men were detailed, under the command of Sergeant Frank A. Worrell, to guard the prisoners. The disbanded mob militia had come up to Carthage to the number of two hundred, with their faces blackened with powder and mud. The Carthage Greys were informed that the assassin band was ready; and it was then arranged that the guard at the jail should load with blank cartridges and that the mob should attack the prison and meet with some show of resistance.

Within the jail the brethren, Joseph and Hyrum, John Taylor and Willard Richards, were confined in a room upstairs and were busy, during the day, writing letters, conversing and praying and singing. Between three and four o'clock at the Prophet's request, Apostle Taylor sang this sweet and comforting poem:

> A poor wayfaring man of grief,
> Hath often cross'd me on my way,
> Who sued so humbly for relief
> That I could never answer Nay.
> I had not power to ask his name;
> Whither he went or whence he came;
> Yet there was something in his eye
> That won my love, I know not why.
>
> Once when my scanty meal was spread,
> He entered—not a word he spake!
> Just perishing for want of bread;
> I gave him all; he blessed it, brake,
> And ate, but gave me part again;
> Mine was an angel's portion then,
> For while I fed with eager haste
> The crust was manna to my taste.
>
> I spied him where a fountain burst,
> Clear from the rock—his strength was gone,
> The heedless water mocked his thirst,
> He heard it, saw it hurrying on.
> I ran and rais'd the suff'rer up;

Thrice from the stream he drain'd my cup,
Dipped and return'd it running o'er;
I drank and never thirsted more.

'Twas night, the floods were out, it blew
A winter hurricane aloof;
I heard his voice, abroad, and flew
To bid him welcome to my roof.
I warm'd, I cloth'd, I cheer'd my guest,
I laid him on my couch to rest;
Then made the earth my bed, and seem'd
In Eden's garden while I dream'd.

Stripp'd, wounded, beaten nigh to death,
I found him by the highway side;
I rous'd his pulse, brought back his breath,
Reviv'd his spirit, and supplied
Wine, oil, refreshment—he was heal'd;
I had myself a wound conceal'd;
But from that hour forgot the smart,
And peace bound up my broken heart.

In prison I saw him next—condemn'd
To meet a traitor's doom at morn;
The tide of lying tongues I stemm'd.
And honor'd him 'mid shame and scorn.
My friendship's utmost zeal to try,
He asked if I for him would die;
The flesh was weak, my blood ran chill,
But the free spirit cried, "I will!"

Then in a moment to my view,
The stranger started from disguise;
The tokens in his hands I knew,
The Savior stood before mine eyes.
He spake—and my poor name he nam'd—
"Of me thou hast not been asham'd.
These deeds shall thy memorial be;
Fear not, thou didst them unto me."

And when it was done, Joseph asked him to repeat it. He replied that he did not feel like singing. He was oppressed with a sense of coming disaster; but to gratify Hyrum, he sang the hymn again, with much tender feeling.

At four o'clock the guard was changed. A little after five the jailor came in and said that Stephen Markham had been surrounded by a mob and driven from Carthage. A little later there was a slight rustling at the outer door of the jail, and a cry of surrender, then a discharge of three or four guns. The plot had been carried out: two hundred of the mob came rushing into the jail yard, and the guards fired their pieces over the heads of the assailing party.

Many of the mob rushed up the stairs while others fired through the open windows of the jail into the room where the brethren were confined. The four prisoners sprang against the door, but the murderers burst it partly open and pushed their guns into the room. John Taylor and Willard Richards, each with a cane, tried to knock aside the weapons. A shower of bullets came up the stairway and through the door. Hyrum was in front of the door when a ball struck him in the face and he fell back, saying:

I am a dead man.

As he was falling, another bullet from the outside passed through his swaying form, and two others from the doorway entered his body a moment later. When Hyrum fell, Joseph exclaimed, "Oh, my dear brother Hyrum!" and opening the door a few inches he discharged his pistol into the stairway—but two or three barrels missed fire.

When the door could no longer be held, and when he could no longer parry the guns, Elder Taylor sprang toward the window. A bullet from the doorway struck his left thigh. Paralyzed and unable to help himself, he fell on the window sill and felt himself falling out, when by some means which he did not understand at the time he was thrown backward into the room. A bullet fired from the outside struck his watch and the watch saved his life in two ways; it stopped the bullet, which probably would have killed him, and the force of the ball in striking it threw him into the room. The watch stopped at sixteen minutes and twenty-six seconds past 5 o'clock. After he fell into the room, three other bullets struck him, spattering his blood like rain upon the walls and floor.

Joseph saw that there was no longer safety in the room; and thinking that he would save the life of Willard Richards if he himself should spring from the room, he turned immediately from the door, dropped his pistol and leaped into the window. Instantly two bullets pierced him from the door, and one entered his right breast from without, and he fell outward into the hands of his murderers exclaiming:

Oh, Lord, my God!

When his body struck the ground, he rolled instantly upon his face—dead. As he lay there, one of the mob, barefooted and bareheaded, wearing no coat, with his trousers rolled above his knees and his shirt sleeves above his elbows, seized the body of the murdered Prophet and set it against the south side of the well curb. Colonel Levi Williams then ordered four men to shoot Joseph. Standing about eight feet from his body they fired simultaneously. The body slightly cringed as the bullets entered it, and once more Joseph fell upon his face. He had smiled with sweet compassion in his countenance as he gazed upon his murderers in the last moment of his life; and this was the expression when the face was set in death.

When Joseph fell from the window, the mob on the stairway rushed down and out of the building to find him; and it was this which saved the lives of Willard Richards and John Taylor. Willard started to leave the room, thinking all were dead but himself; but Elder Taylor called to him. He returned, took up the body of John, which was bleeding from four ghastly wounds, and carried him into an inner dungeon cell and placed him on a filthy mattress which was lying there, saying: "If your wounds are not fatal, I want you to live to tell this story."

Nearly all the inhabitants of Carthage followed the mob in their flight of horror. The governor came to Carthage in the night, wrote an order for the citizens of Nauvoo to defend themselves, and then the miserable coward fled to Quincy.

Having provided as well as possible for the wounds of John Taylor, on the morning of the 28th of June Dr. Richards started for Nauvoo with the bodies of the martyrs. They were met by thousands of lamenting Saints whose wailings ascended unto the ears of Almighty God. Ten thousand people were addressed by Apostle Richards, Colonel Markham and others who admonished them to keep the peace and trust to the law for a remedy for the awful crimes which had been committed, and when the law failed, to call upon God in heaven to avenge them of their wrongs.

The bodies of the martyrs were taken to the Mansion House and cared for by loving friends. The loved ones of the dead Prophet and Patriarch were first admitted and fell upon the dear faces and kissed them and begged for one more word of comfort.

Early the next morning the bodies were placed in coffins covered with black velvet, and the caskets were then placed in rough pine boxes. The doors were thrown open, and ten thousand people walked through the mansion and gazed upon the martyred clay. All this time the people were in constant expectation of an attack by the mob army upon the defenseless city.

At night the house was closed, and then the coffins were lifted out of the boxes and concealed in an apartment of the mansion while bags of sand took their place in the outer caskets. A mock funeral was held; the boxes were carried in a hearse to the graveyard and there deposited in the earth with the usual ceremonies. The course seemed necessary because the enemies of Joseph and Hyrum had taken a ghastly oath to steal the remains.

At midnight the bodies were taken in their caskets from the Mansion House by Dimick B. Huntington, Edward Hunter, William D. Huntington, William Marks, Jonathan H. Holmes, Gilbert Goldsmith, Alpheus Cutler, Lorenzo D. Wasson, Philip B. Lewis and James Emmett to the Nauvoo House, the foundation of which was then built, and they were interred in the basement.

Immediately afterward, a terrific storm of rain came on, accompanied by thunder and lightning. The tears of heaven obliterated all traces of the newly dug graves, and the bodies remained there in safe repose until a later time when they were removed elsewhere.

The woe of the Saints cannot be described. They were menaced with extermination. Their Prophet and Patriarch were dead. Only two of the apostles were there, and one of these was supposed to be dying.

The enemies of truth were sure that they had now destroyed the work. And yet it lives, greater and stronger after the lapse of years! It is indestructible, for it is the work of God.

And knowing that it is the eternal work of God,

we know that Joseph Smith,

who established it,

was a Prophet

holy and

pure.

⌒

Anecdotes and Sayings
of the Prophet

"Seek ye wisdom from the best books."

"The cause of human liberty is the cause of God."

"We will never be justly charged with the sin of ingratitude."

"Baptism is a covenant with God that we will do His will."

"All men will be raised from the grave by the power of God, having spirit in their bodies and not blood."

"Our affections should be placed upon God and His work more intensely than upon our fellow beings."

"I will walk through the gates of heaven, and claim what I seal and those that follow me and my counsel."

"I understand some law, and more justice, and know as much about the rights of American citizens as any man."

"All children are redeemed by the blood of Jesus Christ, and the moment they leave this world they are taken to the bosom of Abraham."

"The Lord once told me that what I asked for I should have. I have been afraid to ask God to kill my enemies, lest some of them should, peradventure, repent."

"Beware, oh earth! how you fight against the Saints of God and shed innocent blood; for, in the days of Elijah, his enemies came upon him, and fire was called down from heaven to destroy them."

"Sectarian priests cry out concerning me and ask: 'Why is it that this bladder gets so many followers and retains them?' I answer: 'It is because I possess the principle of love. All that I offer the world is a good heart and a good hand.'"

"I am a rough stone. The sound of the hammer and chisel was never heard on me until the Lord took me in hand. I desire the learning and wisdom of heaven alone."

"I asked a short time since for the Lord to deliver me out of the hands of the governor; and if it needs must be to accomplish it, to take him away; and the next news that came pouring down from there was that Governor Reynolds had shot himself."

Speaking of the death of Judge Higbee, a just and good man, Joseph said: "Who is there that would not give all his goods to feed the poor, and pour out his gold and silver to the four winds to go where Elias Higbee has gone?"

At Far West, Missouri, on the 4th day of July, 1838, the liberty pole was struck by lightning and shattered into splinters. Joseph walked around on the fragments, saying: "As that pole was splintered, so shall the nations of the earth be."

Soon after the nomination of the Prophet for the Presidency of the United States, Apostle George A. Smith related that Elder Farnham heard the people in St. Louis say: "Things have come to a strange pass; if Joseph Smith is elected President, he will raise the devil with Missouri, and if he is not elected he will raise the devil anyhow."

An angry sectarian in Kirtland commanded fire to come down out of heaven to consume the Prophet and his house. Joseph smiled and said: "You are one of Baal's prophets; your god does not hear you."

A visitor who remarked that the people had been gathered from the four quarters of the earth, of different races and creeds, asked the Prophet: "Mr. Smith, how do you govern these people?"

"I teach them correct principles and they govern themselves."

"Salvation cannot come without revelation; it is in vain for any man to minister without it. No man is a minister of Jesus Christ without being a prophet. No man can be a minister of Jesus Christ except he has the testimony of Jesus, and this is the spirit of prophecy."

The Prophet was preaching in Philadelphia, when a man called out for a sign and would not let Joseph proceed peaceably with his sermon. After having vainly warned the man of what Christ said concerning sign-seekers, the person still persisting, Joseph said to the congregation: "This man is an adulterer."

"It is true," cried another, "for I caught him in the very act"; and the sign-seeker afterwards confessed that the charge was correct.

"The Saints can testify whether I am willing to lay down my life for my brethren. If it has been demonstrated that I have been willing to die for a Mormon, I am bold to declare before heaven that I am just as ready to die in defending the rights of a Presbyterian, a Baptist, or a good man of any other denomination; for the same principle which would trample upon the rights of the Latter-day Saints would trample upon the rights of the Roman Catholics, or of any other denomination who may be unpopular and too weak to defend themselves."

"There are two Comforters spoken of. The first Comforter is the Holy Ghost. . . . Now what is this other Comforter? It is the Lord Jesus Christ Himself. When any man obtains this last Comforter, he will have the personage of Jesus Christ to attend him, or appear unto him from time to time, and even He will manifest the Father unto him. They will take up their abode in Him, and the visions of the heavens will be opened unto him, and the Lord will teach him face to face, and he may have a perfect knowledge of the mysteries of the kingdom of God; and this is the state and place the ancient Saints arrived at when they had such glorious visions."

Sunday, March 10, 1844—"I prophesy in the name of the Lord that Christ will not come this year; and I also prophesy in the name of the Lord that Christ will not come in forty years; and if God ever spoke by my mouth He will not come in that length of time. Jesus Christ never did reveal to any man the *precise* time that He *would* come."

"The Savior, Moses, and Elias gave the keys of the priesthood to Peter, James and John, on the Mount, when they were transfigured before Him. . . . How have we come at the priesthood in the last days? It came down in regular succession. Peter, James and John had it given to them, and they gave it to others." [The Prophet and Oliver Cowdery].

The Laws and Fosters and Higbees had threatened to kill Joseph, alleging that he was a false prophet and they would do well to rid the world of him. He preached a funeral sermon upon Elder King Follett, on Sunday, the 7th day of April, 1844. Referring to the murderous hate of his enemies he said:

"If any man is authorized to take away my life because he thinks and says I am a false teacher, then, upon the same principle, we should be justified in taking away the life of every false teacher; and where would be the end of blood? and who would not be the sufferer?

"But meddle not with any man for his religion; and all governments ought to permit every man to enjoy his religion unmolested. No man is authorized to take away life in consequence of difference of religion, which all laws and governments ought to tolerate and protect, right or wrong. Every man has a natural and, in our country, a constitutional right to be a false prophet as well as a true prophet. If I show, verily, that I have the truth of God, and show that ninety-nine out of every hundred professing to be religious ministers are false teachers, having no authority, while they pretend to hold the keys of God's kingdom on earth, and was to kill them because they are false teachers, it would deluge the whole world with blood."

Elder O. B. Huntington relates the following circumstance, which was detailed to him by Father Zera Cole while they were at work for the dead in the Logan Temple:

"Brother Cole was with the Camp of Zion, which went up to Missouri in 1834. While traveling across a vast prairie, treeless and waterless, they encamped at night after a long and wearisome day's march. They had been without water since early morning, and men and animals suffered greatly from thirst, for it had been one of the hottest days of June. Joseph sat in his tent door looking out upon the scene. All at once he called for a spade. When it was brought, he looked about him and selected a spot, the most convenient in the camp for men and teams to get water. Then he dug a shallow well, and immediately the water came bubbling up into it and filled it, so that the horses and mules could stand upon the brink and drink from it. While the camp stayed there, the well remained full, despite the fact that about two hundred men and scores of horses and mules were supplied from it."

Elder William Cahoon also told Brother Huntington of this incident.

"There are but a few beings in the world who understand rightly the character of God. The great majority of mankind do not comprehend anything, either that which is past or that which is to come, as it respects their relationship to God. . . . If a man learns nothing more than to eat, drink and sleep, and does not comprehend the designs of God, then the beast comprehends as much. If men do not comprehend the character of God, they do not comprehend themselves. I want to go back to the beginning, and so lift your minds into a more lofty sphere and a more exalted understanding than what the human mind generally aspires to.

"I want to ask this congregation—every man, woman, and child—to answer the question in their own hearts, what kind of a being is God? Ask yourselves; turn your thoughts into your hearts and say if any of you have seen, heard, or communed with Him. This is a question that may occupy your attention for a long time. I again repeat the question, What kind of a being is God? Does any man or woman know? The scriptures inform us that 'This is life eternal, that they might know thee, the only true God, and Jesus Christ whom thou hast sent.'"

On the 25th day of June, 1844, at about half past nine A.M., after repeated solicitations from the Prophet for a personal interview, Governor Ford came to Carthage Jail, in company with Colonel Geddes, and the following conversation occurred, as reported by Apostle John Taylor:

GOVERNOR: "General Smith, I believe you have given me a general outline of the difficulties that have existed in the country in the documents forwarded to me by Dr. Bernhisel and Mr. Taylor; but, unfortunately, there seems to be a great discrepancy between your statements and those of your enemies. It is true that you are substantiated by evidence and affidavit, but for such an extraordinary excitement as that which is now in the country, there must be some cause, and I attribute the last outbreak to the destruction of the *Expositor,* and to your refusal to comply with the writ issued by Esq. Morrison. The press in the United States is looked upon as the great bulwark of American freedom, and its destruction in Nauvoo was represented and looked upon as a high-handed measure, and manifests to the people a disposition on your part to suppress the liberty of speech and of the press; this, with your refusal to comply with the requisition of a writ, I conceive to be the principal cause of this difficulty, and you are, moreover, represented to me as turbulent and defiant of the laws and institutions of our country."

GENERAL SMITH: "Governor Ford, you, sir, as governor of this state, are aware of the prosecutions and persecutions that I have endured. You know well that our course has been peaceable and law-abiding, for I have furnished this state, ever since our settlement here, with sufficient evidence of my pacific intentions, and those of the people with whom I am associated, by the endurance of every conceivable indignity and lawless outrage perpetrated upon me and upon this people since our settlement here, and you yourself know that I have kept you well posted in relation to all matters associated with the late difficulties.

"If you have not got some of my communications, it has not been my fault.

"Agreeable to your orders, I assembled the Nauvoo Legion for the protection of Nauvoo and the surrounding country against an armed band of marauders, and ever since they have been mustered I have almost daily communicated with you in regard to all the leading events that have transpired; and whether in the capacity of mayor of the city, or lieutenant general of the Nauvoo Legion, I have striven, according to the best of my judgment, to preserve the peace and administer even-handed justice to all; but my motives are impugned, my acts are misconstrued, and I am grossly and wickedly misrepresented. I suppose I am indebted for my incarceration here to the oath of a worthless man that was arraigned before me and fined for abusing and maltreating his lame, helpless brother.

"That I should be charged by you, sir, who know better, of acting contrary to law, is to me a matter of surprise. Was it the Mormons or our enemies who first commenced these difficulties? You know well we did not; and when this turbulent, outrageous people commenced their insurrectionary movements, I made you acquainted with them, officially, and asked your advice, and have followed strictly your counsel in every particular. Who ordered out the Nauvoo Legion? I did, under your direction. For what purpose? To suppress these insurrectionary movements. It was at your instance, sir, that I issued a proclamation calling upon the Nauvoo Legion to be in readiness, at a moment's warning, to guard against the incursions of mobs, and gave an order to Jonathan Dunham, acting major general, to that effect. Am I then to be charged with the acts of others; and because lawlessness and mobocracy abound, am I, when carrying out your instructions, to be charged with not abiding law? Why is it that I must be made accountable for other men's acts? If there is trouble in the country, neither I nor my people made it, and all that we have ever done, after much endurance on our part, is to maintain and uphold the Constitution and the institutions of our country, and to protect an injured, innocent and persecuted people against misrule and mob violence.

"Concerning the destruction of the press to which you refer, men may differ somewhat in their opinions about it; but can it be supposed that after all the indignities to which we have been subjected outside, that this people could suffer such a set of worthless vagabonds to come into our city, and right under our own eyes and protection, vilify and calumniate not only ourselves, but the character of our wives and daughters, as was impudently and unblushingly done in that infamous and filthy sheet? There is not a city in the United States that would have suffered such an indignity for twenty-four hours. Our whole people were indignant, and loudly called upon our city authorities for a redress of their grievances, which if not attended to, they themselves would have taken the matter into their own hands and have summarily punished the audacious wretches, as they deserved.

"The principles of equal rights that have been instilled into our bosoms from our cradles, as American citizens, forbid us submitting to every foul indignity, succumbing and pandering to wretches so infamous as these. But, independent of this, the course that we pursued we considered to be strictly legal; for, notwithstanding the insult, we were anxious to be governed strictly by law, and therefore convened the city council; and, being desirous in our deliberations to abide law, summoned legal counsel to be present on the occasion.

"Upon investigating the matter, we found that our city charter gave us power to remove all nuisances; and, furthermore, upon consulting Blackstone upon what might be considered a nuisance, that distinguished lawyer, who is considered authority, I believe, in all our courts, states, among other things, that a libelous and filthy press may be considered a nuisance and abated as such.

"Here then one of the most eminent English barristers, whose works are considered standard with us, declares that a libelous and filthy press may be considered a nuisance, and our own charter, given us by the legislature of this state, gives us the power to remove nuisances; and by ordering that press abated as a nuisance, we conceived that we were acting strictly in accordance with law. We made that order in our corporate capacity, and the city marshal carried it out. It is possible there may have been some better way, but I must confess that I could not see it.

"In relation to the writ served upon us, we were willing to abide the consequences of our own acts, but were unwilling, in answering a writ of that kind, to submit to illegal exactions sought to be imposed upon us under the pretense of law, when we know they were in open violation of it.

"When that document was presented to me by Mr. Bettisworth, I offered in the presence of more than twenty persons, to go to any other magistrate, either in our city or Appanoose, or any other place where we should be safe, but we refused to put ourselves into the power of a mob.

"What right had that constable to refuse our request? He had none according to law; for you know, Governor Ford, that the statute law in Illinois is that the parties served with the writ 'shall go before him who issued it, or some other justice of the peace.' Why, then, should we be dragged to Carthage, where the law does not compel us to go? Does not this look like many others of our prosecutions with which you are acquainted? And had we not a right to expect foul play?

"This very act was a breach of law on his part—an assumption of power that did not belong to him, and an attempt, at least, to deprive us of our legal and constitutional rights and privileges. What could we do under the circumstances different from what we did do? We sued for and obtained a writ of *habeas corpus* from the municipal court, by which we were delivered from the hands of Constable Bettisworth and brought before and acquitted by the municipal court.

"After our acquittal, in a conversation with Judge Thomas, although he considered the acts of the party illegal, he advised, that to satisfy the people, we had better go before another magistrate who was not in our church.

"In accordance with his advice, we went before Esq. Wells, with whom you are well acquainted: both parties were present, witnesses were called on both sides, the case was fully investigated, and we were again dismissed.

"And what is this pretended desire to enforce law, and these lying, base rumors put into circulation for, but to seek, through mob influence, under pretense of law, to make us submit to requisitions that are contrary to law, and subversive to every principle of justice?

"And when you, sir, required us to come out here, we came, not because it was legal, but because you required it of us, and we were desirous of showing to you and to all men that we shrink not from the most rigid investigation of our acts.

"We certainly did expect other treatment than to be immured in a jail at the instance of these men, and I think, from your plighted faith, we had a right to, after disbanding our own forces and putting ourselves entirely in your hands: and now, after having fulfilled my part, sir, as a man and an American citizen, I call upon you, Governor Ford, and think that I have a right to do so, to deliver us from this place, and rescue us from this outrage that is sought to be practiced upon us by a set of infamous scoundrels."

GOVERNOR FORD: "But you have placed men under arrest, detained men as prisoners, and given passes to others, some of which I have seen."

JOHN P. GREENE, CITY MARSHAL: "Perhaps I can explain. Since these difficulties have commenced, you are aware that we have been placed under very peculiar circumstances; our city has been placed under a very rigid police guard; in addition to this, frequent guards have been placed outside the city to prevent any sudden surprise, and those guards have questioned suspected or suspicious persons as to their business.

"To strangers, in some instances, passes have been given to prevent difficulty in passing those guards. It is some of those passes that you have seen. No person, sir, has been imprisoned without a legal cause in our city."

GOVERNOR: "Why did you not give a more speedy answer to the posse that I sent out?"

GENERAL SMITH: "We had matters of importance to consult upon. Your letter showed anything but an amicable spirit. We have suffered immensely in Missouri from mobs, in loss of property, imprisonment and otherwise.

"It took some time for us to weigh duly these matters. We could not decide upon matters of such importance immediately, and your posse were too hasty in returning. We were consulting for a large people and vast interests were at stake.

"We had been outrageously imposed upon and knew not how far we could trust anyone; besides, a question necessarily arose, how shall we come? Your request was that we should come unarmed. It became a matter of serious importance to decide how far promises could be trusted and how far we were safe from mob violence."

COL. GEDDES: "It certainly did look from all I have heard, from the general spirit of violence and mobocracy that here prevails, that it was not safe for you to come unprotected."

GOVERNOR: "I think that sufficient time was not allowed by the posse for you to consult and get ready. They were too hasty, but I suppose they found themselves bound by their orders. I think, too, there is a great deal of truth in what you say, and your reasoning is plausible: yet I must beg leave to differ from you in relation to the acts of the city council. That council, in my opinion, had no right to act in a legislative capacity, and in that of the judiciary.

"They should have passed a law in relation to the matter, and then the municipal court, upon complaint, could have removed it; but for the city council to take upon themselves the law making and the execution of the law is, in my opinion, wrong; besides, these men ought to have had a hearing before their property was destroyed, to destroy it without was an infringement of their rights, besides, it is so contrary to the feelings of American people to interfere with the press.

"And furthermore, I cannot but think that it would have been more judicious for you to have gone with Mr. Bettisworth to Carthage, notwithstanding the law did not require it. Concerning your being in jail, I am sorry for that, I wish it had been otherwise. I hope you will soon be released, but I cannot interfere."

GENERAL SMITH: "Governor Ford, allow me, sir, to bring one thing to your mind, that you seem to have overlooked. You state that you think it would have been better for us to have submitted to the requisition of Constable Bettisworth and to have gone to Carthage.

"Do you not know, sir, that that writ was served at the instance of an anti-Mormon mob, who had passed resolutions and published them to the effect that they would exterminate the Mormon leaders; and are you not informed that Captain Anderson was not only threatened when coming to Nauvoo, but had a gun fired at his boat by this said mob in Warsaw, when coming up to Nauvoo, and that this very thing was made use of as a means to get us into their hands, and we could not, without taking an armed force with us, go there without, according to their published declarations, going into the jaws of death?

"To have taken a force would only have fanned the excitement, as they would have stated that we wanted to use intimidation, therefore we thought it the most judicious to avail ourselves of the protection of the law."

GOVERNOR: "I see, I see."

GENERAL SMITH: "Furthermore, in relation to the press, you say that you differ from me in opinion; be it so, the thing, after all, is only a legal difficulty, and the courts I should judge competent to decide on that matter.

"If our act was illegal, we are willing to meet it, and although I cannot see the distinction that you draw about the acts of the city council, and what difference it could have made in point of fact, law, or justice between the city council's acting together or separate, or how much more legal it would have been for the municipal court, who were a part of the city council, to act separate, instead of with the councilors.

"Yet, if it is deemed that we did wrong in destroying that press, we refuse not to pay for it, we are desirous to fulfill the law in every particular, and are responsible for our acts.

"You say that the parties ought to have a hearing. Had it been a civil suit, this of course would have been proper; but there was flagrant violation of every principle of right, a nuisance, and it was abated on the same principle that any nuisance, stench or putrefied carcass would have been removed.

"Our first step, therefore, was to stop the foul, noisome, filthy sheet, and then the next, in our opinion, would have been to have prosecuted the man for a breach of public decency.

"And furthermore, again, let me say, Governor Ford, I shall look to you for our protection. I believe you are talking of going to Nauvoo; if you go, sir, I wish to go along. I refuse not to answer any law, but I do not consider myself safe here."

GOVERNOR: "I am in hopes that you will be acquitted; but if I go, I will certainly take you along. I do not, however, apprehend danger. I think you are perfectly safe, either here or anywhere else. I cannot, however, interfere with the law. I am placed in peculiar circumstances, and seem to be blamed by all parties."

GENERAL SMITH: "Governor Ford, I ask nothing but what is legal. I have a right to expect protection, at least from you; for, independent of law, you have pledged your faith, and that of the state, for my protection, and I wish to go to Nauvoo."

GOVERNOR: "And you shall have protection, General Smith. I did not make this promise without consulting my officers, who all pledged their honor to its fulfillment. I do not know that I shall go tomorrow to Nauvoo, but if I do, I will take you along."

The governor left after saying that the prisoners were under his protection, and again pledging himself that they should be protected from violence, and telling them that if the troops marched the next morning to Nauvoo, as he then expected, they would probably be taken along, in order to ensure their personal safety.

Appendix

Note 1

Family of Joseph Smith, Sr.

NO.	NAME	WHEN BORN	WHERE BORN	WHEN DIED	WHERE DIED	FATHER'S NAME	MOTHER'S NAME
1	Alvin Smith	11 Feb. 1798	Tunbridge, Orange Co., Vt.	19 Nov. 1823	Palmyra, Ontario, N. Y.	Joseph Smith, Sr.	Lucy Mack
2	Hyrum Smith	9 Feb. 1800	Tunbridge, Orange Co., Vt.	27 June 1844	Carthage, Hancock, Ill.	"	"
3	Sophronia Smith	18 May 1803	Tunbridge, Orange Co., Vt.		Coalchester, McDonough, Ill.	"	"
4	Joseph Smith	23 Dec. 1805	Sharon, Windsor Co., Vt.	27 June 1844	Carthage, Hancock, Ill.	"	"
5	Samuel H. Smith	13 Mar. 1808	Tunbridge, Orange Co., Vt.	30 July 1844	Nauvoo, Hancock, Ill.	"	"
6	Ephraim Smith	13 Mar. 1810	Royalton, Vt.	24 Mar. 1810		"	"
7	William Smith	13 Mar. 1811	Royalton, Vt.	13 Nov. 1893	Osferdock, Iowa	"	"
8	Catherine Smith	8 July 1812	Lebanon, New Hampshire	1 Feb. 1900	Fountain Green, Ill.	"	"
9	Don Carlos Smith	25 Mar. 1816	Norwich, Vermont	7 Aug. 1841	Nauvoo, Hancock, Ill.	"	"
10	Lucy Smith	18 July 1821	Palmyra, N. Y.	9 Dec. 1882	Coalchester, McDonough, Ill.	"	"

Family of Hyrum Smith

NO.	NAME	WHEN BORN	WHERE BORN	WHEN DIED	WHERE DIED	FATHER'S NAME	MOTHER'S NAME
1	Lovina Smith	16 Sept. 1827		8 Oct. 1876	Farmington, Davis, Utah	Hyrum Smith	Jerusha Barden
2	Mary Smith	27 June 1829				"	"
3	John Smith	22 Sept. 1832	Kirtland, Ohio			"	"
4	Hyrum Smith	27 Apr. 1834	Kirtland, Ohio	1843	Nauvoo, Hancock, Ill.	"	"
5	Jerusha Smith	13 Jan. 1836	Kirtland, Ohio			"	"
6	Sarah Smith	2 Oct. 1837	Kirtland, Ohio	6 Nov. 1876	Ogden, Weber, Utah	"	"
7	Joseph F. Smith	13 Nov. 1838	Far West, Caldwell, Mo.			"	Mary Fielding
8	Martha Ann Smith	14 May 1841	Nauvoo, Hancock, Ill.			"	"

Family of Joseph Smith, the Prophet

NO.	NAME	WHEN BORN	WHERE BORN	WHEN DIED	WHERE DIED	FATHER'S NAME	MOTHER'S NAME
1	Julia M. Smith (adopted daughter)	30 Apr. 1831	Ohio			Joseph Smith	Emma Hale
2	Joseph Smith	6 Nov. 1832	Kirtland, Ohio			"	"
3	Frederick G. W. Smith	20 June 1836	Kirtland, Ohio	1862	Nauvoo, Hancock, Ill.	"	"
4	Alex. H. Smith	2 June 1838	Far West, Caldwell, Mo.			"	"
5	Don Carlos Smith	13 June 1840	Nauvoo, Hancock, Ill.	Aug. 1841	Nauvoo, Hancock, Ill.	"	"
6	David Hyrum Smith	18 Nov. 1844	Nauvoo, Hancock, Ill.			"	"

NOTE 2

"As you pass on the mail road from Palmyra, Wayne County, to Canandaigua, Ontario County, New York, before arriving at the little village of Manchester, say from three to four, or about four miles from Palmyra, you pass a large hill on the east side of the road. Why I say large, is because it is as large, perhaps, as any in that country.

"The north end rises quite suddenly until it assumes a level with the more southerly extremity, and I think I may say, an elevation higher than at the south, a short distance, say half or three-fourths of a mile. As you pass toward Canandaigua it lessens gradually, until the surface assumes its common level, or is broken by other smaller hills or ridges, water courses and ravines. I think I am justified in saying that this is the highest hill for some distance round, and I am certain that its appearance, as it rises so suddenly from a plain on the north, must attract the notice of the traveler as he passes by. The north end (which has been described as rising suddenly above the plain) forms a promontory without timber, but covered with grass. As you pass to the south, you soon come to scattering timber, the surface having been cleared by art or wind; and a short distance farther left, you are surrounded with the common forest of the country. It is necessary to observe that even the part cleared was only occupied for pasturage; its steep ascent and narrow summit not admitting the plow of the husbandman with any degree of ease or profit. It was at the second mentioned place where the record was found to be deposited, on the west side of the hill, not far from the top, down its side; and when I visited the place in the year 1830, there were several trees standing —enough to cause a shade in summer, but not so much as to prevent the surface being covered with grass, which was also the case when the record was first found."

NOTE 3

The record of these inhuman proceedings is made up mainly from the mobs' own official report of their doings.

NOTE 4

The revelation in our day of the doctrine of baptism for the dead may be said to have constituted a new epoch in the history of our race. At the time the Prophet Joseph received that revelation, the belief was general in Christendom that at death the destiny of the soul was fixed irrevocably and for all eternity. If not rewarded with endless happiness, then endless torment was its doom, beyond all possibility of redemption or change. The horrible and monstrous doctrine, so much at variance with every element of divine justice, was generally believed, that the heathen nations who had died without a knowledge of the true God and the redemption wrought out by His Son, Jesus Christ, would all be eternally consigned to hell. The belief upon this point is illustrated by the reply of a certain bishop to the inquiry of the king of the Franks, when the king was about to submit to baptism at the hands of the bishop. The king was a heathen, but had concluded to accept the form of religion then called Christianity. The thought occurred to him that if baptism was necessary for his salvation, what had become of his dead ancestors who had died heathens. This thought framed itself into an inquiry, which he addressed to the bishop. The prelate, less politic than many of his sect, bluntly told him they had gone to hell. "Then, by Thor, I will go there with them," said the king, and thereupon refused to accept baptism or to become a Christian.

When the Latter-day Saints received the gospel, and learned that there is but one way by which men can be saved, their thoughts turned to their dead ancestry. What would be their fate in the great hereafter? In many cases they knew their parents, grandparents, and other relatives had been persons who conscientiously lived up to the light they had received and served

God to the best of their ability. The words of the Prophet Malachi, as quoted by the angel Moroni to the Prophet Joseph, were literally fulfilled:

> Behold, I will reveal unto you the Priesthood, by the hand of Elijah the prophet, before the coming of the great and dreadful day of the Lord.
>
> And he shall plant in the hearts of the children, the promises made to the fathers, and the hearts of the children shall turn to their fathers; if it were not so the whole earth would be utterly wasted at his coming. (Joseph Smith 2:38–39.)

As predicted, Elijah the Prophet did come. The hearts of the fathers were turned to the children, and the children to the fathers, according to the promise. Then came the revelation of God's plan for the salvation of the dead who had passed away without the opportunity of receiving the ordinances of the gospel, administered by those whom God had authorized to perform them in His name. Peter's words were explained, where he says:

> For this cause was the gospel preached also to them that are dead, that they might be judged according to men in the flesh, but live according to God in the spirit. (I Peter 4:6.)

Also Paul's to the Corinthians, in which he alludes to baptism for the dead:

> Else what shall they do which are baptized for the dead, if the dead rise not at all? why are they then baptized for the dead? (I Corinthians 15:29.)

God's justice and mercy were vindicated. The comprehensive and far-reaching character of the atonement of the Lord Jesus was made plain, and the children of men had renewed cause to extol the glorious plan of salvation provided for the redemption of the human family. Jesus had died for all. His vicarious atonement had broken the bands of death. In a limited sphere, by the revelation of the sublime doctrine of baptism for the dead, His brethren and sisters had the glorious privilege accorded them of becoming saviors, and contributing to the general salvation of the race. They, also, could vicariously officiate for those who had died without the opportunity of obeying baptism and other ordinances essential to salvation, administered by legally authorized servants of God.

NOTE 5

The Illinois Springfield *Register* said of the Prophet's candidacy:

GENERAL JOSEPH SMITH A CANDIDATE FOR PRESIDENT

It appears, by the Nauvoo papers, that the Mormon Prophet is actually a candidate for the Presidency. He has sent us his pamphlet, containing an extract of his principles, from which it appears that he is up to the hub for a United States bank and a protective tariff. On these points he is much more explicit than Mr. Clay, who will not say that he is for a bank, but talks all the time of restoring a national currency. Nor will Mr. Clay say what kind of a tariff he is for. He says to the south that he has not sufficiently examined the present tariff, but thinks very likely it could be amended.

General Smith professes no such fastidious delicacy. He comes right out in favor of a bank and a tariff, taking the true Whig ground, and ought to be regarded as the real Whig candidate for President, until Mr. Clay can so far recover from his shuffling and dodging as to declare his sentiments like a man.

At present we can form no opinion of Clay's principles, except as they are professed by his friends in these parts.

Clay himself has adopted the notion which was once entertained by an eminent grammarian, who denied that language was intended as a means to express one's ideas but insisted that it was invented on purpose to aid us in concealing them.

The Iowa *Democrat* said:

A New Candidate in the Field

We see from the Nauvoo *Neighbor* that General Joseph Smith, the great Mormon Prophet, has become a candidate for the next Presidency. We do not know whether he intends to submit his claims to the National Convention, or not; but, judging from the language of his own organ, we conclude that he considers himself a full team for all of them.

All that we have to say on this point is that if superior talent, genius and intelligence, combined with virtue, integrity and enlarged views, are any guarantee to General Smith's being elected, we think that he will be a full team of himself.

The Missouri *Republican* believes that it will be death to Van Buren, and all agree that it must be injurious to the Democratic ranks, inasmuch as it will throw the Mormon vote out of the field.

Index

New Evidences of Christ in Ancient America

by Blaine M. Yorgason, Bruce W. Warren, and Harold Brown

In 1947 California lawyer Tom Ferguson threw a shovel over his shoulder and marched into the jungles of southern Mexico. Teamed with world-class scholar Bruce Warren, they found a mountain of evidence supporting *Book of Mormon* claims. Now the reader can follow their adventure as they unearth amazing archaeological discoveries and ancient writings, all of which shut the mouths of critics who say such evidences do not exist. In this volume, the newest archaeological evidences are also presented.

Endorsed by Hugh Nibley.

Hardcover, $24.95   ISBN: 0-929753-01-1

Look for it in your favorite bookstore,
or to obtain autographed copies, see last page.

Or order online at:
www.stratfordbooks.com

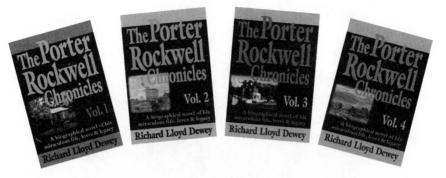

The Porter Rockwell Chronicles
by Richard Lloyd Dewey

This best-selling, historically accurate biographical novel series renders Porter's life in riveting story form, bringing it alive for adults and teens alike.

Volume 1 begins with his childhood years in New York where he becomes best friends with the future Mormon prophet Joseph Smith. The story continues through Porter's settlement with the Mormons in Missouri, where he fights against mobs and falls in love with and marries Luana Beebe.

Volume 2 covers the turbulent first four years in Nauvoo, where he continues to fight mobs and becomes Joseph Smith's bodyguard.

The Nauvoo period of his life draws to a close in Volume 3 as his best friend Joseph is murdered and his wife Luana leaves him and remarries, taking his beloved daughter Emily with her. Porter must bid a heartbroken farewell as he and the Mormons are driven from Nauvoo and flee west.

Volume 4 continues with his first ten years in Utah, where he is joyously reunited with his daughter Emily, takes on the U.S. Army in a guerilla war, and enters a new phase of adventures as U.S. Deputy Marshal.

Volume 1 (ISBN: 0-9616024-6-5)   Hardcover, $23.88
Volume 2 (ISBN: 0-9616024-7-3)   Hardcover, $23.88
Volume 3 (ISBN: 0-9616024-8-1)   Hardcover, $23.88
Volume 4 (ISBN: 0-9616024-9-X)   Hardcover, $24.88

*Look for them in your favorite bookstore,
or to obtain autographed copies, see last page.*

Or order online at:
www.stratfordbooks.com

Jacob Hamblin:
His Life in His Own Words

Foreword by Richard Lloyd Dewey

Far from the gun-toting reputation of super-lawman Porter Rockwell, Jacob Hamblin was known in early Western history as the supreme peacemaker.

No less exciting than Porter's account, Jacob's adventures encountered apparent Divine intervention at every turn, a reward seemingly bestowed to certain souls given to absolute faith. And in his faith, like Porter, Jacob Hamblin was one of those incredibly rare warriors who are *absolutely fearless.*

His migrations from Ohio to Utah with life-and-death adventures at every turn keep the reader spellbound in this unabridged, autobiographical account of the Old West's most unusual adventurer among Native Americans.

In his own words, Jacob Hamblin bares his soul with no pretense, unveiling an eye-witness journal of pioneer attempts to co-exist peacefully with Native brothers, among whom he traveled unarmed, showing his faith in God that he would not be harmed.

Easily considered the most successful — and bravest — diplomat to venture into hostile territory single-handedly, Hamblin takes the reader into hearts of darkness and hearts of light.

Softcover, $10.95   ISBN: 0-9616024-5-7

Look for it in your favorite bookstore,
or to obtain autographed copies, see last page.

Or order online at:
www.stratfordbooks.com

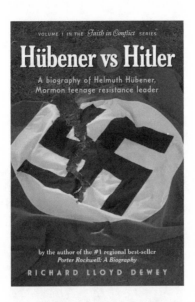

Hübener vs Hitler

A Biography of Helmuth Hübener, Mormon Teenage Resistance Leader

REVISED, SECOND EDITION

by Richard Lloyd Dewey

Nobel Laureate author Günther Grass said Hübener's life should be held up as a role model to every teen in the world. Regional best-selling author Richard Lloyd Dewey (*Porter Rockwell: A Biography*) holds up Hübener's life as a light not only to all teens, but to adults as well.

As an active Latter-day Saint, young Hübener recruited his best friends from church and work and established a sophisticated resistance group that baffled the Gestapo, infuriated the Nazi leadership, frustrated the highest judges in the land, and convinced the SS hierarchy that hundreds of adults—not just a handful of determined teens—were involved!

While other books have told the story of the group of freedom fighters Hübener founded, this is the first biography of Hübener himself—the astounding young man who led and animated the group. The inspiring, spell-binding, true story of the youngest resistance leader in Nazi Germany.

Hardcover, $27.95   ISBN: 0-929753-13-5

Look for it in your favorite bookstore,
or see last page for ordering info.

Or order online at:
www.stratfordbooks.com

The Kade Family Saga, Volume 1:
In Quest of Zion

by Laurel Mouritsen

Hardcover, $19.95   ISBN: 0-929753-07-0

Sure to delight *The Work and the Glory* fans, the *Kade Family Saga* series of historical novels is steeped in likeable, life-like characters in the fictional story of the Kade family and their adventures spanning from Missouri to the Great Salt Lake basin.

In Volume 1, *In Quest of Zion*, we are introduced to the much-travailed Lydia Dawson, who meets the intriguing Mr. Kade, who writes for *The Evening and the Morning Star*—controversial newspaper for the Mormons, who have recently arrived in Missouri. The reader is pulled into their lives as they endure persecution, physical confrontations with enemies, and eventually deadly battles. The external threats are only half the story, though, as they struggle simultaneously with the emotional conflicts in their relationships.

Told with the skill of a masterful storyteller against a historically accurate backdrop, this story is at once exciting, heart-wrenching, and very satisfying.

Look for it in your favorite bookstore,
or see last page for ordering info.

Or order online at:
www.stratfordbooks.com

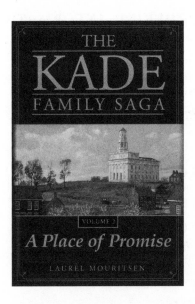

The Kade Family Saga, Volume 2:
A Place of Promise

by Laurel Mouritsen

Hardcover, $25.95 ISBN: 0-929753-08-9

The compelling story of the Kade family continues in this second
volume of the series.

The Kades' two older children, James and Elizabeth, are growing
into young adults in the peaceful riverside town of Nauvoo, Illinois,
in the 1840s. When traitors plot to murder the Prophet Joseph Smith,
James learns of it. Danger and intrigue mount as James strives to shield
the Prophet from assassination.

Meanwhile, Elizabeth faces dangers of a spiriual nature when she
begins associating with friends who will lead her away from the gospel
and bring her into open conflict with her family. During a trip to
Montrose, she comes in contact with a young Sauk and Fox Indian; their
paths will cross again in a surprising twist of events.

As the peace of Nauvoo is being destroyed by foes from within
and without the Church, brother and sister are on a collision course
that will shatter their family and have repercussions for generations of
Kades to come.

Join the Kades in all the color and pageantry, intrigue and suspense,
of old Nauvoo. Its legacy as a place of promise will stir your heart and
deepen your appreciation for the early Saints.

*Look for it in your favorite bookstore, or see last page for ordering info
or order online at:* **www.stratfordbooks.com**

ORDERING INFORMATION

New Evidences of Christ in Ancient America $24.95
by Blaine M. Yorgason, Bruce W. Warren, and Harold Brown.
Hardcover, 430 pp. ISBN: 0-929753-01-1

Porter Rockwell: A Biography $22.95
by Richard Lloyd Dewey.
Hardcover, 612 pp. ISBN: 0-9616024-0-6

The Porter Rockwell Chronicles, Vol. 1   (Reg. $27.50) $23.88
by Richard Lloyd Dewey.
Hardcover, 490 pp. ISBN: 0-9616024-6-5

The Porter Rockwell Chronicles, Vol. 2   (Reg. $27.50) $23.88
by Richard Lloyd Dewey.
Hardcover, 452 pp. ISBN: 0-9616024-7-3

The Porter Rockwell Chronicles, Vol. 3   (Reg. $27.95) $23.88
by Richard Lloyd Dewey.
Hardcover, 527 pp. ISBN: 0-9616024-8-1

The Porter Rockwell Chronicles, Vol. 4   (Reg. $27.95) $24.88
by Richard Lloyd Dewey.
Hardcover, 568 pp. ISBN: 0-9616024-9-X

Jacob Hamblin: His Life in His Own Words $10.95
Foreword by Richard Lloyd Dewey.
Softcover, 128 pp. ISBN: 0-9616024-5-7

Hübener vs Hitler *(Revised, Second Edition)* $27.95
A biography of Helmuth Hübener, Mormon teenage resistance leader,
by Richard Lloyd Dewey. Hardcover, 594 pp. ISBN: 0-929753-13-5

The Kade Family Saga, Volume 1: In Quest of Zion $19.95
by Laurel Mouritsen.
Hardcover, 396 pp. ISBN: 0-929753-07-0

The Kade Family Saga, Volume 2: A Place of Promise $25.95
by Laurel Mouritsen.
Hardcover, 389 pp. ISBN: 0-929753-08-9

FREE SHIPPING & HANDLING
Utah residents, add 6.25% sales tax.

Send check or money order to:
Stratford Books
P.O. Box 1371, Provo, Utah 84603-1371

Or order online at:
www.stratfordbooks.com

Prices subject to change.